Phyllis Richardson is the a.... of several books on architecture
and design, including the highly successful *XS* series, *Nano
House*, and *Superlight*, published in the UK by Thames and
Hudson. She has written on architecture, urban development
and travel for the *Financial Times*, the *Observer*, and *DWELL*
magazine. And she has published many reviews of literary
fiction in the *TLS* and other journals. She is the co-ordinator of
the Foundation Year in English and Comparative Literature at
Goldsmiths, University of London.

HOUSE OF
FICTION

From Pemberley to Brideshead,
Great Houses in English Literature

PHYLLIS RICHARDSON

unbound

First published by Unbound in 2017
This paperback edition first published in 2019

Unbound
Level 1, Devonshire House, One Mayfair Place, London W1J 8AJ
www.unbound.com

Chapter opener illustrations © Harriet Winterburn
Photographs and images within the text are the author's own
where not otherwise credited.

Every reasonable effort has been made to trace the owners of
copyright material reproduced herein. The publisher would like to apologise
for any omissions and will be pleased to incorporate missing
acknowledgments in any further editions.

Text Design by Ellipsis

A CIP record for this book is available from the British Library

ISBN 978-1-78352-693-2 (trade pbk)
ISBN 978-1-78352-379-5 (limited edition)
ISBN 978-1-78352-380-1 (trade hbk)
ISBN 978-1-78352-381-8 (ebook)

Printed in Great Britain by Clays Ltd, Elcograph S.p.A

2 4 6 8 9 7 5 3

For Lucas, Emile, Mason and Avery

'. . . with a pleasure which is both sensual and intellectual we shall watch the artist build his castle of
cards and watch the castle of cards become a castle
of beautiful steel and glass.'

Vladimir Nabokov, *Lectures on Literature*

'Now my aim is clear: I must show that the house is
one of the greatest powers of integration for the
thoughts, memories and dreams of mankind.'

Gaston Bachelard, *The Poetics of Space*

Contents

INTRODUCTION

The House of Fiction's Many Windows

Why do we enjoy reading about houses? Is it voyeurism, curiosity about how other people live, especially those in grander spaces than our own? Or is it to learn about the past, to get inside not just the rooms but other people's lives? Why do writers create memorable houses in fiction? Is it to provide a sense of identity, as Walter Scott did in an age when a man was distinguished by the land and house from which he got his name? Or does a house convey ideas of character, as Charles Dickens's minutely detailed residences often reflected the quirks of his multifarious fictional personalities? Do fictional houses offer us meaningful symbols of social status or envy, as with Jane Austen's Pemberley, or some tangible link to the past as so ardently forged by writers like Evelyn Waugh?

Houses in fiction do all of these things. In addition, they are sometimes used to draw attention to aesthetic debates. The architecture and art critic John Ruskin comes in for scrutiny in novels by E. M. Forster, Thomas Hardy, Ford Madox Ford and Julian Barnes. He hovers in the background of *The Forstye Saga*, as Robin Hill and its detractors reflect the controversy over designs for the White House, built in London by the avant-garde architect Edward Godwin for the painter James A. M. Whistler. (Whistler lost the house to debts accrued in suing Ruskin for slander.) Henry James had a particular regard for the artful qualities of the English country house, while John Galsworthy was the first to propose the liberating possibilities of a new style of architecture. However, in the post-war period, that positive vision of modern design was overturned. Social ills engendered by convenience-driven design, and powered by consumer ideals, were brutally depicted by writers such as Anthony Burgess and J. G. Ballard. And the idealistic view of the English country house has been challenged in recent decades by such writers as Kazuo Ishiguro, Ian McEwan and Alan Hollinghurst. If fictional houses have an aesthetic role, they also act as a prism for focusing and diffracting the concerns of the world in which they were built.

The poet Andrew Motion said that 'a house gives shape to a story', and that 'the physical limits of a house are a way of imposing structure for good or ill'. Of certain novels, they 'create a universe and reflect and confirm character.'[1] In one of our oldest English stories, the *Beowulf* poem, recorded sometime before the end of the first millennium, the conflict begins not with the legendary battles between tribes, but when the monster Grendel invades the new hall built by Hrothgar, heir of Shield Sheafson, 'scourge of many tribes'.[2] The 'fortunes of war favoured Hrothgar', we are told, so, of course, 'his mind turned/to hall-building'. He names his great mead-hall 'Heorot', and it is 'meant to be a wonder of the world for ever'. Grendel, like any grudging outsider, 'nursed a hard grievance' as he heard 'the din of a loud banquet' inside the hall to which he was not a guest. And so he waits until the men are asleep and creeps inside to slay them.[3] It is an extreme form of envy, but the sense of community and hospitality offered by the mead-hall is there in writers from Scott to James to Waugh, as is the destruction at the hand of disgruntled outliers.

It is in the preface to the New York edition of *The Portrait of a Lady* that Henry James offered his analysis of the 'house of fiction'. Recounting how he had worked on the novel in Florence and Venice, he wrote of the 'ceaseless human chatter' that came in through the windows in his rooms on Venice's Riva Schiavoni as he struggled in the 'fruitless fidget of composition'.[4] It was from this vantage point that he arrived at the 'single character' for his novel.[5] Considering the many variations with which he might treat that character, he concludes: 'The house of fiction has in short not one window, but a million'; each one can be pierced 'by the need of the individual vision and by the pressure of the individual will'.[6] James carries on at length with the metaphor, which is, of course, not a reference to any actual house. But as James's artists all look out from their metaphorical windows, all seeing something different, my focus in this book is on looking in. The houses written about here are both fictional and real, the house of the artist but also that of his or her creation. Many are symbolic, and many serve metaphorical purposes. All help to create atmosphere and work towards communicating an artist's notion of time, place, character, society, even spiritual fulfillment, but through an 'individual vision' usually informed by a house the writers knew well and to which they felt some strong connection.

This book is concerned with British authors writing about British houses. Henry James was an American-born writer who became so absorbed in British culture that he took on citizenship of his adopted home. James wrote with particular

admiration of the English country house, a setting so prominent in novels as to have inspired its own very British genre,
'country house fiction'. The British may not have the monop-
oly on house-centred stories, but the literature, from its earliest incarnations, is filled with thinking, writing, and imagining
houses in ways that betray a particular consciousness of house
and home, and of the cultural and spiritual bonds they represent. They say that an Englishman's home is his castle, that is,
the place he rules unequivocally. It could be argued that writers have the same power in the pages of their work and in the
houses they build there.

In *Tristram Shandy*, the confines of the cottage make for the
farcical encounters inside, and was probably influenced by the
parsonages that Laurence Sterne lived in, particularly the
house later dubbed 'Shandy Hall'. Horace Walpole designed
all of the 'Gothic' elements of Strawberry Hill along with a
group of aesthetically minded friends, and these came to
inform the Gothic novel as we know it. The Gothic house was
later re-animated by Charlotte Brontë, Charles Dickens,
Daphne du Maurier and Agatha Christie from houses they
experienced; some were objects of personal obsession. Walter
Scott built his beloved home, Abbotsford, in the Scottish
Baronial style, which reflected the kinds of manorial houses
that are key to many of his romatic tales, but also symbolised
his own desire to inhabit the role of Scottish laird. Jane Austen
led us through the drawing rooms and tea tables of Regency
England and showed us the trend for improving houses and
gardens, all the while whispering in our ears about how the
laws of property were so unjust to women. Thomas Hardy
was an architect before he became a writer, helping to restore

many a Gothic church, building schools and eventually his own house. E. M. Forster's father was an architect too and built the last house that the writer truly loved, a relationship he channelled into his lyrical rendering of the eponymous cottage in *Howards End*.

John Galsworthy's father was a part-time property developer, who commissioned three great houses in Surrey that the family lived in at one time or another. Galsworthy was living in Chelsea when it was full of artists' studios, while inventing what is probably the first avant-garde house in British literature. Virginia Woolf, mourning the early deaths of her mother, sister and brother, unlocked fictional rooms that were hazy with memories and voices from her own past. Ford Madox Ford and Evelyn Waugh wrote about the ruinous effects of modern life on the English landed gentry and their great estates. In the late twentieth century, it was not only single houses that gave stories an imaginative framework, mood and atmosphere, but also the urban apartment block and suburban development. J. G. Ballard and Julian Barnes made architecture and planning into determining factors for their characters' behaviour and aspirations.

'The symbol for England is the house whose name gives the title to [*Howards End*],' wrote the American critic Lionel Trilling. 'Like the plots of so many English novels, the plot . . . is about the rights of property.'[7] Forster was so taken with Trilling's assessment that he quoted it himself in his explanations of the abiding question of the novel: 'Who shall inherit England? The business people who run her or the people who understand her?'[8] Probably no other novel reveals the English love of a good house more than *Howards End*. But Trilling has a fair point about the rights of property in English fiction generally. The issue of inheritance rears up in the stories of Jane Austen, Walter Scott and, to some degree, Charlotte Brontë. It becomes a supreme motivating factor in the design of Galsworthy's *Forsyte Saga*, and in Ford Madox Ford's *Parade's End*. Finally, the inheritors are called to account by Ford, and by Waugh in *Brideshead Revisited*. Forster also lamented that the old certainties about property and inheritance were threatened by the materialism of the modern age; but these modern writers could have taken warning from their predecessors that there were never any guarantees where property was concerned.

And yet people would continue to feel that ownership was one of life's great achievements, if not an assurance of happiness. Ironically, it is the offer of some kind of meaningful connection to other human beings, as well as to the place itself, which causes many characters to cling fast to their property. As Margaret Schlegel says, 'round every knob and cushion in the house sentiment gathered'.[9] In the later twentieth century, instead of a great house being destroyed by conflagration erupting from human strife, it is preserved due to its commercial value. These houses suffer the ignominy of being turned into schools, rest homes and holiday resorts. So in this scenario, instead of going up in flames, Hrothgar's great hall would survive and become derelict, only to be snapped up by a savvy entrepreneur and turned into a Viking-themed, boutique hotel.

People speak of the rootlessness of modern society, and it is easy to see in the writers from the latter half of the twentieth century that the enduring connection to place is not so much a contemporary concern. Rather, in order to write convincingly of such connections, many authors reach back to the past. Of course, writers have long done such reaching to pluck out issues we might find charming, romantic or unenlightened, and hold them up to our modern but nostalgia-prone critical view.

We might ask ourselves what our domestic arrangements today will say about us as characters in the fiction of generations to come. Will it be our requirement for multiple bathrooms, our penchant for open-plan living, our ever-increasing demand for energy and automation that tells future readers about our priorities? As we look askance at Jane Austen's focus on marriage and inheritance, will an audience decades hence, confronted with the deleterious effects of global warming, shiver at our wasteful habits as seen through our love of domestic convenience, painstakingly detailed by some twenty-first century Dickens or Galsworthy? Perhaps future house fictions will be mostly filmic, rather than written. Will the nostalgia for the English country house, as indulged in the current proclivities for costume drama, continue to inspire further re-imaginings of lives lived in past centuries in grander settings and for which we safely know the answers to the question 'what happened next'?

Whatever we pass on from our current concerns for living spaces, it seems the interest in fashioning stories from a view through someone else's windows is not about to diminish anytime soon. Whether it presents us with scenes from the palace scullery, the penthouse living room, or between the thin walls of the apartment block, the house in fiction will offer what it always has: a million windows onto the lives of others.

Shandy Hall

ONE

Shandy Hall:
The Birth of the House in Fiction

Is it not a shame to make two chapters of what passed in going down
one pair of stairs? For we are got no farther yet than to the first landing, and there are fifteen more steps down to the bottom . . . for aught
I know, there may be as many chapters as steps . . .

Tristram Shandy

The Life and Opinions of Tristram Shandy, Gentleman is an
eighteenth-century novel about a man's attempt to tell the
story of his own life, beginning with his conception. It also
follows his father's attempts to raise and educate the ideal
child.[1]* As we know, Walter Shandy's efforts fail, and the narrative, subject to continual interruptions and digressions, also
fails to give the reader any sort of satisfyingly linear tale
about what has made our hero, Tristram, what he is. This
stubborn irregularity is central to the novel's enduring appeal,
and the digressions are at least partly inspired by a house
whose close quarters give rise to moments of being interrupted: by a thumping across the floor overhead; a crash in
the kitchen, which is audible in the parlour; a squeaking door

---

* This is a preoccupation that is also annoyingly familiar to anyone who spends much time
among the British or American middle classes of the twenty-first century.

hinge breaking in on a nap and conversation intruded upon by news and events within and without the house.

Readers familiar with the theatrical farce of the seventeenth and eighteenth centuries will know how houses with connecting rooms and passages work to create mishap and misunderstanding. And though *Tristram Shandy* isn't exactly a bedroom farce, the elements of bawdy humour and misapprehension merging under one roof are clearly alluded to. Laurence Sterne uses the house's intimacy to squeeze comic tension from each room, like piling an assortment of people into a lift and then pressing the 'hold' button to see what erupts. Sterne presses the button at intervals throughout the book, holding characters together in the parlour, on the stairs, in Uncle Toby's sentry box, until something gives way, with a laugh or a sigh or yet another winding digression. Wherever the narrative line wanders, the characters are fixed firmly in the setting of the house, usually sat in diverting conversation by the fire. The novel isn't about a house, but it certainly draws us into a house, a rather small house, where the passing along the stairs, the noise from the bedroom above, the rush to the kitchen or in from the yard are all seen, heard and felt by whomever else might be at home, and by the reader sat there alongside them.

First published in 1759, *Tristram Shandy* was written by an obscure country parson and it shook the literary world (such as it had become in the forty or so years since *Robinson Crusoe* appeared) and the keepers of social decorum. Many people immediately understood and appreciated Sterne's inverting of the standard narrative, the rollicking humour, even the Rabelaisian ribaldry and nonsense. They laughed as the narrator struggles to be born, so he (and we) can properly begin the story of his life, and at his frustration with his parents for being distracted by the question of whether Shandy *père* had remembered to 'wind the clock', thus disturbing the 'animal spirits' during the act of his conception. They appreciated that this distraction led to a novel of 'digressions', which the narrator claims 'incontestably, are the sunshine; – they are the life, the soul of reading!'[2] Nor did they quibble about a novel that, the writer explains, 'is digressive, and it is progressive too, – and at the same time'. And they bought up the first two hundred copies from the bookseller John Hinxman at the Sign of the Bible in Stonegate, York, quicker than you can say 'Ταρασσει τoὺς Ἀνϑρώπους oὐ τὰ Πράγματα, αλλα τὰ περι τῶν Πραγμάτων, Δογματα'.*[3]

Of course, there were those who objected to the first two volumes and to the seven that followed. Four years before he brought out *The Castle of Otranto* (like *Tristram*, published anonymously at first), Horace Walpole noted in his curmudgeonly way that Sterne's work was 'a kind of novel . . . the great humour of which consists in the whole narration always going backwards'. Without conceding much amusement, he says: 'I can conceive a man saying that it would be droll to write a book in that manner, but have no notion of his persevering in executing it.'[4] More serious attacks were made about its indecency. The wife of the Dean of Down claimed that her husband was so 'angry with the author of *Tristram*, etc. and those who do not condemn the work as it deserves; it has not and will not enter this house.'[5] She adds to her kins-

---

* 'Men are disturbed not by things, but by their opinions about things', Epictetus, epigraph to the first volume of the novel, which Sterne used in the Greek.

woman, who it seems had let the book enter *her* house (or at least knew someone who had), 'especially now your account is added to a very bad one we had heard before'.

It taunted, titillated, scandalised and amused. One reviewer commended the author's 'original and uncommon abilities in that manner of writing', but wished he had been 'more sparing in the use of indecent expressions . . . Nay, even downright gross and obscene expressions.'[6] Even after raising hackles initially, Sterne refused to temper his writing. As his biographer Arthur Cash explains, he 'would not be deterred from expressing his comic vision of man's inner life, which included the absurd intrusion of sexual awareness or desire into the thoughts and feelings of people who would rather be free of these disturbances'.[7] It is not hard to imagine all kinds of intrusions that come to anyone living in a small house and overhearing what's said in passageways or on the stairs. Picture Sterne in his study at Shandy Hall or sitting in the parlour, with his wife, daughter and servants about, friends stopping by, and you get the idea that eavesdropping (real and imagined) is a way of life.

Dr Johnson also took exception to the book and the man, calling Sterne 'the Contemptible Priest'.[8] But Sterne won the admiration of many, including Joshua Reynolds (who painted his portrait), William Hogarth (who agreed to illustrate two scenes of *Tristram*) and thinkers such as Voltaire and Diderot. The novel also earned its impoverished author a small fortune. One of the earliest and most valued perks it brought was the tenancy of a cottage that Sterne later referred to as 'a delicious retreat', his 'Philosophical Hut', and which his friends dubbed 'Shandy Hall'.

For his fictional family, Sterne had chosen the name 'Shandy', a term in the Yorkshire dialect used to denote something 'crack-brained' or 'odd', as Patrick Wildgust, current curator at Shandy Hall, puts it. (Others ascribe a lewder interpretation, which would not have been unthinkable for Sterne.) Either way, it is just one example of the author's mixing of the high-minded and lowbrow that gives the novel its particular humour and complexity. Juxtaposing the name 'Shandy', the equally undignified (or as Walter Shandy says, 'abhorrent') 'Tristram' and the abundance of bawdy humour with the epigraph by Epictetus (left untranslated from the Greek), the discourses in Latin and the meditations on learned philosophers, Sterne forced the kind of contrasts that help make the story, characters and situations so 'laugh-at-able'. Containing all of this learned lunacy and providing some anchor to its meanderings is the home of the patriarch of the story, Walter Shandy, brother to Uncle Toby, husband to the labouring Mrs Shandy, father of the benighted Tristram.

In 1760, soon after news of his authorship of the popular volumes became known, Sterne wrote to Catherine Fourmantel, a young singer and his paramour at the time, relating the good news that he had been awarded the living as parson at Coxwold. This preferment included residence in a little medieval cottage belonging to Lord Fauconberg, for which he would pay a small rent. The cottage occupied a picturesque position in the Vale of York, had a large garden and was located just along the road from the church:

My dear Kitty. Tho' I have but a moment's time to spare, I wd not omit writing you an Acc'ount of my good Fortune;

my Lord Fauconberg has this day given me a hundred &
sixty pounds a year, wch I hold with all my preferment;
So that all or the most part of my Sorrows and Tears are
going to be wiped away.[9]

At the time, Sterne was visiting London, making arrangements
for further publication and being wined and dined by the
fashionable people who found it fashionable to become
acquainted with the author of the ribald, digressive tale of
Tristram. He goes on to mention that he has had 'a purse
of Guineas given me Yesterday, by a Bishop', and that 'from
morning to night my Lodgings . . . are full of the greatest
Company – I dined these 2 Days with 2 Ladies of the Bedchamber – then with, L[d] Rockingham, L[d] Edgecomb – Lord
Winchelsea, Lord Littleton, A Bishop – &c &c'.

This early success was built on the first two volumes of the
book, which he had to pay to publish himself, copies of which
he sent to the booksellers Robert and James Dodsley in
London to sell in their shop at the sign of the Tully's Head in
Pall Mall. Coming to London after publication, Sterne visited
the shop, posing as a prospective buyer, and enquired after the
book. On being told 'there was not such a Book to be had in
London either for Love or money', he realised that at the age
of forty-seven, after more than twenty years of working as a
modestly paid village vicar, he had finally arrived.[10] Sterne had
left his parish in Yorkshire a writerly parson and entered
London as a literary celebrity. Indeed, as Sir Thomas Robinson of Newby, later Baron Grantham, wrote of Sterne to his
son in 1760: 'He is in Vogue. He is the man of Humour, he is
the toast of the British Nation.'[11]

An eighteenth-century engraving of the Coxwold cottage that came to be known as 'Shandy Hall', and which came with the living awarded to Sterne in 1760.

When he wrote the letter to his 'dear Kitty', Sterne had recently secured a deal with the Dodsleys to purchase the copyright of the first two volumes for £250, as well as an agreement to publish two volumes of sermons* and further volumes of *Tristram*.[12] The sermons were supported by a list of 642 subscribers, and the package totalled some £650, or well over £100,000 in today's money.[13] So the preferment from Lord Fauconberg, along with the little cottage in Coxwold, was something like icing on the cake. In addition, the position of the cottage, 'removed from the bogs of the Great

---

* The first volume of sermons was provocatively ascribed to Sterne's alter ego, 'Yorick', the ill-fated parson of the novel, and a character Sterne inhabited as the narrator of *A Sentimental Journey*.

Forest', would be better for Sterne's health, the air being drier.[14] But Sterne was never one to tell a bald truth when a dressed-up deviation could be had, and while he threw himself into the life of a London literary celebrity, he came to see the cottage as the storied home of the solitary parson-writer, a character he would develop to friends and associates.

To illustrate the suddenness of Sterne's success, in 1759, while living at the vicarage in Sutton-on-the-Forest, he had approached Robert Dodsley, sending the manuscript of the first volume with a letter, stating:

With this You will recve the *Life & Opinions of Tristram Shandy*, wch I choose to offer to You first . . . The Plan, as you may well perceive, is a most extensive one, – taking in, not only, the Weak part of the Sciences, in wch the true point of Ridicule lies – but every Thing else, which I find Laugh-at-able in my way.[15]

He went on to say that if this first volume sold, 'the World . . . will fix the Value for us both', and that the second volume would be ready by Christmas. He finishes by offering it for £50. Any writer who has ever sent a manuscript 'naked into the world' will know the feeling of hope and trepidation that such a move engenders, and the disappointment when the response is something other than glowing. Robert Dodsley may have found the text 'laugh-at-able' in places, but he also found the fee too high for a single volume and would not take it on. Sterne worked away on revisions for the next few months, and then wrote to Dodsley that he was going to print the book in 'a lean edition, in two small volumes . . . at my own expense'.[16] Up to this point Sterne had been a popular preacher, but his only experience as a writer was in composing sermons and political pamphlets, the latter on behalf of his uncle Jacques Sterne, the Archdeacon of Cleveland and Precentor of York.

Sterne's financial state was always precarious, but this wasn't surprising, as he had spent most of his young life in poverty. Although his father had been born into the lower gentility, he hadn't gained wealth by profession (as a soldier) or marriage. A clever, if mischievous, student, Laurence earned a place at Cambridge and was ordained as soon as he was of age, in order to begin earning a living. He was given his first parish at Sutton-on-the-Forest in Yorkshire and supplemented his income through pamphlet-writing and giving additional sermons at York Minster, which paid him £1 each.[17] Ever anxious to increase his earnings, Sterne was soon maintaining two 'livings', at Sutton-on-the-Forest and at Stillington, both in North Yorkshire and each worth about £30 per year.

Although he became adept at writing political satire, or more precisely, writing up pamphlets that made pointed attacks on the political opponents of Jacques Sterne or his beloved Whigs, Sterne tired of involving himself in his uncle's squabbles, ecclesiastical and otherwise, and decided to opt out of this journalistic role. So he knew he had to find some other way of adding to his income. Meanwhile, Sterne and his wife Elizabeth mourned several infant deaths (they had one surviving daughter), while they also clashed in personality. He continued to enrage and torment her with his infidelities, and she fell ill with attacks of madness (or depression) and, like her husband, suffered from tuberculosis. In one story, handed down years after the fact by a family friend, John Croft, Elizabeth found her husband *in flagrante* with a maid and, after pulling him out of bed onto the floor, became delusional, referring to herself as the 'queen of Bohemia'.[18] Sterne lived with an even more severe tubercular condition than his wife, which sometimes erupted in pulmonary hemorrhages. These left him bed-bound for days at a time, and were commonly treated by being 'bled', as eighteenth-century medical practice dictated. When literary success came, it must indeed have seemed like a gift from above.

The connection of Sterne to the current Shandy Hall is one that moves fluidly from fact to fiction, as one imagines with the author of such a self-consciously narrated novel. Sterne penned a dedication to the first London edition of the novel (1760) that sets the man firmly in his cottage surroundings, engendering that writerly character he imagined himself to be. The book was, he says, 'written in a bye corner of the kingdom, and in a retired thatch'd house, where I live in a constant endeavour to fence against the infirmities of ill health, and other evils of life, by mirth'.[19] As he hadn't yet moved to the cottage at Coxwold, it may well be that Sterne was thinking of the cottage in Sutton-on-the-Forest, where he had been living for the past twenty years, or he could have been referring to the house he took in the Minster Yard in York, just before moving to Coxwold and where his wife and daughter continued to spend winter months. Or it could just be that Sterne was creating yet more fantasy around the personage of the author-character Tristram/Yorick/Sterne. However, the contrast that those few lines conjure between the tenant of the naïve dwelling, located in an out-of-the-way 'corner of the kingdom', and the author who became the toast of London's elite was not accidental. It played to Sterne's love of contrariety and was no subtle clue to his satisfaction with how far he had come, and how quickly, from country parson to acclaimed wit.

Though the reference may initially have been his own invention, Sterne came to view the 'Thatch'd Cottage' of his 1760 dedication and his Coxwold dwelling as one and the same, and both as his creative home. In 1767, after a particularly difficult journey to Coxwold, during which he was made to stop several times owing to his illness, he inserted a relieved note in his journal: 'arrived at my Thatchd Cottage the 28th May'.[20] While architectural historians might argue that Sterne's house in Coxwold never actually wore a thatched roof, the comment goes some way to explaining just how much Sterne identified himself with the persona of that original dedication and how much he wanted others to perceive the author as the witty curate of Shandy Hall.

Whatever the particular references it inspired, the house was key to the progress of his writing. Following the publication of the first two volumes, Sterne worked steadily at his cottage throughout 1760 and 1761, producing volumes III and IV within months. In 1760, shortly after moving in, he wrote to the Bishop of Gloucester: 'I am just sitting down to go on with my Tristram.'[21] To his friend Mrs Fenton, he wrote that he wished 'I was at your elbow – I have just finished one volume of Shandy and want to read it to someone who I know can taste and relish the humour.'[22] By November he had completed the drafts of volumes III and IV, which were published in January 1761. Following another busy year of writing at Coxwold, volumes V and VI came out in December. After that, while Sterne spent the better part of two and a half years travelling around the Continent, visiting old and new-found friends, volumes VII and VIII suffered, only to be completed when he returned to Coxwold in August 1764. A month later, he wrote to his banker, Robert Foley: 'I am now returned to my Philosophical Hut to finish Tristram.'[23]

Once back in his Shandean quarters he made quick work, turning out a draft of the volumes by mid-November, which were published in January 1765.[24] He may have been alone, but he peopled the house with the personages of his vivid imagination. Volume IX, which contains 'the Amours of my uncle Toby' and on which Sterne had been working at various points over three or four years, was finally published in 1767. It is in the first chapter here that Tristram the narrator tells us – as he sits 'this 12th day of August, 1766, in a purple jerkin and yellow pair of slippers, without either wig or cap on, a most tragicomical completion' – of his father's hopes and fears for his son.[25] It is not hard to envisage Sterne sat just so in his study, contemplating his own hopes and fears for his future.

To be sure, *The Life and Opinons of Tristram Shandy* is not about a house in the sense that Jane Austen wrote about houses, or in the way that Daphne du Maurier presented the house as having some psychic presence, or even in the way that E. M. Forster saw it as offering a sense of continuity and meaning. It sits a little like the London townhouse of Virginia Woolf's Clarissa Dalloway, as a place where people come together and, though they may not communicate in a way we find sensible or satisfying, it is to these rooms – the parlour, the kitchen, the stairs – that they bring their stories and desire to connect, however spuriously. The fictional Shandy Hall certainly has its own presence in the novel, as most of the elements of the story unfold while Walter Shandy and Uncle Toby are seated in the parlour, engaged in one of many discussions of 'hobby-horsical' topics, on everything from the nature of time to the importance of names (and noses) and the technicalities of modern warfare, to name but a few.

Though it would be simplifying the novel to suggest that

One of two illustrations produced by William Hogarth for *Tristram Shandy*. Corporal Trim reads a sermon on conscience to Walter Shandy, Uncle Toby and a sleeping Dr Slop.

Sterne tied each event to the particularities of this or any other house, the interior details do unquestionably invite the reader into the domestic setting. The house becomes something like a stage set, and Sterne/Tristram as narrator is very much 'the noisy arranger of the stage'.[26] As Walter and Toby sit and talk, the maid Susannah pounds across the floor overhead in aid of Mrs Shandy, who is struggling in childbirth. In between bouts of discourse and small notices about the progress of Tristram's birth, Walter Shandy fiddles with his coat pockets by the fire, considering the two knobs of the chairback, which the narrator uses to illustrate the twin faculties of wit and judgment, according to the writings of the philosopher John Locke.[27]

Most of the 'current' action of the novel happens inside and around a house that certainly feels similar to the type and dimensions of Shandy Hall. The claustrophobic atmosphere, brought about by the combination of a woman in labour and the constant miscommunication and misdirected movements between the other characters, all happening in close proximity, is key to the tension and the farce of the novel. In the parlour with Walter and Toby, while Dr Slop tries fruitlessly to untie the knots Obadiah has made in his bag of instruments, we hear 'the trampling overhead increase', as Mrs Shandy 'groans' audibly.[28] We later see Walter, flung across his bed (with one toe tapping the chamber pot) in distress at the news that his son's nose has been accidentally damaged by Dr Slop's newfangled forceps, while Toby tries to soothe him.[29] Then the narrator helpfully confides that to explain his father's distress, 'I must leave him upon the bed for half an hour and my uncle Toby in his old fringed chair sitting beside him.'[30] And there his image sits as if in still frame, as Sterne muses on another digression, actor and reader both suspended until the narrator takes up the action again.

The narrative that refuses to move decisively forward (like the child Tristram, who seemingly refuses to be born) is mirrored by characters who, for example, spend several chapters descending the stairs. By the time the child is finally born, Walter and Toby have fallen asleep in the parlour in front of the fire, only to be wakened by the noise of the door hinge. But it is not the parlourmaid delivering the good news, of course, it is Corporal Trim, carrying a pair of jackboots from which he has made some mortars for Toby's battle re-creation. The adult Tristram, as inept as his father at house repairs, later informs us that the door hinge is squeaky still. As for the faulty sash window that has been denuded of its lead weights, which Trim has commandeered for the battle, and is responsible for young Tristram's accidental circumcision later on, we can only assume that it will not have been mended either.

The narrator draws attention to the immediate props of the house in ways we might now call 'postmodern' intrusions, as when Tristram asks: 'Is it not a shame to make two chapters of what passed in going down one pair of stairs? For we are got no farther yet than to the first landing, and there are fifteen more steps down to the bottom . . .'[31] Emphasising the stage-like atmosphere of the story, the narrator cries out for the assistance of a 'critick' to help move the action along. He will give a crown to anyone who can 'help me . . . get my father and my uncle Toby off the stairs, and to put them to bed'.[32] We can easily imagine the narrative being enacted as a modern drama set within a house, in which members of the audience are called upon to fetch a book or a bootlace. Almost every digressive turn is brought back to a house, as in the very beginning when even sex becomes associated with furniture, in the object of the clock that Walter decides needs to be wound just about as often as he needs to have conjugal relations with his wife (that is, once a month).

Yet the story is not entirely 'house-bound', as it were. The narrative leaves the house, metaphorically, as different digressions take hold, such as Slawkenbergius's tale of Diego of the abundant nose, and Corporal Trim's pathetic narration of the death of LeFever. The characters also leave the house physically. At the news that Susannah has misdelivered Walter's choice of name to the curate, so that the boy is registered as 'Tristram' rather than the nobler 'Trismegistus', Walter takes himself out of the house to walk to the fish pond and back again. Later, Uncle Toby and Trim visit their model fortifications, and Toby is 'attacked' by the widow Wadman in his sentry box. The men also go off in a 'cavalcade' to find out about having the child's name changed, and return unsuccessful in their mission. And Tristram relates details from his own journeys abroad (as he, like his creator, tries to outrun Death). But for the final scene, we and the Shandy family are back in the parlour, where Walter, Toby, Mrs Shandy, Dr Slop and Obadiah are present to hear the parson Yorick pronounce that this story 'of a Cock and a Bull' is 'one of the best of its kind I ever heard'.

The house is the locus for the physical movements while the mind travels, thus the overall arc is brought back to the centuries-old image of people sitting by a fire, listening to a tale. As readers, our imaginations too wander out from the house, but our gaze returns to the immediate surroundings as the narrator points out the details of a curtain or a skirting board. However much the plot dances and dips (as Sterne illustrates in the graphics of volume VI), it always returns to the comforting scene of Walter and Toby sitting in their chairs, talking (whether *at* or *to* each other is almost beside the point), at home, in the parlour. And it is not too much to say that the house becomes a touchstone for the narrative, in a way that the actual cottage became a place of realignment and creative productivity for Sterne.

The Coxwold cottage had a changeable effect on the author. Initially, it was an idyll, a reward that symbolised his success after years of trials and frustration. Then, once he gained some notoriety and began to enjoy his life of celebrity in London, Sterne sometimes found the house confining, too far removed from the heady social goings-on of the metropolis, which, even in his many days of illness, he was loath to be removed from. Towards the end of his life, which came so quickly, Sterne resigned himself to its simple pleasures, which he enumerated in letters and a journal, while making additions and alterations to the house and awaiting the return of his last illicit love, Eliza Draper, with whom he imagined sharing his final days at Shandy Hall.

As he settled into life as a successful writer and occupant of the house in Coxwold, Sterne's newfound largesse brought him further domestic enjoyments and some degree of peace, though he would upset that too with time. He wrote to his friend, John Hall-Stevenson, who lived at nearby Skelton Castle: 'I go on with Tristram – I have bought seven hundred books at a purchase dog cheap – and many good – and I have been a week getting them set up in my best room here.'[33] A couple of months later, he portrayed a writer's idyllic existence at Shandy Hall to a young lady friend: 'I return to my new habitation, fully determined to write as hard as can be.' He explained that his house was 'within a mile of his [Lord Fauconberg's] seat, and park, which was 'a very agreeable ride out in the chaise, I purchased for my wife'. As well as presenting Elizabeth with the chaise, he had also splashed out on his daughter Lydia, who was nearly fourteen: 'Lyd has a poney which she delights in.' At work on volumes V and VI, he sets a similar scene of domestic harmony: 'I am scribbling away at my Tristram. These two volumes are, I think, the best . . . My Lydia helps to copy for me – and my wife knits and listens as I read her chapters.'[34]

Once in residence, Sterne made some changes to the house. It was originally built in the fifteenth century, but was altered substantially in the seventeenth, with the floor inserted to create the upstairs rooms, and rooms and hallways partitioned.[35] Though Lord Fauconberg had given Sterne the position as curate, he still paid rent of about £12 per year. In 1761 Lord Fauconberg agreed to Sterne's request to build a stable, which was probably going up while he was writing volume V.[36]

The couple's marital problems meant that Sterne often lived at Shandy Hall on his own, writing his novels and, until his illness prevented him from preaching in public, his sermons. He also wrote the scores of letters to friends and admirers that give us an idea of his thoughts, his preoccupations and his own view of his life and work. But Sterne's return from a lengthy trip to the Continent in 1767 marked a particular change in his attitude and circumstances, a more settled embrace of the peaceful existence in his 'Thatch'd cottage'. He had come back to Coxwold very ill, but intent on finishing the manuscript for his whimsical travelogue, *A Sentimental Journey*. He was again full of joyful musings on the beauty, tranquillity and abundance of his home. In June, he wrote to a friend: 'I am as happy as a prince at Coxwould – and I wish you could see in how princely a manner I live – 'tis a land of plenty. I sit down alone to venison, fish and wild fowl, or a couple of fowls or ducks, with curds, and strawberries, and cream, and all the simple clean plenty which a rich valley . . . can produce.'[37] After a visit to John Hall-Stevenson at Skelton, he wrote: 'Am got home from Halls to Coxwould – O 'tis delicious retreat! Both from its beauty, & air of Solitude; & so sweetly does every thing abt it invite yr mind to rest from its labours – and be at peace with itself & the world.'[38]

It is at this time that a good deal of refurbishing work to the house was being carried out. Four 'half rooms' were created in the extension at the western elevation, contained in a two-storey brick addition with a parapet on top and a niche between the doorways, which has a distinctively Georgian style. It is this more composed, elegant side that, balanced by the massive medieval chimney breast, along with the other smaller stack from Sterne's study at the opposite end, creates the slightly wonky but pleasantly 'Shandean' character of the house. The upstairs bedrooms were also renovated, including the large bedroom at the southwestern side, which would have been Sterne's, and the upstairs fireplaces were refurbished.[39]

Whether or not he had a direct say in all of the building work, Sterne presented some of it in his letters and journal as a gift for Eliza Draper, the young woman with whom he had fallen madly, ridiculously, in love. Of the many improvements, he wrote to her that he had added a coach house: 'My Chaise is so large – so high – so long – so wide . . . That I am building a coach house on purpose for it – do you dislike it for this gigan-tick Size?'[40] (Read that as you will.)

Sterne met the twenty-three-year-old Eliza in 1767. She was unhappily married, but had followed her husband in his posting to India. The two corresponded and Sterne kept a jour-nal of his communication to her, which he thought to publish (possibly in emulation of Jonathan Swift's *Journal to Stella*, 1766). In one of several letters and entries enumerating the changes he has made to accommodate her, Sterne writes, even as he awaits a visit from his own wife and daughter:

I have made you, a sweet, Sitting Room (as I told You) already – and am projecting a good Bed-chamber adjoining it, with a pretty dressing room for You, which connects them together – & when they are finishd, will be as sweet a set of romantic Apartments, as You ever beheld – The Sleeping room will be very large – The dressing room . . . will be little – but Big enough to hold a dressing Table – a couple of chairs . . . wth spare Room to hang a dozen petticoats – gowns, &c – & Shelves for as many Bandboxes . . .[41]

Sterne did, in fact, prepare a 'sweet sitting room' at Shandy Hall for Eliza, which is above his own study and still remains largely as he had it, though empty of whatever 'pretty' furnishings he may have acquired for it. A window looks out to the south over fields, and a separate room at the back, over the old kitchen, would have been her dressing room and was once fitted with basins for dressing a wig. The panelling beneath a dado and a cast-iron fireplace surround are all of the period. Whatever one thinks of Sterne's philandering or of his pining for a much younger married woman, there is some poignancy in this room, in the feel of his letters and his fussing over the decor.

The idea that Eliza and Sterne would live together at Shandy Hall was a hopelessly absurd prospect on many fronts: they were both married, she was very much younger, and though Elizabeth Sterne was ill with consumption – as he noted to Eliza, 'my wife cannot live long' – she would outlive him by five

Sterne's study at Shandy Hall as it is today. Writing from the house he called his 'philosophical hut', Sterne declared himself 'as happy as a prince'.

years. As he was well aware, his own health was in serious decline, and it was unlikely he would live to see another summer at Coxwold, or anywhere else.

Today, the old stone-floored kitchen with hearth is a sort of display room for Sterneana, left much as it would have been in the eighteenth century. Forward, facing the southerly aspect and now the road, Sterne's study is also much as he would have known it, apart from the editions of his books lining every wall, and beckons a writer to sit and conjure something outlandish and wonderful, as some have been invited to do in recent years. The books, as Patrick Wildgust explains, would probably have been in the parlour, now a snug room with an opening in the wall panel revealing the cottage's medieval origins. The little wood stair doesn't boast anything like the fifteen steps to the landing that Walter and Toby could spend so much time pausing and prevaricating on. However, the parlour at the west end of the house, where Sterne added on, is in fact below the bedroom, and a door formerly led outside, from where Walter might well stroll off to the fish pond. Sterne's coach house is probably the outbuilding that runs north, adjacent to the main house.

Wildgust, who has been curator since 2004, has added a few appropriately quirky touches to the house, such as the large entrance gate and handrail sculpted in imitation of the convoluted plotlines, as drawn by Sterne/Tristram (in volume VI) to illustrate the story's adamantly non-linear narratives. Although the diminutive size of the house belies the grandiose title of 'hall', it is of appropriate dimensions for the close proximities of the novel. There are some satisfying trappings of its famed eighteenth-century occupant, who, nearing six feet in height, must have found his square-shaped study quite cosy, and certainly must have knocked his wig askew on more than one occasion when passing down the stair or through the low thresholds.

Tristram Shandy has endured not only for its humour and 'hobby-horsical' digressions, but also for the vast scope of its attentions, from religious and philosophical to medical and base humanity. In its slapstick ribaldry it takes something from the plays of seventeenth-century Restoration comedy. And it came at a time that saw an explosion in popular literature and the novel becoming part of the national culture. But it also took a turn away from some of the popular early novels, including Samuel Richardson's epistolary *Pamela, or Virtue Rewarded* (1740) and Henry Fielding's picaresque *Tom Jones* (1749), both of which centre the action on grand country residences and questions of moral behaviour. Although Tristram's family home has the grand name of 'Shandy Hall', it is obvious that this is not a large manor of elaborate public rooms, with wings for various purposes and many servants, apart from the harried Susannah and Obadiah.

In Richardson's novel, the virtuous Pamela is imprisoned by her lusty employer, Mr B, at his vast Lincolnshire estate, where he attempts to wear down her virtue, but then is won over by her steadfast morals. His stately pile was probably imagined as something along the lines of Castle Howard, which was designed by John Vanbrugh, an architect who was in high demand in the early eighteenth century (and who was also the author of saucy Restoration comedies). *Tom Jones* is the story of a lucky bastard (in the literal sense). He turns out to be the son of a large landowner, and it is his good deeds that eventually allow him to inherit the family seat. Fielding was born at Sharpham Park, an eighteenth-century Palladian villa in Somerset; later, the family moved to East Stour in Dorset, the home of his mother's family. But Fielding also knew Hagley Hall and Prior Park, both large neo-Palladian stately homes of his friends and supporters, George, 1st Baron Lyttelton, and Ralph Allen, respectively. *Tom Jones* (dedicated to Lyttelton) contains what is believed to be the first fictional mention of a Gothic house, in Squire Allworthy's mansion: 'the *Gothick* stile of Building could produce nothing nobler'.[42] Allworthy's Paradise Hall was an 'imaginative synthesis' of Sharpham and Prior Park with a nod to Sanderson Miller, an architect and proponent of the Gothic revival, who had designed a rotunda and 'ruined castle' for Lord Lyttelton at Hagley Hall.[43] Fielding had an eye for a good house and a pen for lashing his enemies, which he did in his poem the *Vernoniad*, which mocks Robert Walpole's governance, his house Houghton Hall and his art collection: 'a huge dark lantern hung up in his hall/and heaps of ill-got pictures hid the wall'.

Some might argue that the real beginning of the house of fiction came not with Sterne or Fielding, or even Richardson, but with the publication of what is considered the first novel in the English language. Written in 1719, Daniel Defoe's *Robinson Crusoe* tells the story of an Englishman who is shipwrecked on an island for twenty-eight years. To appeal to his audience of rising merchant-class readers and dissenting religious groups who valued hard work over idle privilege, Defoe made sure to enumerate the ways in which his hero survives

From the Collection at Hagley Hall

Hagley Hall, the Worcestershire home of George, 1st Baron Lyttelton, friend and patron of Henry Fielding, was of a size and stature more in keeping with fictional manors of the period.

by paying heed to Providence and applying diligence and ingenuity to create his own island kingdom: harvesting fruit, killing game, herding and domesticating goats, and even managing to grow crops from a few stray crumbs of grain.

First, however, Crusoe gets to work in building himself a home. Defoe spends many pages describing in painstaking detail the way Crusoe chooses the spot for his abode (in the partial shelter of a cave), and conceives a design for a palisade fence to keep intruders out and himself protected within. He spends eighteen days 'in widening and deepening my cave, that it might hold my goods commodiously', and builds a warehouse area, or 'magazine', as well as 'a kitchen, a dining-room, and a cellar'.[44] Crusoe is so successful at his construction and domestication – making tools, a table and chair and clay pots for cooking, and weaving baskets for storage –

that he builds a second home on another part of the island, which, in the tradition of his aristocratic kinsmen, he modestly calls 'my country-house'.

Of course, Defoe had never been to a tropical island, let alone built himself a house, but he knew what it was like to fear homelessness. He was a self-published pamphleteer, whose criticisms of the government often got him into trouble (spells of bankruptcy, and imprisonment for criticising the High Church), and he had to rely on friends in high places to get him out. He was neither a squire of the landed gentry nor a tenanted farmer, but he was a canny observer of his own times and capitalised on the appeal of the story of building and filling a new house with the necessities of homemaking, long before such processes became a staple of early evening television viewing.

A lot had happened with the novel between 1719 and 1759, and it continues to evolve into our own century, so much so that discussions of the limits or even 'death' of the genre are difficult to fathom. Sterne was as much a contrarian as Fielding or Defoe, and that spirit was captured in the wonderful 2005 film, *Tristram Shandy: A Cock and Bull Story*. Only one scene was actually filmed at Shandy Hall (in it, Stephen Fry poses as a curator named Patrick taking a phone call in Sterne's study). Otherwise, the production was shot in a variety of grander houses and gardens: Blickling Hall, Gunthorpe Hall, Heydon Hall and Felbrigg Hall in Norfolk, and Deene Park in Northamptonshire. At one point, a member of the fictional film crew remarks that the house they are using is much too grand to be the Shandy Hall of the book, but makes the film sexier. And indeed even the garden – where the widow Wadman (Gillian Anderson) walks with Uncle Toby (Rob Brydon), hoping, somewhat salaciously on her part, to see precisely 'where' he was injured in the Battle of Namur – is on a much grander scale than the garden of Shandy Hall, which Sterne enjoyed so well. Small spaces are great for squeezing in comedy and drama, but not for film crews.

'There will be just time, whilst my uncle Toby and Trim are walking to my father's, to inform you that Mrs Wadman had . . . made a confident [*sic*] of my mother,' Tristram begins the penultimate chapter.[45] So we read on, conscious they will at any moment reach the door of the house and interrupt the story again, and anxious to know what secrets have passed 'behind the garden wall'. But as Toby enters the room with 'marks of infinite benevolence and forgiveness' and sits himself down by the fire, we know that wherever it takes us in the realms of history, philosophy, anatomy or astronomy, the conversation will be a delight.

Strawberry Hill

TWO

Strawberry Hill:
The Invention of the Gothic Novel

'A Gothic chapel and an historic castle are anodynes to a torpid mind.'
Horace Walpole

Picture a medieval stone castle, perched on a craggy cliff-face, its walls impenetrable, its turrets and battlements shrouded in grey mist. Now put yourself in a darkened corridor, listen for the echo of strange footsteps, a blood-curdling cry. The setting is eerily familiar in the twenty-first century, but the combination of intimidating architecture and supernatural activities was first used to terrify readers nearly 250 years ago. The haunted house or enchanted castle that we now know from stories and film can be traced back to an English penchant for Gothic styling, which began to emerge in the middle of the eighteenth century. And the tales of terror that we associate with these buildings got their popular start in an early novel that electrified readers with its spine-tingling mixture of modest maidens and occult forces. Of course, the tale of an endangered damsel had been seen before in chivalric narrative poems and romances, but this tale was not a formal exercise in verse and had some elements of realism that earlier stories lacked, making it even more disturbing. The setting was very specific, the architecture was in a style that people knew vaguely from old churches and ancient tales, but it was still strange enough to thrill and beguile.

The Castle of Otranto, written by Horace Walpole in 1764, is widely accepted as the first Gothic novel in English. It was certainly the first to be inspired by an author's love of Gothic architecture, as he used details from his own extraordinary 'Gothic villa', Strawberry Hill, to paint in the background. Walpole's love of Gothic architecture and the atmosphere it engendered became not only a design style, but also a lasting component of the fiction. The novel was soon followed by another tale linked with an architectural sensation, this time by William Beckford, who also created the legendary house Fonthill Abbey. Walpole and Beckford shared a few other important similarities: both were wealthy aesthetes and had secret passions that kept them on the margins of polite society, and both created extreme monuments to their creative vision that helped to fix the romance and mystery of Gothic designs in the popular architectural and fictional imagination.

Horace Walpole has become a somewhat obscured figure in Britain. He is often confused with his father, Sir Robert Walpole, the country's first and longest-serving prime minister. *The Castle of Otranto* is now almost unheard of among the general reading public, but it provided the inspiration for centuries of writers, from the sensationalists of the later eighteenth century to writers like Jane Austen, Charlotte Brontë and Charles Dickens to Bram Stoker and Daphne du Maurier, and a whole genre of stories and films, right up to the modern fantasy of wizard academies decked with talking portraits. Walpole's inspiration for the enchanted setting of his novel was the house and collection that he created for himself at Strawberry Hill in Twickenham, the first Gothic Revival house in England, which galvanized an architectural trend of its own.

Walpole, a fervently articulate politician and social commentator, has provided subsequent generations with a window on eighteenth century Britain through his extensive letters, memoirs and political pamphlets.[1] His witty and sometimes scathing commentaries on society, politics, art and culture, and smouldering installments of gossip, are entertaining in their own right, but particularly compelling because he was so firmly connected to the established political and social elite of the time. Serving as an MP for decades, he took some rather progressive moral stands, being against slavery, as well as opposed to wars with France and with the British colonies that became the United States. Of course, there was a private side to Walpole, and his vast correspondence includes some very telling letters to someone, as biographer Tim Mowl argues, who was secretly the love of his life: Henry, 9th Earl of Lincoln, once described by George II as 'the handsomest man in England'. Strawberry Hill not only gave Walpole the chance to indulge his creative fantasies, but also a place to retire to with like-minded friends, away from the frenetic gossip of London society.

Looking for a summer retreat*, Walpole at first leased the little house in 1747 (aged thirty) from Elizabeth Chevenix,

---

* Walpole also had a house in London

who had a 'toyshop', selling small trinkets in Charing Cross. Within a couple of years he had set about redesigning it with the help of a group of learned friends he dubbed the 'Strawberry Committee', or 'Committee of Taste'. These included John Chute, an avowed aesthete and architectural enthusiast who enjoyed helping to plot out renovations and additions for the grand houses of his friends. Chute had inherited a grand house of his own, The Vyne in Hampshire, built by Henry VIII's Lord Chamberlain, in 1754. While living there, Chute's sons William and Tom became friendly with the children of the local vicar, George Austen, and The Vyne would influence a different strand of the English novel through the vicar's younger daughter, Jane.

During his travels in Europe and around his home country, Walpole developed a passion for a hallowed medieval past and became enamoured of the Gothic style, which he emulated in the elaborate remodelling of his little retreat. The origins of Gothic style lie in the ecclesiastical architecture of France and a spate of buildings that went up in the twelfth and thirteenth centuries, from village churches to the abbey of Saint-Denis and the cathedrals of Notre Dame in Paris and Chartres. Not only did the Gothic appear in public places of worship, but it was also a popular choice for private chapels built by prominent families of the period. The style came to England, where it was known as the Perpendicular, in early church buildings, such as the cathedrals at Wells and Glastonbury (Gothic elements built over Anglo-Norman structures), and at Westminster Abbey, and was also prominent in university halls and chapels, as at Eton, Oxford and Cambridge. Its hallmark is its verticality, enhanced by tapering spires, pointed arches and ribbed vaulting. Decorative elements often include refined carved stonework, intricate tracery, trefoil windows and stained glass. But the Gothic was not as wholly mimicked in England as in other places in Europe. English attitudes towards the French models were, according to some historians, 'ambivalent, casual, even critical'.[2]

By embracing the Gothic as a domestic fashion in the mid-eighteenth century, Walpole was bucking an earlier trend for neoclassicism, which was popular with English gentlemen who had returned from the Grand Tour under the spell of the sixteenth-century Venetian architect Andrea Palladio. Indeed, many of the residences in Twickenham were called 'villas' in reference to their Italian inspiration and showed the restrained neoclassicism and symmetry espoused by Palladio. Lord Burlington's Chiswick House, built in 1729, was perceived by many at the time to be the apotheosis of taste. Walpole, perhaps a bit competitive, admitted: 'I give myself a Burlington-air, and say, that as Chiswick is a model of Grecian architecture, Strawberry Hill is to be so of Gothic.'[3] His 'model' featured tall, pointed arches and ribbed vaults; narrow, curving 'ogee' and flowery quatrefoil windows; thick, stone walls (or the illusion of them), capped by battlements and corner steeples. He even created a crenellated tower with a cone-topped turret. And to all of this he added a riot of stained and painted glass and tracery designs that made his Gothic far less austere and much more virtuosic and flamboyant than what had inspired it.

Walpole's only novel, like his house, took an existing model and turned it into something far more spectacular. His fictional tale also has its origins in earlier designs, such as the

Strawberry Hill house after its transformation into a 'little Gothic castle' by Horace Walpole. Engraving by Paul Sandby, *c.* 1774.

legends of chivalric romance that sprang from the medieval quest tradition. But at the time he was writing, the novel itself was a new literary form, one that was much more flexible and adaptive than we sometimes allow for even today. *Robinson Crusoe*, considered the first English novel, was only forty-five years old when Walpole published *The Castle of Otranto* in 1764. The first volumes of Laurence Sterne's bawdy, meandering *Life and Opinions of Tristram Shandy*, still one of the most experimental novels ever written, had appeared five years previously and further volumes were still in progress. Walpole's tale, inspired by his love of Gothic architecture and the mystical atmosphere it created, was completely different, but it is safe to say that at this moment in literature, a lot of what was being written was completely different from what had come before. It was a good moment for inventing a genre.

Highlighting its 'toyshop' origins, Walpole referred to the higgledy-piggledy assortment of rooms across two small, attached houses as 'a little play-thing-house', or 'bauble'. Well before he began his novel, before his plans to remodel the house as his own 'Gothic castle' were underway, he was thrilled with his new abode, located in an area populated with the summer 'villas' of other prominent folk. Though in his love of Gothic he may have played the peculiar individualist, socially, Walpole liked to be where the action was. In this summer playground of the rich and notable, he had snapped up the last lot available that offered a clear view to the Thames, later recording that 'dowagers as plenty as flounders inhabit all around'.[4] The admired bluestocking (and Walpole's sometime nemesis) Lady Mary Wortley Montagu had a house nearby, as did her second cousin Henry Fielding, and other distinguished members of the artistic and social classes enjoyed summer houses in fairly close proximity. Alexander Pope once had a house only a couple of hundred yards away, which Walpole had visited as a child; in an early letter describing the wonders of his new neighbourhood, he wrote, 'Pope's ghost is just now skimming under my window by a most poetical moonlight.'[5] Having learned that the area had once been known as Strawberry Hill Shot, Walpole decided to adopt the bucolic title 'Strawberry Hill'.

By 1764, when he wrote *The Castle of Otranto*, Walpole had expanded and recast the house into a Gothic setting, with its imitation stone details and atmosphere of 'hallowed gloom' that became the backdrop for his novel. By today's standards, the novel is ridiculously unreal and a bit hokey (though it would be hard to dismiss it on those grounds, given much of what has been printed in the genre). Though based on earlier, mainly French, chivalric romances, Walpole's work was less ponderous, more action-packed and, admittedly, a quicker read than those drawn-out legends and narrative poems. There had also been some stories set in gloomy Gothic settings in the decades before, but they failed to capture the reading public in anything like the way that Walpole had managed.

As with the authors of some of the earliest stories that have come down to us, Walpole claimed to have been inspired by a dream. But rather than falling into a reverie while in some enchanted glade, as was a popular trope in Middle English poetry, he was captivated by his own architecture. He wrote that he had been inspired by the moody stair hall which had been created by Richard Bentley, a gentleman architect and member of the Strawberry Committee. Its Gothic features were drawn from an engraving of Prince Arthur's Chantry in Worcester Cathedral, the walls painted to resemble thin, elongated stone arches, and elaborate balustrades carved from wood in imitation of stone tracery.[6] Here, Walpole had established his formidable collection of arms and armour, and it was of these relics that he dreamed. 'I had thought myself in an ancient castle,' he wrote to his friend, the Reverend William Cole, 'and that on the uppermost banister of a great staircase I saw a gigantic hand in armour.'[7]

The story was not without its literary references. Critics of the time gave credit to Walpole's use of classical and Shakespearean elements, and his writing was far too sharp to be prosaic. But he had fun with the tale, publishing anonymously and claiming it had come from 'mysterious origins'; the first edition was titled *The Castle of Otranto, A Story. Translated by William Marshal, Gent. From the original Italian of Onuphrio Muralto, Canon of the Church of St Nicholas at Otranto*. The original preface states that the work was 'found in the library of an ancient catholic family in the north of England' and 'printed at Naples, in the black letter, in the year 1529', speculating that it must have been written 'between 1095, the æra of the first crusade, and 1243, the date of the last, or not long afterwards'.

With his detailed (and fictitious) preface, Walpole wanted very much to place readers in the mindset of a genuine 'Gothic' story. This wasn't just a device for fooling people. The first readers would not have been prepared for a novel like this, so he was probably wise to alert them with the mask of mysterious provenance, even though it later made his critics unhappy. He also wanted his readers to pay particular attention to the deliberately antique and accurately described setting, pointing out (in case they failed to notice) that 'the scene is undoubtedly laid in some real castle', since 'the author seems frequently, without design, to describe particular parts [of the house] . . . these and other passages are strong presumptions that the author had some certain building in his eye'.[8] Of course, it was all done very much 'with design', and the author did have a certain building in his eye: Strawberry Hill.

'In the evening I sat down and began to write, without knowing in the least what I intended to say or relate,' Walpole later said. But then, he continued, 'the work grew on my hands', and he finished the tale, in a continuous, engrossed state, in two months.[9] He was not the first or last writer to say he composed his masterwork in some sort of rush of artistic fervour.* But he was cleverer than his story of charging through his tale in a blind run suggests, and he worked hard to give it the atmosphere of ancient chivalry, mysticism and terror that 'some real castle', which was still ancient enough to provoke such reactions, would provide. As for the story itself, the language is archaic and the conceits grandiose, but there are elements that even a modern horror junkie would respect.

The novel tells the story of the egomaniacal Manfred, prince of Otranto, and begins with the wedding day of his son, Conrad. The boy is 'a homely youth, sickly and of no promising disposition', but Manfred has pinned the hopes for his own fortunes and the continuation of his bloodline on the marriage of his son to the daughter of a wealthy lord.[10] On the day of the wedding, a giant, disembodied battle helmet, 'a hundred times more large than any casque ever made for a human being', suddenly floats down into the castle courtyard, crushing poor Conrad and Manfred's carefully wrought plans along with him. Upon discovering this, 'the horror of the spectacle, the ignorance of all around how this misfortune happened, and above all, the tremendous phaenomenon before him, took away the prince's speech'. But rather than mourning his son, or even wondering how a giant helmet got into his castle, Manfred quickly decides to wed his would-be daughter-in-law, Isabella, himself. At this declaration, the plumes on the giant helmet begin twitching. 'Look, my lord!' Isabella cries. 'See heaven itself declares against your impious

---

* Some thirty years later, Samuel Taylor Coleridge professed to have written his poem *Kubla Khan* while not only in a dream state, but one induced by opiates.

intentions!' To which Manfred replies, 'Heaven nor hell shall impede my designs' (cue evil chuckle), and dispatches his wife with an order for divorce and a trip to the nearest convent with shocking efficiency.

But Manfred's schemes soon come undone. Isabella escapes his clutches by following a secret door (the lock being revealed by a singular shaft of moonlight) into a hidden underground passage to the sanctuary of a church, where she falls under the protection of a kindly priest. Manfred remains undeterred, and demands that the girl be found and returned to him, accusing his wife Hippolita, 'an amiable lady', and daughter Matilda, 'a beautiful virgin', of plotting against him and helping her to escape. After scolding the women for their betrayal (not taking into account, perhaps, that this is the wife he has

Private Collection/AS

The stair hall and 'armoury' at Strawberry Hill, with walls painted to resemble Gothic stone-work. It was the collection here that Walpole credited with inspiring *The Castle of Otranto*.

just abandoned), Manfred locks them in a tower. But then another signal of Manfred's dark secret appears in the form of an armour-clad arm, which descends on the castle, this time crushing an innocent servant. Finally, a whole giant knight appears, and Manfred and co. finally get the message that there is some sort of spiritual misdeed that demands atonement before people can stop being slaughtered by over-sized appendages. The story ends with Manfred, still determined to have his way, accidentally killing his own daughter, then losing everything anyway, because, as it turns out, he has come by his title, riches and power illegitimately, and so a cosmic wrong will be righted.

The reviews of the first, anonymous edition, praised the 'accurate and elegant' language and the 'keenest penetration, and most perfect knowlege [sic] of mankind' in what reviewers believed was a rediscovered medieval manuscript.[11] However, those same reviewers later baulked on finding that they had been duped by a well-known man of letters. The *Monthly Review* stated: 'When this book was published as a translation from an old Italian romance, we had the pleasure of distinguishing in it the marks of genius,' but 'that indulgence we afforded to the foibles of a supposed antiquity' could not be extended to a modern work 'in a cultivated period of learning'. It went on to admonish the author, 'a refined and polished genius', for 're-establishing the barbarous superstitions of Gothic devilism!'[12] So to their minds an old and mysterious tale was great if it was, in fact, old and mysterious, but not so if it was a clever imitation.

Walpole thought Gothic devilism was all great fun, however, particularly as it was his own house and collection that had played a part in it. In addition to being prompted by his armoury, he credited one of his paintings with provoking another mystical scene in the novel, when the portrait of Manfred's grandfather 'uttered a deep sigh and heaved its breast' and 'quit its pannel [*sic*]', before descending onto the floor 'with a grave and melancholy air'.[13] Such things may be an everyday occurrence at Hogwarts, but in the mid-eighteenth century the idea of a portrait coming to ghostly life was a more sensational concept. Pleased with his scenes of terrifying fantasy, Walpole wrote, somewhat giddily, to his friend William Cole in 1765: 'When you read of the picture quitting its panel, did not you recollect the portrait of Lord Falkland, all in white in my gallery?'[14]

For Walpole it wasn't the house as it was found (medieval or otherwise) that had captivated him, as was the case for other writers such as Charlotte Brontë (Norton Conyers), Charles Dickens (Restoration House) or Daphne du Maurier (Menabilly). It was the Gothic as Walpole himself had re-created it that got his literary wheels turning. *His* arched windows and wall paintings, *his* bits of coloured glass, *his* four-poster bed with its black and white ostrich feathers, *his* collections of everything from painted miniatures to arms and armour and what a contributor to the *General Magazine and Impartial Review* in 1791 called 'a collection of capital pictures', were the sources of his literary Gothic.[15] And while these designs and objects might have been well known to Walpole and his friends, they were still fantastical when presented to a reading audience as part of such a frightening narrative. (It must be said that the house, particularly after its recent restoration, is still quite provocative and could inspire even the most reasoned mind to imagine all sorts of strange goings-on.)

Though the Gothic tale depends on the elements of mystery and the 'unknown', Walpole and his Strawberry Committee approached the design of the house with precision. In the execution of his remodelling, Walpole was happy to use pattern books to create the *illusion* of stonework with paint and wood instead of the real thing, and to use papier mâché instead of plaster, because it was cheaper and faster. He wasn't interested in making exact replicas of anything, but he was absolutely committed to a certain style and atmosphere. The Gothic here was more important as a stage-setting than as a real revival of the historic architecture. What Sterne did in fiction Walpole was creating in physical detail. In fact, Walpole willingly admitted, 'My buildings, like my writings, are paper, and both will be blown away in ten years after I am dead.'[16] Nonetheless, as he toured the great houses of England, he was clear about what kind of building was acceptable. In a letter to his friend, Richard Bentley, he wrote in 1754 of a visit to Belhus, a substantial Tudor house in Essex belonging to Lord Dacre, which had lately been 'improved': 'What he has done is in Gothic, and very true, though not up to the perfection of the committee.'[17]

On that trip Walpole also visited 'the famous plantations and buildings of the last lord Petre', which he found to be 'the Brobdingnag of bad taste. The unfinished house is execrable.'[18] He was also less than pleased with Chalfont, the house belonging to Col. Charles Churchill and Lady Maria Walpole, Horace's illegitimate half-sister. This may have been a case of personal displeasure, but writing to his lifelong friend George Montagu, Walpole was unsympathetic to the couple and their home: 'The house and grounds are still in the same dislocated condition; in short, they [the couple] finish nothing but children.'[19] In later correspondence, he goes on to demolish Moor Park, a Palladian-style mansion in Hertfordshire, whose gardens had been laid out by 'Capability' Brown, and Blenheim Palace, designed by Vanbrugh for the first Duke of Marlborough. The latter, he says, 'looks like the palace of an auctioneer, who has been chosen king of Poland, and furnished his apartments with obsolete trophies, rubbish that nobody bid for'. And he goes on: 'The place is as ugly as the house, and the bridge, like the beggars at the old duchess's gate, begs for a drop of water, and is refused.'[20]

Though he may have been more outspoken than most, Walpole was not entirely alone in his taste; it was not unheard of to add Gothic elements to suburban houses at the time. The Gothic style that had come down through the High Church was already being revived by the nobility and the rising merchant class, who wanted to suggest some connection to ancient bloodlines. As Walpole had noted in his letters, the owners of Belhus and Chalfont, which had 'Mr Bentley's Gothic stable', had made their own Gothic additions and most people accomplished this by using the same kind of pattern books that Walpole consulted at the beginning of his project. But nothing was being done to the extravagant or detailed degree of Strawberry Hill.

Walpole's letters are full of ideas for his 'little Gothic castle'. He wrote to George Montagu in 1749 that he had seen some 'arms in painted glass' in the broken-down chapel of the church at Cheneys. 'As these are so neglected', he said, 'I propose making a push and begging them of the duke of Bedford.'[21] This was one of dozens of such 'pushes' that Walpole made to outfit his house in Gothic splendour and build his collection of art inside it. The Gothic Revival in England wouldn't take hold for another fifty years or so, reaching its apogee with A. W. N. Pugin's upward-seeking designs for the Houses of Parliament. So Walpole's own efforts and the designs that made their way into his fictional castle, though much more elaborate, were a reflection of a taste that was creeping around the margins of English buildings in the late eighteenth century.

For Strawberry Hill, Walpole strove to reproduce a sense of what he called 'gloomth' (gloom and warmth), which he felt was key to the allure of Gothic cathedrals. On his first trip to France, he was captivated by Chartreuse, a Carthusian monastery in Paris (now destroyed). He tried to copy elements from French cathedrals, such as Rouen, as well as designs from English churches. Walpole was not a religious man, however he loved the ritual, the ornate symbolism and theatricality of the High Church and its architecture. It was the kind of architecture, like his fictional castle, that invites strange and dramatic happenings. He filled the the ground-floor hall with stained-glass windows featuring the figures of saints, and when an explosion at a gunpowder mill a few miles away caused the windows to shatter, he wrote to a friend, 'The two saints in the hall have suffered martyrdom.'[22]

In the novel, Walpole called on both the fortified and ecclesiastical references: the story involves the intercession of a friar and a subterranean passage leading to a church, where

Isabella takes refuge. In this, he was following some of what had come before, as the darkened recesses and dimly lit niches of Gothic architecture lend themselves so well to a good horror story. But thereafter, these spaces became lasting ingredients in the Gothic novel. Walpole also enjoyed the trappings of the church: he and his friends were known to dress up in monk's garb to play-act in his deliberately monastic spaces, both revelling in and mocking the Christian rites, in much the same way that he revelled in and also played on the tropes of the Gothic in his novel. Were there some aspects of the occult in the original formations of Gothic buildings? There are perfectly reasoned, historic answers to such questions, but

Horace Walpole posing in the library at Strawberry Hill. The bookcases were framed in elaborately carved timber painted to mimic carved Gothic arches and pilasters.

then there is the human imagination, and Walpole liked to let his run, which is why his novel and his house are such great fun.

Like Manfred, Walpole wanted to establish a house that would be remade into his own ancestral seat, but without having a legitimate ancestor to claim as its creator. So although he had already successfully converted the façade to a suitably Gothic one, and added and recast rooms in the Gothic style, he decided to create other rooms fit for 'state' occasions. The most flamboyant of these is the Gallery, which was and, thanks to its recent restoration, is again a piece of Gothic confectionery, with niches framed in elaborate tracery and topped by gilded baldachins modelled on the tomb of Archbishop Thomas Bourchier in Canterbury Cathedral. A riotous, lacey fan-vaulted ceiling, made from papier mâché and based on the side aisle of Henry VII's chapel at Westminster Abbey, was painted white and gilded. The room was lined in rich, crimson damask wall-coverings, which, together with the swirling white and gold plasterwork, all reflected in mirrored glass, made for a heady experience, especially when seen by candlelight. While Walpole found the space made him 'ashamed of my own magnificence', others have perceived it as a gaudy indulgence. His most recent biographer, Tim Mowl, compares its decorative effect to 'a whore's boudoir'.[23]

Here, Walpole also set up the country's first private printing press, the Strawberry Hill Press, which he used to publish his pamphlets and his novel. He also printed in 1784 *A Description of the Villa of Horace Walpole*, a detailed guide to the house and its collections, so that people would understand and better appreciate the vast array of art and objects he had so carefully accumulated. His rooms and collections were among the finest in the country, and Strawberry Hill became one of the most famous houses in Europe. Because of its notoriety and Walpole's willingness to open it to the public, crowds of people visited the house during the fifty years of his residence there, and surely more had heard of it and seen the 'description', if not the actual house. The Gothic Revival, at least in people's imaginations, was building.

As for Walpole's other creation, the modern Gothic novel, it directly influenced other works that combined architecture and fantasy during his own lifetime and beyond. In 1796 a young writer called Matthew Gregory Lewis produced a speedily written novel called *The Monk*, which played on a nightmarish monastic background and featured a creaky castle, a violated maiden, ghostly visages and an unusual villain in the form of a woman who disguises herself as a novice in order to seduce a young priest. *The Monk* shocked with its depictions of violence, devilry, murder, rape, incest and a bleeding nun, and so was a great success with readers, including the poet Samuel Taylor Coleridge, who admired it as 'the offspring of no common genius', but found some parts to be of 'a low and vulgar taste' and a novel that 'if a parent saw in the hands of a son or a daughter, he might reasonably turn pale'.[24]

Ann Radcliffe, who published her first Gothic novel in 1789 but found fame with *The Mysteries of Udolpho* in 1794, is considered the more direct heir to Walpole. Her novel also takes place in a faraway land, and although she achieved her terror-charged atmosphere as much through the landscape (perilous mountain passes and rugged coastal cliffs) as through architecture, the title refers to a castle in the Italian Apennines. (By now the exotically named castle has already become a popular hook in fiction.) There, the heroine, Emily St Aubert, is held captive, along with her aunt, who is banished to the 'east turret' and eventually dies. She comes upon a room filled with 'instruments of torture', finds a dead body and appropriately faints, before accomplishing an unlikely escape.[25] Emily St Aubert meets all of the requirements of the Gothic heroine, being 1) innocent, 2) young, 3) orphaned and 4) beautiful. The eponymous castle, as well as Chateau-le-Blanc, where she finally finds refuge, were probably based on the author's reading, rather than on any building she knew directly, as it is not likely that she travelled on the Continent before the novel was published.

Radcliffe's already popular works gained even more notoriety when Jane Austen created Catherine Morland, in *Northanger Abbey*. Of course, a great deal is known about Austen and her gift for capturing the manners and morals of Regency society (see chapter 3). Her genre was not the Gothic, but, having read Ann Radcliffe, she did produce a delightful parody of the style and of its readers, who had, by the time of her writing, around 1803, become so familiar as to be considered legitimate targets for ridicule, albeit gentle. At the beginning of *Northanger Abbey*, Catherine argues the merits of *The Mysteries of Udolpho* with her friend's rather dull brother John Thorpe, who dismisses novels generally, provoking a defense of both; at the time, novels were not considered worthwhile reading material for well-born young ladies. When Catherine is finally invited to the abbey belonging to the family of the handsome Henry Tilney, she can barely contain her excitement at fulfilling a Gothic-inspired dream. Familiar with Catherine's reading habits, Tilney asks whether she is 'prepared to encounter all the horrors that a building such as "what one reads about" may produce'.[26]

Catherine answers Tilney's prod as if reading straight from a page of ghostly fiction, saying that she needn't be frightened of the house, as 'it has never been uninhabited and left deserted for years, and then the family come back to it unawares, without giving any notice, as generally happens'. But Tilney goads her further: 'No, certainly. We shall not have to explore our way into a hall dimly lighted by the expiring embers of a wood fire.' Nor will there be 'gloomy passages into an apartment never used since some cousin or kin died in

Private Collection/AS

Fonthill Abbey, with its soaring, twenty-five-storey central tower, painted by the Romantic artist John Martin, *c*. 1823.

it about twenty years before'. However, he continues, she may be awakened by 'a violent storm', which will drive her out to a 'subterraneous communication between your apartment and the chapel of St Anthony'.[27] In addition to 'gloomthy' passages and empty apartments, the secret tunnel, which was Isabella's path to freedom in *The Castle of Otranto*, has by now become a hallmark of the genre. It is thought that Northanger was probably inspired by the ruined Netley Abbey in Hampshire, a Cistercian monastery converted in the Tudor period into a private manor house. Netley Abbey was in a state of abandonment by the time Jane Austen would have visited around the turn of the nineteenth century, but it continued to attract artists and writers, especially those of the Romantic movement, who were in thrall to its picturesque ruins.

Walpole's legacy of a Gothic literary-architectural obsession also has a descendent in William Beckford, author of the little-known novel *Vathek*, and better known as the creator of Fonthill Abbey. Beckford became fabulously wealthy at the age of nine, when his father died in 1770. The boy inherited a country house, 'one of the greatest fortunes in Europe' and an income from his father's Jamaican plantations.[28] Bright and well educated, he published *Vathek* (written in French) in 1782. Translated into English and published in London in 1786, the novel was influenced both by *The Castle of Otranto* and by the fashion for Orientalism engendered by the recent popularity of Lady Mary Wortley Montagu's *Letters from Turkey*, written during her residence there as wife of the British ambassador, and by the equally popular tales of *The Arabian Nights*.

The eponymous Vathek is a greedy caliph who seeks super-natural powers and performs hideous deeds in order to achieve them. He casts innocent children to their deaths and finds amusement in the abasement of those who are loyal to him, all the while feasting and indulging his sensual appetites. In pursuit of the powers of the dark arts, Vathek ventures from his mighty tower and palace at Samarah to find the sub-terranean 'palace of fire'. The idea of the two palaces (and the splendour of the travelling retinue) held an intoxicating charm for a reading public who had become just familiar enough from those recent accounts of the East to be engaged with, rather than alienated by, their lavish exoticism.

Like Walpole, Beckford claimed to have written the book in a fever of inspiration, saying 'the fit I laboured under lasted two days and a night'.[29] While it is likely that the writing took longer than that, the feverish atmosphere is believable, as the tale took its cue, Beckford said, from an extravagant coming-of-age party he had thrown for himself at Fonthill Splendens, the grand house he had inherited. Beckford's father had been a friend of Walpole, and the elder Beckford, like Walpole's father, had built his own grand country house, which attracted visitors from around the country and bestowed a sense of architectural grandeur on his only child. Built in the Palladian style, Fonthill Splendens was a massive house with a giant front portico, approached by a double-stair enclosed with stone balustrades. Colonnades connected to two further pavil-ions topped with cupolas. Of the interiors, it was the great Egyptian Hall and the Turkish Room that were the most remarkable. The former was eighty-five feet long, with many low, vaulted passages coming off of it, and probably inspired the Hall of Eblis in *Vathek*. The Turkish Room reflected the popularity among the upper classes for the decor of the East, as portrayed in accounts such as those by Lady Mary Wortley Montagu, and had a golden coved ceiling, painted with arabesques and flowers, an oversized Persian carpet, silk draperies and a profusion of mirrored glass that amplified the effect of the room to a dizzying experience. One visitor remarked on 'the utmost profusion of magnificence', marred by 'the appearance of immense riches almost too tawdrily exhibited'.[30]

In the Christmas season after his twenty-first birthday, the young Beckford held a private festival that consisted of three days of food, drink, music and play-acting in a 'delirium of delight', all carried out at Fonthill Splendens, which had been lavishly decorated with theatrical scenery, curtained off from prying eyes and daylight.[31] Tales of the party scandalised polite society, or at least those members who hadn't been invited. *Vathek* is peppered with similar scenes of extended bacchanal, interspersed with moments of grotesque barbarism, making way for a moralistic ending that enabled the book to get past public censure (in a way that Beckford himself could not). Though the story is not considered wholly Gothic, the elements of horror and fantasy have a lot in common with the genre, and as the builder of the great Gothic folly Fonthill Abbey, Beckford assumes a rightful place in the Gothic canon. Perhaps foretelling his own majestic designs, Beckford describes how Vathek found his father's palace of Alkoremi 'far too scanty' and made sumptuous improvements, adding 'five wings, or rather other palaces, which he destined for the particular gratification of each of the senses'.[32] Beckford would later take down Fonthill Splendens to build Fonthill Abbey, whose central tower would, in fact, bear a tragic similarity to Vathek's own tower of 1,500 steps, from where 'he beheld men not much larger than pismires; mountains than shells; and cities, than bee-hives'.[33] Like Fonthill Abbey, the fictional tower does not stand for long.

Vathek garnered enthusiastic reviews and was greatly admired by figures such as Lord Byron, but the author had little time to enjoy his success. He was forced to take himself and his new wife off to exile in Europe after being accused of conducting a homosexual liaison with the fifteen-year-old William 'Kitty' Courtenay, 9th Earl of Devon, with whom Beckford had been besotted for several years. On his return to the family home towards the end of the century, Beckford began work on one of the most extensive and extravagant indulgences of private building in the country.

Begun in 1796, the new house that would replace the Palladian Fonthill Splendens was designed by James Wyatt, an architect who began his career as a neoclassicist but then embraced the Gothic style (Wyatt had also created some designs for Strawberry Hill). By its completion in 1812, Fonthill Abbey would have induced a feeling of awe in Walpole himself. Beckford, too, had travelled extensively in Britain and Europe, and shared Walpole's admiration for medieval architecture, particularly that of the French Carthusians, an admiration that found expression in Fonthill Abbey. Containing eighteen bedrooms, as well as various parlours, vaulted corridors, galleries and a suitably Gothic cloister, the house was not composed of five 'palaces of the senses', but was nonetheless grandiose. It was laid out in a cruciform shape, with four wings coming off of an octagonal centre, and stretched 312 feet in length from north to south, and 270 feet from east to west. But it was the enormous height of its octagonal turrets (120 feet) and its central tower, which rose to 276 feet (more than twenty-five storeys for a modern building) that gave the Fonthill its startling presence.[34] Contemporaries noted the building's poetical spirit, delicate, tapering towers and collection of vertically striving shapes, which evinced an ethereal quality, especially when shrouded in the mists of the Wiltshire countryside. Artists, notably J. M. W. Turner, rushed to paint it.

Beckford lived a fairly solitary life at Fonthill Abbey; his two young daughters, whose mother had died in childbirth, lived in a separate house in the grounds. Unlike Walpole, he seldom entertained guests. Having been stung early on by public condemnation of his exploits, it is likely that he dared not allow himself the temptation of large, boisterous company. The Abbey may not have been fully occupied, but it was extravagant, from the Eastern Postern Tower in the south transept to St Michael's Gallery, with its walls washed in 'palest pink', the Great Dining Room, the Crimson Drawing Room, the Great Drawing Room, the Octagon Room, the Lancaster Rooms, and the Oratory, painted and draped in purple, scarlet and gold.[35] Beckford furnished all of the interiors splendidly. As he had mixed ingredients of English Gothic fiction and Arabian tales in his novel, he combined elements of Gothic (Christian) architecture with the Oriental objects that had become popular among the educated classes (and which were enumerated in the palatial splendours of *Vathek*). He complemented his large collection of art with intricate stucco painted to look like stonework, window- and door-hangings in great lengths of purple and crimson velvet, massive Turkish carpets and specially commissioned pieces of furniture. Mimicking the powers of his fictional caliph, Beckford indulged in dramatic effects to amaze his (infrequent) guests, creating a long, vaulted hall with no windows and a set of double doors that he had rigged to swing back when he stamped his foot on a certain plank, shouting 'Open!' as he did so.[36]

Like Walpole, Beckford strove to establish links with a historic past. The great hammerbeam ceiling was dotted with supposedly ancestral shields, and he claimed that the seventeenth-century ebony 'state bed' had belonged to Henry VII and that some other ebony chairs once belonged to Cardinal Wolsey.* However, despite the elaborate dressing, most of the rooms were either inaccessible by the winding stairs or uncomfortably damp and chilly. It was recorded that servants often tended sixty fires at once to keep the internal temperature of the occupied rooms bearable. But the vistas of the spires in the landscape and of the views through the vaulted interiors were said to be breathtaking.

By 1805, with his estates in trouble and the costs of the abbey continuing to rise as steadily as its shapely spires, Beckford found himself in financial trouble. In 1822 he sold the 'Holy Spulchre', as he called it, for a healthy £330,000. He had become less enamoured of the building, finding that it had not answered his passions after all. It seems he would have recalled his own portent: when Vathek ascends his great tower, he is dismayed to observe that 'he saw the stars [still] as high above him as they appeared when he stood on the

---

* The bed and many other furnishings were bought by George Lucy at the Fonthill sale of 1822 and went to Charlecote Park Park near Stratford-upon-Avon.

Private Collection/AS

King Edward's Gallery in the north wing of Fonthill Abbey. The elaborate decoration included flowing purple and scarlet drapery, walls covered in red damask and carved oak ceiling.

surface of the earth'.[37] In a nice Gothic twist to the tale, a few years later Beckford is said to have received a deathbed confession from the contractor who had worked for Wyatt. The dying man allegedly revealed that he had not laid the foundations for the tower correctly and that it was probably unstable. The new owner, Mr Farquhar, was informed, but paid no heed. The tower fell later that year, crushing the centre octagon and the Great Western Dining Room. When Farquhar was told what had happened, he replied coolly that it was a good thing, since the house had been too large for him anyway.[38] Later excavations showed that the tower's foundations were adequate, but that the building work had been less than perfect.

Though it was eventually demolished (only part of the gate-house and a small part of the north wing remain) Fonthill Abbey lives on, like a ghostly presence, in paintings, drawings and poetry. If the name sounds like it should be a novel itself, that's probably because, as scholars Barbara Benedict and Deirdre Le Faye have reckoned, between 1784 and 1818 there were 'no fewer than thirty-two novels' published that contained the word 'Abbey' in the title. And the trend didn't show any signs of slowing in 1818.[39] It is as if Beckford's greater gift to the Gothic tradition was his fallen abbey, rather than either the built object or his galloping tale of Oriental treasure and necromancy. (He went on to build another, somewhat less spectacular, tower in Bath, where he lived after leaving Font-hill.) But the very nature of the Gothic story – the supernatural happenings, the gloomy halls, the terror-inducing encounters with the spirit world – were all present in his novel, which, along with the poetic ruins of his abbey, helped to sustain the genre for a new generation.

Part of that new generation were the Romantic writers, some of whom took inspiration from *Vathek* and *The Castle of Otranto*, while others followed new directions. Mary Shelley's *Frankenstein* (1818), while focusing more on physical and psycho-intellectual terrors than supernatural ones, nevertheless plays on the chilling drama of an inhuman stalker and a frenzied chase through a dreamlike landscape. Thomas Love Peacock, a friend to Byron, Shelley and Coleridge and a frequent guest at their intellectually charged gatherings, wrote novels that played on the Gothic penchant for haunted houses, but were more about satirising liberal-intellectual discourse than any demonic presences. His books *Headlong Hall*, *Crotchet Castle* and *Nightmare Abbey* sound like classics of the horror genre, and their Gothic-inspired settings are drawn in fanciful detail. But these settings were just convenient backdrops from which to poke fun at the self-congratulatory high-mindedness of Peacock's Romantic friends, such as the poet Percy Bysshe Shelley and his circle as well as politicians and scientists. In the half-ruined castle, a group of characters – a nobleman, a vicar, an ichthyologist, perhaps, and one or two other pseudo-intellectuals – share a passion for reforming the world through disputations of 'metaphysical romance and romantic metaphysics' that are not worlds away from the debates at Shandy Hall.[40] It wasn't until the middle of the nineteenth century that a bestseller, Charlotte Brontë's *Jane Eyre*, came along to marry, once again, Gothic romance and architecture, as well as the tale's protagonists.

The Gothic story, as Walpole shaped it, became about transcending limits: those of the old-fashioned legend (of the early romances), the classically inspired morality tale, even the popular realism of Defoe, Fielding and Richardson. The Gothic architecture he embraced started off by defying the most popular trends of the time and later evolved into something that drew on real historic patterns, but was enlivened by pure fantasy. Of course, what Walpole and Beckford did in building their fantasies was not totally unheard of at the time. Many a country squire indulged in building ornate follies in their estate parks, including Stowe, in Buckinghamshire, whose Gothic Temple dates from 1741, Goldney Hall, Hagley Hall, and many others. But Walpole and Beckford instigated a cultural cycle of creating in life something that mirrored their literary imaginations and then presenting both to the world at large. Not many years later, Walteer Scott would inhabit a similar cycle of creation in his romanticising of Scottish history while building himself a Baronial hall at Abbotsford.

Of course, for Walpole and Beckford, there were other motives behind these extraordinary architectural feats. Both were rich, highly intelligent and creative men. They were also both homosexual and lived at a time when sodomy was still a capital offense, and both were threatened with exposure of their inclinations to the wider public. Their near-obsession with their fantasy buildings is seen by many cultural commentators to reflect an urge for unchecked expression that was not allowed in their daily life – an exuberant rebuttal to censorship, perhaps. Gothic fiction, with its psychosexual overtones, is an apt channel for such expression.

The authors of these first Gothic novels not only tell us about their own preoccupations with houses and the accomplishments of their fantasies, but also reflect the bourgeois passion for building and improving houses that was beginning to take hold in the eighteenth century. With a different style of house came different modes of socialising, in which young people had more freedom to intermingle. By the Regency period building houses had become something of a national pastime for the wealthy, and brought with it a taste for dinners, balls and assembly dances. They may have appeared less frightening than the dimly lit corridors of a ghostly manor, but for the characters, particularly the women who were caught up in them, those rooms could be every bit as intimidating.

Chawton Cottage

THREE

Pride and Property:
Women and Houses in Regency England

'And of this place,' thought she, 'I might have been mistress! With these rooms I might now have been familiarly acquainted! Instead of viewing them as a stranger, I might have rejoiced in them as my own . . .'

Pride and Prejudice

Jane Austen is one of those figures who is often viewed through the wrong end of a telescope from the modern age towards a seemingly estranged past. She never married, lived her entire adult life with her mother and sister and seemed at home with the idea of female dependence and subservience. Her novels all end with a good-hearted heroine triumphing over obstacles and marrying for love, occasionally above their own station. But Austen was an active participant in her own social scene. She also had acute powers of observation, and while she accepted the society she lived in, she could also lampoon its participants and preoccupations with cutting accuracy and fulsome humour. She did not directly challenge the fixation on marriage and property that was so much a part of her social set, but concentrated her author's lens so powerfully on the expectations and accepted rules of engagement, so to speak, that readers see the questions clearly for themselves. Questions such as, why must all women, even the clever independent ones, be compelled to find men to marry them? Austen begins five of her six completed novels by explaining her characters' relationships to their properties and what kind of predicament these cause,* whereas in *Northanger Abbey* the title tells us the name and style of house that is at the centre of the story.

Jane Austen wrote and was published during the Regency period in England, when the Prince of Wales acted as regent while his father, George III, was declared too unstable to govern. The Regency lasted only from 1811 to 1820, but a longer period – affected by the prince's lavish lifestyle against the backdrop of uncertainty generated by the French Revolution and the Napoleonic Wars – can be identified from around 1789 to 1830. It was a time when the Prince of Wales, later George IV, a profligate character who enjoyed food, drink and parties as much as any modern tabloid celebrity, defined the tastes and habits of the upper classes. The man who once spent an entire morning watching the fashion trendsetter Beau Brummel tie a cravat and, on being declared regent, gave the largest, most expensive party the British had ever seen, also had an interest in doing up houses. He commissioned first Henry Holland and then John Nash to design a seaside retreat at Brighton for himself and his mistress, Mrs Fitzherbert, in an extravagant Chinese-Indian style, and had his London lodgings, Carlton House, substantially augmented into an opulent palatial residence. On becoming king in 1820, he sold

---

* Her unfinished novel, *Sanditon*, also opens with a named house, and concerns property speculation at a seaside resort in the years following the Battle of Waterloo.

Carlton House to fund a scheme to turn Buckingham House into the much grander Buckingham Palace.

The spendthrift prince wasn't the only one with a fever for building. Some of the grandest houses in Britain were being constructed, or 'improved', during the Regency period by architects such as Robert Adam and John Nash, as members of the court did their utmost to imitate the prince's extravagances. New houses took their places alongside Kedleston Hall ('the glory of Derbyshire'), Syon House, Osterley Park, Chatsworth House (which was being enlarged), Blenheim Palace, Castle Howard – houses that had become the great symbols of English power and glory. These elaborated residences also became the settings for the social life of the elite, with all of its drama and intrigue. In his classic study *Life in the English Country House*, Mark Girouard names the period from 1720 to 1770 as that of 'the social house' and 1770 to 1830 as 'the arrival of informality', referring to the new arrangements and sizes of rooms, which allowed for more frequent and less programmed gatherings. The landed gentry ensured that their country houses had rooms big enough to hold gatherings that in the past might have only happened in London, and their many rooms and servants made it possible to host friends for weeks or even months at a time.[1] Visitors moved in a train of coaches packed with cases, servants, gifts and gossip, carried from one fashionable house to another.

In addition to the space offered in such massive homes, improvements in roads, turnpikes, carriage and coach transportation made such extended visits more feasible, especially for women, who were less likely to make long-distance journeys on horseback or in the earlier, less comfortable carriages.[2] Advances in transport also enhanced the speed and efficiency of the postal service, which meant that information and chatter between houses travelled faster and more frequently. Letter writing was an intrinsic part of eighteenth-century life, and Jane Austen was a particularly diligent and entertaining correspondent. If, for example, she went to stay with her brother Edward at his large estate Godmersham in Kent, she and her sister, Cassandra, wrote to each other every three or four days, despite having to mind the expense. The habit of letter-writing naturally influenced the fiction of the time, most directly in the epistolary novel, or 'novel-in-letters'. Two of Austen's predecessors (and literary influences), Samuel Richardson and Fanny Burney, both wrote novels (*Pamela*, *Clarissa* and *Evelina*) that consisted of epistolary sequences. Austen herself initially composed *Sense and Sensibility* as a series of letters, and it is thought that some of her other novels were also originally conceived in this way. She may have abandoned the idea of telling her stories wholly through letters, but by having her characters spend long periods at other people's houses, Austen allowed herself the opportunity to fly personal notes from house to house, filled with the news, intimate matters and whiffs of any household scandal, as well as descriptions of their hosts' decorative tastes.

With the trend for grand houses came a taste for 'entertainments'. In the late eighteenth century, the charismatic Georgiana, Duchess of Devonshire, an intimate of the Prince of Wales, led the 'ton', or high society, and became a model society hostess. But it was her son, the 6th Duke of Devonshire, 'an incessant giver of house parties', who added the long North Wing to Chatsworth House and had a private theatre built to further entertain his many guests. Chatsworth was among a string of large country houses, among them Wynnstay in Denbighshire, Wargrave in Berkshire and Blenheim Palace in Oxfordshire, to have such an extravagant construction for entertainment.[3] Amateur theatricals were also popular among the lower gentility, even at the Austen rectory. In *Mansfield Park* the young Bertrams take advantage of their father's absence (the grim Sir Thomas is no fan of such frivolity) and decide to construct a temporary stage in the billiard room. Of course, they are advised against it by the ever-sensible Fanny Price, and the reveal is a comic scene in which the blustering Sir Thomas, returning home unexpectedly, stumbles onto the

Private Collection

The rectory in Steventon, Jane Austen's family home until the age of twenty-five, in a sketch by her niece Anne Lefroy.

stage by accident and finds himself standing opposite 'a ranting young man' (Tom junior's friend Mr Yates in thespian mode), 'who appeared likely to knock him down backwards'.[4]

Austen's portraits of country houses were painted with an eye for the property rights, rituals and manners they occasioned. Points of architecture and landscaping are detectable but not marked out with as fine a brush. As the architectural historian Nikolaus Pevsner said, she is 'without exception vague, when it comes to describing buildings', adding ruefully that Austen tells us even less of the interiors than the exteriors.[5] And yet, somewhat ironically (and due only somewhat to the efforts of film-makers), anyone who has read one of her novels has a clear sense that there is a particular house, or houses, at its heart. The details that she does provide, however 'vague', have entranced a train of serious scholars, from Pevsner to the novelist Vladimir Nabokov, who assiduously mapped out the plan of Mansfield Park and the house and grounds of neighbouring Sotherton Court, as well as various other details from the novel.[6]

And Austen was certainly not vague about the importance of houses. Her heroines all aspire to marriage and a comfortable home as a matter of some urgency, a condition with which she was well acquainted. She knew what making a good marriage or otherwise acquiring property meant to women of her time, and she wasn't afraid to make the point. She knew the room arrangements and the etiquette of both large estates and parsonages, as well as the intricacies of inheritance law, and she reflected popular domestic trends, such as the fad for amplifying houses and ornamenting their grounds, and for touring those great houses filled with the furnishings and artistic trophies of the very rich.

Entailment, the condition by which a property is tied to a male heir for succeeding generations, was still widely practised at the time Jane Austen was writing. This meant that an inheritance and property could pass over a female relative – a wife or daughter, say – in favour of the next male in the family, even if he is only a distant relation. Austen presents the issue head-on in *Pride and Prejudice* and *Sense and Sensibility*, demonstrating how a woman of some wealth could find herself penniless on her father's (or husband's) death, with her well-being wholly dependent on the male heir. In *Sense and Sensibility*, that heir happens to be the Dashwood sisters' otiose brother, John, whose opinions are so easily manipulated by his grasping wife. When Mrs John Dashwood 'installed herself mistress of Norland', John's mother and sisters were quite quickly 'degraded to the condition of visitors'.[7] Austen spends several pages at the beginning of the novel explaining the means by which Norland, though not technically entailed, will be passed on to John Dashwood and then to his young son, leaving his mother and sisters dependent on a small income and his grudging support.

The Bennet women in *Pride and Prejudice* are similarly endangered, as Longbourn is entailed and Mr Bennet's cousin, the priggish Mr Collins, is next in line to inherit. As Mr Bennet informs his family, 'When I am dead [Mr Collins] may turn you all out of this house as soon as he pleases.'[8] Mrs Bennet lets us know perhaps a little of how Austen feels on this score when she says of Mr Collins and his new wife, 'Well if they can be easy with an estate that is not lawfully their own, so much the better. *I* should be ashamed of having one that was only entailed on me.'[9]

Tellingly, when the fickle Maria Bertram decides to stick with her engagement to Rushworth after all, 'she pledged herself anew to Sotherton' – not the man exactly, but his house anyway.[10] Similarly, Mary Crawford considers Tom Bertram has 'almost everything in his favour' as a potential spouse, 'a park, a real park five miles round, a spacious modern-built house, so well placed and well screened as to deserve to be in any collection of engravings of gentlemen's seats in the kingdom'. It wants, she notes, 'only to be completely new furnished'.[11] In her portraits of women trying to marry well, Austen was not emphasising the shallowness and greed of young women in society (or not in all cases). For women in England in the late eighteenth century, the ownership of property meant personal security, but in a wider public sense rules of ownership were seen as being key to social order and peace in general; the obsession with property, getting it, improving it and showing it off, was all around.[12]

As well as improving their property, it was common practise for members of the upper classes to go on the Grand Tour, as Austen's brother Edward was allowed to do. These wealthy wanderers typically returned with a haul of furnishings, artworks and other souvenirs, for which they needed a suitably grand exhibition space. Such displays were not only for friends and family, but also for the wider public. Since the Elizabethan period, the great houses had attracted well-heeled tourists who came to study these fabulous collections of architecture and Continental art. During the Regency, this sort of touring became increasingly popular, with some houses even producing guidebooks detailing their important features.* Horace Walpole produced such a guide for Strawberry Hill in 1784. As Elizabeth Bennet and her aunt and uncle find when they visit Pemberley, thinking that Mr Darcy is not at home, there was usually an informed housekeeper on hand, who, for a small fee, would show visitors around and tell them about the house and its collections. Although Austen probably never ventured much beyond the South of England, it's likely that she visited or at least knew about Stowe, home of the Viscount Cobham, and one of the most popular garden attractions at the time, which may have informed her sharp-eyed view of the improvements planned for Sotherton.

The Georgian period of house-building and expanding was also a time when socialising between the families of the upper echelons became both more organised and somewhat less formal than in the past, and this was very important to Austen's plotting. In their enlarged and lavishly decorated rooms, genteel society gathered for dinners, balls, assemblies, masquerades, routs, drums, *ridotto* (a dance combined with a concert) and gambling, all of which are brilliantly described by writers like Austen and her coeval society novelist, Fanny Burney.[13] Austen sent her characters to such social events in order to create the interactions that would advance her plot, as well as providing space – like visits to country houses and afternoon tea – for some choice moments in the comedy of manners. But her private observations on these occasions were much more biting (and humorous) than what made it

---

* Among the earliest was a guide for Stowe in Buckinghamshire, published by Benton Seeley in 1744.

into her fiction. In 1800 she wrote to Cassandra of one such ball:

> Miss Iremonger did not look well, & Mrs Blount was the only one much admired. She appeared exactly as she did in September, with the same broad face, diamond bandeau, white shoes, pink husband and fat neck. [...] The General has got the Gout, and Mrs Maitland the Jaundice. – Miss Debary, Susan & Sally all in black [...] made their appearance, & I was as civil to them as their bad breath would allow me.[14]

Austen herself was not averse to staying at a party until the early hours and in a letter from 1798 she describes a ball attended by her early love interest, Tom Lefroy: 'There were twenty Dances & I danced them all, & without any fatigue.'[15] She attended balls at the assembly rooms in Basingstoke, as well as at several great houses, including Manydown, Hurstbourne Park, Kempshott, Greywell Hill, Oakley Hall, Ashe Park, Chilham Castle and Goodnestone, the house in Kent belonging to her brother Edward's in-laws. She wrote to Cassandra in 1800: 'I believe I drank too much wine last night at Hurstbourne; I know not else how to account for the shaking of my hand today. [...] – we began at 10, supped at 1, & were at Deane [Park, a house belonging to friends] before 5.'[16] As with the trend for new kinds of dances and entertainment, the protocols for socialising among the elite were evolving from more staid 'assemblies' (gatherings of 'polite persons' for conversation, and perhaps card games) to balls, at which people also dined and played cards.[17] The Austen siblings took part in these rituals with alacrity, sometimes at the homes of wealthier friends, sometimes in public assembly rooms.

Although there was some relaxation of socialising, in the heady atmosphere of extravagant fashions and famously extravagant personalities, high society tried to maintain a hold on power and order via strict codes of conduct. As we know from the array of scandals that emerged, however, in practice these were often more about the appearance of propriety than the reality, at least in some circles. People interacted with others in keeping with the relative distinction of their wealth or family ties. The house party, those prolonged visits of groups of guests or entire families, was a great facilitator of such meetings. (It was during one such visit, while he and his wife were guests at Powderham Castle in Devon, that William Beckford was accused of assaulting the young William Courtenay, see chapter 2.)

Austen's characters often participate in similarly extended visits, though with slightly lesser degree of scandal. Sir John Middleton of Barton Park 'delighted in collecting about him more young people than his house would hold' and it is in his home that the Dashwoods meet Colonel Brandon, Mrs Jennings and the Palmers, all of whom are his resident guests.[18] The Dashwood ladies, become somewhat itinerant after losing their home to the male heir, John, a condition that echoes Austen's own experience after her father made over his living and rectory to his eldest son. Marianne and Elinor spend over two months with Mrs Jennings in London, then move onto stay with the Palmers at Cleveland, 'a spacious modern-built house, situated on a sloping lawn',[19] and it is during a long visit with her aunt and uncle at their house Lambton that

Elizabeth Bennet learns of her younger sister's elopement, by letter from her sister Jane.* House parties became not only a way for leisured society to pass the time, but also a way for parents and matchmakers to bring together young people of similar 'connections' and 'breeding'. Elinor Dashwood comes to know Edward Ferrars after he has been staying 'several weeks' at Norland, and when Jane Bennet is invited to Mr Bingley's house Netherfield, it is so his sisters can look her over at their leisure.[20]

When Lady Catherine de Bourgh admonishes Elizabeth Bennet, asking if she does not 'consider that a connection with you must disgrace [Mr Darcy] in the eyes of everybody, a young woman without family connections or fortune', it was to mark her out from the crowd she had seemingly infiltrated. (For this injustice, Austen could call on her own thwarted love affair with a young man who was meant for a wealthier match.) Tellingly, Elizabeth and Jane Bennet become long-term guests at Netherfield by chance, rather than invitation. Jane has been asked for a short stay, but falls ill and cannot return home, whereupon her spirited sister Elizabeth comes to nurse her. Here, the Bennet sisters effectively gate-crash the gathering at Netherfield, causing all sorts of awkwardness on both sides of the social divide.

Jane Austen's life, like that of her fictional characters, was lived in and around the houses of the very wealthy and the middling members of the educated classes. Born in 1775, the seventh child and second daughter of a clergyman and his

---

* Austen's 'vagueness' is apparent here, as she also describes Mr Collins' parsonage as 'a handsome modern building, well situated on rising ground'.

wife (who was marginally his social better), she grew up in a lively household. Her parents went on to have another son after Jane, and to this brood were added half a dozen or so school-age boys whose fees as boarding students provided a much-needed supplement to the Reverend George Austen's income.[21] Nevertheless, they lived in a sort of modest gentility. George Austen, while not profligate, was never quite able to live within his means and often borrowed from relatives to keep his large family in good circumstance. However, despite the fact that they could not afford the trappings of wealthy society, their standing was such that they still moved comfortably within it, and were well acquainted with families that boasted grand houses and substantial property, all of which had an impact on Austen's fiction.

THE RECTORY AT STEVENTON

The first property that had any importance to Jane Austen was, of course, the house she grew up in: the rectory at Steventon in Hampshire. This was a plain sturdy structure, built in the early seventeenth century and renovated in the 1760s for the Austen family. It had seven bedrooms, a central hearth and a pretty, trellised porch. The house was surrounded by fields, where her father farmed, and by gardens, where Mrs Austen grew vegetables. There were also many trees – elms, firs, and chestnuts; Jane's characters often take note of such things. Overall, the aspect is not so unlike her final, beloved home at Chawton or Mrs Dashwood's Barton Cottage, or the famously unglamorous rectory to be taken over by the noble Edmund Bertram in *Mansfield Park*. Austen clearly had a fondness for a well-kept cottage, as she did for a well-appointed mansion.

The sprawling rooms at Steventon accommodated not only all of the Austen children and their boarders, but also, later, brothers returning from university with friends and relatives, who stopped for days or weeks at a time. During these visits, it was not uncommon for the family and guests to perform plays, either of their own creation or those that were popular at the time. Unlike the production so heavily frowned upon in *Mansfield Park*, these theatricals were greatly enjoyed by family and friends, all of whom were avid readers of any new fiction or drama. Though the rectory is no longer standing, some sketches exist and, in any case, it is almost better to imagine this house full of bright, competent children, tumbling through the halls and practising their fine sense of wit and their stage personas on one another, all diligently rehearsing their lines against their improvised sets and backdrops.

The rectory at Steventon has another point of significance: it was where Jane Austen lived when she entertained the one suitor about whom she expressed any sincere emotion, or rather, a giddy sense of being in love. Sadly, Tom Lefroy the young man in question, was quickly sent away from Steventon before any promises could be exchanged. He too was from a modest, but aspirational, family, and when his parents got wind of the blossoming courtship they acted quickly to remove him from danger, having decided that he should marry a woman of greater means than a clergyman's daughter, however clever she may be.

The rectory was also the home that she lost when her eldest brother James became a vicar and her father decided to hand over his living and the family home to his son. In 1801, when Jane was twenty-five, George Austen took his wife and daughters off to rented accommodation in Bath, where it was supposed Jane and her sister, Cassandra, might find husbands. Jane Austen never recorded her thoughts on leaving the rectory, but stories exist that she nearly fainted on hearing the news of their move. And her fiction writing, which was inspired by her life there – she had begun her first three novels, and probably finished drafts of at least two – seems to have slowed considerably after the family's departure. Although her letters from this time were not preserved, perhaps there is something of her feeling in Marianne Dashwood's grief at being forced to leave her childhood home: 'Oh! happy house, could you know what I suffer in now viewing you from this spot, from whence perhaps I may view you no more! – And you, ye well-known trees!'[22]

However plain or snug, it is the rectory, and perhaps her final home at Chawton cottage, that influenced the sanctuary Austen described for her female heroines. Although Elizabeth Bennet and Emma Woodhouse end up marrying into rich estates, Austen had a penchant for settling her heroines into cottage parsonages. Arriving at Mansfield Park as a child and poor relation, Fanny Price finds that 'the grandeur of the house astonished, but could not console her', for her homesickness. The rooms are 'too large for her to move in with ease', and, worried lest she damage some expensive item, 'she crept about in constant fear of something or other'.[23] Luckily, Fanny gets to live with Edmund Bertram in the parsonage at Mansfield. Catherine Morland (with Henry Tilney at Woodston) and Elinor Dashwood (with Edward Ferrars at Delaford) also find their happy endings shrouded in the cosy familiarity of Austen's own beginnings. The Dashwood ladies find respite at pretty Barton Cottage, which Mrs Dashwood intends to enlarge, though it already has four bedrooms, two garrets and two parlours. It is not a parsonage; in fact, Austen cheekily admonishes it for not being picturesque enough: 'As a cottage it was defective, for the building was regular, the roof was tiled, the window shutters were not painted green, nor were the walls covered with honey-suckles.' A few additions, Mrs Dashwood concludes, 'will make it a very snug little cottage', though 'I could wish the stairs were handsome'.[24]

THE VYNE

Full as it was, the life of the family was hardly confined to the beloved rectory. One of the first grand houses on the list of Austen touchstones is The Vyne in Hampshire, now in the care of the National Trust. It was built during the reign of Henry VIII for his Lord Chamberlain, Lord Sandys, and was visited several times by the king before being passed to the Chute family, who owned it for more than three hundred years. The house is indeed a grand affair, with a soaring portico flanked by rambling wings. The interior is full of (now restored) neoclassical panelling, pristine coffered ceilings, halls lined with busts of historic figures, all befitting eighteenth-century classical revival. There is a long gallery, covered in honey-toned oak, which is the oldest such room in England. There is also a rather magnificent dining parlour that, in Austen's time, could have doubled as a ballroom. The house's grand staircase was added in the mid-eighteenth century by John

Chute, a close friend of Horace Walpole and prominent member of Walpole's 'Committee of Taste' (see chapter 2). Though the Austens belonged to a lower social set than the Chutes, the Austen brothers were friends with Thomas Chute, who also knew, and danced with, Jane and Cassandra. They probably danced together at Basingstoke, but possibly also at The Vyne, which had ample room for such entertainments.

It was Thomas Chute's older brother William who, in 1790, inherited the grand house, making him a very good catch indeed for any woman who could lure him away from his bachelor pursuits towards a more settled existence. Austen began writing *Pride and Prejudice* in around 1796 or so; her oft-quoted observation that 'a single man in possession of a good fortune must be in want of a wife' is widely believed to have been inspired by William Chute's arrival at The Vyne. He is mentioned in her letters, but usually in her ironic, offhand fashion: 'Wm. Chute called here yesterday. I wonder what he means by being so civil.'[25] His accession to the fortune must certainly have generated a flurry of speculation among her social group but the new lord of the manor was more interested in fox hunting than in social events, and he chose his wife from among the daughters of his political hunting pals, rather than from his or his brother's dancing partners. It is unlikely that the young Jane Austen ever fancied herself a potential candidate for the title of Mrs William Chute (she was only fifteen at the time), but the circumstances of his inheritance and marriage were among the significant events in her social circle that helped to forge the social topography of her stories.

For Austen was well aware of the fact that, for most women, the only route to property and financial security was through marriage. Things could become interesting for a widow left in charge of her own fortune, as John Dashwood's mother-in-law, Mrs Ferrars, demonstrates. It is she who arranges the marriage for her son Edward, a marriage he refuses, thereby losing his right to the family inheritance and 'the Norfolk estate, which, clear of land-tax, brings in a good thousand a-year'.[26] For families like the Dashwoods, it was the male heir who was usually charged with maintaining the women of the family. But he did not always keep his promises, as John Dashwood demonstrates, and as one of Jane's female ancestors had learned the hard way.

When her husband, a man of some property, died, Jane's great-grandmother Austen (née Elizabeth Weller), found herself an abandoned widow with young children. Though her husband had charged his own father (who had inherited everything on his son's death) with providing for his wife and family, the deal soon fell apart. The father objected to looking after his daughter-in-law and grandchildren, and his neglect eventually led to them living in penury. George Austen's own father, and his siblings, only received an education because their mother, showing some of the tenacity that Austen herself would inherit, rented out her family home, and took a job as a housekeeper at a boys' school, which earned her a living, as well as tuition for her sons.[27] Her only other means of salvation would have been to find a suitable husband willing to take on a woman with children who brought no income with her, not an easy task.

BATH

When George Austen retired in 1801, Jane (twenty-five) and Cassandra (twenty-eight) were whisked off to live in Bath. It could hardly escape their notice that their own mother and aunt had been taken to Bath in similar circumstances – as marriageable young women whose relations hoped to snag a suitable husband from among the visitors in the popular spa town.

Most of Austen's letters from this period were destroyed by her devoted but censorious sister, but in *Northanger Abbey* we can get a glimpse of what Austen thought of her new home. Here, she allowed herself some rather wonderful moments ridiculing the social niceties and changing fashions of Bath, which had become much less fashionable by the time she and Cassandra were brought there. Mr Tilney sums up the monotony of what passes for social etiquette when he says to Catherine Morland: 'I have hitherto been remiss, madam, in the proper attentions of a partner here; I have not yet asked you how long you have been in Bath; whether you were ever here before; whether you have been at the Upper Rooms, the theatre, and the concert; and how you like the place altogether.'[28] We do know that the Austens lived at three addresses before George Austen died. However, it seems the sisters had little affection for the place. 'It will be two years tomorrow since we left Bath for Clifton', Jane wrote to Cassandra in 1808, 'with what happy feelings of Escape!'[29]

GODMERSHAM

After George Austen's death, Mrs Austen and her daughters lived a peripatetic existence, moving from temporary accommodation to long visits with relatives. The Austen boys contributed towards the upkeep of their mother and sisters, but not in a way that alleviated the need for the women to hone their habits of frugality, or, in Jane Austen's words, practise 'Vulgar Economy'. Her letters from this period are full of references to the prices of cloth, thread and foodstuffs, and of remaking worn-out clothing. Some change in the family fortunes came when her brother Edward, who had been adopted by wealthy, childless cousins, inherited their substantial fortune and estates, becoming Edward Austen-Knight. One of these, Godmersham, became his family home. His mother and sisters were often invited for extended visits, many of them during or shortly following the birth of yet another of Edward's children. (He and his wife Elizabeth had eleven altogether; she finally expired with the birth of the last, in 1808, at the age of thirty-five.)

In Edward Austen's day, Godmersham had 5,000 acres of land (today it still has 2,000). The house was built in 1732 by the Knight family, who added two wings in the 1780s before Edward inherited the property in 1797. It still has several wings and was built in an elegant Regency Italianate style. It is closed to the public, but a public footpath through the property affords a view of its immense space and grandeur. It is sometimes speculated that the more famous Chatsworth was the inspiration for Pemberley, since Austen has Elizabeth

Bennet visit there, but it was at Godmersham that Austen had personal experience of living in such a large house, with its many rooms, servants and large entertainments. She spent many hours writing letters in the library, and the vicarage, still extant on the property, is thought to have inspired Mr Collins' house. As Pevsner pointed out, Austen does not provide an overabundance of interior description of her fictional houses, but she makes clear what is important. Certainly her time at Godmersham, and at Goodnestone House, another large property belonging to Edward's in-laws, informed her discriminating eye. Elizabeth Bennet admires Pemberley not because it is overly grand, but because it is just right. She enjoys the 'lofty and handsome rooms' not because they are lavish but because they afford a view, 'from every window there were beauties to be seen'. She approves of Darcy's taste in furnishings because it 'was neither gaudy nor uselessly fine; with less of splendour,

© Godmersham Park Heritage Centre

The 1785 painting Godmersham Park in Kent the Seat of Thomas Knight Esqr by W. Watts was used by the Bank of England for the design of the new £10 note.

and more real elegance, than the furniture of Rosings'.[30] By contrast, Mr Collins praises the extravagant interiors of Rosings 'with a rapturous air', particularly the chimneypiece, for which Lady Catherine de Bourgh has paid £800.[31] It is an extravagant sum, as Pevsner relates, given that suitably grand chimneypieces were acquired in the mid-eighteenth century for Woburn Abbey and Longford Castle for between £200 and £300.[32] Here Elizabeth (and Austen) is taking a moral sounding from the degree of household extravagance to determine the depth of Darcy's character.

Whether or not the décor at Godmersham showed 'real elegance', the place was luxurious to Austen. Writing in 1813, she described a sense of contentment there: 'We live in the Library except at Meals & have a fire every Eveng.' Later, she says, 'I am now alone in the Library, Mistress of all I survey.'[33] Though she was a welcome visitor to Godmersham, she was very much the poor relation – note her mention of a fire every evening, which would have been a significant expense in her own household. Fanny Price is not allowed a fire at Mansfield Park, and must shiver alone in her 'little white attic' room until Edmund Bertram insists on the extravagance of a little warmth. (Later, Jane Eyre's loitering in the upper floors of Thornfield Hall would recall Fanny's consignment to the marginal spaces of the house.*)

Austen's perception of life at Godmersham was one of noticeable ease. In 1813, she wrote, 'I have no occasion to think of the price of Bread or of Meat where I am now; – let me shake off vulgar cares & conform to the happy Indiffer-

---

* Charlotte Brontë claimed not to have read *Mansfield Park*, or anything by Jane Austen, before writing her novel. When she did read them, she was not a fan.

ence of East Kent wealth.'[34] By contrast, writing from the rectory in 1798, she complained: 'People get so horridly poor & economical in this part of the World, that I have no patience with them. – Kent is the only place for happiness, Everybody is rich there.'[35] At another quiet moment in the library at Godmesham, Jane enumerated her household blessings: 'At this present time I have five Tables, Eight and twenty chairs & two fires all to myself'.[36]

A few days later, Austen remarks again on the comfort of her surroundings: 'Having half an hour before breakfast – (very snug, in my own room, lovely morng, excellent fire, fancy me).'[37] She was treated kindly at Godmersham and, though she may have bristled, she was offered the hand-me-downs or lesser articles belonging to her wealthy sister-in-law. So it is easy to see how she could write of the finer lifestyle while sympathising with poorer relations, such as Fanny Price. However, Austen often enjoyed her time at Godmersham, making trips into Canterbury and attending dinners and parties at nearby Goodnestone. But it is doubtful that she envied her sister-in-law, for she was witness to the hardships of Elizabeth's almost continual state of pregnancy. Furthermore, Jane Austen did have her own chance to be lady of the manor, but she turned it down.

MANYDOWN

The Bigg-Wither family were longtime friends of the Austens from their time in Steventon, and the Austen children were frequent guests at dinners and balls the family gave at their great house, Manydown, in Hampshire. It was after the Austens had removed to Bath that an invitation in 1802 brought Jane for a particularly important stay at Manydown. There, she was offered what might be termed the opportunity of a lifetime.

Harris Bigg-Wither, the dull and awkward but kind younger brother of the family (who was made even less confident by a stammer) asked Jane Austen to marry him. Though five years older, and immeasurably wiser, she at first agreed to the proposal. If she married, Manydown, with its Tudor wing and ample grounds, would have been hers to command; her time, rather than being consumed by attending her hypochondriac mother or her brothers' wives and children, would, with the consent of her husband, be hers to direct as she pleased. But after accepting the offer, she spent a night in the throes of her better conscience and decided she could not honestly follow through. Austen was never offered another opportunity to marry; Harris Bigg-Wither married two years later and had ten children.

For all of her disappointments, Jane Austen never seemed to kick against the established hierarchy of her world, but she showed her misgivings and drew attention to the fact that the dream of marrying into a grand country estate might go wrong. It often needed some inspiration from a relative outsider like Elizabeth Bennet or Fanny Price to set things to rights. However, Elizabeth's triumph was to accede to the stately home, not to disparage it. And the temptation, even for Austen, to accept a less than desirable marriage for the security of a great house and all the trappings must have been enormous. When Willoughby sets out to seduce Marianne Dashwood, he takes her on a secret visit to Allenham Court, confident of impressing her with the estate he is due to inherit.

To Marianne, the delights of the 'charming house' trump any notion of impropriety in the unchaperoned visit with Willoughby. To be sure, they have got the gossips' tongues wagging, but Marianne intends to drown them by out by regaling Elinor with the merits of the house, including the 'remarkably pretty sitting room upstairs', which is described in typically imprecise style as 'of a nice comfortable size for constant use'. Like Mary Crawford at Mansfield Park, Marianne is already imagining the improvements she will make at Allenham as Willoughby's wife ('with modern furniture it would be delightful'), but Austen knows better than anyone that not every young woman in love gets her man, or his family home.[38]

STONELEIGH ABBEY

In 1806, while the Austen women were still moving between the houses of their relations, Mrs Austen paid a visit to her

Stoneleigh Abbey as it is today. On her first visit, Jane Austen's mother remarked that the house was so large 'that we cannot find our way about it'.

cousin, the Reverend Thomas Leigh. The Leigh family was considered to be of a higher rank than the Austens, and when Mrs Austen (née Cassandra Leigh) married Jane's father, it was thought to be a step below her best opportunities. There was an acute awareness among the family of the greater wealth and standing of the Leighs, one symbol of which was Stoneleigh Abbey.

When the Hon. Mary Leigh died in 1806, a possible dispute about the will meant that Thomas Leigh was encouraged to put forward his claim to Stoneleigh in person, and somewhat in a hurry. He was joined in this giddy pursuit by Mrs Austen and Jane. It was an experience that could only have sharpened the author's preoccupation with houses and the right of inheritance. Mrs Austen wrote to her daughter-in-law of the wonders of Stoneleigh, counting out its features in a way her daughter had once done at Godmersham:

> Now I wish to give you some idea of the inside of this vast house – first premising that there are forty-five windows in front, which is quite straight, with a flat roof, fifteen in a row. You go up a considerable flight of steps to the door, for some of the offices are underground, and enter a large hall. On the right hand is the dining-room and within that the breakfast-room, where we generally sit; and reason good, 'tis the only room besides the chapel, which looks towards the view. On the left hand of the hall is the best drawing-room and within a smaller one.

These rooms, however, were 'rather gloomy with brown wainscot and dark crimson furniture'. Unlike her literary daughter,

Mrs Austen was anything but vague. She noted the 'smaller drawing-room', which was 'the state-bedchamber' and had a 'high, dark crimson velvet bed, just fit for an heroine' (perhaps one such as Catherine Morland, we might surmise). There were the 'old gallery', the parlours, three staircases and 'two small sitting-rooms', as well as 'twenty-six bedchambers in the new part of the house and a great many, some very good ones, in the old'. Finally, she added, 'every part of the house and offices is kept so clean, that were you to cut your finger I do not think you could find a cobweb to wrap it up in.'[39] The house was so large 'that we cannot find our way about it', she complained. 'I have proposed [Mr Leigh] setting up direction posts at the angles.'

Stoneleigh was impressive; as Pevsner called it, 'a monumental ensemble in the tradition of Chatsworth'.[40] It had been built as a Cistercian abbey in the twelfth century and by 1561 had fallen to 'a roofless ruin', but was enlarged with a new wing by Edward, 3rd Baron Leigh after his return from the Grand Tour in 1711. Then the large Jacobean house built of red sandstone was joined by a new wing built in the Baroque style, which took six years to complete and cost the princely sum of £3,000. Altogether the ensemble contained numerous private and public rooms, including the Saloon, one of the great Georgian rooms in Britain, with a ceiling and walls covered in fine Rococo plasterwork depicting the Labours of Hercules. Gold-painted columns dressed in faux-marble lined the room lit by gilt chandeliers and by generous windows hung with gold draperies. The Georgian addition also contains a library (the State Bedroom during Austen's time) and the chapel, which was likely the model for the chapel at Sotherton in *Mansfield Park*.

There are other hints of Sotherton at Stoneleigh. In 1809 the garden designer Humphry Repton proposed a scheme for a vast park at Stoneleigh, most of which was not undertaken, but significant alterations to the River Avon were achieved. In the period when the gentry were not only adding to their houses, but also carrying out lavish schemes in their parks and gardens, such a project might include digging out valleys to create vistas and even rerouting streams or rivers to enhance the tour of the grounds, which were often dotted with architectural follies. Stowe, the most famous and elaborate of these, was among 250 estates undertaken by the great landscape designer Lancelot 'Capability' Brown. His successor was Repton, whose works are so admired by Mr Rushworth in *Mansfield Park*. Speaking of a neighbouring estate that has recently been reshaped by Repton, Mr Rushworth says, 'Smith's place is the admiration of all the country; and it was a mere nothing before Repton took it in hand. I think I shall have Repton.'[41]

As the visitors tour the grounds of Sotherton, Austen takes aim at this popular taste for exteme gardening and the eager tourists who flocked to experience it. Mary Crawford notes in jaded tones, 'I have looked across the ha-ha til I am weary. I must go and look through that iron gate at the same view, without being able to see it so well.'[42] Alarmed at the idea of cutting down an avenue of trees merely to satisfy a fashion in landscaping, Fanny says it is a shame to lose the woods, and citing William Cowper, a favourite poet of Austen's, muses, 'I should like to see Sotherton before it is cut down.'[43] In a similar vein of criticism towards the fashion for too much contrivance, Elizabeth Bennet admires the grounds of Pemberley. Like Mr Collins' parsonage, it too is 'a large, handsome stone building, standing well on rising ground'. It also had:

'a stream of some natural importance [that] was swelled into greater, but without any artificial appearance. Its banks were neither formal, nor falsely adorned . . . She had never seen a place for which nature had done more, or where natural beauty had been so little counteracted by an awkward taste.'[44]

It is also pointed out that rather than being 'laid out with too much regularity', like Sotherton, the grounds of Donwell Abbey, the estate belonging to Mr Knightley in *Emma*, have also been left in a pleasingly natural condition. As opposed to having artificial vistas carved through forests and hills, it enjoys 'all the old neglect of prospect' and 'an abundance of timber in rows and avenues, which neither fashion nor extravagance had rooted up'.[45] Austen, who enjoyed the various woods on the Godmersham estate, and was fond of the small woodland around the rectory, seems partial to more natural vistas.

CHAWTON

Mrs Austen and her daughters had to wait several years after he received his inheritance from the Knight family before Edward finally helped them to a home of their own. In 1809 he gave his mother the choice of two permanent houses, one near Godmersham, the other a cottage in the village of his estate at Chawton, in Hampshire. Mrs Austen chose the cottage at Chawton, which had previously belonged to Edward's bailiff, and it became the last home any of the women inhabited. Edward had seldom used Chawton, the large house of the estate, which Jane called 'the Great House'. But once his mother and sisters were installed in the village, his stays there became more frequent, and Mrs Austen and her daughters often made the walk up to the main house from their own tidy cottage. It is thought that Jane derived some of the description of the house and grounds of Mansfield Park from those at Chawton, particularly the view from the wood-panelled dining room, where a wide window seat is an ideal place from which to look out and imagine.

Chawton is a handsome Elizabethan manor house, large but not so sprawling as Godmersham, and today exhibiting some of the homely charm that Austen found there. Its rooms are well proportioned and warm, now lined in restored seven-

Chawton cottage became the author's last home and the place where she completed and published all of her novels.

teenth-century oak panelling and filled with period furniture and replica fabrics. Ancestral portraits line the walls and stained-glass coats of arms chart the descendants of the Knight family (whose name Edward acquired in 1812).* At the cottage, Edward made a few alterations for his mother and sisters, moving the entrance away from the road and adding a large window over the garden, and it became a haven of creative endeavour for Jane. Here, she took up her pen once more and wrote or revised all of her novels and saw all of them published. She experienced the first intimations of fame and, more importantly, an acknowledgement of herself as a fully fledged writer while living here. The squat, seventeenth-century brick house on the main village road has been the Jane Austen's House Museum since 1949, and still preserves the simple, ordered rooms that the Austen women enjoyed. But though they are pleasant enough and the garden charming and the whole set up inviting, this was not a large house and must have felt a bit crowded at times.

The Austen women were joined by their longtime friend Martha Lloyd, it not being uncommon for unmarried women to lodge together, and sometimes by overnight guests. Despite there being six bedrooms in the cottage, Jane never enjoyed 'a room of her own', that basic need for women writers later identified by Virginia Woolf. The sisters continued to share a bedroom, as they always had. There was no 'study', so Jane did her writing in the dining parlour, a public room whose notoriously squeaky door Austen insisted on leaving unoiled, so that she would be alerted to visitors. But for Austen, who

---

* Rescued from being turned into a hotel by developers in the late 1980s, it is now the Chawton House Library, dedicated to early women's writing.

famously described the scope of her fiction as a 'little bit (two Inches wide) of Ivory on which I work with so fine a Brush', it seems a sense of serenity brought about by a settled existence was sufficient. One can imagine a long-awaited feeling of settled calm, the satisfaction of having a home that gave her the mental and emotional capacity, if not great physical space, to produce the books that defined a period and sensibility in English literature. In July 1809, she composed a poem to her brother Francis, which anticipated happy days ahead at Chawton:

> The many comforts that await
> Our Chawton home, how much we find
> Already in it, to our mind;
> And how convinced, that when complete
> It will all other Houses beat
> That ever have been made or mended,
> With rooms concise, or rooms distended.[46]

Because Austen's female characters did all strive to marry well, and were concerned with what Ralph Waldo Emerson referred to as 'marriageableness', many find her plots somewhat frustrating. But as Margaret Anne Doody has argued, her heroines, like the women of her time, are 'constricted and abused by an unjust property system', and 'taught by society' that husbands are important not because they 'are good or lovable in themselves, but because they are the means to money and houses'.[47] Ironically, marriage can mean freedom for the woman in question – freedom from worrying where she might live, freedom to run her own household (if in concert with an agreeable, uxorious spouse), freedom from the constant plotting of her family and friends to find her a suitable husband. Of a visit to Ash Park in 1800, Austen wrote that 'to sit in idleness over a good fire in a well-proportioned room is a luxurious sensation'. Chawton may not have provided the amenities of Ash Park or Godmersham, but it offered luxury of another kind.

As much as the eighteenth century was a golden age for the English country house, it is also considered the great age of the novel. Of all the authors of the time (Richardson, Smollet, Sterne, Fielding, Defoe), Fanny Burney was one of the most successful. Her stories foreshadow Jane Austen's in that they are novels of manners that often take a satirical view of social conventions. Burney, too, used visits between grand houses to further her plots and engender the writing of letters to describe it. By the time Burney was writing, in the 1770s, the country house had been incorporated into a fluid movement of visitors, guests and residents that was still common decades later, when Austen opened that world to a new readership.

Burney's novels are rambling romances, highly entertaining but prone to melodrama and lacking the refined plot structure that Austen achieved. They show naïve young women navigating the minefields of upper-class social and courtship rituals while casting a somewhat critical eye on the pleasure-seeking vices of eighteenth-century London. Like Austen, Burney placed her young heroines in positions to experience country houses and acquire them through fortuitous marriages earned through their virtuous behaviour. *Evelina, or a Young Lady's Entrance into the World* (1778) is an epistolary novel very much in the Cinderella tradition, which tells the story of an orphaned young woman who manages to marry well. When she enters 'society', Evelina's kind and generous nature is easily preyed upon by its more practised members. The plot mainly turns on her choice between two suitors: one who is less than honourable (by the name of Willoughby), and another who is the picture of moral rectitude. The novel was originally published anonymously, since it was not seemly at the time for women to be identified as authors. *Cecilia* (1782) was even more popular, prompting three editions within a year and providing Austen with the title for *Pride and Prejudice*.[48]

Fanny Burney grew up in her father's house in Poland Street in London. A musical scholar, Dr Burney was at the centre of a lively and intellectually engaged social circle that included Samuel Johnson and the actor David Garrick. The family were also frequent guests at Chessington Hall in Surrey, which belonged to Samuel Crisp. That house was demolished in the nineteenth century, but it probably influenced Howard Grove, the home of Evelina's friend and protector Lady Howard, or the home of her rescuer, Lord Orville. The family also lived in St Martin's Street, in a house that had been home to Sir Isaac Newton, who had built a glazed observatory on the top floor. Burney wrote: 'Sir Isaac's identical observatory is still subsisting, and we show it to all our visitors.'[49] She also recorded, 'It is my favourite sitting place, where I can retire to read or write any of my private fancies or vagaries.'[50] That it does not appear in her novels is no surprise, since she was trying to maintain her anonymity as an author.*

---

* The house in St Martin's Street was demolished in the 1913 and replaced by the Westminster Reference Library. A commemorative plaque details its notable residents.

Burney also spent time in one of the grandest houses in the kingdom: in 1786 she was made Second Keeper of the Queen's Robes and went to live in apartments in the Queen's Lodge at Windsor Castle. By this time her most popular books were behind her, but she had already set an invaluable precedent as a social commentator and woman writer, so much so that Virginia Woolf called her 'the mother of English fiction'. However, centuries on, it is a truth 'universally acknowledged' that it was Jane Austen, a clever young woman without fortune, who made us sensible to the prejudices of marriage and property in her lifetime.

Abbotsford ·

FOUR

Ancient and Romantic:
Walter Scott's Baronial Halls

'It had been built at a period when castles were no longer necessary, and when the Scottish architects had not yet acquired the art of designing a domestic residence.'

Said of Tully-Veolan, in *Waverley*

He was the first literary celebrity, the inventor of the historical novel in English and reinventor of the Scottish Baronial style, helping to usher in the Scottish tourism industry. His vision of an old Scotland shrouded in chivalric romance was wildy popular in his time. Yet today Walter Scott is viewed with great scepticism, even derision. This is partly to do with what is seen to be his over-the-top Scottishness, the fact that he celebrated a type of Highland hero that veered too easily toward cliché, and that his passion for preserving the quaint manners, speech and dress of the Highlands and the Borders was too emphatic to hold any real currency. Yet Scott was a political pragmatist, a dedicated Unionist, whose novels concluded that Scotland's rich national heritage was best preserved and maintained as part of a British kingdom. Abbotsford, his own neo-Gothic castle, where he lived for twenty-one years, also represented this dual allegiance and fanaticism.

97

From his early days, Walter Scott's imagination thrilled to historic landscapes and houses. Those he visited as a tourist or guest – Craighall Castle, Dalkeith Palace, Bruntsfield House, Traquair, Tullibody – influenced his fictional descriptions of architecture, history and baronial decor, right down to the coats of arms in the stained-glass windows. These houses all symbolised a real, physical connection to the past, to the manners and traditions that he celebrated in his romances. Still other places – Melville Castle, Drumlanrig, Bothwell, Bowhill – inspired his own building ambitions, which he indulged at Abbotsford, the house that gave him almost as much pride as his writing, and which he laboured intensely during the last years of his life to hold on to.

Scott was born in Edinburgh in 1771, and lived in the College Wynd area of the city. His father was a Writer to the Signet, or solicitor, and his mother came from a family of medical men and was an enthusiastic and wide reader.[1] Edinburgh was in a period of great material change in the late eighteenth century. The erection of the New Town began in the 1770s, with the leveling of some areas to make way for the construction of harmonious neoclassical terraces and squares, so Scott's later building ambitions were in keeping with a general renewal of the building fabric at the time.

As a small boy Walter was sent to stay with his grandparents at their farm Sandy Knowe, about thirty miles southeast of Edinburgh. He had become lame in one leg owing to what was thought to be a fever, but was probably polio, and it was hoped that the countryside rambles and fresh air would work some homespun magic on his poor health. Scott's ancestors

had leased the original dwelling, Smailholm Tower, in 1645, but when the family built the house at Sandy Knowe, the tower was abandoned and Scott first saw it as a pleasingly romantic ruin. It was during his time at Sandy Knowe that Scott first heard the old ballads, folk songs and oral tales that would continue to enchant and inspire him for the rest of his life. His Aunt Janet read and sang to him, and his grandmother regaled her wide-eyed grandson with stories of border skirmishes and family lore. Scott later recalled:

> My grandmother in whose youth the old border depredations were a matter of recent tradition used to tell me many a tale of Wat of Harden, Wight Willie of Aikwood, Jamie Tellfer of the fair Dodhead, and the other heroes, merrymen all of the persuasion and calling of Robin Hood and Little John.[2]

These may not be household names for the contemporary reader, but to young Walter their exploits had the enticing ring of adventure and noble struggle. And they started a slow-burning fire that was fed in later years by his reading of German and French romances, and by his exploring further this land of legend into which he'd been born. At Sandy Knowe, Walter also learned of his great-great-great grandfather, who was knighted by James I of England and VI of Scotland, but then fined by Cromwell for his loyalty to the king. He was told stories of his great-grandfather, known as 'Beardie', who was involved in the 1715 Jacobite uprising, the attempt of James Francis Edward Stuart, the 'Old Pretender', to regain the throne that his father, the Catholic king James II and VII, had been forced to abandon in 1689.

The Jacobite cause found support among a number of Scots, who objected to the casting out of King James and the reign of the German branch of the royal family, beginning with the accession of George I to the British throne in 1714. 'Beardie' was known for having refused to shave his facial hair until a Stuart was back on the throne. At the nearby manor house of Traquair in Peeblesshire, the 5th Earl of Traquair similarly vowed to close the 'Bear Gates' to his property until a Stuart again became king. The last Jacobite attempt to seize the throne was in 1745, when the many Scottish troops fighting on behalf of the Old Pretender's son, Bonnie Prince Charlie, were brutally crushed at the Battle of Culloden, an event that takes centre stage in Scott's first novel, *Waverley*. As it happened, the Pretender never took the throne, the beard grew, the Traquair gates remained shut.

At the age of about twelve, again in delicate health, Scott was sent from Edinburgh to stay with his Aunt Janet, now living in the village of Kelso. Here he claimed to have been particularly inspired by 'the ruins of an ancient abbey, the more distant vestiges of Roxburgh Castle, the modern mansion of Fleurs [Floors]', which 'is so situated as to combine the ideas of ancient baronial grandeur with those of modern taste'.[*] It was at this point in his young life, Scott later wrote, that 'the ancient ruins or remains of our fathers' piety or splendour, became with me an insatiable passion'.[3] It was the land and the ruins that got him, along with the stories of splendour, acts of 'piety', or bravery, like those he had read about or been told by his grandmother and Aunt Janet.

---

[*] Floors was altered in the 1820s and '30s in a manner similar to the Gothic baronial style Scott would employ at Abbotsford.

Already, he could reimagine a scene vividly in story form: 'Shew me an old castle or a field of battle and I was at home at once, filled it with its combatants in their proper costume and overwhelmed my hearers by the enthusiasm of my description.'[4]

In 1786, at the age of fifteen, Scott was apprenticed to the legal profession, working for his father, and was sent to attend to a client called Alexander Stewart, who lived at Invernahyle.[*] It was Scott's first visit to the Highlands, and he was powerfully taken with the scenery, 'that inimitable landscape', which seemed to him almost unreal, and with the person he was sent to meet. Stewart had been in the thick of the Jacobite uprisings of 1715 and 1745, had personally engaged in a duel with the celebrated Highland chief, Rob Roy Macgregor, and, to Scott's delight, he was not shy in relating tales of his exploits.[5] As James Reed has it, 'when Apprentice Scott first visited those habitations, both in the Borders and in the Highlands, the breath of those who lived and died there in the Scottish troubles after 1688 was still warm upon them'.[6]

Scott qualified as an advocate in 1792, but he continued his forays into the Border regions, indulging his taste for folk ballads and his antiquarian collecting impulses and visiting some of the more notable abodes of his native land. He was a guest at Penicuik, a grand Palladian house that was the family seat of his friend William Clerk. There, Scott probably noted the ceiling of the saloon had been elaborately decorated with

---

[*] Alexander Stewart was said by Scott to have come to the aid of 'an officer of the King's forces', as does his fictional hero Waverley, and was pardoned under the Act of Indemnity, similar to Baron Bradwardine.

scenes from the *Poems of Ossian*, by the Scottish poet James Macpherson, rather than with Greek or Roman images befitting its neoclassical architecture* Scott also visited Menstrie Castle and Tullibody in Clackmannanshire, which belonged to George Abercromby, the grandfather of another friend, also called George. The elder Abercromby had his own stories to tell about run-ins with Rob Roy in Stirlingshire.[7] Scott also visited Flodden Field and Loch Katrine (the setting for his poem, *The Lady of the Lake*), and stayed with the Rattray family, relatives of William Clerk, at Craighall Castle, a sixteenth-century sandstone fortress in Perthshire that looms dramatically over one of Scotland's deepest ravines. These excursions fed Scott's imaginative hunger for connections to a Scottish past filled with images of triumph and grandeur.

In 1797 Scott married Charlotte Carpenter (or Charpentier) and, while working steadily at his legal duties, began preparing a collection of old Scottish ballads for publication (with the help of some like-minded antiquarian friends). *The Minstrelsy of the Scottish Border* grew from one volume to three, and with its publication in 1802, Scott established himself as more than just a lawyerly mind. These were celebrations in song of age-hallowed events, many of which had never been written down, but which Scott had managed to record (and sometimes 'enhance') for future generations. They were heroic, romantic, tragic, quaint, and the reading public found them irresistible.

Scott also found space in the collection for his own composi-

---

* Macpherson claimed that the poems were translated from the Galic verses of a third-century bard. They were very popular, though it was later shown that most of the poems were Macpherson's own work.

tions, a few ballads written 'in imitation of the old style'. In *Cadyow Castle*, Scott's fascination with the symbolic and associative power of a named dwelling begins to emerge. It tells the story of an old and bloody battle, and the title links it to a specific fortress, one of those 'remains of our fathers' piety or splendour' that so inspired him. Another romance of a historic house, produced a few years later, *Rokeby* is a tribute to the home of his friend and fellow antiquarian J. B. S. Morritt, whose family seat was Rokeby Park, not a storied castle, but an eighteenth-century Palladian-style country house in Teeside, Co. Durham. Here Scott was following a tradition reaching at least as far back as the English Renaissance, when Ben Jonson wrote *To Penshurst* praising the 'ancient pile' of the family of Sir Philip Sidney.

Later, in Scott's first, best-selling novel *Waverley*, the centrepiece of both ancient ties of the past and the Anglo-Scottish reconciliation is the Baron Bradwardine's home, Tully-Veolan. It is one of several houses in Scott's novels that are key to the tension of the drama, representing the seat of ancient bloodlines, traditions and family inheritance, imbued with cultural significance and threatened with destruction. This became a standard plot device for Scott. The chieftain's own Glennaquoich in *Waverley*, Osbaldistone Castle in *Rob Roy*, the Bertram family seat, Ellangowan, in *Guy Mannering*, and Ravenswood and the eerie Wolf's Crag in *The Bride of Lammermoor* are all similarly endangered and are emotive touchstones for the dramatic force of the novels.

While still in his early days as a ballad collector/composer, Scott embarked on the lifestyle of a true Scottish gentleman by establishing his own country residence. While renting a house for his family in Edinburgh, he also took up the tenancy at a small country house at nearby Lasswade, owned by his friend William Clerk, which was not far from Melville Castle and Dalkeith Palace, the homes of Henry, 1st Viscount Melville, and the Duke of Buccleuch, respectively. He then took a house at Ashestiel, located in the Ettrick Forest. Here, Scott finished work on the first ballad of his own making, *The Lay of the Last Minstrel*. It was published in 1805, around the time that he went into business with the printer James Ballantyne, an enterprise that, along with the purchase of land, would consume a large portion of his increasing profits. He also completed the epic poems *Marmion* (1805) and *The Lady of the Lake* (1810) while at Ashestiel, where he honed his writing regimen, which involved a pre-dawn start and long walks into the countryside.

The Lay of the Last Minstrel was written in the form of a tale being recited by an old bard in the late seventeenth century, and tells the story of the Duke of Buccleuch's (and Walter Scott's) ancestor, 'the bold Buccleuch', mentioning his seat at 'sweet Bowhill' and making careful reference to the loyal service provided by Scott's own ancestors to repel the invading English troops.* Heavily influenced by German romanticism and the popular medieval revival, it sets out that framework that would be echoed later on in the plots of Scott's novels: an old noble family, caught up in the political strife of the period, experiences some reversal of fortune, leaving the family seat in peril, so that it is incumbent upon an estranged but determined heir to re-establish the family's good name and recover

---

* Scott was distantly related to the Duke of Buccleuch, who had supported Scott in his professional (legal) ambitions, as both descended from Walter Scott, who had been created 1st Lord Scott of Buccleuch in 1606.

the old demesne, all the while paying homage to the nobility of its lineage and honouring the manners of the revered past. The Arthurian overtones, with the idyllic Camelot at the centre, had significance beyond the written page, as Scott began to imagine his own similarly noteworthy residence.

The poem was extremely popular, selling fifteen thousand copies in five years.[8] There had never been a poem that grabbed the attention of the reading public quite like it; even the prime minister, William Pitt, was keen on the work. It did so well that John Constable, Scott's publisher at the time, offered him 1,000 guineas for his next work, a move some cite as the first 'advance' ever paid to an author.[9] Scott's notoriety gained him new friends and admirers at home and abroad. During a visit around the Scottish isles in 1810, Scott and his wife were 'were treated with something like feudal splendour' as the guests of the Laird of Staffa, that remarkable vertical 'pillar island' in the Inner Hebrides, whose home was on nearby Ulva. According to Scott, the laird's men received the visitors in formal fashion, 'under arms and with a discharge of musketry and artillery'. Scott was particularly pleased to be addressed by a man who praised him in Gaelic as 'the great bard of the lowland border'.[10] It is a scene worthy of Scott's own invention (and perhaps there is a bit of that in his account), the laird's piper was 'in constant attendance on our parties and wakened us in the morning with his music'. Scott would later employ his own piper at Abbotsford to play on the terrace in the evenings.[11]

Scott's own ambition to accede to the part of Scottish laird began to come into focus when, in 1811, he purchased the farmhouse and estate at Cartleyhole on the Tweed, which he renamed 'Abbotsford'. The farm, near Melrose Abbey, included about one hundred acres, cost something like £4,000, and 'extend[ed] along the banks of the Tweed for about half-a-mile'.[12] It was suggested to Scott that this was a place where the monks used to ford the river, hence his arrival at the more romantic-sounding moniker. He tried to emphasise the practicality of his purchase, saying that the land afforded him more opportunities for planting and farming. Yet Scott was not nearly as practical in his financial affairs as he tried to make himself appear. Unfortunately for him, neither were his business partners, who were also piling up debts.

Scott was now house-proud. No longer a temporary country tenant, he was, like his titled friends, attached to a named country residence of his own, and he eagerly announced his purchase to friends and family. To John Morritt (of Rokeby Park), he said: 'I have bought a small farm value about £150 yearly with the intention of "bigging myself a bower" after my own fashion.' His plans for renovating the old farmhouse at this point were modest: 'If I can get an elegant plan for a Cottage it will look very well, and furnish me with amusement for some time.'[13]

If he was in search of ideas for playing the part of the laird and building himself a noble seat, Scott did not have to look far. He was indebted to both the Duke of Buccleuch and Lord Melville, for their patronage, and visited both socially. Lord Melville was a powerful figure, known as 'the uncrowned King of Scotland', and he and the Duke of Argyll, who plays such an important role in *The Heart of Midlothian*, are viewed as having 'managed' Scotland for the English king.[14] Lord Melville had obtained his estate – the former seat of Mary, Queen of Scots, just outside Edinburgh – through marriage to the fourteen-year-old daughter of its late owner, a trading tycoon. In

1786, he proceeded to demolish the old medieval castle and replace it with a grand, new Gothic-style building designed by James Playfair, whose architect son created some of the most admired buildings of Edinburgh's New Town in the 1820s.* The elder Playfair worked mainly in the neoclassical style, the prevailing fashion of the day, which was being overtaken in the late eighteenth century by a turn towards Gothicism (Scott himself was an admirer of *The Castle of Otranto*). Lord Melville obviously preferred the new Gothic and began a grand building, which was completed in 1791. The castle has an imposing centre block with crenellated roof and two side wings with hulking solid turrets, but lacks anything like the personal quirks of style that Scott would stamp on Abbotsford.

Scott, in his early years of publishing ballads, was also a guest at Bothwell, a fourteenth-century castle belonging to the Douglas family. In the early eighteenth century Bothwell House had been constructed near the old castle, but in 1787 Archibald Douglas, later 1st Baron Douglas, demolished it and built another grand residence in the neoclassical style, also designed by James Playfair.[15] It was while staying at Bothwell in 1808 that Scott composed his ballad *Young Lochinvar*. Dalkeith Palace, the home of the Duke of Buccleuch, was also built in the neoclassical style. But if the architecture of every house did not directly inspire Scott's own designs, it is easy to see how these grand households prompted him to entertain his own ideas of castle-building and nurtured the desire to establish an antique-style family seat in the modern era. The significance of an ancient residence, even one newly rebuilt, as

---

* The National Gallery of Scotland and the Royal Scottish Academy among them.

a symbol of power and authority, held tremendous attraction, and the historic house or castle as the symbol of the noble past and the guardian of culture that Scott valued so highly, became more prominent in his writing.

Scott's grandiose schemes for Abbotsford were soon bubbling away, agitating the pool of more practical plans. In 1811, he wrote to his wife's brother, Charles, of a recent visit to their newly acquired property: 'I assure you we were not a little proud of being greeted as laird and lady of Abbotsford.'[16] He got on with 'planting and enclosing', making undramatic changes to the old house, but he was also buying more land. He wrote to his friend Robert Surtees that work on the house and land had 'interfered with my literary labours', but was now 'like to impel me toward them: for if I build I must have money'.[17]

1815 engraving of Traquair house in Peeblesshire, home of Walter Scott's dear friend Louisa Stuart, and a model for Tully-Veolan in his first novel, *Waverley*.

A grave financial crisis in 1813, during which his publishing venture showed some worrying debts, meant that Scott was obliged to petition friends, including the Duke of Buccleuch, John Morritt and his publishers, for letters of credit. This crisis, however, did nothing to check his ambitions or his eagerness to spend time in grand houses. In a letter to Matthew Hartstonge, in which he asks for 'advance on security of £500', he also talks of his recent visit to Drumlanrig Castle, still an impressive 'large Gothic quadrangular building' in pink sandstone dating from the late seventeenth century, where he and Charlotte spent ten days with the Duke and Duchess of Buccleuch.[18] The couple celebrated Twelfth Night in 1814, again as guests of the Buccleuchs, this time at Dalkeith Palace. In early 1815, he wrote to his friend Morritt, informing him that he was buying a plot at Kaeside, near Abbotsford, which would cost 'about £3,000'.[19]

As Scott liked to tell it, the story of Waverley sat forgotten in a drawer and was only rediscovered in 1813 while he was searching for fishing tackle. This version of the book's origins made an auspicious connection between it and Abbotsford, for it was here that Scott says the manuscript reappeared, enhancing the romance of both. Other evidence suggests that the novel was deliberately shelved in 1805 after Scott solicited friends' comments and found them so discouraging that he put it away and only took it up again when he was in need of new material and form. By 1813 the world of popular epic poetry had been rocked by the dashing figure of Lord Byron, and it is reasonable to assume that Scott thought it prudent to leave the field to his more charismatic rival, turning his attention to producing a kind of novel that would build on the success and appeal of his ballads.

Yet, while he enjoyed being known as the collector and author of folk ballads, Scott did not feel that being named as a novelist was appropriate for a man of his standing in the legal establishmen, nor did he want to be checked for the apparent Jacobite sympathies of his characters. So his *Waverley; or, 'Tis Sixty Years Since* was published without an author's name, and subsequent books (until 1827) were ascribed only to 'the author of *Waverley*'. That the author was anonymous did nothing to stem the popularity of the stories. *Waverley* and its successors enjoyed the kind of international notoriety that was only approached much later in the century by Charles Dickens, and is still, even in our age of global media, something of a rarity. As Andrew Hook put it, Scott's novels 'made an impact upon the reading public and literary culture of Europe and America unequalled by any literary phenomenon before'.[20]

In *Waverley*, Scott was able to combine his love of landscape and ruins and his desire to pay homage to the manners of the old Scots with a (seemingly contrary) appreciation of the British establishment. Its importance is largely symbolic. The hero, Edward Waverley, as Scott admitted privately and as most readers would agree, is a 'sneaking piece of imbecility', but he manages to battle through his rollicking adventures, befriend the most important clan chief of the Highlands, be taken into the confidence of the Young Pretender, and still stand tall as the epitome of English courage and honour.[21] Edward's main fault seems to be his unrestrained romantic impulse: he sees in the landscape something irresistibly poetic, and in the Highland rebels all that's noble and heroic. Though he later understands the dangers of indulging such romantic visions and backing them with weapons, he nonetheless allows readers to glimpse a period and atmosphere of tantalising drama and adventure. As the story progresses, it is Waverley's ability to switch sides in the argument with such alacrity that irks.

A young, impressionable English nobleman, Waverley joins the king's army in Scotland, where he becomes embroiled in the second Jacobite uprising in 1745, as the subtitle 'Sixty Years Since' indicates. Once in Scotland, Edward is shown great hospitality by the proud, imperious, but ultimately kind-hearted Baron Bradwardine, a firm adherent to the Jacobite cause. While a guest at Bradwardine's beautiful old castle-house, Tully-Veolan, Edward becomes acquainted with some Highlanders, who eventually introduce him to the famed Highland chief, Fergus Mac-Ivor Vich Ian Vohr. In time, his admiration for Fergus is only matched by his ardour for the chieftain's sister, Flora, a committed fighter in her own right. Edward also becomes enamoured of their cause and ends up at the Battle of Preston, fighting against his own former regiment, on the side of the Highlanders and Bonnie Prince Charlie. But as the battle rages and the discipline of the Highlanders crumbles, Edward comes to comprehend the gravity of his actions and returns to the English fold and his position in the establishment.

Forging those connections between character and place, Scott often adheres to the tradition that a man's name and the appellation of his house are interchangeable: Edward Waverley of Waverley-Honour is just Waverley; Baron Bradwardine is referred to as Tully-Veolan by his intimates, we are told, 'or more familiarly, Tully'.[22] Correspondingly, the Baron refers to Fergus Mac-Ivor as 'Glennaquoich', after his remote and picturesque fastness in the Highlands. John Oldbuck, the anti-quarian of the eponymous novel, is pleased when he is called by the name of his property, Monkbarns, as we are informed, 'distinguishing him by his territorial epithet [is] always most agreeable to the ear of a Scottish proprietor'.[23] These estates are the giant lynchpins in Scott's scheme of cultural history and their loss threatens dangerous times for their rightful inheritors, and by extension for the citizenry at large.

Of the various homesteads that anchor the events of his novels, it is Tully-Veolan, whose charms and destruction are described in most loving, painful detail, and that best illus-trates the threat to a romantic but critical ancient heritage. Inspiration for the house came from 'various old Scottish seats', as the author of *Waverley* footnotes helpfully. He notes

The 'Bear Gates' at Traquair are echoed in the 'rampant bears' of Tully-Veolan. In 1744, the 5th Earl of Traquair vowed to shut the gates until a Stuart King was crowned in London.

Bruntsfield House[*] and Old Ravelston (an estate that includes a Z-plan[†] tower house), both in Edinburgh, as well as the nearby House of Dean, as providing 'some of the peculiarities of the description' of Tully-Veolan. And he adds, rather cryptically, that 'the author has, however, been informed, that the House of Grandtully resembles that of the Baron of Bradwardine still more than any of the above'.[24] Scott's son-in-law and first biographer, John Lockhart, later noted that Craighall Castle and Traquair House were also influential.

Grandtully Castle, a sixteenth-century Z-plan fortalice (or fortified house), with an added modern mansion, located near Pitlochry in Perthshire, has the hallmarks of the Scottish Gothic that so pleased Scott, but it is Traquair, the fortified manor house thirty miles to the east of Abbotsford, in his well-trodden border region, which has the most details in common with Tully-Veolan. Dating back to the early twelfth century, the house shows more refinement than some of the other suggested models, with its whitewashed exterior, high-pitched roof and neatly defined courtyard. The family home of one of Scott's close friends, Lady Louisa Stuart, Traquair projects the sense of strength and elegance that Scott invested in Baron Bradwardine's beloved Tully-Veolan, as well as its symbolic importance in the events of 1745.

The approach to Traquair is also similar to that described in the story: the 'upper gate of the avenue' is marked by pillars of stone, topped by 'two rampant Bears, the supporters of the family of Bradwardine'.[25] The famed 'Bear Gates' of Traquair, added by the 5th Earl of Traquair in 1738, and closed by him

---

[*] Bruntsfield House is now part of James Gillespie's High School.

[†] A design with a rectangular structure at the centre and towers set on a diagonal at either side.

in 1744 'till a Stuart King was crowned', are still standing and still locked shut. They do not sit under an archway, as described in the novel, but they do mark the entrance to an avenue lined by a double row of 'ancient' trees. Traquair has the 'steep roofs and narrow gables' and 'corners decorated with small turrets' of many fortified houses of its time, and consists of 'two or three high, narrow, and steep-roofed buildings'. There is no bear fountain, as at Tully, but there is a rather serene 'well pond'. Another note from the author makes clear that the walled garden of the fictional Tully-Veolan was modelled on one at Ravelston.[26] Most authors call on a variety of buildings for inspiration, but it was obviously important to Scott, the antiquarian and collector, to make clear at least some of his sources, or to point out that there were real houses that had inspired those of his literary imagination.

Traquair may have also influenced Osbaldistone Hall, the eponymous home of the family at the centre of intrigue in *Rob Roy*. This house, too, becomes a pawn in political, religious and familial strife. Its upper-level library and secret escape stair are used both by Rashleigh Osbaldistone, a committed Jacobite, and all-around nasty piece of work, and by the local Catholic priest, Father Vaughan. Practising the Catholic faith was still dangerous in the early eighteenth century, particularly as Catholics were often viewed as sympathisers to the Jacobite cause. Like Osbaldistone Hall, Traquair has a very notable library, with a collection filling two separate rooms. The room next to the library was indeed 'the priest's room', and is equipped with access to a secret stair concealed behind a corner bookcase. In the event of a raid, the stair allowed the priest time to descend from the top floor to the grounds and escape into the woods unobserved.*

Not surprisingly, the setting of Tully-Veolan stirs the young Edward, who finds 'the solitude and repose of the whole scene ... almost romantic'.[27] He also calls it 'this solitary and seemingly enchanted mansion', qualities shared by both the more isolated Craighall Castle, and by Traquair.

As events unfold, Tully-Veolan is first defiled, then confiscated, then restored. It is nearly destroyed by marauding English soldiers, who show themselves to be little better than barbarians. As Edward approaches the house after the English victory, he sees that 'the place had been sacked by the king's troops'. Most cruelly of all, 'the carved Bears, which were said to have done sentinel's duty upon the top for centuries, now, hurled from their posts, lay among the rubbish'.[28] The troops had also tried to burn the house to the ground. They were unsuccessful, but 'the towers and pinnacles of the main building were scorched and blackened; the pavement of the court broken and shattered; the doors torn down entirely, or hanging by a single hinge; the windows dashed in and demolished; and the court strewed with articles of furniture broken into fragments'. As a final dread summary, the narrator relates that 'the accessaries [*sic*] of ancient distinction, to which the Baron, in the pride of his heart, had attached so much importance and veneration, were treated with peculiar contumely'.[29]

It is as if through the damage wrought to the old mansion, Scott is signalling the difficult transition from old Scottish clan system to modern British union, but in ensuring it is repaired

---

* The trappings of the Catholic service at Traquair were hidden in secret compartments around the 'priest's room', with vestments in white cloth, so that they could be camouflaged as bedding.

with the help of the English colonel, he is insisting that the change can be a restorative force for good. As David Daiches has explained, Scott may have seen 'the movement towards enlightened progress in Scotland as both inevitable and desirable', but he also knew this wasn't without its cost.[30] Because of Baron Bradwardine's Jacobite sympathies, Tully-Veolan is taken away from him and handed to a distant male heir, as its entail dictates. Edward manages to engineer the restoration of the house's fabric and gardens *and* return it to the Baron. He then settles down to marry Bradwardine's mild, virtuous daughter Rose, whom he brings to live at Waverley-Chase, his English home, thus weaving Scots and English, Tory and Jacobite, into one harmonious family.

This vision of the destruction of Tully-Veolan came as Scott sat in his new surroundings at Abbotsford, though he had yet to build his new study or any of the features that would give it its later idiosyncratic grandeur. Whether he was imagining the loss of great houses he knew or of his own newly secured manor, he wanted readers to shiver at the possibility of such cultural devastation. The English, he seemed to be saying, were not all perfectly civilised beings, but the true English gentlemen, like the great Scottish chieftains, could be entrusted with looking after the country's built heritage.

With success came further indulgence in Scott's collecting habits. He bought more antiques, more land, and his plans for Abbotsford grew from the 'elegant cottage' to that of a neo-Gothic castle. In 1815 he published *The Lord of the Isles* and *Guy Mannering*, and by 1816 the work at Abbotsford took a much more grandiose turn. His relic-hunting had gained a new purpose, that of decorating his baronial-style home. Among the new treasures he acquired in 1812 were a gun that had belonged to Rob Roy himself, 'a long Spanish barrel'd piece with his initials R. M. C. for Robt. Macgregor Campbell', and a sword 'given to the great Marquess of Montrose by Charles I'.[31] He was also reclaiming bits and pieces from old buildings that were being torn down in Edinburgh to make way for new developments.

In 1816 Scott obtained 'some capital triangular stones from the Old Tolbooth of Edinburgh'. A medieval building, the Old Tolbooth had served various municipal purposes, including as a jail, renowned for the beating and torture of its inmates. The Tolbooth features prominently, and ominously, in the novel Scott would produce a couple of years later, *The Heart of Midlothian*. So perhaps keeping the pieces nearby gave him particularly close inspiration. These capitals would be used to top off some windows 'with fleur de lis and thistles at the upper angle', and he had also got hold of 'the old Tolbooth door' and 'the gate of the Parliament house'. He intended to use the door for his wash house and the gate as 'a sort of screen . . . to the east of the house'.[32] Still mindful of the grand houses belonging to his social betters, in the same letter, he mentions that he is keen to have 'a belt of granite and free-stone like that at Bowhill'.[33]

With works going on all over Edinburgh, Scott found such scavenging easy. 'They are pulling down so many of the old places here that carved stones are to be had for the asking,' he explained, and added that he had secured 'several scutcheons in the College which came down this summer'. He would also be watching out for some 'fine Gothic niches &c' and 'a projecting octagon window', which he might get after the proposed demolition of the west end of St Giles' church. Scott had already acquired 'a Gothic front to a well', which came from 'some debris dug out of the rubbish of the Abbey at Melrose'.[34] He would use it to decorate his own well, where 'it makes a tolerable deception and looks 300 years old'. Less appealing perhaps was a door knocker made from the foot of a deer, mounted in silver and sent to Scott by his brother, who had killed the animal.

Scott's acquisitive drive for his new home seemed to know no bounds. Daniel Terry, an architect-turned-actor who admired Scott and served as a liaison between the author and his architects, also contributed much to Abbotsford's decor. In a lengthy letter to Terry, Scott asks whether his friend thinks 'a commodity of real old stained glass can be picked up in London'.[35] In another he tells Terry that has found 'a very fine Quarry of Whin stone', which was 'producing specimens . . . as dark & fine a blue as that at Bowhill'.[36] His kinsman's home is clearly on his mind as he builds, and past money troubles (and any that might be accruing) are clearly not.

As Scott elaborated his plans for Abbotsford, he worked with several architect-designers, and finally settled on William Atkinson, who carried out most of the major work. Having first decided to make due with alterations to the original farmhouse, adding a dining room, armoury, anteroom and study, along with windows, doors and all manner of decoration, he finally decided, in around 1820, after buying yet more land, to demolish the old building and give free rein to his new vision. A new drawing room overlooking the Tweed, a great library, study and entrance hall were created, and the whole made to resemble a fortified baronial mansion: smaller, but not less impressive, than Drumlanrig; more ornamented than Traquair; more stylishly Gothic than Melville Castle; less romantically isolated than Craighall. With its many bays and turrets, bartizans and crow-stepped gables, pointed arches and crenellations, patterned stonework and manicured garden, Abbotsford is a wonderfully fanciful agglomeration of elements. On the outside, these pieces speak of an attempt to revivify an older architectural order, but most potently they speak of Scott's love affair with the varied traditions, legends and lore of ancient Scotland.

There is a definite air of Gothicism in the final designs, but it was Scottishness more than the Gothic that Scott wanted to emphasise. In 1816 he expressed his preference for an exterior

© The University of Edinburgh

Abbotsford in Scott's lifetime. He sought to create something 'less Gothic & more in the old-fashioned Scotch stile which delighted in notch'd Gable ends and all manner of bartizans'.

that Edward Blore had worked (from designs by James Skene), for 'being less Gothic & more in the old fashioned Scotch stile which delighted in notch'd Gable ends and all manner of bartizans'.[37] He was also after an authentic ad-hoc effect. In a letter to the poet and playwright Joanna Baillie, Scott wrote of his 'private dislike to a regular shape of a house'. He conceded, however, that 'it would be wrong headed to set about building an irregular one from the beginning', since the irregularity he admired in other buildings usually came from centuries of habitation and adaptation. He had no love of 'the cut-lugged bandbox with four rooms on a floor and two storeys rising regularly above each other'; in other words, the neoclassical style. He preferred the quirky 'outs and ins' of the farmhouse with its several additions (he hadn't yet knocked it down and begun a wholesale reinvention) and the 'odd variety of snug accommodation', but he still wanted something that would bespeak his status and rank. He told Miss Baillie: 'The front I intend shall have some resemblance to one of the old-fashioned English halls which your gentleman of £500 a year lived comfortably in former days.'[38] Former days, indeed: Scott was certainly spending more than this on property, bric-a-brac and alterations, so it is unclear whether he meant to be quaint or disingenuous.

The house, the collections and Scott himself were a magnet for the friendly and the curious. Abbotsford was often full of visitors and overnight guests, so much so that he complained at times of the toll it took on his writing efforts. One feature he incorporated into the design of the house was in answer to this public-private conundrum. A small door in the corner of his gallery-library above the study leads up to his dressing room, meaning that, like the 'ghostly' Father Vaughan, he could move between rooms quietly, without running into any houseguests.

When the publishing house of James and John Ballantyne failed in 1826, it should not have come as a surprise, given previous scares and the 'fatal amateurishness and recklessness' with which the business had been conducted.[39] Constable also suffered bankruptcy, and Scott was accountable for debts amounting to £126,000, or more than £10 million in today's money.[40] 'My extremity is come', he wrote in his journal on 18 December 1825. 'I suppose it will involve my all.'[41] He worried the creditors would not only take his land and goods, but also his home: 'I have half resolved never to see the place again.'

But rather than part with his 'Dalilah', as he often referred to Abbotsford, Scott sold off what other assets he could: the extra land and his house in Edinburgh, along with its furnishings. Employing his legal accuity, he constucted a deed trust for his debts, which meant that his creditors let him stay on at Abbotsford while writing novels to pay them off. By 1830 he achieved the return of his 'furniture, plates, linens, paintings, library' and other 'curiosities' that had stayed in the house, but had become the creditors' assets.[42] His wife, Charlotte, took the fall with less fortitude and died in 1826.

To pay his debts, Scott intensified his productivity, publishing several novels, histories and volumes of tales in a fevered pace of work. His last, *Castle Dangerous*, was published in 1831 and he died the following year after a series of strokes. Abbotsford came to exemplify his success, as well as his position as a writer and elevation to the seat of the new laird, but also, in some ways, perhaps, his demise. Yet Abbotsford was not just a personal achievement. Architecturally, it also popularised a style that was reproduced again and again elsewhere. In Scotland, bartizans and pointy turrets abound in later designs for places like Skibo Castle (rebuilt for the American industrialist Andrew Carnegie at the turn of the twentieth century), and at Balmoral, the Scottish retreat acquired by Queen Victoria in 1852 and redesigned by William Smith under the close supervision of Prince Albert. The carousel of baronial towers and protuberances can be found as far afield as New Zealand, in some municipal buildings and in the country's 'only castle', Larnach, in Dunedin, built in 1874 (the city also boasts a suburb called 'Waverley'), and in Ireland, Canada and the US, not to mention Edward Blore's designs for Vorontsov Palace in the Crimea.

Although Scott thrived on historical legends and artefacts, he embraced progress with enthusiasm. He became chairman of the Edinburgh Oil and Gas Company, and Abbotsford was one of the first buildings in Scotland to have gas lighting installed. We may have Scott to thank for the over-popularisation of the Scottish tartan and baronial mansions, but he was also an early adapter of the modern concept of strength in diversity. The novels, beginning with *Waverley*, helped Scott to express his divided loyalties, his passion for Scottish traditions and culture and his loyalty to the British king.[43] That division finds expression in Abbotsford, the new house built to look like an old Scottish manor and filled with relics from both English and Scottish history, such as Rob Roy's gun and the Marquess of Montrose's sword: he thought a 'dialogue' between them 'might be composed with good effect'.[44] This was a tricky undertaking when so many Scots were still smarting from the brutality of the Highland Clearances, and the Battle of Culloden only 'sixty years since'. But from his study in his *dulce domum*,* at his desk (modelled on John Morritt's desk at Rokeby Park), he gave Scottish castles and Highland heroes to the imaginations of legions.

Of course Scott didn't invent historical fiction all on his own, nor did he originate the idea of putting a house at the heart of a good story. Scott had read Horace Walpole, Jane Austen, and probably any number of the books inspired by the Gothic trend and produced at the end of the eighteenth century (see chapter 2). One writer, Maria Edgeworth, had a particular influence on Scott. Her novel, *Castle Rackrent* (1800), takes place in Ireland and is considered the first regional novel in English, something that Scott saw could be exploited in his own part of the world.[45] He acknowledged this debt, noting in his 'postscript' to *Waverley* that his intention was 'to emulate the admirable Irish portraits drawn by Miss Edgeworth', with whom he later became friends.[46]

Scott may have taken more than the regional flavour of Edgeworth's writing. As the title implies, there is a house at the centre of her novel, too. While it may seem to draw on the audience for the Gothic, Edgeworth's tale is more concerned with worldly sins. The loyal family steward is a comic-romantic figure called Thady Quirk, whose use of local vernacular probably also influenced Scott. Quirk chronicles the story of

---

* 'Home Sweet Home', title of the seventieth chapter of *Waverley*.

the Rackrent family through several generations, as they lose their estate through a combination of bad luck and worse behaviour. Unlike Scott or Austen, Edgeworth didn't see the need for a saviour to appear – whether galloping on a noble steed or demurely gliding into the parlour – to rescue Rackrent for future generations. Edgeworth went to live at her father's house at Edgeworthstown in Co. Longford when she was a teenager, and stayed there for most of her life, writing novels, children's stories and memoirs.

The house as the centre for historical fiction would get a boost in the 1920s when Virginia Woolf used Knole, the vast Tudor mansion belonging to the family of her friend, and

National Trust/Essenhigh Corke

The Great Hall at Knole in Kent, 1904. The Tudor mansion was the ancestral home of the writer Vita Sackville-West and inspired the setting for *Orlando*.

lover, Vita Sackville-West. Orlando, the gender-shifting, time-travelling protagonist of her novel, maintains his/her tie to the house as Vita, owing to an entailment, was unable to. Returning to the house in the present day (1928), Orlando envisions those centuries of life that have passed through its rooms. She sits at 'the end of the gallery with her dogs couched round her, in Queen Elizabeth's hard armchair', and has a vision of people 'laughing and talking', 'statesmen in colloquoy; and lovers dallying in window-seats'. There are people eating and drinking at the long tables wreathed in wood smoke. Orlando sees them 'dancing a quadrille', and then 'fluty, frail, but nevertheless stately music' begins. The whole cycle of life has occurred here: 'a coffin was borne into the chapel. A marriage procession came out of it.' There are 'armed men with helmets', who have come from Flodden and Poitiers. Peering further into the past, Orlando makes out, 'beyond the Elizabethans and the Tudors, someone older, further, darker, a cowled figure, monastic, severe, a monk, who went with his hands clasped, and a book in them, murmuring'. In her vision, the house, like those perhaps more fancifully rendered by Walter Scott, presents a pageant of vibrant living history to the readers of the present.[47]

Norton Conyers

FIVE

Madwoman in the Attic, Author in the Dining Room: The Haunts of Charlotte Brontë

'I like Thornfield: its antiquity, its retirement; its old crow-trees and thorn-trees . . . and yet how long have I abhorred the very thought of it; shunned it like a great plague-house!'

Mr Rochester, *Jane Eyre*

In 1847, using the male pseudonym Currer Bell, a clergyman's daughter from a small village in Yorkshire published *Jane Eyre*, a novel that 'set all London talking'.[1] The story caused a sensation, not for its eerie elements of Gothic tales – a great house, ghostly movements, a terrified virgin and the threat from some unnatural, malevolent force – but for the sheer passion of its heroine. Many people thought it 'immoral', others described the heroine, determined to seek a better life than the one she was born to, as distinctly 'angry', and found her perhaps more unsettling than the house or its ghoulish inmate.[2] And though some may have suspected that Currer Bell was, in fact, a woman, what they could not guess was that the female author, Charlotte Brontë, possessed a similarly fierce desire for self-determination.

That self-determination meant that while Charlotte Brontë remained rooted to her family home in Yorkshire, she would not forsake her dream of reaching out to the minds and imaginations of much more worldly readers with her pen. And if her life became a struggle to be both separate from the world and fiercely making her mark *in* it, that opposition is vividly reflected in her attachment to Haworth parsonage and her invention of Thornfield Hall. The parsonage was an isolated refuge and a hive of creative energy; Thornfield has become a byword for a young woman's intellectual and emotional awakening, as much as for Gothic horror. The invention of Thornfield was also different from historical romances. Unlike Walter Scott's Tully-Veolan, Thornfield is not a heroic guardian of the past; rather, it is a space for psychological and emotional exploration.

Like her Gothic-leaning predecessors, Brontë captivated readers by offering a mysterious dwelling to explore. Though it was not in the ancient style of a medieval castle or church, Thornfield features crucial Gothic elements: the darkened stairs and low-ceilinged corridors, and tucked away on the top floor, the supposedly uninhabited rooms signalling secrets and mystery. Like Jane Austen's *Northanger Abbey* and Ann Radcliffe's *The Mysteries of Udolpho*, the novel is both Gothic and romantic; there is a sense of terror, but also a happy marriage. But Jane is different, and so is her response to those spooky spaces. Far from being immediately intimidated by Thornfield, Jane Eyre is intrigued and grateful to be a resident there. To her, the house offers sanctuary, a promise of happiness, and only later a hovering threat. Unlike the frail Gothic heroines of old, Jane is no shrinking violet: on first hearing Bertha Rochester's maniacal laugh, she is more inclined to reasonable explanation than hysterics. If it appeared suddenly in her midst, all the floating armour of Otranto would be confidently batted away. And yet the house and its mystery are key to Brontë's narrative: it is the crucible for Jane's love affair with Mr Rochester and for her first experience of being valued for her intelligence and insight; it hosts her induction into the world of madness; and it is the frame for the compelling action of the novel.

Thornfield Hall was not modelled on any place that the author called home. Charlotte Brontë grew up in much more modest circumstances. Haworth parsonage is now a well-kept and popular literary landmark, but in her youth the sparsely furnished house, perched in the hilltop village hard by the cemetery, offered no abundance of physical comforts. The Reverend Patrick Brontë came from a crofting family in Co. Down, Ireland, and had raised himself up by being educated to the church. His was not the rollicking household of the Reverend George Austen. Described by many as a stern eccentric and by Elizabeth Gaskell as a man of 'antique simplicity', he did not allow his children anything that might be deemed 'luxury'.[3] Charlotte Brontë's great friend Ellen Nussey later remarked that the home was 'scant and bare indeed', and that 'there was not much carpet anywhere'.[4] She also noted that Mr Brontë's 'horror of fire forbade curtains to the windows', so these were covered in wood shutters. Such 'accessories to comfort and appearance' only arrived after Charlotte redecorated some of the rooms after earning her own sums from her writing and before her marriage in 1854.

Mrs Gaskell, who became friends with Charlotte and, after her death in 1855, her first biographer, commented on the grim plainness that was coupled with a bright, intellectual atmosphere in the Brontë home. 'The place tells of the most

Haworth parsonage today looks more inviting than in Charlotte Brontë's lifetime, when her friend Ellen Nussey pronounced it 'scant and bare indeed'.

dainty order,' she wrote, 'the most exquisite cleanliness.'[5] She, too, recorded Mr Brontë's insistence that the children were clothed humbly, else they might 'foster a love of dress' or other comforts. She also made note of the 'pleasant old fashion of window seats all through the house',[6] where it is easy to imagine Charlotte absorbed in her book, like little Jane Eyre reading in the window seat at Gateshead, or her sister Emily conjuring figures in the moors that spread out below.

It may have been clean and tidy, but in such a windswept place, with so few rugs and curtains, it probably wasn't always warm. The children's Cornish aunt, Elizabeth Branwell, who came to live with them after the death of their mother, was said to have found the stone floors so cold that she wore 'pattens' indoors and could be heard 'clicking up and down the stairs'.[7] These were removable wooden platforms attached to the bottom of shoes to protect them from mud and wet, and were usually reserved for outside use. The spare interiors were somewhat in keeping with late-Georgian and early Victorian style but the abstemious atmosphere was also down to the beliefs of the Brontë patriarch. In her descriptions of the decor of Gateshead, especially the 'red-room', and of the well-appointed interiors of Thornfield, Charlotte Brontë certainly gifted her characters more lush living spaces than those she had grown up with.*

Overlooking the moors that Emily Brontë painted as so passionately charged in *Wuthering Heights*, the parsonage was the centre of a strong family community. For Charlotte and her siblings, it was an isolated existence, but one that pulsed with life and colour when the children created stories together. Mr Brontë was almost as fervent about his children's education as he was about their asceticism; they were allowed to read, and did read, voraciously and freely. That passion was channeled early on into creating and writing about imagined worlds, which they peopled with their own characters and adventures. They were encouraged in their writing by their father (who had published his own small collections of verses), spinning tales set in elaborately detailed fantasy lands called 'Angria' and 'Glass Town', or 'Versopolis'. In the manuscript of a play written by the children, *Tales of the Islanders*,

---

* This is obviously not the case in all of her writing; for example, Robert Moore's mill cottage in Shirley is less than luxurious.

the thirteen-year-old Charlotte described the origins of the story in a passage that vividly relays the physical and artistic atmosphere of the Yorkshire home: 'One night about the time when the cold sleet and stormy fogs of November are succeeded by snow-storms and high-piercing winds of confirmed winter,' she recalls, 'we were all sitting round the warm blazing kitchen fire.' The children, not wanting an early bed, had been having a quarrel with their housemaid, Tabby, 'round the propriety of lighting a candle'. In this battle, Tabby 'came off victorious, no candle having been produced'.[8] Nevertheless, the children carried on with their play about different islands and their rulers, inventing characters and settings out loud to one another in the darkened kitchen.

From a young age, Charlotte Brontë had a taste for wondrous architecture of the imagination. This was at least partly inspired by popular engravings of fantastic cityscapes and biblical scenes created by the Romantic artist John Martin, of which Mr Brontë had three prints hanging in his study. In a similarly fantastic vein, Charlotte described her Glass Town as a city 'lying in splendour and magnificence', with a palace that 'was majestically towering in the midst of it, and all its pillars and battlements seemed in the light of the moon as if they were transformed into silver by the touch of a fairy's wand'.[9] Here, her fancy leans more towards William Beckford's tower than Horace Walpole's gloomy Gothic, but the rapture of dreamy creation is common to all three.

In their earliest years the children spent many hours in a small, upstairs bedroom, performing plays and writing in their 'little books'. As they grew older and their brother, Branwell, struggled with his thwarted ambitions and alcohol abuse, the girls (Charlotte, Emily and Anne) set up their literary activities in the dining room. Each had her own portable writing desk, and it was their practise to write and share their progress with each other as they paced around the dining table. Many letters, diary pages and poems were composed here in this cooperative fashion, along with the novels *Jane Eyre*, *Wuthering Heights* and *Agnes Grey*. Later Charlotte would come to experience life in more luxurious surroundings (such as those she re-created in Gateshead and Thornfield Hall) through her work as a governess and as the invited guest of friends Ellen Nussey and Mary Taylor. But in these early years the only extravagance was that of the imagination.

The creative spirits of the Brontë children came to bud in a climate of rigid simplicity, scarcity and sorrow. The children's mother died in 1821 when Charlotte was five years old and the youngest child, Anne, was just a toddler. At about the age of eight, Charlotte was sent to the Clergy Daughters' School at Cowan Bridge, fifty miles away on the border of the Lake District. There she, and later Emily, joined their elder sisters, Maria and Elizabeth. The school had been set up to educate the children of the poorly paid clergy, like Mr Brontë, but it was run by its Calvinist head on the lines of very meagre and strict provision for its resident pupils. Charlotte later described the constant gnawing cold and hunger, and she never forgave the harsh treatment meted out to pupils, especially towards her eldest sister, Maria. Her intense feelings of unhappiness at the strict regime and its scant comforts emerge in her depiction of Lowood School in *Jane Eyre*.

While attending the school, both Maria and Elizabeth became sick and eventually died, aged twelve and eleven, from tuberculosis, in 1825. Charlotte and Emily were taken back home to live, but were said to be 'stunted' by the prolonged exposure to cold and malnourishment, not to mention the trauma of losing two sisters in the space of a few months only a few years after the death of their mother. Charlotte later attended Roe Head School in Mirfield, where she had a happier experience and where she met her lifelong friends, Ellen Nussey and Mary Tayor. But, like her sisters, she was never happy being away from home. Whether because of their traumatic experiences at Cowan Bridge, suffering the deaths of so many family members at such a young age or the relative seclusion in which they lived, none of the Brontë children ever left the parsonage for good. As Mrs Gaskell explained, 'it appeared that Emily at least could not live away from home, while the others suffered much from the same cause'.[10]

Though content to live out her days in Haworth, Charlotte still had her own aspirations. She was keenly aware of the need to earn money for herself, as well as for the household. She also knew that should their father die, not only would his children be without a protector, but without a home, since the parsonage would be offered to the next curate. Decades after the Austen women had been forced into a dependency on family for shelter and care, the future for unmarried women was still dangerously precarious. Charlotte bristled at the narrow opportunities available to (or acceptable for) a young woman of her social standing, since realistically her career choices came down to working either as a teacher or governess. She tried both, and still aspired to publish her writing. In 1836 she sent some verses to the poet laureate, Robert Southey, for his consideration and advice. His answer was not encouraging. 'Literature cannot be the business of a woman's life: & it ought not to be,' he wrote. 'The more she is engaged in her proper duties, the less leisure time she will have for it.'[11] The full contents of the letter were more sympathetic than this extract suggests, as Southey was as much concerned with the difficulty for anyone, not just a woman, of earning a living at writing. But Charlotte was clearly frustrated by the occupations she was forced by economic circumstances and gender to pursue.

In 1835 she took up a teaching post at her former school Roe Head, but was not inspired by her pupils or her place. She became restless and depressed by what she perceived as her 'bondage', but nonetheless devoured detail and relished the occasions when she had time to let her imagination run.[12] And though she claimed in her angrier diary entries to feel contempt for her students, she was known to entertain them with ghost stories in the evenings, and told Ellen Nussey of 'the singular property of "seeing in the Night time", which the ladies at Roe head used to attribute to me'.[13] It helped that the school was thought to be haunted by a ghostly woman who inhabited the disused top floor. Charlotte found the idea much less horrifying than her charges, and she didn't mind the fright it gave them. It would be good fodder for her own eerie concoction later on.

By 1838, Charlotte had given up her position at Roe Head and returned to Haworth, saying, 'my health and spirits had utterly failed me'.[14] The next year she tried again to earn her own money, taking work as a governess with the Sidgwick family at Stone Gappe, an imposing brick manor house of three storeys set in terraced grounds in Lothersdale, North

Yorkshire. It was another place that failed in pleasing her, but not in giving her ideas for her fiction. Charlotte wrote that 'the country, the house, and the grounds are . . . divine', but lamented that she had 'not a free moment or a free thought left to enjoy them in',[15] her time and thoughts all being spent on the 'pampered, spoilt and turbulent children' she was engaged to look after.[16]

Gateshead Hall, Jane Eyre's first home, with the Reed family, was probably inspired by Charlotte's time as a governess at Stone Gappe. Although she doesn't provide many details about Gateshead, its ground-floor breakfast room with the window seat, its lodge and long path from the coach road are all present at Stone Gappe. Charlotte was not abused by the Sidgwick family, as the child Jane is by the Reeds, but her let-

© The Brontë Society

The Rydings, Birstall, near Huddersfield was home to Charlotte Brontë's friend Ellen Nussey. Its castellated parapet roof was probably woven into the design of Thornfield Hall.

ters attest to the fact that she was deeply unhappy there, both with the work imposed on her and with the social life, which she felt ill equipped to engage with. Mrs Sidgwick, she said, 'cares nothing about me except to contrive how the greatest possible quantity of labour may be squeezed out of me'.[17] Charlotte's crippling shyness ('a reserved wretch', she called herself) meant that she couldn't begin to join in polite conversation, even when invited to take part. 'I used to think I should like to be in the stir of grand folks' society but I have had enough of it,' she concluded.

Charlotte lasted only three months with the Sidgwicks, and then worked briefly for the White family, of Upperwood House in Apperley Bridge, about fifteen miles east of Haworth. Here, too, she soon pined for home, or better opportunities. Later, having read of her friend Mary Taylor's travels and adventures, Charlotte admitted feeling 'such a vehement impatience of restraint & steady work, such a strong wish for wings – wings such as wealth can furnish – such an urgent thirst to see – to learn – to know'.[18] It is in similar moods of frustrated ambition that Jane Eyre elects to pace the attic corridors and roof of Thornfield Hall rather than attempt to join the company of her social betters.

While attending a language school in Brussels with Emily (in hopes of acquiring skills and experience to set up their own school at home), Charlotte became enamoured of her employer, Constantin Heger, who ran the school with his wife. The girls left under a cloud, and all three sisters were back at Haworth in 1843. The parsonage was yet again the centre of their creative endevours. There, they set themselves to work, not in opening a school, but in putting together a volume of poetry to be published under the noms de plume of Currer, Ellis and Acton Bell. This was followed by the submission of Anne's novel *Agnes Grey*, Emily's *Wuthering Heights* and Charlotte's *The Professor* for publication. The first two novels found publishers, but *The Professor* (based on Charlotte's time in Brussels) was rejected. Undaunted, Charlotte turned her formidable imaginative powers to create something altogether different from a tale of unrequited love.

Jane Eyre was a bestseller. William Makepeace Thackeray (to whom Charlotte would later dedicate the second edition), claimed that he was 'exceedingly moved and pleased' by the novel, and that he had 'lost (or won if you like) a whole day in reading it', in the midst of a busy time with his own printers.[19] Other reviewers found it 'deserves high praise, and commendation',[20] and put it 'at the top of the list to be borrowed'.[21] Queen Victoria was a fan, and in the US there was 'Jane Eyre Fever'.[22] There were some naysayers, of course: some found in Jane far too passionate a heroine; others thought her inconsistent, but noted 'scenes of suppressed feeling, more fearful to witness than the most violent tornadoes of passion'.[23] Studies of the novel since reveal it as revolutionary in its presentation of a woman who refuses to shrink her aspirations to the limits of her gender and social class. And it is after she arrives at Thornfield that Jane begins to stretch her intellectual muscles and spread her metaphorical wings.

Thornfield is the place where Jane's mind and emotions rise to maturity. She is finally allowed to exercise her vibrant intellect, not as Adele's governess, but in her verbal sparring with Rochester. And despite his not being handsome, she feels herself becoming strongly attracted to the man, who is nevertheless a tribute to the Byronic heroes of her juvenile fiction. Like many a Gothic manse, Thornfield exerts a power over her, but it is not initially an ominous presence, as would befit a stirring Gothic tale. On arrival, Jane describes Thornfield in pleasing tones as 'a gentleman's manor-house ... battlements round the top gave it a picturesque look'.[24]

But Thornfield is also homely. Jane's first impression, on meeting Mrs Fairfax in the kitchen, is a pointed contrast to the atmosphere of other Gothic settings and to her previous experiences at Gateshead Hall and Lowood School. She calls it a 'beau ideal', and Mrs Fairfax is certainly no Mrs Danvers. Sitting in a 'snug small room', by a 'cheerful fire', the housekeeper was 'occupied in knitting; a large cat sat demurely at her feet ... A more reassuring introduction for a new governess could scarcely be conceived.'[25] Of course, in keeping with a good Gothic story, the picturesque scene does take a menacing turn. Jane's descriptions begin to mix admiration with wariness. She may bravely stride through the passages and up the stairs of Thornfield, but we readers are on cautious tiptoe behind her praying the candle doesn't suddenly blow out:

> The staircase window was high and latticed; both it and the long gallery into which the bedroom doors opened looked as if they belonged to a church rather than a house. A very chill and vaultlike air pervaded the stairs and gallery, suggesting cheerless ideas of space and solitude.[26]

Thornfield is not the first large house with a threatening air that Jane encounters in her young life. Although a poor orphan, she does not suffer her early deprivations in an impoverished dwelling; rather, it is amid the poisoned grandeur of Gateshead Hall that her aunt, Mrs Reed, and her cousins make little Jane the target of their insults and mistreatment. Gateshead provides a suitably terrifying moment of Gothic horror when little Jane is locked in the sinister 'red-room', in which 'the blinds [were] always drawn down' and the fire was seldom lit. Here, we find a mahogany bed draped in red damask, and a wardrobe with a 'certain secret drawer', among other items of mystery. Being locked inside this room – where Mr Reed had 'breathed his last' – as punishment for her insolence has an understandably terrifying effect on the child.[27] Charlotte Brontë ratchets up the scare factor by degrees and soon Jane faints away, like a true Gothic heroine. (However, Brontë is careful to point out that the sense of injustice is almost as gripping as the fear.) It is not clear that any such room existed at Stone Gappe or at Upperwood House, however, Charlotte's experiences at the Roe Head school, the great old house where she boarded as a pupil and then a teacher, also contained rooms associated with haunted lore. And this was not the only place associated with tales of a woman's ghost wandering the rooms of the top floor.

In a curious moment that tells us something of Brontë's views about being raised in poverty, Jane is asked by the kindly doctor whether she would like to go to 'poor relations', if she had any, rather than stay with 'Aunt Reed', whom she hates. Jane tells us: 'Poverty looks grim to grown people; still more so to children.' She doesn't think poor people 'have the means of being kind', and she doesn't want 'to grow up like one of the poor women I saw sometimes nursing their children or washing their clothes at the cottage doors'.[28] Clearly for Charlotte and for her heroine, a warm, comfortable home had visceral importance, not as a guarantee of love, perhaps, but as a bulwark against other, more feared dangers (cold, hunger, illness, death). At Thornfield, there is luxury but also more modest comfort. Jane enjoys the contrast of her own simple room with 'that wide hall, that dark and spacious staircase, and that long, cold gallery'. Her chamber is a 'safe haven': in the morning, as the sun shines through, she finds it 'a bright little place', with 'gay blue chintz window curtains . . . papered walls and a carpeted floor, so unlike the bare planks and stained plaster of Lowood'.[29] It's also unlike the bare stone floors and curtainless windows of the parsonage.

As Jane views the splendours of the house, readers get to enjoy a voyeuristic thrill through her eyes. The dining room is 'a large, stately apartment, with purple chairs and curtains, a Turkey carpet, walnut-panelled walls, one vast window rich in stained glass and a lofty ceiling, nobly moulded'. But this is only the prelude to the riches of the drawing room, which she views through a 'wide arch corresponding to the window'. Both are hung with 'a Tyrian-dyed curtain'. Jane thinks she glimpses there 'a fairy place, so bright to my novice eyes appeared the view beyond'. Yet she acknowledges:

It was merely a very pretty drawing-room, and within it a boudoir, both spread with white carpets, on which seemed laid brilliant garlands of flowers; both ceiled with snowy mouldings of white grapes and vine-leaves, beneath which glowed in rich contrast crimson couches and ottomans; while the ornaments on the pale Parian mantelpiece were of sparkling Bohemian glass, ruby red; and between the windows large mirrors repeated the general blending of snow and fire.[30]

The white carpets and red glass, that 'snow and fire', have great symbolic significance in the novel, but they may also say something about Charlotte Brontë's own contrasting character. One of Mrs Gaskell's friends, who met Charlotte at the home in Haworth, remarked on her similarity to her character Jane Eyre. She wrote to Mrs Gaskell that 'there is something touching in the sight of that little creature entombed in such a place, and moving about herself like a spirit, especially when you think that the slight still frame encloses a force of strong fiery life, which nothing has been able to freeze or extinguish'.[31] It is poignant that she chooses such a word as 'entombed', suggesting that Charlotte was not really alive in that place, or that her spirit, at least, was coldly confined there.

On Jane's first day at Thornfield, Mrs Fairfax gives her a tour, which allows the reader, again, to have a really good look around the house: 'I followed her upstairs and downstairs, admiring as I went; for all was well arranged and handsome.' Walking along with Jane, we are shown everything from top to bottom; we even pass along the rooms on the third storey, where we will later find the first Mrs Rochester locked away. At this point, Jane notes only that, 'though dark and low', the rooms were 'interesting from their air of antiquity. The furniture once appropriated to the lower apartments had from time to time been removed here, as fashions changed.'[32]

A thoroughgoing tour guide, Mrs Fairfax even takes Jane

'on to the leads', where she is encouraged to follow 'up a very narrow staircase to the attics, and thence by a ladder and through a trap-door to the roof of the hall'. Here, she observes a landscape that is not at all like the steep windswept moorlands of home, but more like the tamed gardens and parkland of estates Charlotte Brontë had visited: 'Leaning over the battlements and looking far down, I surveyed the grounds laid out like a map: the bright and velvet lawn closely girdling the grey base of the mansion; the field, wide as a park, dotted with its ancient timber.' All is as peaceful as 'the church at the gates, the road, the tranquil hills, all reposing in the autumn day's sun'. Her summation: 'No feature in this scene was extraordinary, but all was pleasing.'[33]

But now comes the first sign that something in this placid scene is amiss. Jane descends into the comparative blackness of the attic spaces, travels the narrow staircase to the darkness of the third floor, which was now 'black as a vault'. The passage between the front and back rooms is 'narrow, low and dim, with only one little window at the far end', reminding her of 'a corridor in some Bluebeard's castle'.[34] To needle our suspense, she does not hurry through the unknown, but keeps herself on the edge of potential danger, saying, she 'lingered' there. Of course, we might think that Jane should do anything but hang around. However her refusal to be cowed by an unlit passage shows her standing up to Thornfield and whatever horrors it may offer. She is too sensible to fear the dark for its own sake, and her 'lingering' affords her the opportunity to hear 'a curious laugh; distinct, formal, mirthless', which then 'set off in a clamorous peal that seemed to wake an echo in every lonely chamber'. The source is clear: 'I could

143

have pointed out the door whence the accents issued.' But even this, explained as the weird behaviour of the seamstress Grace Poole, does not scare off our heroine.

Rather than having her flee, Brontë gives us more of the house, the rooms in the attic, the rooftop, where Jane later returns and looks 'out afar over sequestered field and hill' and 'longed for a power of vision which might overpass that limit'. It is as though the author wants to be sure we are seeing all that is enticing about Thornfield rather than just scaring us, and Jane, away. Even in its mystery the house holds some allure for Jane, but not in its great rooms. Struggling with an independence of mind that challenged contemporary ideas of women's roles and ambitions, Jane experiences moments of 'restlessness' when 'my sole relief was to walk along the corridor of the third storey, backwards and forwards'.[35] If she lays claim to any part of the house, it is not in the downstairs drawing room (though she may admire it) where the society ladies prance and giggle, or the large 'saloon' where Rochester and his guests dine with 'ten footmen . . . running to and fro', but in these liminal spaces that Charlotte Brontë must have known in her roles as governess: the attic, the stairs, the nursery, the schoolroom, the library.[36] It is, ironically, in the unsocial corridors of Thornfield, precariously near to the first Mrs Rochester, that Jane feels 'safe in the silence and solitude'.

In constructing the fictional designs of Thornfield Hall, Charlotte appears to have amalgamated a few residences she visited in the 1830s and '40s. The Rydings in Birstall, near Huddersfield, was the home of her friend Ellen Nussey, and

Charlotte first visited with her brother, Branwell, in 1832. Though not a terribly large house – it certainly wouldn't take ten footmen, plus guests, in the dining room – it has five bays and, perhaps most importantly, a castellated parapet roof, like the one Jane describes at Thornfield, 'the grey and battlemented hall'. Charlotte and her brother were both taken with the house and its location. Branwell pronounced it 'paradise', while Charlotte later wrote to Ellen: 'Rydings is a pleasant spot, one of the old family Halls of England, surrounded by Lawn, and wood-land speaking of past times and suggesting (to me at least) happy feelings.'[37]

Though visits to The Rydings provided Charlotte with the experience of living in a larger and more comfortable house

© Peak District National Park Authority

Charlotte visited North Lees Hall in 1845 and learned the story of the Eyre family, who had built it. She was also told of a madwoman kept on the upper floor, who had died there in a fire.

than she was used to, a more like model for Thornfield is North Lees Hall, in what is now the Peak District National Park in Derbyshire. Charlotte visited North Lees in 1845, while staying at the vicarage in nearby Hathersage with Ellen Nussey, whose brother was the vicar there. This Elizabethan tower house is taller, with three storeys, and has a crenellated roof, which can be accessed from the attic floor inside. It also enjoys a more isolated setting, which would have been even more striking in the 1840s, and suggests some of the seclusion of Thornfield. Sitting on a little rise, the house offers wide views over woodland and green hills. It could be this view that Charlotte was thinking of when Jane 'climbed three staircases, raised the trap-door of the attic . . . and looked out afar over sequestered field and hill'.[38]

North Lees was built in 1590 by a family by the name of Eyre. At the time Charlotte visited, the family still lived there and, as biographer Claire Harman describes, she and Ellen were guided around the house by a widow called Mary Eyre, who 'showed them a tall cabinet decorated with heads of the twelve apostles'.[39] This particular item appears in chapter XX, when Jane sits beside the wounded Richard Mason, bathing the wounds inflicted by his mad sister, waiting for the return of Mr Rochester and the surgeon. There she notices 'a great cabinet opposite – whose front, divided into twelve panels, bore in grim design the heads of the twelve apostles'. Mary Eyre also told Charlotte and Ellen the story of 'a former mistress of the house', who 'had gone mad and been kept in a padded room on the top floor, where she died in a fire that had damaged the house severely'.[40] Harman notes further that the pair went to the parish church, where 'they admired the ancient brasses of these Eyres, and the tomb of Damer de Rochester'.

Inside North Lees there is indeed a heavy, spiralling staircase (though of elm, not oak) and windows with thick stone transoms and leaded mullions typical of the period. But its internal spaces are not nearly as lofty as those described at Thornfield, and the top floor simply isn't large enough to contain many rooms, even those that might be 'narrow, low and dim'. For those spaces, we must look to another visit that is not recorded by Charlotte herself.

During her difficult post with the Sidgwicks, Charlotte visited Swarcliffe, near Harrogate, a house belonging to John Greenwood, the father of Mrs Sidgwick. Decades later, Ellen Nussey is said to have reported that during this time Charlotte had a fateful encounter with a house called Norton Conyers, outside Ripon.[41] A Jacobean manor house with a great hall dating to the fourteenth century, Norton Conyers had belonged to the Graham family since 1624. The lease was later taken over by Mrs Sidgwick's brother Frederick, making it not unlikely that the Charlotte's employers knew of the house and that they would have visited when staying in the area in 1839.

At the time of Charlotte's purported visit, the house had come down to Sir Bellingham Graham, 7th Baronet, who had a reputation as a vain and profligate figure. According to Sir James Graham, the current owner and resident of Norton Conyers, Bellingham was 'the bad one'. He gambled, kept mistresses (fathering several illegitimate children) and ultimately lost his ancestral home, allowing it to be picked up by Frederick Greenwood in 1865. (The 8th baronet managed to get it back in 1879.)[42] It is unlikely that Charlotte would have met Bellingham himself, as he had inherited several other properties, along with Norton Conyers, and was never there for long. But his troubled, Byronic character may have been partly responsible for the scandalous past and proud bear-ing of Mr Rochester. Certainly, Ellen Nussey reported that Char-lotte had been particularly struck by elements of the house, the oak staircase, the suits of armour and yet another story of a madwoman confined to one of the upper rooms.[43]

No direct evidence exists to link Charlotte to Norton Conyers, and arguments for other models continue to be put forward, such as Thurland Castle, only two miles from Cowan Bridge, which Charlotte might have seen but never entered.[44] Details do suggest that connections between Norton Conyers and Mr Rochester's home are fair. It is, like Thornfield, more like 'a gentleman's manor-house, not a nobleman's seat'.[45] The staircase coheres with Jane's description of Thornfield, as does the arch off the main hall, which frames the window. The arch spans the bottom of the wide oak staircase and marks where the medieval house would have ended. The 'staircase window', which is 'high and latticed' and, like the long gallery, 'looked as if they belonged to a church rather than a house', are also to be found at Norton Conyers, whose tall stair window is set with stained glass panels bearing the armorial devices of vari-ous ancestors.

Though the curving Dutch gables and lack of crenellation do not correspond to the description of Thornfield, the view from the roof does take in the church tower, as Jane sees when she first goes up onto the leads with Mrs Fairfax. The 'spacious staircase' and 'long, cold gallery' can also be found at Norton Conyers. The voluminous hall, hung with an array of family portraits through the centuries, rings true, and one of these, a man in armour by Sir Peter Lely, *c.* 1650, was possibly the painting Jane describes as 'a grim man in a cuirass'. This room could certainly stand for the 'stately apartment, with . . . walnut-panelled walls' and a 'lofty ceiling, nobly moulded', as in Thornfield's dining room, and its mantelpiece could be taken for 'Parian', or bisque, porcelain.[46]

The most tantalising of the many corresponding details is the concealed staircase that leads from the first-floor gallery to the attic rooms on the top floor, which was rediscovered and revealed by Sir James and Lady Graham in 2004. It is thought the staircase was installed in the late seventeenth century to provide a direct route for servants from their quarters to the gallery. The Grahams believe that it was probably in use

Norton Conyers, near Ripon, lacks the battlements of Thornfield, but its interiors and concealed staircase are key features of Mr Rochester's house.

during Charlotte Brontë's visit, though are unsure when it was blocked up; as Sir James recalls, 'it was still used when I was a boy'. The stair leads to an enfilade of little rooms. As the 7th Baronet had recently sold another property and removed its furnishings in some of the attic rooms of Norton Conyers, Charlotte may indeed have seen furniture stored there, as Jane notes. As the farthest attic room is well removed from the stair, and only reached by travelling through the others, Sir James notes that it would have been 'quite a lonely place to be'.[47]

This is the stair Mr Rochester would have used in chapter XX, when Richard Mason is attacked by his crazed sister: 'A chamber door opened: some one [sic] ran, or rushed, along the gallery. Another step stamped on the flooring above, and something fell; and there was silence.' The secret stair would have allowed Rochester to go from the gallery quickly to the attic room above the guests' quarters on the first floor without being seen on the main staircase. After the commotion quiets down, Jane observes that 'the door at the end of the gallery opened, and Mr Rochester advanced with a candle: he had just descended from the upper storey'.[48] Here, he would have come from the main stair appearing in the normal way, to calm his shaken guests.

Judging that the sounds have come from the room 'above mine' (on the third floor), Jane thinks she has heard more than the others and understands that it was not merely 'a servant's dream'. On the third floor, Rochester opens a 'small black door' to a room hung with tapestry, which 'was now looped up in one part, and there was a door apparent, which had been concealed'. This description agrees somewhat with the attic rooms at Norton Conyers, which are linked to one another, rather than being set on either side of a corridor. The linked rooms are used to effect by Brontë when Jane is tending the injured Mason in one room but can hear, through the door beyond, a horrific 'snarling, snatching sound, almost like a dog quarrelling'. Left sitting in the room with her patient while Rochester runs to fetch the surgeon, Jane ruminates: 'Here then I was in the third storey, fastened into one of its mystic cells; night around me; a pale and bloody spectacle under my eyes and hands; a murderess hardly separated from me by a single door', a lonely place indeed.[49]

George Henry Lewes, the noted critic, dramatist, novelist (and married lover of George Eliot), criticised *Jane Eyre* for having 'too much melodrama and improbability', but he warmly credited its 'remarkable beauty and truth'. In terms Walpole would have appreciated, Lewes also expressed admiration for 'the reality stamped upon almost every part', which is not only confined to 'the characters and incidents, but . . . is also striking in the description of various aspects of Nature, and of the houses, rooms, and furniture'.[50] Lewes goes on to speculate: 'In her delineation of country-houses and good society there is the ease and accuracy of one who has well known what she describes.' Of course, Charlotte Brontë was not a habitué of great houses, but she had spent time in some and was a keen observer of all she witnessed, both the people and the surroundings.

While the architecture and atmosphere of Thornfield Hall is not as extreme as those created by Walpole or William Beckford, the house is as necessary to the exciting atmosphere of

Jane's evolution as Manfred's castle or Vathek's tower is to theirs. Charlotte Brontë also shares with both earlier writers a penchant for characters who are dissatisfied with the limits of their station and strive for powers and distinction that seem just beyond their grasp. In the earlier novels, the many rooms and passages of the house or castle become emblematic of a frantic and frustrating quest for power. For Jane Eyre, the house's secrets are revealed in a search for self-fulfillment. Beyond its rich ornament, the obstacles it poses are real and conquerable, though necessitating destruction (by fire), that allows for rebirth.

Even as a successful author, Charlotte Brontë continued to live at Haworth parsonage. In spite of achieving fame, Charlotte still felt uncomfortable going about among strangers, so the

The dining room at Haworth Parsonage, where the Brontë sisters often gathered to write and read their work to one another. Charlotte redecorated after her marriage in 1854.

readers and critics came to her. The parsonage became a place of pilgrimage both before and after her death. Having survived the deaths of Branwell, Emily and Anne in 1848–9, Charlotte married her father's curate, Arthur Bell Nicholls, in 1854. She made a few changes to the family home, since even though she was to be married, she was still not leaving Haworth. She enlarged the main bedroom for herself and her new husband, and decorated the downstairs dining room, the room where the children used to gather to write and discuss their work over so many years. For this room, where Charlotte now received her visitors, or paced alone with only the ghosts of her siblings, she chose new wallpaper and curtains, which, as Ellen Nussey noted, Mr Brontë still objected to, 'but it was not forbidden'.[51] She created a study for Arthur from what was a storeroom. A fireplace was added, and she enjoyed doing it up. As she wrote to Ellen, 'I have been very busy stitching – the little new room is got into order now and the green and white curtains are up – they exactly suit the papering and look neat and clean enough.'[52]

Tragically, Charlotte died only eight months after her marriage, not from the consumption that took most of the members of her family, but possibly from illness owing to extreme morning sickness (*hyperemesis gravidarum*). Her husband was left to look after the serially bereft Mr Brontë, who had survived his wife and all of his six children. Responding to Mrs Gaskell's *Life of Charlotte Brontë*, published in 1857, Charlotte's friend Mary Taylor wrote to the author that the book gave 'a true picture of Melancholy life'. Noting some of the reviews, Mary wondered that none of the critics 'seems to think it a strange or wrong state of things that a woman of first-rate talents, industry, and integrity should live all her life in a walking nightmare of "poverty and suppression"'.[53]

Unlike Jane Austen, Charlotte Brontë did not reward her heroine with a settlement in a small country parsonage, which, to her, perhaps, was not much of a reward. Jane Eyre finds not only a devoted husband, but also a large, comfortable house to be mistress of. Ferndean, where she goes to live with Rochester after their marriage, is smaller than Thornfield, but is still a manor house, 'a building of considerable antiquity, moderate size, and no architectural pretensions, deep buried in a wood'.[54] She would avoid any intimations of poverty, but in keeping with Charlotte's abiding need for separateness, Ferndean is located in an 'ineligible and insalubrious site'. It is thought to have been inspired by the location and setting, if not the architecture, of Wycoller Hall in Lancashire, a place Charlotte and her sisters were said to have visited frequently, though it lies about nine miles from the parsonage. Its romantic ruins were used to illustrate an early edition of *Jane Eyre*. When she wanted to give her impassioned heroine a happy ending, it seems Charlotte chose to remove her from the bewitching, far-off setting of her early tempestuous love affair and bring her closer to home.

Ghost stories, tales of haunted houses and murder mysteries were to become popular genres towards the latter half of the nineteenth century. Charles Dickens sought to partake of this popularity in his last, unfinished novel, *The Mystery of Edwin Drood*. His friend Wilkie Collins, in *The Moonstone* and *The Woman in White*, brought accomplished writing to the burgeoning mystery genre. Not all, or many, addressed the moral or social concerns that Charlotte Brontë brought to light in *Jane Eyre*. Certainly, her sister Emily's novel *Wuthering Heights* combined passion with the supernatural, but Anne's *The Tenant of Wildfell Hall* brought the named house and nascent feminism to bear with another strong-willed female character who seeks refuge in an ominous-seeming mansion. The Gothic romance would generate still more branches and devotees among both the literary elite and the wider reading public in the new century.

Restoration House

SIX

Charles Dickens:
A Child's View of Home

'This is Gadshill we are coming to, where Falstaff went out to rob those travellers, and ran away' . . . said the very queer small boy . . . 'ever since I can recollect, my father, seeing me so fond of it, has often said to me, "If you were to be very persevering and were to work hard, you might some day come to live in it."'

Charles Dickens, 'Travelling Abroad', 7 April 1860

A few days before his death in 1870, Charles Dickens walked from his house at Gad's Hill Place in Higham, Kent, to nearby Rochester. It was a journey of about three miles, but for a man who routinely walked several miles a day, this was no great distance. What was of more significance was the fact that he had returned to scenes of his childhood for his last novel, *The Mystery of Edwin Drood*. Dickens had spent a crucial period of his early life in nearby Chatham, exploring the marshes and towns along the Medway near his home. He later recalled that this was the happiest time of his youth, as there was relative stability in the family: John Dickens still had a job in the Navy Pay Office, the family lived in a modest but respectable home, and young Charles, a bright and ambitious child, regularly attended school.

A significant event from this period was recounted several times by Dickens later in life. It was the story of his first glimpse of Gad's Hill Place, where he would spend the last dozen years of his life. He described how he 'spied' what seemed to him a very grand house while on a walk with his father. In the passage quoted above, Dickens presents himself as the new owner of the house being greeted by a young boy, who is similarly enamoured of Gad's Hill. The boy is, in fact, a vision of his own 'queer small' self, and the account relates his sense of both wonder and pride at achieving his childish dream. In a letter to a friend written just after he had moved into the house, Dickens recalled his father had told him 'that if I ever grew up to be a clever man, perhaps I might own that house, or such another house'.[1] John Dickens was by all accounts a clever man, but that did not prevent the fecklessness that resulted in his being imprisoned in the Marshalsea for debt, and in his twelve-year-old son having to leave school and go to work in a shoe-blacking factory.

When Dickens made his last trip to Rochester, it was June 1870. He was a fifty-eight-year-old father of nine children, and had separated from his wife, Catherine, twelve years previously. He had been living at Gad's Hill for the past ten years or so with his daughter Mary ('Mamie') and his unmarried sister-in-law, Georgina Hogarth. (The fact that his wife's younger sister had decided to stay on to run the household after Dickens had so abruptly, and publicly, split with Catherine had become a fact of family arrangement, no longer much remarked upon.)

At the time he was also a hugely successful author, who could have stretched to a much grander house. Indeed, when he acquired Gad's Hill Place in 1857, there was no indoor plumbing, the roof leaked and there was not sufficient water supply for the household. To solve this, a well had to be dug, and, as the house sat on a hill, the excavations ran deep, to some 217 feet. Once water was finally found, Dickens claimed that the first glass of the stuff had come at a cost of about £200.[2] Given that the entire purchase price was just under £2,000, this one improvement might have been deemed an extravagance.

But this house held an allure for Dickens that trumped other luxuries or mere practicalities. On finding it was for sale and that he might be able to purchase it, he could barely contain his delight. Again, Dickens told versions of the same story. The scene involves an evening walk from Gravesend in 1855, after a birthday dinner with friends. Dickens took the road to Rochester (the main London to Dover road), and passing over Gad's Hill, once again spied the house of his fancy. This time, through a snowy landscape, he saw a sign advertising the house for sale. He later explained to his friend and editor William Wills that the house was 'a dream of my childhood', and asked Wills to look into the purchase for him.[3]

Dickens's fiction is almost as full of quirky living spaces as it is eccentric characters. Those we are most familiar with come from the teeming streets of London, but his return to the neighbourhoods of his youngest memories presented two houses of particular importance: Gad's Hill Place, the home of his childhood dream, and Restoration House, the rambling mansion that he probably also saw as a boy and a house that still provokes some of the most vivid associations in literature. Dickens had already written eleven novels and was at work on *A Tale of Two Cities* when he moved into Gad's Hill, but his next novel demonstrated the depth of feeling the return to Kent had ignited about ideas of home and childhood. *Great Expectations* (1861), his second autobiographical novel, was one of the first to present the world from a child's point of view.

That Dickens came to write it after settling himself at Gad's Hill shows us how a writer who was the champion of the poor, particularly poor and abused children, came back to examine his own beginnings. While in *David Copperfield* he presented his life as a rags-to-riches story, in *Great Expectations* he shows us that the boy who wishes only for riches will be sorely disappointed. We might be tempted to read the promise of Gad's Hill as an antidote to Miss Havisham's Satis House; however, Dickens's own life by this point was too conflicted to ascribe a happy equilibrium to his time there.

Gad's Hill Place makes few appearances in his fiction. But it is there, for example, in the touching scene from *A Christmas Carol* (1843), when Scrooge is taken to visit his own past. Scrooge and the spirit come upon 'a mansion of dull red brick, with a little weathercock-surmounted cupola on the roof', much like Gad's Hill. In the story, this is the school of Scrooge's youth, but the passage foreshadows some of the decay of Miss Havisham's house. The school is 'a house of broken fortunes', the rooms inside 'cold and vast' and there is a 'chilly bareness'. Scrooge, like his creator, is powerfully affected by the boyhood memories stirred by the visit here. Not 'a latent echo in the house' nor 'a drip from the half-thawed water-spout', not even 'the idle swinging of an empty store-house door, no, not a clicking in the fire', none of these things went unnoticed by the embittered old man. Rather, they fell upon his heart 'with a softening influence, and gave a freer passage to his tears'.[4]

If Dickens is responsible for the British nostalgia for the Victorian house, it isn't because he tried to make it glamorous or inviting, but because he made it irresistibly potent for children, and for adults recalling their youthful impressions. Most Dickensian interiors are crowded, dimly lit, often suffused with something like mustiness. Always they say something about the characters at hand, whether they are charming 'little' cottages or, like evil Daniel Quilp's premises, 'a small rat-infested dreary yard ... in which were a little wooden counting-house burrowing all awry in the dust as if it had fallen from the clouds and ploughed into the ground'.[5] It is easy to recall Mr Brownlow's cosy fireside in *Oliver Twist*, Lady Dedlock's drafty drawing room in *Bleak House*, Mr Peggotty's fantastically incongruous dwelling in the hull of an old boat, which young David Copperfield deems 'beautifully clean inside and as tidy as possible', in short, 'a perfect abode'.[6]

Houses for Dickens were the fabric of his fiction. Presenting them through a child's eyes, he drew comic and tender portrayals, such as David Copperfield's early memories of his cottage home before the arrival of Mr Murdstone. From his infant memory, David recalls:

Here is a long passage – what an enormous perspective I make of it! – leading from Peggotty's kitchen to the front-door. A dark store-room opens out of it, and that is a place to be run past at night; for I don't know what may be among those tubs and jars and old tea-chests.[7]

It is an enchanting description of spaces that once seemed so large and scary to a child; now, of course, understood to be of reasonable size and commonplace. We laugh knowingly at the enlarged perspective, the fear of the dark and the need to 'run past' areas where imagined menace looms in shadow. Dickens plays on the naive sense of awe and the mature self-awareness to great effect. He helps us to see how our childish perspectives may shape our own ideas of comfort or fear, welcome or distress and how these impressions last well into our adult lives.

In his own life, Dickens insisted on a neat and tidy house, and it is a habit shared by his most virtuous characters, whatever their circumstances. In *The Old Curiosity Shop* Kit Nubbles's virtue and that of his poor mother is conveyed by their home, 'an extremely poor and homely place, but with that air of comfort about it' that 'cleanliness and order can always impart in some degree'.[8] In fact, Mrs Nubbles's tidiness helps land Kit a well-paid job with the Garland family, as Mrs Garland is 'quite sure [Mrs Nubbles] was a very honest and very respectable person', owing to 'the appearance of the children and the cleanliness of the house'.[9] When Kit arrives at his dream employment, it is a fairytale setting, 'a beautiful little cottage with a thatched roof and little spires at the gable-ends, and pieces of stained glass in some of the windows almost as large as pocket-books'.[10] For Kit, who has often had little to eat, the kitchen was 'such a kitchen as was never before seen or heard of out of a toy-shop window, with everything in it as bright and glowing, and as precisely ordered too, as Barbara [the little housemaid] herself'.[11]

Dickens describes many pleasant dwellings in diminutive terms. They might have 'pocket-book' windows, or look like something out of a 'toy-shop' or 'doll's house', linking little-ness with neatness, and both with childlike fancy. Another paean to 'littleness' and tidiness is the newly dubbed 'Bleak House', prepared by Mr Jarndyce for his recently married ward, Esther Summerson. It has a 'pretty little orchard, where the cherries were nestling among the green leaves' and is 'a rustic cottage of doll's rooms'. Outside is a 'little rustic veranda, and underneath the tiny wooden colonnades, garlanded with woodbine, jasmine and honeysuckle'.[12] Such quaint comforts are a luxury for most of Dickens's characters, especially the children. Images of safe, comfortable homes to the 'Tom-all-alones', the 'Marthas', the 'Sissys', the 'Esthers', are like Orien-tal fantasies to a more privileged dreamer. While some characters like Esther Summerson, Florence Dombey and David Copperfield are rewarded with safe and happy homes, others, like Oliver Twist and Kit Nubbles, are introduced to a nurturing home only to have it snatched away by evildoers (though they find happiness in the end). For all such charac-ters, a place of modest, or 'little', comforts is a pleasure to be savoured, as young David Copperfield reminisces happily about his aunt Betsey Trotwood's welcoming parlour, which was 'as neat as Janet or my aunt':

The old-fashioned furniture brightly rubbed and polished, my aunt's inviolable chair and table by the round green fan in the bow-window, the drugget-covered carpet, the cat, the ket-tle-holder, the tall press guarding all sorts of bottles and pots, and, wonderfully out of keeping with the rest, my dusty self upon the sofa, taking note of everything.[13]

Some of the poorest children in Dickens's vast menagerie, like Little Nell and Pip, come to lament the loss of even their very modest households, as Dickens did when his family left Chatham for London. The angelic Little Nell transcends the surroundings of her grandfather's overfilled shop and living quarters, 'singing through the dim rooms, and moving with gay and lightsome step among their dusty treasures, making them older by her young life and sterner and more grim by her gay and cheerful presence'.[14] But young Charles, as he later told his friend John Forster, couldn't muster so much cheer when his family moved to London. Life became a struggle, he was no longer sent to school, and from his 'back garret' in Bayham Street, Dickens thought of 'all that I had lost in losing Chatham, what I would have given if I had anything to give, to be sent back'.[15]

From *Great Expectations*, readers will recall Miss Havisham's ghostly drawing room, but other spaces are chock-full of the evidence of their inhabitants' follies, virtues and vices. There is Mr Pumblechook's quarters, 'which were of a peppercorny and farinaceous character, as the premises of a corn-chandler and seedsman should be'. Pip guesses that Mr Pumblechook must be 'a very happy man indeed, to have so many little drawers in his shop'; again highlighting the wonder in 'little' things.[16] The mysterious Mr Jaggers' office is 'a most dismal place', with its 'dreadful' death masks perched on a shelf, its chair of 'deadly black horsehair, with rows of brass nails round it like a coffin.'[17]

Like much in *Great Expectations*, Satis House comes out of Dickens's early years growing up near Rochester. The marshes, the dismal graveyard, the prison ships and the decayed grandeur of Miss Havisham's Gothic mansion are all rooted here. Satis House took its name from one house in Rochester, but its shape from another house in the town, Restoration House, a grand agglomeration begun in the Tudor period with a gated courtyard, ivy climbing the chimney, a warren of stairs and several windows that were barred or blocked. It was also next to a brewery, Woodhams, established in 1750.[18] This appears in the novel and is explained by Herbert Pocket, who notes that Miss Havisham's over-indulgent father was a brewer.[19]

Apart from its role in the story, Restoration House has a history reaching back several hundred years before Dickens ever noticed it, and has its own tales to tell. The name was given to the house after a visit by Charles II in 1660, who was on his way to London to reclaim his throne after fifteen years in exile in Europe.* Some elements of the building were constructed as early as 1454, but the more substantial and elegant part of the house dates from around 1587. The various 'dark' staircases noted with trepidation by Pip recall the odd assortment at Restoration House, which were introduced over centuries of additions and changes. Though Satis House is probably a composite drawn from other places of the

---

* A vertical shaft following the chimney structure down from what is now called 'the King's Bedchamber' is alleged to have been an intended escape route.

author's experience, Dickens's close friend and first authorised biographer, John Forster, affirmed that the author 'took Satis House' from Restoration House, which 'had a curious attraction for him'.[20]

Satis House looms large in the novel, focussing the Gothic mood conferred by the marshes, the prison ships and Jaggers's disturbing office. Its inmate, Miss Havisham, has a near-supernatural presence. She is legendary to the locals, the neighbourhood eccentric familiar to children and adults, and known as 'Miss Havisham up town . . . an immensely rich and grim lady who lived in a large and dismal house barricaded against robbers, and who led a life of seclusion'.[21] Pip learns that this eerie manor is called 'Satis', meaning 'enough', and while Estella proclaims its derivation – 'Greek, or Latin, or Hebrew' – the reader is aware of the irony: it is, of course, not enough. And as Dickens was pointing out, for some people (perhaps himself) no amount of money, or house, ever would be.

The story of a half-crazed, wealthy recluse going round in her tattered wedding finery was conflated from different stories that Dickens had heard or read. But his approach to the novel was more inventive in presenting the early parts of the story from the point of view and through the voice of a very young boy. Pip's fearful rendering of Miss Havisham and her 'large and dismal house' have the ring of childish honesty, a nice contrast with the absurd deference shown by the adults. Pip's story, introduced in his own 'infant tongue', carries the full measure of childish terror, as Magwitch, 'a fearful man, all in coarse grey, with a great iron on his leg', crawls out of the marshes and seizes Pip by the chin. The unfiltered naive view also gives us our impressions of the forge and its harsh mistress, Mrs Joe, as well as the awesome strangeness of Satis House.

Like the boy who found the passage from Peggotty's kitchen to be 'a place to be run past at night', Pip is frightened and disturbed by Miss Havisham's cobwebbed quarters. The first impression is not promising:

[The house was] of old brick, and dismal, and had a great many iron bars to it. Some of the windows had been walled up; of those that remained, all the lower were rustily barred. There was a court-yard in front, and that was barred; so, we had to wait, after ringing the bell, until some one should come to open it.[22]

As with any good Gothic mansion, what is inside the walls is even more forbidding than the external landscape, but what is outside is a harbinger of evils within. Pip notices that in the brewery yard 'the cold wind seemed to blow colder than outside the gate. There it made a shrill noise, howling 'like the noise of wind in the rigging of a ship at sea'.[23] The sound recalls the hulking prison ships, with which we have already made a grim acquaintance. The brewery is no longer making beer of any kind, Estella tells him, 'for that's all done with, and the place will stand as idle as it is, till it falls'. But there is more: 'As to strong beer, there's enough of that in the cellars already, to drown the manor house.' Such an apocalyptic vision of the house sinking into its own beer stores is comparable to the climax of *The Fall of the House of Usher* (1839) by the American maestro of terror, Edgar Allan Poe, whose cursed house is swallowed into the tarn. The image conjured by Estella foreshadows the destruction of the house, though by very different means, at the end of the book.

The interiors of Satis House also adhere to classic scenes of Gothic gloom and ruin. The passages 'were all dark'; there is only a single candle burning. Estella takes this up 'and we went through more passages and up a staircase, and still it was all dark, and only the candle lighted us', until, at last Pip finds himself 'in a pretty large room, well lighted with wax candles'.[24] This is Miss Havisham's dressing room, and the extravagance of candles cannot make up for the lack of daylight. In an armchair nearby sits 'the strangest lady I have ever seen, or shall ever see'. There she is, dressed in satin, lace and silk, 'all of white', with her veil and bridal flowers and jewels still in place. Her half-packed trunks and other dresses are 'scattered about'. Pip conjures a laughable (to us) comparison of her shrunken form to a skeleton he has once seen. But instead of being locked away in her madness, like Bertha Rochester, Miss Havisham has doused all of Satis House with the festering murk of cherished vengeance.

A watercolour of Restoration House from 1849 shows a pleasant-looking grand manor, with none of the decay that Dickens paints so vividly. Yet it is very possible that a house that was made up of components assembled over 400 years, and which had changed ownership several times (passing through ten different owners in the previous century) might have had some tumbledown aspect. And less is known about the state of the house in the period Dickens would have seen it than in other parts of its long history.

Restoration House as it appeared in the nineteenth century, when Dickens would have seen it. Its brickwork, barred windows, 'passages and staircases' appear in Satis House.

What Dickens thought of the house, beyond Forster's claim that it had a 'curious attraction', is impossible to know. The author himself left no record of any visit there. Some further details of Satis House, however, correspond to the Tudor manor. On his second trip to Miss Havisham's, Pip is taken to 'quite another part of the house':[25] at the end of a passage he finds himself in 'a small paved court-yard', and on the opposite side he sees a 'detached dwelling-house, that looked as if it had once belonged to the manager or head clerk of the extinct brewery'. There is no such basement passage at Restoration House, but the 'dwelling-house' quite possibly referred to one of the buildings belonging to the brewery at the back. Today, the gardens are pleasantly elegant, with lawns, paths, hedges, beds and parterres stretching towards the site of the old brewery yard. However, in a neglected state, it's not hard to see how the ample grounds could have inspired Miss Havisham's cold and colourless garden.*

On a later visit to Satis House, Pip says, 'I crossed the staircase landing, and entered the room she indicated.' Here, 'wintry branches of candles on the high chimney-piece faintly lighted the chamber'. He continues:

> 'It was spacious, and I dare say had once been handsome, but every discernible thing in it was covered with dust and mould, and dropping to pieces. The most prominent object was a long table with a tablecloth spread on it, as if a feast had been in preparation when the house and the clocks all stopped together.[26]

If Miss Havisham's dressing room was the room now dubbed the King's Bedchamber at Restoration House, then the place reached by crossing the landing would have been what is now the Great Chamber, a roomy first-floor hall, which would make a splendid venue for a celebratory feast. Its moulded panelling is from the 1680s and its narrow pine floorboards were probably installed as a ballroom floor in the late eighteenth century, so would have been in place in Dickens's time.

In the 1970s and '80s, Restoration House was owned by the comedian and ventriloquist Rod Hull, who took the house's association with the novel to the extreme, even decorating the Great Chamber with the trappings of a wedding

---

* The current owners are keen to reinstate some historic elements, such as the 'cherry garden' noted by Samuel Pepys during a visit in 1667.

banquet. As Pip tells us, the table in Miss Havisham's room has an épergne at the centre, which is covered in cobwebs and looks 'like a black fungus'. Miss Havisham blithely points out that this is where she will be laid out when she dies, and 'they shall come and look at me here'. So this impressive banquet room becomes a mourning room in waiting, as the severely decayed grandeur of Satis House embodies the empty promises of wealth and class. Miss Havisham is extraordinarily wealthy, but she is a wreck, physically, emotionally and morally. As Pip notices the 'mice rattling behind the panels', there is an implied comparison with the tidiness of the forge that cedes some bit of admiration for an otherwise not wholly sympathetic portrait of Pip's sister and guardian, Mrs Joe. In Dickens's world, we know, 'cleanliness and order' speak of greater virtues.

Dickens's attraction to Restoration House must have had something to do with its mix of luxury and Gothicism and, most keenly, with the response it might trigger (or perhaps once did) in a child. As a writer, he would have seen very clearly its potential to enliven an atmosphere of enchanting dreams and cruel realities. Windows in the southern 'Oriel Room' were blocked up long ago when another house was built on to the adjoining wall, and these maintain a strange, dead-end appearance. Like the King's Bedchamber and the Great Chamber, these walled-up windows would only have been visible from within, and these details suggest Dickens may well have been inside the house. Given his habit of gaining entry to places that sparked his curiosity or concern – schools, prisons, opium dens – it is not unlikely that he found a way to investigate such an enigmatic dwelling. He may even have been aware of the fact that Pepys had visited some 200 years before. Dickens was such a frequent visitor to Rochester, and so familiar with its streets and buildings (an acquaintance demonstrated particularly in his last novel), that there is an arguable chance he did get beyond the great red-brick façade, the blocked and barred windows, the courtyard and the locked iron gate of Restoration House. Whatever he saw, whenever he saw it, he related through the eyes of a boy whose life had not prepared him for such a combination of splendour and 'sour remembrance'.

Satis House is not the only remarkable dwelling detailed in *Great Expectations*. One of the most amusing and likeable characters, Mr Jaggers's clerk John Wemmick, maintains rigid standards of impersonal sobriety in the office, but retreats at the end of every day to a comfortably odd home. There he cares for his father, the affectionately named 'Aged P', and entertains his beloved, Miss Skiffins. Wemmick's house is another diminutive gem, 'the smallest [Pip] ever saw', but it is also a work of ridiculous design that parodies the great Gothic gloom of Satis House.

The littleness of Wemmick's home is inversely proportional to its charm. It has 'the queerest Gothic windows (by far the greater part of them sham), and a Gothic door, almost too small to get in at'.[27] There is a flagstaff, a tiny moat and a drawbridge. Wemmick has also installed some kind of gun for sounding the time in 'a separate fortress, constructed of lattice-work'. There is a 'bower' that is only 'a dozen yards off, but which was approached by such ingenious twists of path that it took quite a long time to get at'. The whole concoction is reminiscent of Commodore Trunnion's comic abode in Tobias Smollett's *The Adventures of Peregrine Pickle* (1751), a favourite novel of Dickens's boyhood, and it may also have taken some ideas of model armoury from Uncle Toby's fortifications in *Tristram Shandy*. But Wemmick's most immediate influence was probably Horace Walpole's fanciful 'little plaything house', Strawberry Hill, which Dickens had visited in 1839.[28]

The amateur architectural enthusiasm also brings to mind the author's own contrivances at Gad's Hill Place. Shortly before he began writing *Great Expectations* in earnest, Dickens had begun work on additions and improvements at Gad's Hill, which he had purchased in 1856 but had not been able to occupy until 1857. To his friend William De Cerjat, he wrote in 1858: 'At this present moment I am on my little Kentish freehold . . . looking on as pretty an English view out of my study window, as you would find in a long day's English ride.' As he did for many correspondents at the time, he then fell to describing the 'grave red brick house' to which, he claimed in Wemmickian fashion, he had 'added to, and stuck bits upon, in all manner of ways: so that it is as pleasantly irregular, and as violently opposed to all architectural ideas, as the most hopeful man could possibly desire'.[29]

The additions to the sides and top of the house and the digging of the well were not nearly as disorderly or peculiar as he made them sound, but clearly he enjoyed speaking of his new home as some sort of unique concoction of his own making. To Miss Coutts, the banking heiress whom he often petitioned for support of charitable causes, he wrote, 'I want you so much to see it. It is full of the ingenious devices of the inimitable writer.'[30] He also loved to relate the association of the place with the site of Falstaff's robbing and being robbed in Shakespeare's *Henry IV*. Like the 'queer small boy' in the account he wrote for *All the Year Round*, Dickens told De Cerjat happily: 'It's on the summit of Gad's Hill. The Robbery was committed before the door, on the men with the Treasure, and Falstaff ran away from the identical spot of ground now covered by the room in which I write.'[31]

It was a fanciful idea, of course; no one could point to the exact spot of ground where Shakespeare had meant for the robbery to have occurred. But that possibility, along with the proximity of the Sir John Falstaff pub, both structures built in about 1780, was enough to set Dickens's imagination to work, weaving his own house into literary history. To Miss Coutts, he

Private Collection/AS

The Swiss Chalet was delivered to Dickens as a flat-pack kit. It became his writing retreat, reached via a tunnel under the road in front of Gad's Hill Place.

wrote that 'the crowning glory', apart from its association with Falstaff and nearness to the eponymous public house, was the knowledge that he now inhabited the house 'I used to look at . . . as a wonderful Mansion (which God knows it is not), when I was a very odd little child with the first faint shadows of all my books, in my head – I suppose.'[32]

Buying Gad's Hill Place realised a childhood dream and, thanks to his friend, the actor Charles Fechter, Dickens got to realise another dream, that of creating his own work of personalised eclecticism, i.e., building a 'toy' house for himself, in 1865. It arrived in ninety-four pieces, ready for assembly. But, like most flatpack constructions, the 'Swiss Chalet' required a bit of help to put together. This was years after Dickens had written about Wemmick's 'crazy little box of a cottage', and he decided to make the assembled chalet his new refuge for writing. It had two floors, with one room on each. A summer study on the upper floor, reached by an external staircase, was fitted with five mirrors; Dickens remarked to his friend James Fields how they 'reflect and refract in all kinds of ways the leaves that are quivering in the windows and the great fields of waving corn, and the sail-dotted river'.[33] (He also wrote in the study of the main house and in his bedroom, which has a window overlooking the pub and across to Rochester Cathedral in the distance).

The chalet was reached by a tunnel under the road in the front of the house, which was originally created to access the 'wilderness', as the family called the shrubbery on the other side of the road. The tunnel had been created with the help of his brother Frank and friend Henry Austin. There was no drawbridge, but for Dickens, a tunnel was, perhaps, nearly as satisfying. He spent most of the last day of his life sitting at his desk upstairs in the chalet, working frantically to finish off the mystery story whose conclusion has remained a mystery for nearly a century and a half.[34]

As effective as they were in his fiction, particular houses were also important markers in Dickens's own journey from impoverished child to famed writer and performer. He epitomised the successful modern man in that he lived in a number of houses during his lifetime, 'trading up' as his family and means increased. His journey had begun from almost the lowest point imaginable but he managed to move upwards in the way of some of his most hopeful fiction. His course was steady and smooth, if troubled by his inability, in his own eyes, to ever be or have 'enough'.

Dickens's first experience of London was as a boy, living in 'a mean, small tenement', in what he told John Forster 'was about the poorest part of London'.[35] This was a house in Bayham Street, in Camden Town, from where he nursed memories of better days in Chatham. Dickens was just nine years old when the family left Kent for London, but their fortunes had taken a downward turn from already modest circumstances. It was in Camden Town that the boy Dickens began to feel the sting of his family's own privation – the fact that his father had creditors pursuing him – and of the 'struggling poverty' all around.[36] John Dickens was sent to the Marshalsea for debt in 1824, and his wife and younger children soon followed. At that time it was not uncommon for debtors to take their families into the prison with them, since their condition meant that they were unable to pay for other shelter.

However, it was deemed better to put twelve-year-old Charles to work. He was sent to lodge with strangers in Camden, walking two miles each day to his job in the blacking factory on the Thames. After Charles complained of loneliness his father found him a room in 'the back-attic of the house of an insolvent agent' in Lant Street, Southwark.[37] It was nearer to the factory, and meant that he could visit his family in the prison more often. Still, he spent much of his free time roaming the neighbourhood on his own and at times he must have felt as Oliver Twist, 'a poor houseless wandering boy, without a friend to help him or a roof to shelter his head!'[38] Miserable as he was, it was from his observations in and around the streets of London that he began to gather the characters that would emerge as such glorious oddities in his fiction.

Dickens was twenty-five years old and in the first blush of success when he was able to afford his first house. He moved from rooms at Furnival's Inn with his young wife and child to 48 Doughty Street in 1837. It was a respectable terraced house on three floors with a basement (kitchen, scullery and wine cellar) and attic (with nursery and servants' bedroom). The rent was £80 per year, and it was the popularity of *The Pickwick Papers* that made it possible. His family grew alongside his achievements, and Dickens took a much more spacious house at 1 Devonshire Terrace, near Regent's Park, in 1839, for which he paid £800 for a twelve-year lease, plus rent of £160 per year. Here, he concerned himself with the 'smallest' and 'greatest' details of furnishings and decoration, as Forster described it. While on holiday in Italy in 1845, he wrote to his solicitor Thomas Mitton, who was overseeing work on the house, that 'Kate thinks with you, that Green for the hall and staircase is quite out of the question . . . So let it be whatever you and the Decorator think best – not so cold as to be dull, and not so warm as to suffocate the prints.'[39] The house had large public rooms for the elaborate entertainments Dickens loved to host, most including dramatic/comic performances acted by himself, his friends and children.

Ever restive, Dickens moved about in London, often staying at his rooms above the *Household Words* office on the Strand, and taking his family abroad for holidays. He also spent regular periods in August and September in Broadstairs over a period of about fourteen years from 1839. He finished *Nicholas Nickleby* and wrote *David Copperfield* while staying at Fort House (which was largely extended and dubbed 'Bleak House' in 1901, though it had no connection to the house of the novel), or in one of the other houses he rented for his family or at one of the local hotels.

Today, various hotels in Broadstairs claim his tenancy and there are many tributes to Dickens, such as the somewhat bleakly preserved study and dining room at the Bleak House Hotel. Closer to the high street, the very charming Dickens House Museum occupies the house formerly belonging to Miss Mary Pearson Strong. It is (suitably for Dickens) a little house in a small row on the raised terrace above the cove. The parlour is preserved as it was in Dickens's time, when, his son Charley recalled, Miss Pearson Strong 'fed him tea and cakes' and was interrupted by chasing the donkeys from her cottage garden.[40] Of course, Miss Pearson Strong served to inspire the wonderfully intrepid Betsey Trotwood, whose parlour became another reassuringly tidy symbol of home. It is a pitiable image of the young David Copperfield, who, having walked from London in search of his aunt, a relation who might care for him, is forced to sell his waistcoat and sleep outside. Like Oliver, he is another homeless boy: 'Never shall I forget the lonely sensation', says David, 'of first lying down, without a roof above my head!'[41] And we know, as his first readers did not, that Dickens was drawing on close experience.*

After Devonshire Terrace, Dickens moved his family to Tavistock House in Bloomsbury. He took a fifty-year lease and meant this to be his last home. But in 1855 he decided to buy Gad's Hill Place, the only house he would ever own outright. At first he intended to stay there for short breaks, letting it out from time to time. He even envisioned selling it for a good return at some point. But in 1858, when his relationship with the young actress Nelly Ternan began raising questions, he decided to make a complete break with (though not a divorce from) his wife, Catherine. Gad's Hill Place offered sanctuary, a retreat from the public in London and a return to a childhood dream, perhaps even, in theory at least, a simpler existence for a man whose life was becoming increasingly complicated.

But at Gad's Hill, as in other aspects of his life, Dickens defied simplification. His imaginiative intensity moved from writing books to expanding the drawing room, adding bedrooms upstairs, transforming the breakfast parlour at the back of the house into 'a retreat fitted up for smokers into which he put a small billiard table', and outfitting his new study with floor-to-ceiling bookcases, which are still in place.[42] Like Walter Scott, he even indulged in the acquisition of arte-

---

* Most of the details of Dickens's impoverished childhood were unknown to his reading public until John Forster published the biography of his friend after his death.

Private Collection/AS

Gadshill Place

Gad's Hill Place, Dickens' 'Kentish freehold'. As a boy, Dickens was told by his father 'that if I ever grew up to be a clever man, perhaps I might own that house . . .'

facts. He was pleased to report in 1859 that he had got one of the balustrades from the old Rochester bridge, which had been 'duly stone-masoned and set up on the lawn behind the house'.[43] Though he had wrenched the family apart, insisting that the children leave their mother and live with him, he saw the new house as evidence of his parental devotion. 'I hope it is the best thing I could do for the boys', he wrote to his friend W. C. Macready, 'particularly Charley, who will now be able to have country air.'[44] Ironically, Charley was the only one of the nine children who deliberately disobeyed his father and remained with Catherine (though several others were away at school or no longer living with their parents).

At Gad's Hill, Dickens lived with his elder daughters, Katey and Mamie, and with Catherine's younger sister, Georgy, who stayed on after the marital split and acted as head of household. Katey left after marrying Charles Collins, brother of Dickens's good friend, the author Wilkie Collins, in 1860. But the family had many guests, including the Danish writer Hans Christian Andersen, who stayed nearly three months in 1857. Though his split with Catherine ruptured some friendships, Dickens continued to socialise and entertain with the enthusiasm of the house-proud.

But even at Gad's Hill, Dickens had trouble being happy in one place. He continued to stay frequently in London, now at his new offices of *All the Year Round* (having broken with the publishers of *Household Words* over their refusal to print his statement about the breakdown of his marriage in their magazine, *Punch*). He also continued to rent a house in London annually during 'the season' (in spring) for the entertainment of Georgy and Mamie. He alternated these with time at Gad's Hill and overnight visits to Nelly Ternan at her cottage in Slough (where he went by the name of 'Tringham'), and lastly in Peckham. All of these movements were fitted around his writing and an exhausting schedule of sold-out public reading performances.[45]

Yet much as he moved from house to town and back again, Dickens's work continued to signal the importance of a secure, comfortable home, especially for children. In his novels, stories and numerous essays on the conditions of workhouses, prisons and slums, he demonstrated a genuine concern for people who lacked such basic refuge in life. The plight of the urban poor particularly, which he had first 'sketched', living in 'wretched houses with broken windows patched with rags and paper; every room let out to a different family . . . clothes drying, and slops emptying from the windows', continued to occupy his mind.[46] Beset with ideas of the importance of home and the need to help those without one, he threw himself into charitable work aimed at improving the lives of the poor. He even convinced his friend Miss Coutts, the banking heiress, to help him set up and fund a house for 'homeless', or fallen, women, which he helped to oversee from 1848 to 1857.*[47]

Dickens's move to Gad's Hill Place hailed both the culmination of his achievement and the stubborn determination of his later years. It also returned him to the scenes and landscapes of his early life; a time of impressions and experiences that were never far from his imagination became even closer. Though it may not have completely calmed his innate restlessness, his 'Kentish freehold' did afford him some peace: 'The blessed woods and fields have done me a world of good, and I am quite myself again,' he said, after moving from London in 1858.[48] His marital problems notwithstanding, Dickens was more or less settled at Gad's Hill. From here, he finished *A Tale of Two Cities* and wrote *Great Expectations*, *Our Mutual Friend* and *The Mystery of Edwin Drood*, as well as the essays and tales of his later years.

No doubt being back in the surroundings of his own youth, both hopeful and terrifying, added to the verisimilitude of Pip's descriptions and to his awestruck emotions. At Satis House, it seems to Pip that 'the stopping of the clocks had stopped Time in that mysterious place, and, while I and everything else outside it grew older, it stood still'.[49] Perhaps Dick-

---

* This was the year Dickens decided to separate from his wife and set in train a number of other personal and professional ruptures.

ens felt that he could arrest time here, or at least hold on to his boyhood ambition – the clever young man who might grow up to achieve success and the very best home that his youthful fantasy could envision – without having to reconcile the turbulence he had created in his own domestic life. As Forster noted, while Dickens had 'added to, and stuck bits upon' Gad's Hill, the house retained the look of a 'plain, old-fashioned, two-story country house with a bell turret on the roof, and over the front door a quaint neat wooden porch', in this way keeping it 'to the last much as it was when he used as a boy to see it'.[50]

To some, Dickens is the novelist who never grew up, forever seeing the world both in its wonders and its injustices, its gentle natures and its hard prejudices, with the eyes of a child. It is a child's wonder that pervades Pip's description of Satis House, and a child's delight that heightens the achievement of owning Gad's Hill Place. As John Forster wrote of his friend's memories of Chatham and Kent: 'Here the most durable of his early impressions were received; and the associations that were around him when he died, were those which at the outset of his life had affected him most strongly.'[51] Dickens's will decreed that on his death Gad's Hill Place be sold; the pictures and furnishings, too, were sold at auction.[52] His son Charley bought the house and lived there until 1879. In 1924, the house became part of Gad's Hill School.

Rooksnest

SEVEN

For the Love of an English Cottage: Thomas Hardy and E. M. Forster

'To them Howards End was a house: they could not know that to her it had been a spirit, for which she sought a spiritual heir.'

Howards End

Thomas Hardy and E. M. Forster were born nearly forty years and several social strata apart, but they shared a profound love of the English countryside and attached huge symbolic importance to the humble cottage. Both came from 'building' families: Forster's father was an architect, and Hardy, descended from a family of builders, worked as an architect before he became a writer. As Ford Madox Ford and Evelyn Waugh saw the passing of a way of life in the demise of the grand country estates (see chapter 10), Hardy and Forster viewed the rural cottage as the prism through which the pre-modern past could be understood and its most keenly felt traditions preserved.

Of all the writers included in this book, Thomas Hardy is the one who would have been voted most likely to write a novel about the building of a house. He belonged to the fifth generation of a family of master stonemasons, and became apprenticed to an architect at the age of sixteen (confounding the lower expectations of his fellow villagers). He went on to work with well-respected architects of the period, helping to restore old churches, and to build schools and houses. He became a member of the avant-garde Architectural Association in 1862 (aged twenty-two), and was awarded a Silver Medal by the Royal Institute of British Architects for an essay written in 1863.[1*] The cottage he grew up in had been built by his grandfather, and as a successful novelist, Hardy designed his own writer's residence, Max Gate, in 1885.

None of Hardy's fictional houses offers a spiritual touchstone in the way of Forster's Howards End, but his background, as both architect and cottage-dweller, entered into his fiction in other ways. It gave him inspiration for characters, a fine feeling for architectural details and a passion for some kind of authenticity in building, all of which are bound up in the threads of class-consciousness and social justice that are woven throughout his fiction. Some critics have even argued that his plots bear out a certain 'architectural' logic, especially perhaps The Mayor of Casterbridge, which was written while Hardy was working on designs for Max Gate.

Hardy's interest in architecture emerges through characters as well as through details of plot and setting. A Pair of Blue Eyes (1873), his third published work, features an assistant architect, the son of a mason, like Hardy, who is deemed too lowly for the hand of his beloved by her father. The Hand of Ethelberta (1876) presents two brothers, a carpenter and a joiner/house-painter, and A Laodicean (1881) centres on a young woman who inherits a medieval castle and must choose

---

* 'On the Application of Coloured Bricks and Terra Cotta to Modern Architecture'.

between an established local architect and a newly qualified young man from London. Opening with the architect sketching and measuring a village church, as Hardy himself had often done, this story held 'more facts of his own life', he later said, than anything else he wrote.[2] *Jude the Obscure* (1895) presents the would-be scholar who is also a mason, with a mason's tactile appreciation for materials and forms. Moving among the revered buildings of Christminster (modelled on Oxford and Cambridge), Jude 'rambled under the walls and doorways, feeling with his fingers the countours of their mouldings and carving [...] poticoes, oriels, doorways of enriched and florid middle-age design'.[3]

As the critic Norman Page has observed, 'the prominent role given to buildings with distinctive architectural features . . . is the principal legacy bequeathed by Hardy's first career to his second'.[4] In addition, the number of places in and around Dorset that have specific correlation with his fictional towns, churches and houses testifies to his imaginative, as well as his real-life, connections to the place that has become known as 'Hardy Country'. Many authors populate their work with known landmarks, but Hardy's attention to style and construction bespeak a precise appreciation. His *Architectural Notebook* provides a fascinating glimpse into his work at the time, its small pages filled with projects and sketches of ornaments and architectural details, including plans for some labourers' cottages, some of which translated to his writing.[5]

Knapwater House (in *Desperate Remedies*) , for example, matches a description attributed in his *Notebook* to Kingston Maurward in Dorchester, a large estate with a neoclassical manor house at its centre.[6] Hardy's father was contracted to do building work on the estate, and when he was a boy, the wife of the estate owner built a small school for the local children, of whom young Tommy was her special pet. Other structures too come from life. Endelstow House is finely described in *A Pair of Blue Eyes*, as is the barn at Weatherbury in *Far from the Madding Crowd*, probably based on Waterston Manor, in Puddletown, where the elder Hardys were born. In Hardy's fiction as in his life, housing types play a crucial role in defining antiquity, social station, wealth and class. From Jude Fawley's humble home at Marygreen to the d'Urbervilles' manor house, all add their voices to the distinctive chorus of Hardy's tales.

Like most architects, Hardy developed strong feelings about design styles and trends. His characters engage in aesthetic debate, and through them he voices an appreciation for the craft of building. As well as presenting the plight of the struggling architect, *A Laodicean* expresses the tensions between old-fashioned architectural traditions and the rise of more modern ideas, as Paula Power decides whether the castle should be restored in a kind of romantic medieval imitation, or whether modernity should be allowed to show itself. In the end, the castle burns down and her lover proposes a modern house, answering, for Hardy anyway, the conundrum of historic restoration.

In *Jude the Obscure*, Hardy again tackles the 'passion for restoration', which took hold in the earlier nineteenth century. In the stonemason's yard at Alfredston, Jude discovers 'a little centre of regeneration', where 'with keen edges and smooth curves, were forms in the exact likeness of those he had seen

Drawing of his family cottage at Bockhampton in Dorset, by Thomas Hardy. It was built by the author's grandfather.

time-eaten on the walls' at Christminster. These pristine, newly chiselled reproductions are 'the ideas in modern prose which the lichened colleges presented in old poetry'. It is as they age that these ornaments, too, will 'become poetical'.[7] But the lyricism is tempered, as Jude becomes skeptical of the masons' ability to recreate the 'poetical'. As much as he appreciates the 'straightness, smoothness, exactitude' of the newly worked elements, he also finds they lack something that is inherent in the 'irregularity and disarray' of the decayed originals, concluding that what went on in the yard was 'only copying, patching and imitating'. This scene is both a meditation on the skilled work of the stonemasons and a realisation of the futility of their efforts to inspire a similar sense of wonder as that roused by the old monuments. In it, Jude also recognises the inevitability of change. He decides that 'medievalism was as dead as a fern-leaf in a lump of coal; [...] other developments were shaping in the world around him, in which Gothic architecture and its associations had no place'.[8]

Hardy later explained that during the time he worked as an architect's assistant, 'there was one true style of architecture – the style of the thirteenth-century Gothic'.[*] By the time he was writing *Jude*, however, the tide was turning, at least for him. In his veiled autobiography, *Early Life* (purportedly written by his second wife as biographer), Hardy reveals that in assisting with many church restoration projects, he had been 'passively instrumental in destroying or in altering' some of the 'beautiful ancient Gothic, as well as Jacobean and Georgian work', and that this was 'a matter for his deep regret in later years'.[9] He later argued that Victorian architects should not have been so keen to strip away the crumbling ancient remnants and replace them with pristine reproductions.[†] Even earlier, in the composition of *The Laodicean*, Hardy was already weighing the effects of architectural restoration. Paula Power is clear in her objection to replacing Stancy Castle's damaged Saxon-age stones with new reproductions: 'I should prefer an honest patch to any such make-believe,' she says.[10] The young architect George Somerset advances the argument further in his plans for the castle, which did not attempt 'to adapt an old building to the wants of the new civilization'. Rather, he aimed to build a modern house beside and 'slightly attached' to the ancient structure, 'harmonizing with the old; heightening and beautifying, rather than subduing it'.[11]

---

[*] For a time, Hardy worked for Raphael Brandon, author of *Analysis of Gothic Architecture* (1847).

[†] It was this enthusiasm for 'restoration' projects that inspired William Morris to set up the Society for the Protection of Ancient Buildings in 1877, of which Hardy later became a member.

Hardy's change of attitude towards restoration was largely influenced by his lifelong reverence for old buildings. Like Virginia Woolf (whose father commissioned the serial of *Far from the Madding Crowd* for the *Cornhill Magazine*), he had a feeling not only for the age of the stones, but also for the lives that had touched them. As Jude observes of the past residents of the old colleges, 'the brushings of the wind against the angles, buttresses, and door-jambs were as the passing of these other inhabitants'.[12] Similar sensations are echoed in Woolf's own ghostly rendering of the halls and chapels of Cambridge in *Jacob's Room* (see chapter 9), and they resurface in an essay Hardy composed in 1906, in which he discussed the difficulty of 'preserv[ing] an old building without hurting its character'. But Hardy was not a conservation obsessive: 'Life, after all,' he said, 'is more than art, and that which appealed to us in the (may be) clumsy outlines of some structure which had been looked at and entered by a dozen generations of ancestors outweighs the more subtle recognition, if any, of architectural qualities.'[13] It was the life lived in the time-worn buildings, not the structures alone, that mattered, but together they offered ballast in the turbulent seas of a changing world.

Before becoming acquainted with the finer points of architectural discussion, Hardy's deepest inspiration came from his childhood, and was shaped by his early career. He was born at the cottage that still bears his name, at Higher Bockhampton, Dorset, in 1840. At the behest of his ambitious mother, Jemima, he was well educated for a child of his station. Hardy grew up with tales of village life from his grandmother, and was a young boy during the 'hungry forties', when the rural poor suffered the effects of failed harvests and higher food prices in the wake of the Corn Laws. Fortunately, the Hardys had a 'family lifehold' on their cottage and land, so were not prey to the changing whims of the landowner (as most were at the time, including the impecunious Durbeyfields in *Tess*).

A frail and studious young man, Hardy was not deemed fit for the trade of stonemason, like his father, but instead became articled to a local architect, John Hicks. Much of Hardy's work at this time had to do with drawing and measuring old churches, such as St Peter's in Dorchester, which were scheduled for improvements. But in 1862, he set out on his own 'to pursue the art and science of architecture on more advanced lines' in London.[14] There he found a job with the architect Arthur Blomfield, who was in need of 'a young Gothic draughtsman who could restore and design churches and rectory-houses'.[15] (One of his more unusual jobs was to help supervise the removal of corpses from the old St Pancras churchyard when the Midland Railway needed to cut through the site.)[16] One reviewer reported of Hardy in his later years, he was 'considered a promising representative of the young Gothic school that flourished contemporaneously with the pre-Raphaelite movement in painting'.[17]

Hardy's life in London in the 1860s followed a routine of work in the day and reading for self-improvement in the evening (like Jude), still in the hope of gaining university admission.[18] But by 1867, at the age of twenty-seven, he had fallen ill and was back at home in Bockhampton, living 'between architecture and literature'. He continued with his architectural work, some for G. R. Crickmay, an architect based in

Weymouth, doing more church restoration and helping design or supervise work on schools.[19] He was also writing his first novel. *The Poor Man and the Lady* failed to be taken up by a publisher, and his next work, *Desperate Remedies*, was published but without success. Persevering, in 1872 he had some recognition with *Under the Greenwood Tree*, and began work on *A Pair of Blue Eyes*. At the same time, he was still employed as an architect, now working for T. Roger Smith in London, and building schools created by the recently formed London School Board, among other projects.[20]

At the age of twenty-five Hardy had published his first story, in *Chambers's Journal*.[21] 'How I Built Myself a House' is a humorous, fictional account that gently mocks the aspirations of a new class wealthy enough to hire an architect and build their own house, but still mindful of cost. It is told from the point of view of a young husband and father, who expresses the hopes of probably everyone who ever embarked on building their own home: the house 'was to be of some mysterious size and proportion, which would make us both peculiarly happy ever afterwards'. It would also be 'easily accessible by rail'. John finds an architect, Mr Penny, who is known for 'designing excellent houses for people of moderate means', a statement that even in the twenty-first century sets a home-buyer's heart to fluttering. John and his wife happily submit their own 'sketches', and the architect creates a compromise to fit their budget. In the end, the rooms are too small, the added porch nearly blocks up a window and the whole thing runs into hundreds of pounds of 'extras'. Plus ça change, you might say.

This light-hearted response to his new profession marked a contrast to the more sober, romantic concerns that would dominate Hardy's later writing, even, as in *Jude*, his commentary on architecture. His first surviving poem, composed at eighteen, also focuses on a house, but it is a thoughtful, personal reflection. The deleterious effects of social class may be the primary drive (or impression*) of his novels, but 'Domicilium' tells us something of the other abiding current in his fiction, a sensitive reimagining of his rural home:

> It faces west, and round the back and sides
> High beeches, bending, hang a veil of boughs,
> And sweep against the roof. Wild honeysucks
> Climb on the walls, and seem to sprout a wish
> (If we may fancy wish of trees and plants)
> To overtop the apple trees hard-by.

The sensitivity is even more evident in his later poem 'The Self-Unseeing', which shows Hardy's appreciation for place, coupled with an awareness of those who came before:

> Here is the ancient floor,
> Footworn and hollowed and think,
> Here was the former door
> Where the dead feet walked in.

A woman, probably Hardy's mother, sits 'Smiling into the fire', while his father plays his fiddle, 'Bowing it higher'. (All

---

* In response to criticism of *Tess of the D'Urbervilles*, Hardy wrote 'a novel is an impression, not an argument', in the preface to an 1892 edition cited in Harold Orel, ed., *Thomas Hardy's Personal Writings* (London: Macmillan, 1967), 27.

of the men in the Hardy family played string instruments, like the generations of the Dewy family in *Under the Greenwood Tree*.) The Portland flagstones are indeed worn in the Bockhampton cottage, especially under the window where the 'former door' had been, blocked up when the extension where Hardy's grandmother lived was knocked through. Having raised her own family in the three-room main cottage, where Hardy lived with his parents, brother and sisters, his grandmother moved to the extension next door and remained there until her death – so even his childhood home was peopled with lives from the past.

The cottage and the village of Bockhampton resurface in much of Hardy's fiction, as do the details and rituals of rural life. *Under the Greenwood Tree* was the first novel Hardy published under his own name and the first to have even small success. It is a pastoral elegy in prose, introducing readers to the village men's choir, thatched cottages, flagstone floors (occasionally sprinkled with 'the finest yellow sand' for dancing) and whitewashed chimney corners. Here, men brew their own cider, women sew next to the fire, and even in the slightly nicer gamekeeper's cottage in Yalbury Wood there are gaps between the floorboards, so that the young bride getting ready upstairs must overhear the chiding and joking of the wedding party below. The precision of detail conveys extraordinary visions of common happenings. The windowsill of the gamekeeper's cottage is 'between four and five feet from the floor' and the window is 'set with thickly-leaded diamond glazing', which makes for wonderfully distorted views of the people approaching from outside, 'lifting hats from heads, shoulders from bodies'. The ceiling is 'carried by a huge beam traversing its midst', and from it projects 'a large nail, used solely and constantly as a peg for Geoffrey's hat'.[22]

Hardy's affection for the rural cottage never abated, nor did his concern for the poor living at the mercy of landlords who could abruptly cast them out. Tess Durbeyfield is at least partly driven back into the arms of the man who ruined her because her family are evicted from their cottage.* One of Hardy's last published articles was written in support of an appeal by the Royal Society of Arts to preserve the ancient cottages of England. He patiently explains, 'what was called mudwall was really a composition of chalk, clay, and straw', which was then mixed by 'treading and shovelling' in 'a process that had doubtless gone on since the days of Israel in Egypt and earlier', so there is timelessness in the very fabric.[23] Finally, as a gibe to unthinking modernisers, he remarks that it is no surprise that the inhabitants prefer these 'old dingy hovels' to the 'new cottages', as they are better insulated and have better natural ventilation.

Hardy returned again and again to his own family's cottage, even after his marriage. He wrote his first four novels here, and stayed at long intervals while writing the book in which he first adopted the old Saxon name of 'Wessex' to describe the area where most of his characters live out the drama of their common lives. He wrote 'sometimes indoors, sometimes out'; when outdoors and finding himself without any paper, 'he would use large dead leaves, white chips left by the wood-cutters, or pieces of stone or slate that came to hand'.[24]

---

* There is a 'Tess Cottage' in Marnhull, near Dorchester, which Hardy is thought to have used as his reference for the Durbeyfield home.

Perhaps Hardy romanticised this description, but it speaks to his desire to ground the story firmly in the very soil of his Dorset home.

Far From the Madding Crowd, the story of Bathsheba Everdene's attempts to run her farm as she sees fit, marry whom she likes and to be allowed some happiness in her life, had important consequences for Hardy. It brought him his first material success, which enabled him to choose literature over architecture as his career, and to marry the woman he had been courting for nearly four years. In March 1870, Hardy had been sent by his employer to investigate the little church in the town of St Juliot, in northern Cornwall. There he met Emma Lavinia Gifford, the sister-in-law of the rector. They married in 1874, not long after the novel's publication, and for the next nine years lived in a number of houses: first in Surbiton, a suburb of London; then in Swanage and Sturminster Newton in Dorset; then, in the London borough of Wandsworth. Finally, in 1881, they were back in Dorset, 'for reasons of health and for mental inspiration'. Hardy had decided that 'residence in or near a city tended to force mechanical and ordinary productions from his pen'.[25]

In 1883 Hardy purchased a plot near Dorchester for £450 from the Duchy of Cornwall, on a site that could be reached much along the same three-mile path that he had walked every day from the cottage in Bockhampton. Now life did seem to imitate art as Hardy, like Clym in *Return of the Native*, came back to his homeland, but wearing, in his own modest way, the garments of success and prosperity. He drew up plans for a new house originally called 'Mack's Gate', in

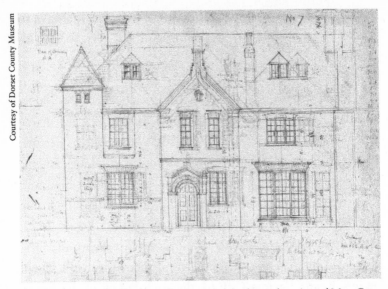

Courtesy of Dorset County Museum

Thomas Hardy's architectural rendering of the front elevation of Max Gate, which he built with his brother and father in 1885.

reference to Henry Mack, the keeper of the old turnpike gate that sat across the road. Max Gate, as it became known, was built by the family firm, namely his father and brother. Referred to as a 'villa', it was larger than a cottage or farmhouse, but certainly smaller than a country manor.

Described by a visitor in 1886 as 'an unpretending redbrick structure of moderate size', Max Gate is not Gothic, or even neoclassical.[26] It is a restrained Victorian house that avoids all of the Queen Anne revival ornament fashionable at the time. The simplicity of its steeply sloping roof, smart red brick and large, many-paned windows veer towards the Arts and Crafts style, though possess nothing of the curving, organic forms of William Morris or Philip Webb. Nikolaus

Pevsner perceived 'no architectural qualities whatever', but there is no doubt that the 'thoroughness of workmanship' Hardy argued for in *A Laodicean* was of utmost importance.[27] In addition to designing the building, he planted 'some two or three thousand small trees' around it and created a vegetable garden, croquet lawn and nut walk, like the one that provides solace to Dick Dewy in *Under the Greenwood Tree*.[28]

In an article written in 1892, Hardy made clear that he 'was resolved . . . not to ruin myself in building a great house as so many other literary men have done'. When the interviewer remarks that his house is 'a very nice one', Hardy replies, 'Well, everything is not as I would have it. I think I shall have to enlarge it. It is difficult to say exactly how a house should be until one has lived in it.'[29] It is not surprising that a man of Hardy's social consciousness didn't aim for a more ostentatious dwelling. As well as highlighting architectural integrity and craft, his stories often emphasise the fateful contrast between the housing of the rich and poor. These are symbols in mud, brick and stone that delineate the degrees between social classes: the Durbeyfields and the d'Urbervilles (*Tess of the d'Urbervilles*); the dwellers in the malthouse and the solitary inhabitant of Boldwood's mansion (*Far from the Madding Crowd*); the gamekeeper, whose cottage is somewhat nicer than the tranter's (which resembles Hardy's own home), and Farmer Shinar's house, which is better than both, but has 'the aspect of a human countenance turned askance' (*Under the Greenwood Tree*).

The chasm between haves and have-nots is perhaps most finely illustrated in *Tess of the d'Urbervilles* through the contrast between the cramped Durbeyfield cottage and The Slopes, the d'Urberville family seat. The Slopes is not 'a manorial house', with people working on the land, but 'a country house, built for enjoyment pure and simple'. It exists completely apart from the livelihood of the community: 'There was not an acre of troublesome land attached to it beyond what was required for residential purposes.'[30] On that residential plot is a thatched cottage, not dissimilar to the one Tess shares with her parents and six siblings. But this cottage, instead of offering shelter to a poor family, has been squandered as a home for Mrs d'Urberville's pet fowl.

So unacquainted is Tess with sprawling estates that she at first mistakes the gatehouse for the house it serves. She observes that 'everything on this snug property was bright, thriving, and well kept', and that 'everything looked like money – like the last coin issued from the Mint'.[31] The Slopes, like Wragby Hall in *Lady Chatterley's Lover*, draws Tess to its grounds out of economic necessity, but once there, she, like Mellors the gamekeeper, becomes the focus of the sexual appetites of the aristocratic resident. In *Tess*, of course, the gender roles are more traditional, and the girl is seduced against her will. D. H. Lawrence presented the grand old house and the social structure it represented as being in decline, impotent and irrelevant in the modern world, like its master. But Hardy still saw these great houses as emblematic of the fatal power their owners wielded over the rural peasantry.

At The Slopes, even the stables were 'fitted with every late appliance', and were 'as dignified as Chapels-of-Ease'.[32] This particular detail draws comparison with one of Hardy's last architectural projects. In 1871–2, while in the employment of Crickmay, Hardy worked on additions to the seventeenth-century Slape Manor, in Netherbury, which had been converted to a manor house in the eighteenth century. Hardy is said to have helped to design the library addition, but his notebook specifies decisions on flooring, and especially notes the design of the coach house, with 'matched and v jointed boarding, suspended by means of strong wrought iron straps & wheels running on a piece of 3 in iron bolted & blocked out from wall & beam to be guided at bottom by means of wt iron guides on a iron bar'.[33] This was a well-appointed coach house, if not quite resembling a chapel of ease. And having been an architect on such a project, as well as the son of a cottage family, Hardy was well aware of the world of difference separating the two.

Almost a decade earlier, in 1863, Hardy had won a prize for the design of a country mansion, and there are plans for another in his notebook.[34] But neither the country houses he designed or knew in life nor those he described in fiction were the kinds of dwellings he would create for himself. When it was first completed, Max Gate was a three-storey house with a steeply sloping roof, dormer windows in the attic rooms, a smallish kitchen, a study and small guestroom, as well as the master bedroom at the front. It was formed of three bays with an extended covered porch at the centre, and inspires words like 'handsome', 'fine', even 'restrained', much like the man himself. It had a separate dining room and a drawing room that is ample but in no way grand. There are classical mouldings and dado rails, simplified neoclassical details on the fireplaces, and overall a feeling of carefully measured indulgence.

Further success and the increased division in his marriage inspired additions in 1894–5, but there was no change to the pragmatic essence of the house. Above the drawing room is Hardy's 'first study', the room in which *The Woodlanders* was written. As improvements and additions were being carried out, he moved to a temporary study at the back of the house. This was an unsatisfying arrangement, but he managed to write both *Tess* and *Jude the Obscure*, his last novels, while working in this interim space. His third and last study was built over the new kitchen addition, and it was here that he wrote the verse drama *The Dynasts*, as well as the large body of poetry that he felt was the real achievement of his career. From this room, which faced east, 'the full moon rising over the tops of the dark pines was a familiar sight'.[35]

Private Collection/AS

Thomas Hardy's study at Max Gate, *c.* 1900. Notice the square centre panes in the windows, which allowed for a clearer view of the trees and sky.

Like Walter Scott, Hardy made use of a 'slyly contrived passage' to allow him to escape visitors unnoticed. Behind the front stair on the ground floor, an exit up a steep staircase leading to Hardy's study was concealed by a sliding door.[36] As a famous writer who valued his privacy, he also designed the upside-down window shades in the dining room: wood panels that can be raised to block the view into the house from outside while still allowing sunlight through the upper panes. Upstairs, however, in his last study, he designed windows with a large, square central pane that allowed broader views of his beloved Wessex surroundings.

The Hardys moved into Max Gate in 1885, and six months later, Hardy was worrying whether building it had been 'a wise expenditure of energy'.[37] From this, we can assume that the house had not made Hardy and Emma 'peculiarly happy', a fact that is not surprising given the tensions that developed early in their marriage. The building works of 1895 included two rooms in the attic to give Emma her own private spaces for reading and sewing, and by 1899, for sleeping, allowing the pair to live separately under the same roof. Emma died in 1912, and in 1914, at the age of seventy-four, Hardy married Florence Emily Dugdale, a woman thirty-nine years his junior who had been his assistant since 1905.

Florence managed some changes to the house, but Hardy's own domestic habits remained fixed in the nineteenth century. Unlike Charles Dickens and Walter Scott, Hardy was not quick to embrace the latest domestic advances. In 1920, at Florence's insistence, he added a bathroom that had hot water on tap, but continued to bathe in a tin bath in his bedroom, filled with water carried up in jugs by the maids. He had included a flush toilet in the first design of the house, but the water, which also supplied the taps, had to be drawn from a well and lugged up to a roof tank. Although Dorchester had electricity by 1901, the Hardys continued to rely on oil lamps and candles until 1924. A contradiction of conveniences was noted by the poet Siegfried Sassoon, who visited in 1921 and described how the famed author 'went up the dark stairs in front of you carrying a silver candlestick, and showed you, with a touch of pride, the new bathroom which has super-seded the previous hip-bath brought into the bedroom before breakfast'.[38]

In addition to Max Gate, Hardy designed Talbothays Lodge, named in honour of the dairy in *Tess*, for his brother and two sisters in nearby West Stafford. The local manor house there, Stafford House, appears as Froom Everard House in 'The Waiting Supper', a story from 1887, 'solidly built of stone in that never-to-be-surpassed style for the English coun-try residence – the mullioned and transomed Elizabethan'. The Lodge shares the plain style of Max Gate, as do nine cottages designed by Hardy that were also erected on the land, previ-ously called 'Talbots', which his father had used for farming.

Unlike his family home at Bockhampton, Max Gate doesn't emerge in any dwelling in Hardy's fiction. Rather, it is the sense of place, a profound connection to the village and house of his birth, and of time that is so bound up in his stories and which kept him in Dorchester. It is a way of life marked by the farming seasons and church holidays, by summer milking, autumn harvesting, Christmas caroling and 'thyme-scented, bird-singing morning[s]' in spring. Hardy's most enigmatic characters – Bathsheba Everdene and Gabriel Oak, Tess

Durbeyfield and Angel Clare, Jude Fawley and Sue Bridehead – all have their own roots in these rhythms and communities of rural England.

Largely because of *Tess* and *Jude*, Hardy is considered one of the most courageous writers of the period. As a freethinker, he questioned the status quo and the injustice of the class system, highlighting the ills of rural poverty and elitism. He never felt comfortable among the great and the good, even in the provincial county town of Dorchester, let alone in London, so Max Gate also represents the separateness that permeates all of his books. The term 'laodicean' refers to one who is undecided or half-hearted, whether in religion or politics, and the title is often seen as a reflection of Hardy's character. The biographer Claire Tomalin calls him 'the time-torn man', as he seems caught between two worlds and, indeed, times. This is in no way better illustrated than in the journey from the homemade house at Bockhampton along a thickly wooded path to the mildly modern Max Gate, or from that house to the progressive new century, which he entered having given up fiction for poetry. He died at Max Gate in 1928 at the age of eighty-seven; Florence Hardy continued living there until her death in 1937.

As Thomas Hardy saw the rural cottage as a symbol of England's humbler but finer traditions, E. M. Forster revered the power of such a house to bind people to each other, and to generations past and present, as well as to provide a cultural anchor in the tempestuous waters of the modern world. Forster's view is highly romantic and infectious. Few can read *Howards End* without feeling a tender longing for a golden afternoon in the garden of an English cottage, hay being cut, ancient trees rustling in a breeze, vines and dog roses trilling over a stone wall, sunlight casting a glow across hummocky green fields. Forster is clear from the first pages that the house's appeal is not stylistic or merely symbolic, but also imaginative, spiritual. Its power in the novel is in evoking the England of the past, and a connection being threatened by a world in motion, where motorcars speed people through a landscape they have no time to appreciate or comprehend. Its imaginative and spiritual energy comes from the vividness of personal relationships and the possibility of connectedness between people and places and over time.

Howards End is a story about a house, but it is also about ideas of property versus home, and the competing forces of liberal intellectualism (represented by the Schlegel family) and exponents of market-driven capitalism (the Wilcoxes). And it is about an ideal of England and Englishness that must draw from these different currents some sort of acceptable compromise that makes civilization fair, just and humane. It is also about 'the end of the age of peace', as Forster described it, and the onslaught of a faster, noisier world.[39] Like Forster himself, the idealistic, bourgeois Schlegel sisters hope that 'this craze for motion' won't last and 'may be followed by a civilization that won't be a movement, because it will rest on the earth', while the successful businessman Henry Wilcox is all about motion, blithely transfering his life and habits from place to place.[40]

Margaret and Helen Schlegel cross paths with the Wilcoxes while on holiday in Germany (home of the sisters' deceased father). On return to England, the younger sister, Helen, is invited to join the Wilcoxes at their country cottage, Howards

End, which she finds, 'old and little, and altogether delightful.' It has 'three attics in a row' above 'three bedrooms in a row'.[41] As a weekend retreat it is charming. As a symbol of civilization at rest, the house presents a serene bulwark against 'the architecture of hurry', but it also has imaginative force that lies in a sense of continuity, giving weight to notions of cultural heritage and inheritance.[42] As an old house, inhabited over several generations, it offers profound ties to living beings across the ages. 'I feel that our house is the future as well as the past,' says Margaret Schlegel, having come, finally, to inhabit the cottage that was intended for her. It is a bold (and hopeful) statement, whose fulfillment resonates in the book's message, 'only connect'. Having agreed, after the death of his wife, to marry the 'prosperous vulgarian' Mr Wilcox, Margaret looks for a way into his soul, 'a rainbow bridge that will connect the prose and the passion'. Without such a bridge, she decides, 'we are meaningless fragments' or, in architectural terms, 'unconnected arches that have never joined into a man':

> Only connect! That was the whole of her sermon. Only connect the prose and the passion, and both will be exalted and human love will be seen at its highest. Live in fragments no longer. Only connect and the beast and the monk, robbed of the isolation that is life to either, will die.[43]

It is the house – Howards End – which will provide this crucial connection to the past, as a relic of history and a vessel for those characteristics of English life that should be preserved for generations to come: the country's agricultural heart and the ways of the yeomanry, from which both Leonard Bast and the first Mrs Wilcox have descended; the intellectual ardour represented by the Schlegels' ample library; the reverence for the wisdom of age, maintained by the house's de facto guardian, Miss Avery; and respect for the power of nature to absorb the bodies of the believers and non-believers alike, to reclaim some of its dominion and its struggle against the encroaching motion-obsessed modernity. These strands, as well as the clash of different ranks of the English middle class, come together in the 'altogether delightful' Howards End.

All of this casts a near-hypnotic aura over the book, which may cause us to forget the real divides and antagonisms that drive the plot, the tension of deceit that balances the fate of Howards End in precarious limbo. The competing moralities of the materialistic Wilcoxes versus the enlightened Schlegels have tragic consequences for Leonard Bast, hovering 'at the extreme verge of gentility' and aspiring to a better life.[44] At the opening of chapter six, Forster defines the class of people who are the focus of his story: 'We are not concerned with the very poor. [...] This story deals with gentlefolk, or with those who are obliged to pretend that they are gentlefolk.' It was about these people, yes, and their different attitudes to property. All people who get to choose where they will live.

In an essay written in the 1950s, Forster said that *Howards End* was about 'a fight for a house', and 'the possessions of England'.[45] He cited the American critic Lionel Trilling, who had argued that the novel asks the question: 'Who shall inherit England?' In answer, Forster saw two options, 'the business people who run her' and 'the people who understand her'.[46] The first and second Mrs Wilcoxes represent the latter group, but both nearly fail to save their beloved house from ruin. In the novel, relations between people are vital, but so are the ties to a place.

Howards End is the childhood home of the first Mrs Wilcox, who much prefers life there to London. Our first glimpse of Mrs Wilcox is at the house, standing outside with her grown children and the family motorcar, where 'she seemed not to belong to the young people and their motor, but to the house, and to the tree that overshadowed it.'[47] During her life she has struggled to keep her husband and children from tainting her refuge with their interventions. After her death, her son contemplates 'how she had disliked improvements' and 'what trouble they had to get this very garage! With what difficulty had they persuaded her to yield them the paddock for it – the paddock that she loved more dearly than the garden itself!'[48] For the woman 'whose life had been spent in the service of her husband and sons', it seems a pitiful fact that they could not preserve her birthplace the way she liked.[49]

To Mrs Wilcox the connection with the family home is a civilising impulse, and its rupture signifies the doleful state of modern life. When she learns that the Schlegels' lease on their home of thirty years will not be renewed, she is bereft on their account. 'It is monstrous,' she says. 'To be parted from your house, your father's house – it oughtn't to be allowed. It is worse than dying. I would rather die.'[50] This seems ironic coming from a woman of means with more than one property to inhabit, but it displays a deep reverence for old alliances and traditions. This core message could well have been spoken by one of Hardy's characters, albeit in a more rustic accent. In our digitally distracted global society such an idea sounds backward-looking and parochial, but for Forster there was something fundamental at stake in breaking away from ancestral roots. He expressed as much on visiting Hinchingbrooke, the Elizabethan manor that had belonged to the family of his friend Lady Faith Culme-Seymour. The house had been sold years before, and during Forster's visit in 1955 it sat empty. Forster was appalled, remarking: 'Houses are important, you know. A house gives security. It is an anchorage.'[51]

Margaret Schlegel understands this, or at least she understands Mrs Wilcox's deep feelings for Howards End. She also knows that Mr Wilcox and the children did not know, or care to understand, that for the woman who nurtured them as wife and mother Howards End 'had been a spirit, for which she sought a spiritual heir'. This is why Mrs Wilcox decides, just before she dies, to leave the house to her friend Margaret, rather than to her own family, who view this as an unjust forfeiture of what is rightfully theirs. Their collective verdict is that Mrs Wilcox 'had been treacherous to the family, to the laws of property', and they choose to ignore her dying wish.

Forster, like John Galsworthy writing only few years earlier, highlights those 'laws of property' that are not so much about legalistic claims as they are about rational mercantile behaviour, the kind that defines the growing English middle class at the turn of the century. The family grievance against leaving Howards End to Margaret Schlegel is levelled at finances, rather than sentiment. Was she to have 'a life interest' or to 'own it absolutely'? How would they be compensated for the 'garage and other improvements that they had made under the assumption that all would be their some day?' The idea is 'Treacherous! Treacherous and absurd!'[52]

Though it is the focus of the novel, Howards End is by no means the only property with which the story concerns itself. The Schlegel sisters share a London townhouse at Wickham Place with their younger brother, Tibby, and are forced into house-hunting when their landlord wants to knock down their home to build 'Babylonian' flats. The landlord, we are told, is not 'spiritually richer' for having built them, for in tearing down the townhouse he has 'split the precious distillation of the years, and no chemistry of his can give it back to society again'. Here, Forster anticipates Ford Madox Ford's 'eighteenth-century Tory', in feeling that 'the feudal ownership of land did bring dignity, whereas the modern ownership of movables is reducing us again to a nomadic horde'.[53]

On his meagre clerk's salary, Leonard Bast is at the impoverished edge of the middle class. His neighbourhood is a harbinger portending the evils of unalloyed development in London. Blocks of flats 'constructed with extreme cheapness' are at either end of the road, and more are going up quickly. An old house was 'being demolished to accommodate another pair', the 'distillation of years' lost again. Forster adds that this kind of scene 'might be observed all over London – bricks and mortar rising and falling with the restlessness of the water in a fountain'.[54] The flat that Leonard shares with his common-law wife Jacky is 'known to house-agents as a semi-basement, and to other men as a cellar'. In these surroundings, amplified by the ruins of the old buildings outside and their disappointing replacements, Leonard reads John Ruskin for self-improvement. After puzzling through this elevated aesthetic discourse, he concludes with grim irony: '"My flat is dark as well as stuffy." Those were the words for him.'[55]

Apart from Howards End, the properties belonging to the Wilcoxes do not evoke any such ponderings. Helen calculates that the Wilcoxes have eight houses, all told, which makes their refusal to act on Mrs Wilcox's wishes for Howards End even more deplorable – they don't need the house; none of them even wants to live in it. As Mr Wilcox tells Margaret, it is 'picturesque enough, but not a place to live in'.[56] Learning of the Schlegels' plight, Mr Wilcox offers them the rental of a house he owns near Mayfair. The interiors smack of pretension: 'the sumptuous dado, the frieze, the gilded wallpaper, amid whose foliage parrots sang [...] the heavy chairs, that immense sideboard loaded with presentation plate'.[57] It is not the thing for the intellectual Schlegels, but Margaret feels she can make it work, until Mr Wilcox proposes marriage and the question of house-hunting comes to a close.

The next Wilcox house on parade is Oniton Grange, a 'grey mansion' near the Welsh border, of the kind that was 'built all over England in the beginning of the last century, while architecture was still an expression of the national character'. Margaret falls in love with Oniton, 'a genuine country house', with a ruined castle in the grounds. It is 'clumsy and a little inconvenient', but again 'she was determined to make new sanctities among these hills'.[58] Unsurprisingly, Mr Wilcox has already decided that Oniton is a bad investment, being on the wrong side of Shropshire, and he is only waiting until after his daughter's wedding takes place there to 'get it off his hands'.[59]

Oniton shares the fate of many such large houses in the period, one that Alan Hollinghurst highlights nearly one hundred years later: it will be sold to 'some fellows who are starting a preparatory school'.[60]

After Margaret marries Mr Wilcox, they return to live at Ducie Street, but rather than use Howards End even as a country retreat, Mr Wilcox decides that they will build a new house in Sussex: 'We are to have a good many gables and a picturesque skyline', says Margaret.[61] The other houses in the Wilcox portfolio belong to the children, who each have a town and country abode. But of all of these properties, it is only Howards End that exerts its force on the characters' fate. As Margaret and Mr Wilcox decide where to live, the Schlegels' belongings are taken to be stored at Howards End. When Helen disappears, Margaret entices her back through a meeting there. It is in the beamed living room where the final tragic action of the novel takes place, the truth of Mrs Wilcox's bequest revealed, where 'Helen's child had been born in the central room of the nine', and where hope for vital connectedness lay.

The description and significance of Howards End is so vital to the story it will come as no surprise that there was a particular house, or houses, that the author held dear. Forster was born in London to an architect father and a mother from a somewhat lower class (her father was a drawing-master).[62] Eddie Forster was a descendent of the Clapham Sect, evangelical Anglican intellectuals who championed the anti-slavery movement in the eighteenth and nineteenth centuries and included Eddie's great-grandfather, Henry Thornton, as well as William Wilberforce. The family home was the eighteenth-century Battersea Rise House on Clapham Common, a 'compact brick house of the age of Queen Anne', with three storeys, additions made by Henry Thornton, some thirty-four bedrooms and a 'fine oval library' lit by a great bow window.[63]

The fact that Marianne Thornton, Forster's great-aunt, did not inherit Battersea Rise, was a slight that Forster would file with his own personal disappointments in his arguments for the importance of family homes. Battersea Rise is at the heart of the biography he wrote of his aunt; for that generation, he said, it was 'a sacred shrine'.

> It satisfied in them the longing for a particular place, a home, which is common among our upper and middle classes, and some of them transmitted that longing to their descendants, who have lived on into an age where it cannot be gratified.[64]

We may quibble with the class distinction, but the sentiment is one that had been crystallising for Forster since he first held it to the light in *Howards End*. He kept the nursery table from Battersea Rise, an oval of dark walnut, six feet by four, with, according to the nursery nurse of the time, no 'nasty corners for her children to knock their heads against'.[65] Forster passed it on to the grandson of his friend and lover Bob Buckingham many years later.[66] The house was demolished in 1907, he explains, 'at a time when development was unusually ruthless'.[67]

Forster's connections with particular houses had other reinforcement. His father worked for the London architectural firm of Arthur Blomfield in around 1870, only a few years

E. M. Forster, c. 1885, aged about six, sitting on a pony next to his mother, Alice 'Lily' Forster in front of his beloved Rooksnest.

after Thomas Hardy had left the office. One of Eddie's few achievements was West Hackhurst, a house designed for his sister Laura at Abinger Hammer, near Weybridge in Surrey. Forster had visited the house frequently since he was a child, and it was there that he lived with his mother for twenty years from 1925. After her death, he was forced to give up the tenancy, another blow to his 'longing for place'. However, this occurred many years after he published his paean to the ancestral home.

The most important house in *Howards End* is the eponymous cottage, and this building, Forster left no doubt, was built from his memories of the house where he spent his boyhood. After his father died of tuberculosis, when Forster was not quite two years old, his mother decided it would be healthier for 'Morgan', as he was called, to be brought up in the country. In 1883 she took the lease on Rooksnest, near Stevenage in Hertfordshire, where they lived for the next ten years. The house had belonged to a family named Howard, who had farmed there for three centuries. An advertisement for the house in 1882 described it as 'containing drawing room, dining room, hall, kitchen, scullery, pantry and larder on ground floor, 4 bedrooms on first floor, good attics, etc; excellent cellars'.[68] In a letter, Mrs Forster noted 'two sitting rooms' and 'a large hall & six bedrooms'; Forster himself later described three. The differences may highlight the fallibility of memory, but there is little doubt of the force of feeling. The importance of the house is clear from the author: 'I took it to my heart and hoped, as Marianne had of Battersea Rise, that I should live and die there.'[69]

Even after they left, Forster and his mother remained friends with the Poston family, who lived at nearby Highfield House. There had been two Mrs Postons at Highfield, as there would be two Mrs Wilcoxes and, as in the novel, it was the first Mrs Poston who defined the connection with the house. Like Margaret Schlegel, the second Mrs Poston also became connected to the life of Highfield, at least in Forster's recollection. She later inhabited Rooksnest with her children, and Forster, who began writing about the house while in his teens, was still returning to visit forty years on.[70]

In the opening pages of *Howards End*, Helen Schlegel writes to her sister, offering a matter-of-fact description of a modestly sized cottage, where she is staying with the Wilcox family:

From hall you go right or left into dining-room or drawing-room. Hall itself is practically a room. You open another door in it, and there are the stairs going up in a sort of tunnel to the first floor.[71]

The layout is not atypical for a cottage of this kind, though Forster described it as 'peculiar', and it certainly follows his description of Rooksnest, where 'five doors opened out of the hall, the dining-room, the door to the lobby leading to the kitchen, the door leading to the porch, the door to the staircase'. And, as Helen finds at Howards End, the stair was hidden by a door, and one could 'double her kingdom by opening the door that concealed the stairs'.[72] Outside, as at Howard's End, there was a wych elm tree with 'three or four fangs stuck deep in the rugged bark', which Forster surmised 'were votive offerings of people who had their toothache cured by chewing pieces of the bark'.[73] As the great tree confers a link to ancient mysticism on the manor at Groby in *Parade's End* (see chapter 10), Forster wrote that the wych elm 'overshadowed' Rooksnest 'with its primitive magic'.[74] By the time of his reminiscence in the 1950s, the tree had been cut down, but the house, he made clear, 'still stands', and 'is Howards End'.

Unlike many writers whose fictional dwellings are an amalgamation of different real-life models, Forster was at pains to describe over and over again how very important the Hertfordshire home had been to him, both in terms of its physical description, as well as its spiritual significance. 'The impressions received there remain and still glow,' he wrote in *Marianne Thornton*.[75] The further emotions he felt, it is safe to say, emerge in the lyrical closing pages of *Howards End*.

There were other homes. Forster boarded at Kent House School in Eastbourne from the age of eleven, while he and his mother, Lily, were living at Rooksnest. But when he was fourteen, Lily sent him as a 'day boy' to Tonbridge School in Tunbridge Wells and moved house to be near him. The pair left Rooksnest for good in 1893, but Forster clearly remained in thrall to the place.[76] When they left, they took with them 'the Rooksnest mantelpiece', which his father had built and which followed them to Tunbridge Wells, before eventually finding a home in his rooms at King's College, Cambridge, where Forster had spent his university years and returned as an honorary fellow in 1946.

Forster had early success with his novels, and had inherited a relative fortune from his father's family as a young man. He was not entirely comfortable with his unearned riches, and although there are no 'very poor' characters in the book, an awareness of privilege permeates *Howards End*, as Margaret sees that the loss of their house is not so grave for them as it might be for someone like Leonard Bast. From his bleak flat, the impoverished young man recalls the Schlegel sisters had 'passed up the narrow rich staircase at Wickham Place, to some ample room, whither he would never follow them'.[77] While decrying 'the particular millionaire' who was going to tear down Wickham Place, Margaret understands enough to note, 'Money pads the edges of things.' She concludes: 'God help those who have none.'[78]

West Hackhurst, in Surrey, was designed by Forster's father, Eddie, for his sister. Forster lived there with his mother from 1925–45.

After Cambridge and time spent abroad, Forster lived with his mother in Weybridge, from 1904 until 1925, in a red-brick villa named 'Harnham'. The house was nearly new, so had none of the continuity of the ages that Forster admired through the pages of *Howards End*, but it was here that he lived while he wrote all six of his novels, and elements of the house and garden are reproduced in the new properties built near the Honeychurch family home, Windy Corner, in *A Room with a View* (1908). Windy Corner bears more resemblance to West Hackhurst, the house built by Eddie Forster at Abinger Hammer, since Lucy Honeychurch's father, 'a prosperous local solicitor', built it 'as a speculation at the time the district was opening up, and falling in love with his own creation had ended up living there himself'.[79] The newly built villas 'Cissie' and 'Albert' more closely resemble Harnham. The village of Summer Street and the little wood in the neighbourhood of the Honeychurch family are taken from the Surrey countryside. The attitudes towards the influx of new residents are taken from Forster's loathing for suburban life. He also manages a dig at popular taste, saying that Mr Flack, the builder of the villas, 'apparition[s] of red and cream brick' with Corinthian columns clinging 'like leeches to the frames of the bow windows', had 'read his Ruskin'.[80]

In 1924, Forster's Aunt Laura died and she bequeathed to her nephew and his mother the existing lease, with thirteen years remaining, for West Hackhurst.[81] Although Eddie Forster had built it, the house was not owned by the Forster family; the ground lease belonged to Lord Farrer. The house was much larger than Rooksnest, with six bedrooms, two chimneys, and north and south verandas. However, as at Rooksnest, modern amenities were lacking. There was no electric light, no gas and no hot water supply. As at Max Gate, servants had to troop upstairs with hot water in copper kettles for bathing.[82] Its design shows something of the nascent Arts and Crafts in its half-timber portion, tiled walls and low-slung roofline, and one wonders whether Eddie might not have had a fulfilling architectural career had he lived past the age of thirty-three. West Hackhurst was isolated from London and from friends, but Forster was attached to it, no doubt owing to its connection to the father he never knew.

To ensure some stability for his mother, Forster asked Lord Farrer for 'some arrangement by which we should not be turned out of W. H. during mother's lifetime'.[83] This was granted, but when Lily died in 1945, Forster was sorely disappointed to learn that the landlord wanted the house for his own daughter, who had been bombed out of her London home. Forster was aggrieved and made his bitterness known. He complained to his lover Bob Buckingham of a lack of sympathy: 'You were much too sharp with me over West Hackhurst,' he argued. 'No doubt our feelings about houses &ct differ – if I hadn't mine I shouldn't have written *Howards End*.'[84] Forster did manage to purchase Piney Copse, an adjoining wood, in order to prevent it being developed. And even this small gesture towards ownership was momentous to him. He wrote in the essay 'My Wood' that 'it is the first property that I have owned', and it caused him to ask, 'What is the effect of property upon the character?'[85] For Forster, worries of avarice and proprietary anxiety – the sound of a snapping twig signalling the threat of an intruder – were at least partly ameliorated by the ability to pass something on to future generations. He bequeathed the nearly four and a half acres of Piney Copse to the National Trust.

At the end of his life, Forster wrote: 'I don't feel of anywhere. I wish I did. It is not that I am déraciné. It is that the soil is being washed away.'[86] His lament for the ties to a physical home and an ancient heritage was not the dream of a man stood against the modern world. In fact, *Howards End* is a modern novel in many ways, and its themes of enlightened liberalism and feminine independence do not hark back to a comfortable, imperialist past. Margaret Schlegel, though she joins herself to a patriarchal boor, expresses a strikingly modern sensibility.

What Forster feared was rampant mechanisation and the

unthinking speed of development, storming through both Leonard Bast's neighbourhood and the genteel environs of Wickham Place, where the 'lofty promontory of buildings' would be 'swept away in time, and another promontory would arise upon their site, as humanity piled itself higher and higher on the precious soil of London'.[87] Nor is the author's attitude anti-capitalist. Margaret recognises that Mr Wilcox's money had saved Howards End 'without fine feelings or deep insight, but he had saved it and she loved him for the deed'.[88] The Schlegel sisters acknowledge that cash is 'the warp of civilization'. But just as important is 'the woof', which for them is their home at Wickham Place, while 'for Mrs Wilcox it was certainly Howards End', the 'holy of holies'.[89]

As if to prove that he was no romantic idealist, Forster wrote a decidedly unromantic appendix to the 1958 edition of *A Room with a View*. Here the author imagines the future life of Lucy and George. During the Second World War, George is a wartime captive in Italy, not always faithful to a wife who is made homeless when their 'little flat in Watford' is bombed. The piece is titled 'A View without a Room', since George wanders through Florence trying to locate the pension where they first met, and though the view is still there, he can't find the room. Lucy, now without a room of her own, 'was glad of the news'.[90] The view, at least, endures, as do the cycles of rural life at Howards End: the meadow being scythed in early summer, the red poppies in July, the cutting of the wheat in August, 'these little events would become part of her year after year'.[91] Forster, like Hardy, finds more than a little solace in that: 'Here men had been up since dawn. There hours were ruled not by a London office, but by the movements of the crops and the sun.'[92]

Critics often speak of the elegiac tone of *Howards End*, a paean to life in an idealised countryside. But if the landscape invokes dreamy nostalgia, there is not much idyllic in the people who inhabit it. It is the possibility of a spiritual bond that matters, and is what Forster fears may be lost in the rush of modernity. Unlike Waugh, Forster never disavowed the 'praise of splendours of the recent past' or the 'rhetorical and ornamental language' that Waugh had indulged in *Brideshead Revisited* and later found 'distasteful'.[93] Rather, Forster continued to write feelingly of Rooksnest, West Hackhurst and of the ancestral home, Battersea Rise. Like Howards End, they are neither vessels for ornamental sentiment nor mere items of 'property', but, as Lionel Trilling concludes, places where people with 'failed outer lives' might come together, so that the 'inner life might come to [their] rescue'.[94]

Forster's struggle to deal with his own homosexuality and sense of social awkwardness, coupled with his mother's long widowhood, could not have made their lifelong partnership entirely harmonious. But something in the atmosphere of these places they inhabited together was for Forster worth preserving in fiction and autobiography. If in the modern world the commercial and the spiritual, the moral and the intellectual, 'the prose and the passion', must find a way to cohabit, a house that has a history of coaxing human beings towards connections might offer hope.

The Arts and Crafts movement is not mentioned explicitly by either Hardy or Forster, but it hovers in the background for both writers. In architecture, its veneration for some kind of cultural authenticity grew out of the Romantics' worship of nature and their exaltation of the sublime, which could be found in natural landscapes, Gothic ruins or a shepherd's hut. Arts and Crafts adherents, steeped in the stylised medievalism of William Morris and the instructive aesthetics of John Ruskin, were inspired to relish or try to recreate some ideal of English craftsmanship. Ruskin's views on architectural integrity and the importance of conservation over restoration, most elaborately put forward in his popular treatises *The Seven Lamps of Architecture* (1849) and *The Stones of Venice* (1853), were highly influential in the late nineteenth century and pre-war years. Both Leonard Bast and Lucy Honeychurch become frustrated in trying to apply Ruskinian principles to their surroundings.

In the first of Ford Madox Ford's *Parade's End* novels, Christopher Tietjens's friend and dependent, Macmaster, seeks out the Reverend Duchemin, because he is 'a personal disciple of Mr Ruskin'.[95] Ford's irony is soft compared to Aldous Huxley's in *Crome Yellow* (1921). In that novel, railing against the trend for construction, which has some affinity with nature à la Morris, Mr Scogan laments, 'we now employ our wealth, our technical knowledge' to create 'adaptations of the village hovel'. He pronounces that 'the house of an intelligent, civilised and sophisticated man should never seem to have sprouted from the clods'.[96] Ruskin comes in for much worse fifty years later in Julian Barnes's *Metroland*, when young Christopher's feckless uncle calls him 'Bloody Ruskin' for making too much work of a simple gardening job.[97]

It is easy to sympathise with Mr Scogan's criticism, and yet lyrical associations with an idyllic English vernacular linger, as does the hope that associations with a particular place can still hold the promise of some kind of spiritual fulfillment.

Robin Hill

EIGHT

The House as a Work of Art:
The Aesthetic Visions of John Galsworthy
and Henry James

'You'll never make anything of this!' he said tartly, pointing at the
mansion; 'too new-fangled!'

The Man of Property

As *Howards End* became familiar by way of the soft-focus
film, many people will know the story of *The Forsyte Saga*
through the lush and stylish television adaptation from 2002.
Forty years earlier, a previous series was so popular in Britain
that churches changed the timing of their services to allow
parishioners to catch the Sunday evening episodes. The love
triangle at its heart is unlike any other in literature. Neither
the cold, supercilious husband nor the passionate architect is
singularly compelling, but the fact that they both love the
same woman and are involved in building the same house for
her, a new kind of house that is 'something unique' and deliberately provocative, gives the tangle lasting allure.

Written between 1903 and 1920, John Galsworthy's first trilogy follows the fortunes of the wealthy Forsyte family, namely
those of its most stalwart heir and defender, Soames Forsyte.
Galsworthy carried on his chronicle of the Forsytes, eventually

writing nine books, the last published posthumously in 1934. In the first novel, *The Man of Property* (1906), Galsworthy describes how the Victorian world of wealth and property, gentlemen's clubs and afternoon tea, is on a track of inevitable decline, and he bids it good riddance. Although he doesn't realise it, the house at Robin Hill, which Soames hires the architect Philip Bosinney to design for his wife, Irene, is a potent symbol of a new world that is overtaking the old. Built in a decidedly 'new-fangled' style, it has nothing of the imposing quality of the other Forsyte houses, with their 'rich brown atmosphere' of 'dark green velvet and heavily carved mahogany'. These houses were 'placed at intervals round the Park' and 'watched like sentinels lest the fair heart of this London . . . slip from their clutches'.[1]

Robin Hill is something altogether different, thoughtfully constructed on the page, beguiling to the characters, its modern aesthetic marking a definitive break with the style of both Soames's Forsyte forebears and Galsworthy's own cultural class. Robin Hill sits at the fulcrum of a passionate love affair and the tousle between tradition and innovation. And yet the house's origins were never acknowledged by Galsworthy. For nearly a century, biographers and television researchers have puzzled over his vision for one of the most iconic houses in English literature, and certainly one of first arguments for 'modern' design in fiction. But the author remained silent on the matter. Luckily, some unpublished drawings sitting quietly for decades in the British Library collection have revealed at last the author's fictional intentions, which were more complete than anyone could have known.

Ever since Virginia Woolf dismissed him as a 'materialist',

John Galsworthy has been seen as a writer firmly lodged in the Victorian era.[2] But *The Forsyte Saga* heralded the coming of a new age, one in which women were no longer regarded as property, could have money of their own (the novel makes more than one mention of the Married Women's Property Act) and people married for reasons of love over class.

Around 1904, when Galsworthy began writing *The Man of Property*, he had experience of watching the designing and building of grand houses up close. His father, a successful businessman, became something of a property developer, and built a series of three large houses in Victorian Gothic style in Surrey. He also built the red-brick Kensington Palace Mansions and a terrace of residences in Queen Anne revival style in Regent's Park (dubbed Cambridge Gate) in 1887, but none of these approaches the provocative design of Robin Hill. The author himself didn't boast any designer leanings; he attended Harrow and Oxford and early on was destined for a career in law. Galsworthy may not have been a modernist in his writing style, but the building of Robin Hill, and what it symbolises, is one of the most modern statements in literature from the period. It is through this house of light and air, with a view that inspired a feeling 'like the murmur of bright minutes holding revel between earth and heaven', that Soames inadvertently frees Irene from the trap of a bad marriage. It represents not only an ideal new dwelling, but also a complete work of art, heralding a break with stifling tradition.

Robin Hill may be a new kind of architecture, but Soames only comes to build it because property is in the Forsytes' blood. The Forsyte patriarch made his money building in

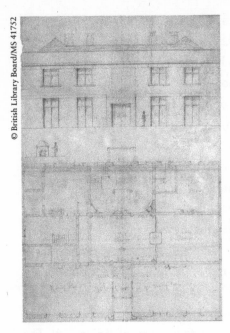

John Galsworthy's own drawings of the house at Robin Hill, which were never published. The plain, unornamented front can be compared to Godwin's designs for the 'White House' in Chelsea.

London and left a legacy to his ten children. It is the children of the ten who are to carry their property and themselves into the twentieth century. For the Forsytes, 'the whole spirit of their success was embodied in [their houses]'.[3] They are in favour of guarding what they own, and where possible acquiring more. Soames's biggest sin is in considering his wife, Irene, as his property also. This attitude is so much in his make-up that even he and his father 'regarded one another as an investment'.[4] When Soames decides to build a house in the country for the enchanting but inscrutable Irene, it is to please her, as she is 'very artistic' (and to keep her away from troublesome influences). He is a collector of paintings, but little understands how this move towards art in building will alter the firmament of his life.

The house's design, argued for passionately by its architect, represents a forward-looking aesthetic that embraces, rather than resists, the modern world. As such, Robin Hill is more different, alluring and exciting than Soames could have possibly imagined. Its airy spaciousness intrigues Soames and befuddles his father and uncles. A mystified Uncle Swithin, upon coming into the 'inner court', filled with natural light from the large end window and the glass roof, applies Forsytean practicality to the ethereal space, remarking, 'Ah! the billiard-room.'[5]

And it is expensive: Soames ends up shelling out £12,400 for the house with all of the decoration (houses in nearby Streatham were being built around the same time for a price of £500 to £1,000).[6] He perceives its material and social advantages, but his uncle Jolyon is the first member of the family to understand that 'poor young Bosinney had made an uncommonly good job' of it. In its peaceful arrangement, Robin Hill gives the ageing patriarch a renewed zest for living: 'He had not felt his age since he had bought his nephew Soames's ill-starred house . . . It was as if he had been getting younger every spring, living in the country with his son and his grandchildren'.[7] Ironically, this aesthetic tranquillity is denied to Bosinney, the architect of the house, and to Irene, its inspiration.

If the real-life model for Robin Hill is a mystery, the transcendent view of beauty and nature coupled with the passion for building can be traced back to Galsworthy's own father's building ambitions at Kingston Hill in Surrey. At the time (as in the time of his most famous novels), Surrey was more like countryside than a suburb of London and the plot was on a hilly rise, overlooking the scattering of development below. John Galsworthy, Sr, built three houses here, and the family moved between them in the years 1868 to 1886. Afterwards, they went to live at 8 Cambridge Gate, a new terrace of houses on London's Regent's Park, which Mr Galsworthy had constructed in partnership with his brother Fred.[8]

In a thoughtful essay on his father written many years after the novel, Galsworthy described the older man's impetus to move his young family out of the city, sentiments that chime with Jolyon's fondness for Robin Hill: 'Selecting a fair and high locality, not too far away from London, he set himself at once to make a country place . . . Quite wonderful was the fore-thought he lavished on that house and little estate stretching down the side of a hill.'[9] The first house, built in 1868, was Coombe Warren, now reached by George Road. Later called Coombe Court, it was owned by the Marquess of Ripon before being demolished in 1931. The second, Coombe Leigh, still stands and is now occupied by Holy Cross Preparatory School.[*] Both reflect the prevailing style of red-brick Victorian mishmash with none of the 'regularity' or subdued elegance of Robin Hill. The third house, Coombe Croft, sited a bit further along George Road, was only lived in by the family for a few years. In 1966, it became part of Rokeby School. From the rear gardens all around here in the 1880s, as at Robin Hill, you could very probably 'see the Grand Stand at Epsom in clear weather'.[10]

---

[*] Pevsner contends that only the lodge of the second house remains, the cottage called 'Robin Hill Cottage'. However, family records state that the second house was called Coombe Leigh. The owners of Holy Cross are certain that this is the house built by John Galsworthy, Sr. It is of an appropriate age and style, so one can only speculate that there has been confusion in the past.

After studying law at Oxford, Galsworthy, either because he was indifferent about his career or had become involved with an unsuitable woman, was sent by his father on a trip to the west coast of Canada. On his return voyage in 1893 on board the *Torrens*, he became friendly with the ship's first mate, a young Polish adventurer called Joseph Conrad. Unbeknown to Galsworthy, Conrad at that time was carrying the manuscript of his first novel, *Almayer's Folly*. Once back in England, the pair became friends and fervent advocates of each other's work. Conrad buoyed up Galsworthy's writing spirits, and Galsworthy often supported the impecunious and perennially unhealthy Conrad and his family with gifts and loans. Through Conrad, Galsworthy joined a literary circle that included Ford Madox Ford and H. G. Wells.

Galsworthy readily acknowledged that the setting for Soames's new house was a childhood idyll. As he later explained: 'In those days . . . Coombe was very different – very much as I describe it at the opening of *The Man of Property*. The site of the Forsyte House was the site of my father's Coombe Warren and the grounds and coppice, etc. were actual'.[11] Although he confirmed that Coombe was the setting for Robin Hill, Galsworthy denied the house had any relation to an existing building. He maintained that 'the house itself I built with my imagination. I still have the plans.'[12] Most biographers have taken him at his word here, but any reader of the novels will be struck by the extravagance of detail lavished on the design of the house, and the exoticism of its unconventional interiors. Then there is the fervour with which Bossiney (nicknamed 'the Buccaneer' by the Forsytes for his adventurous attitude) argues for his ideals, proclaiming the virtues of 'regularity' and ranting against the work of 'Little-master', the popular architect who builds houses 'of the pretty and commodious sort, where the servants will live in garrets and the front door be sunk so that you may come up again'. The airing of the aesthetic argument and the catalogue of style and decor not only of Robin Hill, but also of the fusty Forsyte homes, suggest more than a passing interest in buildings. The author even has Soames, 'the unconscious ironist', notice that Bosinney's tie 'was far from being in the perpendicular'.[13]

In around 1895 Galsworthy began thinking seriously of trying to make his name as a writer. By this time he had met his future wife, to whom he gave most of the credit for his change of heart and his success. The only problem was that when they met and fell in love, Ada was already married, unhappily, to Galsworthy's cousin Arthur. Unwilling to subject his lover to the public humiliation and spectacle of a divorce, he entered into what became a ten-year affair. The diary pages covering this period have been excised and most of Galsworthy's private papers destroyed by Ada after his death, but it is entirely likely that it was during this time that the author found at least some of the inspiration for the design of Robin Hill.

When his father died in 1904, Galsworthy and Ada decided to make their affair public and went away together to Wingstone Manor in Dartmoor (a house they had previously visited in secret) to provoke Arthur to sue for divorce. He quickly obliged. The couple married in September 1905, not long before the publication of *A Man of Property*. Biographers differ sharply in viewing Ada either as a devoted partner or a manipulative hypochondriac. Whatever the true nature of their relationship, it is certain that Ada provided the model for Irene and for the romantic crisis that finds two men in the same family fighting for the same woman. But none of the houses we know he inhabited before or after the secretive period of their affair bear any resemblance to Bosinney's 'ill-starred house'.

While Galsworthy was very fond of Wingstone Manor, and the couple made it their 'country home' for fifteen years, the style is of a simple farmhouse.[14] It was primitive in its comforts, not at all modern, nor were any of the homes at Coombe at all like what Galsworthy describes is being built for Soames and Irene. These houses were all large, rambling Victorian Gothic confections made of red brick, with bay windows and ornamental metalwork (those at Cambridge Gate were only slightly more subdued), and none had the startling simplicity of Bosinney's design.

However, there are clues to the house in Galsworthy's personal life. The character of Bosinney was probably at least partly influenced by his brother-in-law, the portrait artist Georg Sauter. A Bavarian of lower social stock than the Galsworthys and of admirable talent, Sauter stood out in the narrow world of his socially constricted in-laws. Sauter and Galsworthy's sister Lilian lived at 1 Holland Park Road, which became the centre for a sort of literary-artistic community. At around the same time that the members of the Bloomsbury Group were establishing themselves a few miles away, and while Galsworthy was embarking on the first novel of his trilogy, Lilian was holding her own 'salons', attended by people as diverse and well known as James McNeill Whistler, Ezra Pound and Mark Twain.

Lilian and Georg Sauter's house had its own artistic origins, being the former home of the Pre-Raphaelite painter, William Holman Hunt. It had a large, naturally lit studio space, which, though not overly grand or dramatic, could have informed the double-height, glass-roofed hall of Robin Hill. Galsworthy was a frequent visitor, and in 1902, when Ada took the bold step of moving out of her husband's house, she conveniently chose a flat at nearby Campden House Chambers. The following year, Galsworthy moved around the corner to 16a Aubrey Walk.

On the hunt for designs that may have inspired the look and feel of Robin Hill, it is possible that both 1 Holland Park

© British Library Board/MS 41752

The inner court at Robin Hill in an unpublished sketch by John Galsworthy. The double-height proportion and glass roof were probably influenced by painters' studios in Chelsea.

Road and Campden House Chambers had some influence. The latter, designed by Thackeray Turner and Eustace Balfour and no longer standing, was said to have 'affinities' with Arts and Crafts architecture and was described as 'an original and characteristic work'.[15] Lilian's diaries record dining with Galsworthy 'at Ada's', so he knew the building and it is possible that it inspired some of his ideas of a new, simpler style.[16]

There are other, more intriguing possibilities. According to Ada's recollections, around the time Galsworthy began writing in earnest, he had returned to living with his parents in Cambridge Gate, but took 'private quarters' at 2 Cedar Studios, in Glebe Place, Chelsea. He then lived at Lawrence Mansions in Chelsea Embankment.[17] This is a small note in the biography, but the association with Chelsea is one that may have had a much greater impact on Galsworthy's artistic sensibilities than he or Ada acknowledged.

When Soames views the plans of Robin Hill for the first time, his immediate reaction is, 'It's an odd sort of house!' So we know it is out of the ordinary for London in the 1880s. It is not a multistorey Victorian Gothic building, or, being in the country, a common farmhouse like Wingstone. Bosinney is going for what he calls 'regularity', but this turns out to be strikingly innovative. The first plans show 'a rectangular house of two storeys . . . designed in a quadrangle round a covered-in court. This court, encircled by a gallery on the upper floor, was roofed with a glass roof, supported by eight columns running up from the ground'. Told that he should 'cut waste' in the size of the house, Bosinney replies that 'the principle of this house . . . [is] that you should have room to breathe – like a gentleman!'[18] He later adds that 'space, air, light' are his driving aims, a comment that could have come from the most avant-garde modernist decades later.[19]

Bosinney, who alarmed his former employer by 'going off with a knapsack' in order 'to study foreign architecture – foreign!', has developed some very new ideas.[20] He claims that Soames's wife 'shan't be cold', because he has included 'hot-water pipes in aluminium casings', which can be got 'with very good designs'. The use of aluminium in such large quantities was new technology for 1886, when the novel opens (the process for extracting aluminium in an economical way that would make it commercially viable would not be discovered until the end of the decade).[21] Even a dozen years later, when Galsworthy was writing the novel in earnest, cast iron was still the preferred material for plumbing work.

Perturbed by Soames's lack of immediate enthusiasm, Bosinney insists, 'I've tried to plan a house here with some self-respect of its own. If you don't like it, you'd better say so.' The best Soames can manage as a reply, not wanting to encourage expenditure and feeling an 'instinctive' need to conceal his satisfaction, is to stammer that it is 'certainly original'.[22] From the arrangement of the rooms around the courtyard to the inner court itself, it is not like anything we have read about for this period. Even the Arts and Crafts masterpieces do not have such a feature. Galsworthy would have known of architects such as C. F. A. Voysey or Charles Rennie Mackintosh, whose work was becoming popular and who, like Bosinney, were being contracted to decorate interiors as well. That Galsworthy has Bosinney specifically agree to design the interiors, along with the building, shows an awareness of the trend and a desire to present the house as a single, harmonious artistic expression.

Galsworthy would have known of Voysey not least because the architect had built a house for his friend H. G. Wells in Sandgate, Kent, in 1901. Among a long list of other much larger and more significant houses, Voysey also built the large, light-filled Greyfriars House in Guildford, Surrey (not so far from Kingston), in 1896. The massive window overlooking the North Downs and the site on the rise with the view over them resonates with the setting of Robin Hill. But the style is too vertical for the description in the book, especially as Soames asks the architect if it will 'look like a barrack', meaning presumably that Bosinney's design has a block-like shape, rather than the sweeping profile of peaked roof that Voysey often employed.

Charles Rennie Mackintosh may have influenced ideas such as the 'black oak floor' and walls of 'ivory white'.[23] Many designers and architects just before the turn of the century were interested in Japanese designs, which had become popular and led to the trend for dark flooring and light walls. In the novel, these are in contrast to the 'scarlet and green drawing room' belonging to Timothy and the old aunts on Bayswater Road, which was 'full at the best of times' with 'eleven chairs, a sofa, three tables, two cabinets, innumerable knick knacks, and part of a large grand piano'.[24] These are exactly the range of ornaments so prized by Mrs Gereth in Henry James's *The Spoils of Poynton*, which was being written just as Galsworthy was setting out to create his own fiction.

So there are no neo-Gothic arches (such as Ruskin might have favoured in the same period) or classical porticoes, or indeed sweeping rooflines of the Arts and Crafts houses or sculptural decorations acknowledging the nascent Queen Anne revival style. Instead, there is space, light and simplicity. Bosinney outlines the generous proportions of the inner court when he shows Soames the plans. Putting his finger on the centre of the courtyard space, he says, 'You can swing a cat here. This is for your pictures, divided from this court by curtains; draw them back and you'll have a space of fifty-one by twenty-three six.' More light enters the inner court at Robin Hill through the end wall, which, unusually, 'is all window; you've southeast light from that, a north light from the court'.[25] The picture room is where Soames will hang the paintings that he has bought for investment. Galsworthy again holds up the contrast between art and commerce as Soames's cousin, June, accuses him of treating art 'as if it were grocery', thus demonstrating why he would never understand or appreciate the real beauty of Robin Hill.[26]

Like the modernists who will follow him, Bosinney repeatedly stresses the importance of 'regularity' in design, and decries those who 'load [their] houses with decoration, gimcracks, corners, anything to distract the eye', like Timothy's house in Bayswater Road and other residences displaying the hallmarks of Victorian wealth and status. In his opinion, 'the eye should rest; get your effect with a few strong lines'. When Bosinney accuses Soames of wanting a house designed like those of the fashionable architect Littlemaster, it may be that the author was thinking of the vernacular revivalist George Devey, who built the first Galsworthy family home in Surrey, Coombe Warren, and was known for trying to create an effect of a building that was made up of different historic parts. This

The White House, designed by Edward Godwin for the artist J. A. M. Whistler. It was derided for its lack of ornament and pronounced a 'dead house' by the Metropolitan Board of Works.

would have been an anathema to Bosinney's sense of regularity and, to some degree, purity. Or he could have been making a veiled critique of the work of Edwin Lutyens, who became enormously popular with his own vernacular revivalist style. What Galsworthy had built in Chelsea would have been very different.

Ever since J. M. W. Turner rented a house on the Chelsea riverside in 1846, this area of London had become known as 'an artistic and bohemian colony'.[27] William Holman Hunt and Dante Gabriel Rossetti moved here in the 1850s and '60s; John Singer Sargent arrived in 1901. In the sixty years prior to the

First World War, over 1,300 domestic artists' studios were built in the area. In Tite Street, just a few blocks from Galsworthy's bachelor apartment in Glebe Place, there was a veritable village of painters' studios.[28] Then in 1878, Edward William Godwin designed the 'White House' for Whistler, a friend of the Sauters and a founding member of the Chelsea Arts Club, a venue frequented by Lilian (and possibly Galsworthy and Ada).

As it was originally designed, the White House looks astonishingly modern. It has a plain, rectangular façade with a simple, unornamented mansard roof. Inside, it features the Anglo-Japanese elements – dark floors and light walls – similar to those at Robin Hill, which Mackintosh favoured and were popularised by Godwin as a proponent of the Aesthetic Movement, which was at its height in the 1870s and 80s and generated debate about the purpose and worth of decoration. While Bosinney's rhetoric on 'space, air and light' doesn't chime with the more ornate interpretations of Aestheticism, it certainly echoes Godwin's belief that an 'abundance of light, air and cleanliness' was key to good design.[29] The stone cladding and green slate roof that Godwin applied to Whistler's residence appear as Bosinney outlines his own compromises for the design of Robin Hill: 'The house, of course should be built entirely of stone, but, as I thought you wouldn't stand that, I've compromised for a facing. It ought to have a copper roof, but I've made it green slate'.[30]

Godwin designed a series of studios and another house in the same street, at no. 44, for the artist Frank Miles, which he shared for a time with Oscar Wilde, and in 1884 Godwin designed the interior of Wilde's house at no. 16 (now 33). Wilde had spent most of 1882 on a popular lecture tour in the

US, speaking on 'The House Beautiful'. The Wildes' drawing room was painted ivory white and flesh pink with a gilded cornice and a ceiling border of Japanese leather.[31] It is not clear whether Galsworthy visited all or any of these houses, but it is likely that he knew of them, and that he met Whistler through his sister. He also knew other artists, including William Rothenstein, who in the 1890s was borrowing studio space at the house Godwin built for Miles. Galsworthy would also have known of Godwin's struggles with the Metropolitan Board of Works, which initially refused permission for the designs of both the White House and Frank Miles' house until Godwin agreed to add stylised ornamentation to the exterior – precisely the kind of 'decorations and gimcracks' to which Bosinney objects. The White House also would have come to Galsworthy's attention in 1877, when Whistler brought a public (and expensive) libel action against the critic John Ruskin, who had disparaged one of the artist's paintings in print. It became a cause célèbre, and the loss of the action famously bankrupted Whistler so that he was forced to give up the house soon after moving in.

Other architects associated with the Arts and Crafts or Aesthetic movements, such as Philip Webb and Norman Shaw, were also very active in Chelsea and its surrounds in this period, so innovation and its attendant arguments were rife, as was the atmosphere of rigid opposition. Among Godwin's other clients was the actress Lillie Langtry, for whom he designed a house with a double-height studio room. Such an amenity, which until this point had only been requested by artists, was now in demand as a point of fashion.

Looking at the wealth of artistic studios and architectural

experimentation in Chelsea during this period, it is not hard to imagine that this is where Galsworthy arrived at his avant-garde notions of design, particularly the idea of the inner court with its glass ceiling – a room, like those artists' studios, whose primary concern is natural light.

By the time he was writing, another unusual house, in nearby Holland Park, had captured the public imagination. Leighton House was the home of the pre-Raphaelite painter Frederic, Lord Leighton who began work on 'one of the first artistic landmarks' of suburban Kensington in about 1864.[32] A sumptuous paean to orientalism, the lower floor recalls an exuberant middle-eastern palace courtyard, with decorative tiles covering almost every surface. The house's dimensions are not palatial, but Leighton divided the lower floor into two 'halls' and a linking corridor so that the stair hall takes natural light from a top-floor skylight. The Narcissus Hall is lined with iridescent blue tiles designed by William De Morgan, while the shadowy Arab Hall, which displays Leighton's collection of mostly Syrian tiles and mosaics from the fifteenth to the seventeenth centuries, has at its centre a small pool lined in black marble.

Though the design of Robin Hill does not mimic quite this degree of extravagant exoticism, the concept of the internal court ringed with columns and the richness of the décor at Leighton House are more consonant with Galsworthy's creation – lined in 'dull ruby tiles' surrounding a 'sunken basin of white marble filled with water' – than any other known house of the time. Perhaps, most of all, the singularity of artistic vision would have held tremendous appeal for the writer, as he tried to create a new material expression of art and emotion.

*

It was totally consistent with Galsworthy's character and his wish to protect Ada from gossip that he would not make the house that served as the model for Robin Hill public knowledge if it meant revealing the location of their early affair. But it is not too much of a stretch to imagine that Ada visited him in Chelsea. Cedar Studios still exists, two light-filled artists' ateliers set back from Glebe Place (which is still dotted with other studio buildings), shaded by a tangle of trees and accessed by a tiny walkway. It wouldn't have been an unattractive setting for clandestine meetings, as few would have questioned the presence of a lady visiting on her own, in a neighbourhood where artists' models (like the famed Dorothy Dene) came and went with impunity.

View from Narcissus Hall through to the double-height, top-lit stair vestibule at Leighton House in London, c. 1890. The 'inner court' at Robin Hill shares some of its exotic decoration and proportion.

Confirmation of Galsworthy's ideas for the house can be found in the manuscripts collection of the British Library. Among various notes and letters is an oversized folio containing a set of drawings, with a description on the reverse in the author's own handwriting:

Original Plans of the House at Robin Hill
Built by Philip Bossiney architect 1887
For Soames Forsyte, Esq of Montpellier Square, London[33]

These are no sketches on the back of a beer mat, but detailed drawings of a front and rear elevation, and ground- and first-floor plans. In fact, the attention to scale and use suggests that perhaps being a writer was not the only vocation Galsworthy considered in those early days after deciding against a career in law. The front and rear façades are presented in a deliberately plain style, without either Queen Anne revival ornament or stylised Arts and Crafts elements. It is not Mackintosh, Voysey or even Frank Lloyd Wright, but something much more pure, showing precision and 'regularity'. As well as the plans and elevations, Galsworthy made a sketch of the 'inner-court' with the purple leather curtain, and a small detail of the stove that was meant to sit between the court and Soames's picture room. He even included the spaces for the kitchen, pantry, laundry and servants' hall.

While these drawings do not point to a single existing model, they demonstrate how very clearly the author had conceived the house in his own mind, and that he had educated himself in both architectural drawing and a new kind of architecture that probably came from the challenges to aesthetic tradition and lively invention percolating in and around

Chelsea in the early years of the century.

The pain of artistic compromise to suit conventional taste, which Galsworthy also witnessed, is rife in Bosinney's diatribe against the work of Littlemaster, and in the reaction of the Forsytes, who privately admit the success of Robin Hill, while publicly complaining of its cost and strangeness. Galsworthy's genius in the novels is in using this aesthetic tension to mirror the struggles of the main characters to live a life that is truer to their own hopes and desires than rigid social codes of the period would allow. Though Soames is the agent in building the new-style house, he does not appreciate its real 'charm', which is its very newness; he will not be its guardian. Forster notes in *Howards End* the tension in England between the people who 'run her' and those who 'understand her'. Soames has owned Robin Hill, but he doesn't understand it. Not even Irene seems to comprehend its special power.

Though Galsworthy was not the builder of houses that his father was, in creating Robin Hill, he brought the passion of artistic debate to a kind of fiction that could otherwise have died under the heavy furniture of tradition. And it is a discussion that predates and prefigures much of our current understanding of the disruptive event we call 'modernism'. He may have deliberately closed the door on the question of which house might have inspired the uncompromising beauty, the 'balance and symmetry', of Robin Hill, but for modern design, which could herald a new way of thinking, he opened a very large window.

Henry James was born into the American intelligentsia, but lived most of his adult life in England and became a British citizen. He settled in London in 1877 and produced a body of work that is hard to match in its scale and psychological reach. His fiction was of the realist sensibility, but one that was more concerned with psychological and behavioural truths than with the general ills of society. And while he differs radically in many ways from someone like Galsworthy, they share an aesthetic view of houses as works of art. Both exult in an ideal of architectural and artistic integrity that clashes with more vulgar attempts at design and decoration. James wholeheartedly admired English houses and traditions in ways that Galsworthy might have objected to, as praising the old, rather than looking to the new. (Though in the latter tales of the Forsyte family, Galsworthy does express affection and concern for the fate of the old country house.) In this, James was typical of many Americans who see England as a place of traditions instead of progress. He was a fervent admirer of the English country house, writing in 1879:

> Of all the great things that the English have invented and made a part of the credit of the national character, the most perfect, the most characteristic, the only one they have mastered completely in all its details, so that it becomes a compendious illustration of their social genius and their manners, is the well-appointed, well-filled country house.[34]

James's fictional observations are offered not just in appreciation, but also in the debate over the importance of beauty as an end in itself, and as measured against simple materialism in ways that can be compared particularly with *The Forsyte Saga*. Most of his novels present Americans who are beguiled by Europe, and by European manners and machinations. Christopher Newman is perplexed and manipulated by a French noble family in *The American*; the staid Lambert Strether is sent to Paris to retrieve his fiancée's son, but is seduced by a world of refinement and art in *The Ambassadors*; Isabel Archer in *The Portrait of a Lady* is undone by the cunning and sophistication of Gilbert Osmond in partnership with Madame Merle; and Milly Theale is preyed upon by Merton Densher, in league with Kate Croy, in *The Wings of the Dove*. There are many grand houses and estates at stake as James addresses the popular theme of rich Americans applying the medicament of wealth to the resuscitation of old English stately homes. Only in James's view, the Americans are not the swaggering industrialists of the Gilded Age who install themselves in ancient buildings, but their more innocent daughters (perhaps like Consuelo Vanderbilt, whose marriage in 1895 to the 9th Duke of Marlborough ensured that the duke received a share of the Vanderbilt millions and the Vanderbilts got an heir to the eighteenth-century riches of Blenheim Palace). In James's novels, it is the English and Europeans who are scheming to get at the young Americans' money, though the Americans come willingly to the sacrifice.

The demise of Isabel Archer, in *Portrait of a Lady*, does not take place primarily in England; rather, it is her point of departure. The safe haven that she fails to recognise is Gardencourt, the home of her cousin Ralph Touchett, he of the 'ugly, sickly, witty, charming face' and kind disposition. James lingers on the afternoon vision of the house as Ralph takes tea in the garden with his ailing father and his friend, Lord Warburton, a decent man who is master of another beautiful house, Lockleigh. Like all great English country houses, Gardencourt has 'a name and a history', which 'the old gentleman taking his tea would have been delighted to tell you'. But the old man being infirm, James tells us himself 'how it had been built under Edward the Sixth, had offered a night's hospitality to the great Elizabeth . . . had been a good deal bruised and defaced in Cromwell's wars . . . and how, finally, after having been remodelled and disfigured in the eighteenth century, it had passed into the careful keeping of a shrewd American banker'.[35]

Like Darlington Hall in the *The Remains of the Day* (see chapter 13) and countless English houses at the close of the nineteenth century and later, this house has been saved, though crumbling, and 'offered at a bargain' to a rich American. Old Mr Touchett, the American owner of Gardencourt, has lived there for twenty years, so that he 'knew all its points and would tell you just where to stand to see them in combination and just the hour when the shadows of its various protuberances . . . were of the right measure'. It is a loving portrait of a man and a house, the former soon to expire, the latter to be left without an heir owing to the independently minded but ultimately misguided actions of Isabel. Her mistake is in not seeing the value in her cousin, Ralph Touchett, (and Gardencourt) and in refusing Warburton (and Lockleigh) in favour of the more exotic Italophile, Gilbert Osmond, 'a gentleman who studied style', but whose original 'clime and country' is difficult to discern.[36]

In contrast to Gardencourt, the Palazzo Roccanera in Rome, Isabel's home after her marriage to Osmond, is cold and echoey, with 'beautiful, empty, dusky rooms'.[37] She has made over her tremendous fortune to 'a man with the best taste in the world', but who cares little for anyone but himself.[38] Her fortune allows him to buy even more paintings, sculpture and tapestries, but in the chapter of her 'awakening', Isabel finds that the house she shares with Osmond is, in the metaphorical sense, 'the house of darkness, the house of dumbness, the house of suffocation. Osmond's beautiful mind gave it neither light nor air'.[39]

James was not the owner of a grand country house, but he visited and admired a great many. He mentioned Hardwick House, near Pangbourne on the Thames, as the house he had 'vaguely and approximately in mind . . . for the opening of Portrait'.[40] Its owner was an MP by the name of Charles Rose, whom James had befriended in his early months in England. It is a handsome Tudor-period house overlooking the Thames in quiet countryside. It does indeed bear the scars of the Civil War, and did once host Queen Elizabeth I. The author Michael Gorra speculates that James visited the house some time in 1877, just after Rose had taken the lease. On James's suggestion, its image was used as the frontispiece for the 1907 edition of the novel.[41] It was also the model for Toad Hall, as Kenneth Grahame had been a frequent guest.

The inveterate dinner guest, James famously 'dined out 107 times' during the winter of 1878–9, and most of these evenings were spent in the homes of highly placed friends.[42] It was often at these dinner parties that he captured the 'germ' of a story, if not from the setting then from the mealtime gossip. Recalling the visit that supplied the idea for the novel *The Spoils of Poynton* (1897), he explained that 'one Christmas Eve when I was dining with friends' he was told the story of how 'a good lady in the north, always well looked on, was at daggers drawn with her only son [...] over the ownership of the valuable furniture of a fine old house just accruing to the young man by his father's death'.[43]

Although James wrote many novels that were more accomplished and more celebrated, *The Spoils of Poynton* is a wonderful look at the petty delights of house obsessives. In those first pages, James is just as bitingly funny as Jane Austen at her most needle-sharp. Yet despite its being 'a story of cabinets and chairs and tables',[44] he also addresses the issue of women being thrown out of their houses when their sons inherit everything, rather like the fate of Mrs Dashwood and her daughters in *Sense and Sensibillity*: 'The house and its contents had been treated as a single splendid object; everything was to go straight to [Mr Gereth's] son, his widow being assured but a maintenance and a cottage in another county.'[45]

Here, the conflict arises not only from an unsympathetic daughter-in-law and an easily manipulated son, as in Austen's novel, but also from the very possessive, aesthetically minded and determined mother. Poynton, the Gereth residence in the south of England, is a pinnacle of taste, contrasted with the home of Mona Brigstock (young Owen Gereth's intended), which is called Waterbath and is, in Mrs Gereth's view, the picture of vulgarity. If this is a novel about inheritance and deception, it also puts forward more than a few hints about the do's and don't's of interior decoration.

As the story begins, Mrs Gereth is a house guest at Waterbath, but far from being gracious, she is disgruntled by the house's imperfections, which are subject to some rather ill-mannered gossip among the guests. Mrs Gereth feels that

Henry James posing at the garden door to Lamb House in Rye, 'an adorable corner of the wicked earth'.

the house suffers from 'an ugliness fundamental and system-atic, the result of the abnormal nature of the Brigstocks, from whose composition the principle of taste had been extrava-gantly omitted'.[46] Waterbath might have been tolerable if only the family had the sense to leave it alone, but in its current state, the drawing room 'caused her face to burn' and each of her companions 'confided to the other that in her own apartment she had given way to tears'. The source of the weeping is, among other things, the fact that 'the house was perversely full of souvenirs of places even more ugly than itself and of things it would have been a pious duty to forget'. But 'the worst horror', we are told, 'was the acres of varnish, something advertised and smelly, with which everything was smeared'.[47] It seems from this long list of offenses that some of James's evenings with friends were not as impressive as others, and that if he had been round to supper you would be mindful to hide the knick-knacks.

Like Oscar Wilde, who famously used his last breath to criticise the wall-covering, Mrs Gereth is no fan of wallpaper.[48] Nor does she approve of the 'trumpery ornament and scrapbook art, with strange excrescences and bunchy draperies, with gimcracks that might have been keepsakes for maid-servants and nondescript conveniences that might have been prizes for the blind', with which the Brigstocks have 'smothered' the interior of their home. (It seems Mrs Gereth and Philip Bosinney are on the same page, so to speak, with regard to 'gimcracks'.) She also accuses the family of having gone 'wildly astray over carpets and curtains', having 'an infallible instinct for gross deviation' and being 'so cruelly doom-ridden that it rendered them almost tragic'.

Breathless at the shock of it all, we have in contrast the Gereth home, Poynton, and its more elegant charms, collected over twenty-six years of marriage by Mrs Gereth and her deceased husband. Her strong aesthetic sensibility is a burden she must bear, in that 'thanks to the rare perfection of Poynton', and having lived 'in such warm closeness with the beautiful', she was 'condemned to wince wherever she turned'. A cruel fate, indeed. She believes that 'nothing in England' compares to Poynton, that although 'there were places much grander and richer', there was 'no such complete work of art'.[49] And it was all going to be lost: 'She would have to give up Poynton, and give it up to a product of Waterbath – that was the wrong that rankled . . . '[50]

Mrs Gereth's horror is not without cause. In James's particular brand of realism there are always complications bubbling beneath the surface of the practical and plausible. Although Mrs Gereth is ridiculous (albeit entertaining), her soon-to-be daughter-in-law, Mona Brigstock, *is* wholly without taste, and we can sympathise with the discomfort of ceding her control of Poynton. When Mona decides the house should have a winter garden, Fleda Vetch, Mrs Gereth's friend and ally, can only imagine 'something glazed and piped, on iron pillars, with untidy plants and cane sofas'. Fleda worries that this will be akin to the conservatory at Waterbath, where she 'had caught a bad cold in the company of a stuffed cockatoo fastened to a tropical bough and a waterless fountain composed of shells stuck into some hardened paste'. Mona also wants a billiard room, which Fleda foresees with equal horror 'would have, hung on its walls [...] caricature-portraits of celebrities taken from a "society paper"'.[51] It is the devastating equivalent of 'footballers' wives' doing up Chatsworth.

The humour begins to abate after Mrs Gereth has agreed to retire to her allotted cottage in the country, but, alas, she has connived to take the most valuable furnishings of Poynton with her. She is convinced to give them back, however, distraught as Owen weds the tasteless Mona. In a scene familiar to most readers of 'house fiction', our last vision of Poynton is of a house in the process of burning to the ground. Mrs Gereth is not suspected of taking revenge, Mrs Danvers-style; rather, the blaze is blamed on something much more prosaic, 'some rotten chimley or one of them portable lamps set down in the wrong place'.[52] However, if familial relations had a hand, all of the players are to blame.

While James never acknowledged a model for Poynton, he did, rather nastily, name his inspiration for the uncouth Waterbath as 'hideous' 'Fox Warren', in Surrey.[53] A model of Victorian Gothic, with patterned brick and crow-stepped gables, Foxwarren Park calls to mind the houses built by John Galsworthy, Sr, in Kingston. It is full of ornamental details that would offend the finer aesthetic sensibilities of both Mrs Gereth and Philip Bossiney. But if Poynton was a symbol for an excess of aesthetic devotion, then Mrs Gereth is to be condemned, like Gilbert Osmond, for her focus on material beauty over human feeling. And yet, though he shined a harsh light on these material concerns, James himself was not immune to the thrill of possession, particularly when it came to the acquisition of the only property he ever owned, Lamb House in Rye, East Sussex.

James lived in flats in London from the 1860s, first in Bolton Street, Piccadilly, then in De Vere Gardens, Kensington. He frequented the country houses of friends and often spent months out of London, travelling on the Continent or in places like Torquay, which became a common escape. But in 1895 he was offered the chance to rent a small cottage near Rye. The house was called Point Hill, and it was a small, run-down place that sat on a prominence offering a fine view.

James loved its peaceful atmosphere and inspiring prospect. In the preface to *The Spoils of Poynton*, he described how he sat writing on the 'small paved terrace' of this 'cottage on a cliffside', where he had taken himself to finish the book 'in quiet'.[54]

James would have liked to have had Point Hill for his own, but the owner wasn't selling. However, James had also fallen in love with the medieval town of Rye, and with a house set along one of its narrow, sloping streets. In 1897 he learned that Lamb House was available on a long lease and acted quickly to get it. He wrote to his friend, Arthur Benson: 'I am just drawing a long breath from having signed – a few moments since – a most portentous parchment: the lease of a smallish charming, cheap old house in the country.' He carries on, 'It is exactly what I want and secretly, hopelessly coveted', and has 'a beautiful room for you (the "King's Room" – George II's – who slept there).'[55] Lamb House actually had two guest rooms, so that now, finally, he could *host* guests instead of forever *being* one. James planned to spend the months of May to October there, returning in winter to his flat in DeVere Gardens, which had been recently refurbished with new paint and wallpaper, as well as electric light, a development that he was extremely delighted with.[56] But as Lamb House became more of a base, James sold the lease of the Kensington flat and settled in at Rye.

Built in the 1720s in a subdued, early Georgian style, Lamb House is a plain block of red brick, with a garden charmingly secreted behind a brick wall off the winding cobblestone street. An airy 'garden room' once faced onto the street and was dubbed the 'Temple of the Muse' by James, who was particularly fond of it. It had two writing desks: one for the author and another for his secretary. He also had a staff of four, who lodged on the top floor.[57] It can be seen in Mr Langdon's 'square, red-footed' house in *The Awkward Age*, in 'the impressions of a particular period that it takes two centuries to produce'. Here, James completed the three late masterpieces: *The Wings of the Dove*, *The Ambassadors*, and *The Golden Bowl*, and he found himself tremendously content, despite the constant worry of earning enough to sustain it. 'All the little land is lovely roundabout,' he wrote. It was 'an adorable corner of the wicked earth'. As the world seemed to be growing more wicked around him, James expressed himself in ways that channelled Mrs Gerther's sense of still beauty: 'Only Lamb House is mild; only Lamb House is sane; only Lamb House is true.'[58]

On a visit back to the country of his birth in 1904–5, after an absence of twenty years, James noted some of the many changes to 'the American Scene'.* In New York he wrote of the skyscrapers 'standing up to the view . . . like extravagant pins in a cushion already overplanted'. This was the architecture of 'economic ingenuity', and the 'thousand glass eyes of these giants of the mere market' had no appeal for the author.[59] Nor was he enamoured of a new style of interior design that seemed to be taking over, 'the universal custom of the house with almost no one of its indoor parts distinguishable from any other'. In other words, James didn't like rooms that lacked specific character or adhered to modern ideas of

---

* The title of the collected essays from this visit.

uniformity or, heaven forbid, anything approaching open-plan living spaces.

But James's objections were not wholly to do with a stodgy resistance to change. In his notoriously roundabout prose, he worried what such interiors would do to human interaction, offering fewer spaces for discreet chats or the odd tryst. In 'the indefinite extension of all spaces and the definite merging of all functions', he foresaw more than stylistic aggravation and fretted over 'the play of social relation' that was not now possible to conduct in such places 'at any other pitch than the pitch of a shriek or a shout'.[60] Both James and Galsworthy, in their distinct but similarly genteel approaches, ascribed spiritual and social value to the aesthetics of architecture, an argument that would inflame urban theorists throughout Europe in the decades to come.

Talland House

NINE

Rooms of Her Own:
Virginia Woolf's Houses of Memory

'We could fancy that we were but coming home . . . & that when we
reached the gate at Talland House, we should thrust it open, & find
ourselves among the familiar sights again . . .'

The Diaries of Virginia Woolf, 11 August 1905

In 1905, ten years after their mother died, eight years since the
death of their half-sister Stella, eighteen months since their
father had also passed away, and a little over a year after she
herself had made her first attempt at suicide by throwing herself out a window, Virginia Stephen and her siblings made a
pilgrimage.[1] Aged from twenty-two to twenty-six, Vanessa,
Thoby, Virginia and Adrian had recently embarked on an
unconventional living arrangement in London that would give
rise to the legendary Bloomsbury Group of artists and intellectuals. But on this trip they were taking a journey back in
time, to the place where they had spent thirteen idyllic summers as a family. In 1881 their father, the eminent critic and
biographer Leslie Stephen, had discovered Talland House in St
Ives, Cornwall, on one of his many walking expeditions. It
was a three-storey detached house sat on a hill overlooking
Porthminster Beach, with Godrevy Lighthouse visible in the

distance, and from then on, from July to September each year, Stephen installed his large family and an array of guests in the airy seaside house, which would become a touchstone for his youngest daughter's art.

For Virginia Woolf, certain houses were of huge importance and for specific reasons. Her first home in Kensington came to represent the Victorian enigma that she would battle against in her life and writing, while Talland House was a childhood idyll that would inspire her throughout her life. The independent and relaxed lifestyle she was able to pursue in various residences in Bloomsbury gave her the mental space and courage to produce the experimental novels that are her defining achievement. And, finally, the retreat that she and her husband Leonard Woolf had at Monk's House in East Sussex gave her the opportunity to recreate some of the atmosphere that she loved so well of those early days at Talland House, while having private space for herself and a continual stream of family friends, whom she liked to see 'dotted about on the estate'.

It wasn't just the houses themselves that Woolf prized, but the lives that inhabited them. In her childhood and young adulthood, her life was spent in rooms filled not only with a large family, but also with a parade of relatives, her father's scholarly colleagues and her parents' artistic friends. As an adult writer, she was at the centre of a lively social and artistic group that often congregated in her living room or around the dining table. The houses of her past became imaginative constructions that safeguarded scenes and figures from her life, many of whom were taken from her in her youth. Opening the doors to a house in her memory brought back the people who had filled its rooms, their voices and their habits, and helped her to bring them alive in her fiction.

Much of Woolf's fiction reflects this association between characters and houses, but it was in her second novel, *Jacob's Room* (1922), that she began to describe the power of interiors to shape and hold memory. As she experimented further with form and prose style in *Mrs Dalloway* (1925), she carried on exploring how individual lives, with their sorrows and elations, could be imprinted in a room. And in what is arguably one of the greatest modernist novels, *To the Lighthouse* (1927), she revisited the Talland House of her childhood, and allowed the ghosts of her parents, siblings and others to reappear in that treasured setting. It was an act of autobiographical catharsis that also helped to lay some of these ghosts to rest.

Born into England's 'cultural aristocracy', Adeline Virginia Stephen was the daughter of an eminent man of letters and a woman who was in her youth associated with (and served as a model for) the Pre-Raphaelite artists. As a member of the Bloomsbury Group and publisher of new writers through the Hogarth Press, she was at the forefront of the modernist movement in England. Her literary output was formidable: she wrote nine novels, many short stories and biographies, and was a gifted essayist and perceptive critic. All her life she struggled with periods of mental illness that left her bedridden for weeks at a time or were treated by cruel periods of isolation. Yet she was also a highly social person, who, like her parents, enjoyed entertaining friends in her own home.

Her first residence was the Stephen family home in the Hyde Park Gate area of London, where she lived until the age of twenty-two, when her father died. As her nephew and biographer Quentin Bell described it, the house 'had five storeys and to these the Stephens added two further storeys of atrocious design'.[2] These additions were to accommodate the eight children plus servants who eventually lived there. The significance of the house for Woolf was its utter Victorian-ness, from its dark, over-stuffed interiors to the punctiliousness of its routines. In her essay 'A Sketch of the Past', she explains that the house 'in 1900 was a complete model of Victorian society'. Selecting any single day from that year, she said, 'would extract a section of the upper middle class Victorian life, like one of those sections with glass covers in which ants and bees are shown going about their tasks'.[3] There were some hours when 'Victorian society did not exert any special pressure upon us', but then, at 'about half past four', 'the pressure of society made itself apparent as soon as the bell rang'.[4] The maid, in her afternoon dress ('black with a white apron'), would announce the first visitor and the Stephen girls would be expected to make themselves amenable to an array of characters.

These characters would be seated on one side of the 'black folding doors' that divided the drawing room. The doors were 'picked out with thin lines of raspberry red', Woolf explains, as 'we were still much under the influence of Titian'. She also recalls 'mounds of plush, Watts' portraits, busts shrined in crimson velvet, enriched the glow of a room naturally dark and thickly shaded in summer by showers of Virginia Creeper'. Her adult preference for 'sunny' rooms, like those in Bloomsbury and at Monk's House, is understandable. The folding doors have particular significance: 'How could family life have been carried on without them?' Woolf describes how a crisis might be happening on one side of the doors: 'A servant dismissed, a lover rejected . . . or poor Mrs Tyndall who had lately poisoned her husband by mistake come for consolation . . . Mrs Dolmetsch would be telling how she had found her husband in bed with the parlour-maid.' However, the other side of the door 'especially on Sunday afternoons, was cheerful enough. There round the oval tea table with its pink china shell full of spice buns would be found old General Beadle, talking of the Indian Mutiny; or Mr Haldane, or Sir Frederick Pollock – talking of all things under the sun.'[5]

She might baulk at the formalities of Victorian social interactions (and recoil from her elder half-brother's attempts to bring her 'out' into society), but in a more relaxed environment Woolf was eager to be among people. Later, as a successful writer, she tried to reconcile her need both for people and for solitude:

This social side is very genuine in me. Nor do I think it reprehensible. It is a piece of jewellery I inherit from my mother – a joy in laughter, something that is stimulated, not selfishly wholly or vainly, by contact with my friends. And then ideas leap in me.[6]

Woolf found social interaction was crucial. As she became more successful in her solitary employment, these moments were her reward. 'Moreover, for my work now', she wrote in her diary in 1923, 'I want freer intercourse, wider intercourse – & now at 41, having done a little work, I get my wages partly in invitations.'[7] It was this social side, and the constant questioning of it, which had influenced the population and settings of her novels. Woolf's characters don't travel the satisfied social path of mistress of the house that we see both lampooned and aspired to in the novels of Jane Austen. If the world of a novel is a house, Austen's disinherited daughters at least know their way around the rooms and, most importantly, how to set them to rights. Compared to these character's, Woolf's men and women, struggling in a society broken up after the Great War, fumble from space to space, as if they aren't even sure where the furniture should go.

After their father's death in 1904, Vanessa Stephen decided to move herself and her siblings from the house in Kensington to somewhat less grand premises in Bloomsbury. It was a bold decision and one that was viewed with concern by the elder friends and members of the extended family, for whom Bloomsbury, despite being home to the cultural ballast of the British Museum and the British Library, suggested something rather more louche and liberal than the old guard found

Smith College Libraries

Talland House, Cornwall, *c.* 1882–94, the summer residence of the Stephen family from 1881 until 1894, just before Virginia's mother, Julia, died.

appropriate. It was also cheaper, so their limited inheritance could go much further. Still, for women at this time to be living without the guiding influence of a parent or guardian was very unusual; for young adults of the Stephens' social group, it was more than a little unconventional.

The family house at Hyde Park Gate sat near the end of a quiet cul-de-sac, running south from the park. This area of London was associated with the elite segment of the upper middle classes and its houses inhabited by those with an ingrained sense of propriety. Houses ranged around Hyde Park like sentinels of an antique guard. It is worth noting that all of the older generation of siblings in John Galsworthy's *Forsyte Saga* have large houses here, from where, dressed in morning suits, top hats, ballooning crinolines and outmoded hairpieces, they battle to preserve their rigid Victorian standards against the onslaught of the modern era.

Bloomsbury was not exactly an impoverished neighbourhood, but it was a world away from the old establishment of Kensington. Here were workshops and artists' studios. Rather than houses and neighbourhoods orientated towards a single great park, Bloomsbury was (and still is) laid out as a series of garden squares, which made each a more communal experience than looking onto the vast avenues and expanse of Hyde Park. Gordon Square (where the Stephen children went to live) and Tavistock Square (where Woolf later lived with Leonard) were laid out as a pair by the architect Thomas Cubitt in the 1820s.* These houses retain some of the grand

---

* After Vanessa married Clive Bell in 1907, Virginia and Adrian moved to 29 Fitzroy Square. In 1911, they moved to Brunswick Square, where they kept a sort of 'lodging house' for friends including John Maynard Keynes, Duncan Grant and Leonard Woolf.

features of the earlier period, such as tall windows and generously proportioned rooms with high ceilings, and a neoclassical elegance, with their flat fronts rendered in cool white. The feeling of these squares is a certain airy grace, helped by those luxuriant trees that Woolf loved so well.

The move to Bloomsbury constituted a drastic change in lifestyle, opening Woolf's eyes to a freer way of living, unconstrained by the obstacles of Hyde Park Gate: there was to be no folding door, literally or metaphorically, here. Firstly, the siblings surrounded themselves with a younger artistic and scholarly set. The Bloomsbury Group began with Thoby Stephen hosting 'Thursday nights', casual, intellectual salons at their house in Gordon Square. In addition to his sisters and brother, the group consisted of Thoby's friends from Cambridge (and their friends), including Lytton Strachey, Duncan Grant, John Maynard Keynes, Clive Bell, E. M. Forster and Roger Fry. All were aspiring and opinionated, and, sprawled on sofas and chairs talking until 3 a.m., none practised the niceties of the Victorian drawing room or the rigid separation of the sexes. 'We were going to do without table napkins,' Woolf describes their sort of Bloomsbury manifesto later on. 'We were going to paint; to write; to have coffee after dinner instead of tea at nine o'clock.'[8] It may not sound like much of a revolution, but it was: 'Everything was going to be new; everything was going to be different. Everything was on trial.' It was a Rubicon moment: 'the gulf we crossed between Kensington & Bloomsbury was the gulf between respectable mummified humbug & life crude & impertinent perhaps, but living'.[9]

That the group became associated with the place, Bloomsbury, is significant not only because the phrase has become cultural shorthand for a certain elite bohemianism, but also in the way that places were significant for the author and her writing. The house was physically lighter and brighter than her childhood home, which was especially important to Woolf, who later wrote that 46 Gordon Square 'in October 1904 was the most beautiful, the most exciting, the most romantic place in the world . . . The light and the air after the rich red gloom of Hyde Park Gate were a revelation.'[10] The Stephen sisters also carried out a decorative revolution, eschewing the 'red plush and black paint' of their former home. Instead of 'Morris wall-papers with their intricate patterns', the walls were decorated 'with washes of plain distemper. We were full of experiments and reforms.'

Unlike Galsworthy, Woolf never made those non-traditional design details part of her novels. She happily broke with Victorian expectations as she immersed herself in a new lifestyle in Bloomsbury, but did not recreate that break in the physical spaces of her fiction. However, it is easy to understand how these new, comparatively freewheeling experiences – the open debates with men and women, the liberty to use her own judgement about when to eat, sleep, have 'company' – helped give her the confidence to experiment with her own creative vision. Woolf would later famously write that a woman needs 'money and a room of her own in order to write fiction'. Now she had both and set out to write, first as a reviewer for the *Guardian* and the *Times Literary Supplement*, then as a young novelist. In her Bloomsbury quarters we find a scene that has become iconic, spare furnishings draped in her mother's shawls and, in Woolf's top-floor rooms, piles of books visible through a haze of cigarette smoke.

In 1912–13, just after completing her first novel, *The Voyage Out*, Woolf experienced one of the several serious episodes of emotional breakdown that punctuated her life. In response to doctors' orders for quiet and rest, her new husband decided to take his wife away from London. They spent nine years at Hogarth House in Richmond, then a village surrounded by verdant parkland at the southern reaches of the city. It is the house where Virginia Woolf recovered her health and where she and Leonard set up the Hogarth Press, another achievement that bears the stamp of a house. The press (for which they learned to set their own type) turned into a successful literary imprint, and its first full-length book publication was *Jacob's Room*.

By the time she married, Virginia Stephen had already made two attempts to find a retreat that compared with the summer house of her childhood. She rented a small house near the South Downs, which she dubbed 'Little Talland', followed by a larger house nearby at Ashesham. Finally, in 1919, she and Leonard purchased their own country residence, Monk's House, a cottage in the village of Rodmell, East Sussex. 'That shall be our address for ever and ever,' she wrote, after they paid £700 at auction for the house. 'Indeed I've already marked out our graves in the yard which joins our meadow.'[11] While Hogarth House had given her a place to restore herself and, in the Hogarth Press, something to focus on while she regained her strength and confidence, Monk's House was a writer's sanctuary. It was also conveniently located, a bicycle ride away from Vanessa's lively household at Charleston.

By 1920, having settled at Monk's House, Woolf was able to write: 'I'm planning to begin *Jacob's Room* next week with

Virginia Stephen with her parents, Julia and Leslie Stephen, at Talland House, *c.* 1893.

luck.'[12] It was the first novel begun since being besieged by illness after completing *The Voyage Out*. For this work, she would draw on her own deeply felt connections with the past and show the power of familiar interiors to evoke, even briefly revive, the dead, at least within the pages of a novel. Published in the same year as James Joyce's pioneering modernist masterpiece, *Ulysses*, and T. S. Eliot's fractured, multi-conscious elegy, *The Waste Land*, *Jacob's Room* was Woolf's first experimental novel. She used a similar stream-of-consciousness technique to Joyce's, so the narrative drifts from the thoughts and impressions of one character to another, as it presents the portrait of a young man, Jacob Flanders. The story was a remembrance of Thoby, who had died young, though not in the war, and of their friend, the poet Rupert Brooke, who had succumbed to an infection while on his way to fight in Gallipoli.

The novel is an impressionistic record of scenes from Jacob's life as he grows from child to adult. We see the small boy hunting crabs on the beach, the young man fretting over his early love affairs, and the budding intellectual surrounded by friends at Cambridge. We get a glimpse of Woolf's feeling for the connection between people and buildings when Jacob sees himself in relation to his surroundings and feels 'a sense of old buildings and time; and himself the inheritor'.[13] Of the many continuities broken by the Great War, one was the link to such places. Jacob's line of inheritance is ruptured with his death; he will not keep or pass on anything to future generations. The careful description of his empty room tells us this.

And yet it is languidly charged with the physical presence of Jacob and his friends, with the sting of their youthful banter, the sincerity of learned discussion, the scrape of a chair. In the absence of the young men who have gone off to war – and, as in Jacob's case, to die – the room projects the aching atmosphere of loss: 'Listless is the air in an empty room, just swelling the curtain; the flowers in the jar shift. One fibre in the wicker arm-chair creaks, though no one sits there.'[14] The benign ghosts from the rooms of Woolf's own memories are there and would continue to appear in her work, as she struggled to reconcile her sense of living in the present with her intense feeling for the past and the lives of the dead.

In 1910 E. M. Forster published *Howards End* (see chapter 7), a novel whose abiding exhortation was 'only connect', drawing person to person to the land, and the countryside to the house, which held something like a promise to endure. Fifteen years later Woolf produced *Mrs Dalloway*, her masterpiece of post-war alienation and dread. By 1923 Woolf felt well enough, and eager, to live once more in London. She and Leonard left Hogarth House and returned to Bloomsbury, taking rooms at 52 Tavistock Square as their London residence. It was while out walking in her old neighbourhood that she conceived of the idea of *Mrs Dalloway*. Perhaps it was a sign of regaining her mental strength that she felt able to take on the shadows and idylls of her past and to contemplate new stylistic methods in which to render them.

The novel's heroine, Clarissa Dalloway, is the admired Edwardian society hostess whose movements through a London day take the reader backward to her past and abruptly forward to the present, moving laterally to the minds of other characters as they contemplate what it is to feel urgently connected to a brief moment, but also what it is to be alone. The stream-of-consciousness prose parades thoughts, feelings, actions, one after the other, in a flow that the reader must disentangle, or wade through, immersed in the mental processing of each experience. In common with Sterne's Dr Slop from *Tristram Shandy*, Woolf's characters in *Mrs Dalloway* and, later, *To the Lighthouse*, all have minds that can accommodate a flotilla of thoughts 'without sail or ballast'.[15] Through her vibrant, near-giddy impressions of the view from the top of the omnibus, the smell and distinct colour of flowers, the icy quality of the white clouds, Woolf makes the day a tenderly felt thing. The climax, we know from the first page, will be Clarissa's party in the evening. Though some criticise her parties as shallow affairs, Clarissa sees them as 'an offering', bringing people together in the present. And yet, like Woolf's, her thoughts are constantly intruded upon by memories of another house and people from days long ago.

The grand elegance of the Dalloway house, located some-where near Victoria Street in Westminster, is a symbol of the couple's wealth and social position, and was probably mod-elled on 33 Cromwell Road in Knightsbridge. This was the home of Kitty Maxse (née Lushington), an old family friend and socialite whose engagement in the garden of Talland House was overheard and gossiped about by the Stephen chil-dren. Woolf later fell out with Kitty, but her role as popular society hostess probably inspired the character of Clarissa Dalloway.*

Although the focus of the party is the Dalloway mansion, it is the captivating nostalgia of the summer house at Bourton that looms over and links several of the disparate characters to each other. Like Woolf, Clarissa is easily drawn to thoughts of her family's holiday home. In the first lines of the story, a squeaking door hinge triggers the memory of another morn-ing there that was as 'fresh as if issued to children on a beach'. And then, 'What a lark! What a plunge!', as she becomes caught up in the reverie of Bourton, how 'with a little squeak of the hinges', as she has just heard, 'she had burst open the French windows and plunged into the open air'.[16] It is a joyful opening passage, a bright glimpse of pure, sensual delight, and it suggests Woolf's own deeper associations with Talland House.

There is also in *Mrs Dalloway* the satisfaction, if not delight, of making connections between people. 'Here was So-and-so in South Kensington; some one up in Bayswater; and somebody else say in Mayfair,' Clarissa thinks, and she

---

* Kitty Maxse died in 1922 after falling over the banisters in her home. Some suspected suicide.

finds it 'a waste' and 'a pity' that they are separated.[17] So she brings them together under one roof, as Woolf's parents had done at Talland House and in Kensington. But Clarissa also crosses temporal boundaries, feeling past lives in the present. Houses could help keep those connections palpable, as Woolf would demonstrate in *To the Lighthouse*.

While the Victorian constraints of Hyde Park Gate gave Virginia Woolf something to run away *from* and Bloomsbury gave her a place to run *to*, Talland House had a pervasive talismanic charm, formed from a time before the deaths of so many family members and before the bouts of madness that would threaten her sense of self and creativity for the rest of her life. Those early experiences in St Ives offered more than a

The Stephen children went to live at no. 46 Gordon Square in Bloomsbury in 1904, where 'everything was going to be new; everything was going to be different'.

pleasing nostalgia. The memories of thirteen summers perme-
ated Woolf's aesthetic vision, and her abiding sense of the
significance and frightening fragility of human relationships –
relationships that did not necessarily end with death. It also
gave her a familiar setting in her imagination to locate those
people who had gone from her, when just keeping them in her
memory was too difficult or unsatisfying.

In her 1939 essay 'A Sketch of the Past', Woolf revisited
some of her early memories at Talland House, impressions
that set herself and the people she loved firmly in its frame.
The front of the house faced the sea and had two squared
porticoes enclosed in glass, with French windows opening
onto steps down to the lawn. These were topped with pretty
little balconies to the rooms above and the whole nearly covered in rampant vines running up the walls, which shaded
much of the light into the drawing room. She described the
nursery: 'It had a balcony; there was a partition, but it joined
the balcony of my father's and mother's bedroom'. She
remembered there were 'passion flowers growing on the wall;
they were great starry blossoms, with purple streaks, and
large green buds, part empty, part full'. In these moments, or
in her recollections of them, Woolf began to develop her imaginative visual sense: 'If I were a painter I should paint these
first impressions in pale yellow, silver, and green.'[18]

Quentin Bell wrote of his aunt that Cornwall was 'the Eden
of her youth, an unforgettable paradise'. Like Monk's House,
it was no luxury retreat, but its emotive allure was potent.
And life there was often social. As Bell describes the house, it
'was shabby and casual', and often 'untidy and overrun with
people . . . cousins, uncles, nephews, nieces'.[19] Henry James

was a regular visitor, as was the American ambassador James Russell Lowell (who was also Virginia's godfather), and other scholars, painters and philosophers came to visit. As with the strange assemblage at the Ramsay residence in *To the Lighthouse*, these people were added to a household already burgeoning with children and servants: in addition to the four children they had together, Leslie Stephen already had one daughter when he married the young widow Julia Duckworth, who had a daughter and two sons.

Talland House, being of modest size, was probably full of 'life' in the sense that Clarissa Dalloway liked so well. Above the bedrooms and balconies was a mansard-style top floor. The rooms here were probably less finished. Thin plank room dividers, like those described in the Ramsay house, are certainly likely: 'A plank alone separated from each other so that every footstep could be plainly heard and the Swiss girl [a servant] sobbing for her father who was dying of cancer in the valley of the Grisons.'[20] In an early scene that conveys the feeling of people living literally on top of one another, and somewhat reminiscent of Mr Shandy in his parlour, Mrs Ramsay hopes that the too-serious scholar Mr Tansley will not 'bang his books on the floor above [the children's] heads'. Woolf recalled hearing her father, whose study was on the top floor of their Kensington house, dropping his books on the floor. Years before writing *To the Lighthouse*, she recorded in her diary the sensation of knowing another man of letters was upstairs. T. S. Eliot, whose work she greatly admired and whom she had campaigned to help support so that he could quit his banking job and write poetry full time, had come to visit Woolf and Leonard at Monk's House. 'Eliot is separated only by the floor from me,'[21] she wrote with some satisfaction. She wasn't worried about him dropping his books, but she was pleased with his nearness under her roof.

On the eve of another trip to Cornwall in 1921, Woolf asks herself: 'Why am I so incredibly & incurably romantic about Cornwall?' Her answer is 'one's past, I suppose: I see children running in the garden. A spring day. Life so new. People so enchanting. The sound of the sea at night.'[22] Photographs from that earlier time show the family gathered around the steps, setting up for games or sitting in the drawing room with their mother at the centre; a Morris-style paper covers the walls and the faces wear sombre looks. Such serious posture was the practice in photographs of the period, but for later viewers these faces seem to portend the tragic cycle of premature death that will touch first their mother, then their eldest half-sister, Stella, then Thoby, and the periods of madness and imposed isolation (part of the 'rest cure' prescribed for Virginia's illness) that would plague the writer in their aftermath.

It is no wonder her recollections of Talland House have such a mournful tone, yet they were vital threads to a past that Woolf would pluck for soundings of 'moods, memories'. She wondered whether 'things we have felt with great intensity have an existence independent of our minds; are in fact still in existence', and she sought to recapture them in a physical space.[23] It took a number of years of writing before she was able to pull those memories into a coherent creative form.

To the Lighthouse is set in a summer house, though the location is the Isle of Skye, rather than Cornwall. Writing it, the author said, helped to exorcise some of the ghosts she had learned to live with: 'I ceased to be obsessed by my mother. I no longer hear her voice; I do not see her.'[24] In fact, she considered calling *To the Lighthouse* an elegy, steeped as it was in the conditions and emotions of a lost time. Like Waugh's *Brideshead Revisited*, the novel contains a past, which, although it is a somewhat tarnished idyll, is still mourned in the present. In Woolf's novel, as in Waugh's, it isn't just personal losses that are grieved for, but the breakup of the notional 'world' caused by the war and human failure.

The war has happened in the intervening years between the two visits to the summer home that make up the main parts of the novel. In the first section, the rooms of the Ramsays' holiday home are filled with family, friends and near strangers, an assortment of shabby wits and flawed intellectuals like some of those who visited the Stephen family in St Ives or in Hyde Park Gate. Recalling some of the 'great figures' who stood in the background of her childhood, Woolf noted, in addition to Henry James, 'Watts, Burne-Jones, Sidgwick, Haldane, Morley'.*[25] The Ramsays' house guests similarly enrich the interiors with their intellects, hopes and foibles, their stuttering attempts at love or just at common understanding.

As with *Mrs Dalloway*, the two main sections of the novel are tense with the yearnings of people who are desperate to be understood or simply loved by others whose emotions and perceptions are disappointed or otherwise engaged. The painter Lily Briscoe says that the Ramsays' summer home 'was a house full of unrelated passions' Yet they *are* related, painfully so, though they are not often in sync.[26] Also written

---

* Artists George Frederic Watts and Edward Burne-Jones; philosopher and economist Henry Sidgwick; Daniel Rutherford Haldane, president of the Royal College of Physicians, Edinburgh; and John Morley, editor of *English Men of Letters*.

in Woolf's own stream-of-consciousness style, *To the Lighthouse* is an impressionistic rendering, built up of layers of emotion, as Lily Briscoe (or, indeed, Vanessa Bell) might layer colours: some blending, others jarring. The point of view drifts from one character to another without any hard barriers between consciousnesses, again 'offering' that tantalising possibility of connections, that minds, emotions, thoughts might stray towards one another like eager but abashed children. Mr Ramsay epitomises this longing for shared intimacy as he searches, arms outstretched, for his dead wife. The large home filled with family and guests acts as a sort of alembic, into which Woolf poured her disconnected characters and observed as they bounced from one to another, like atoms failing to collide and then fusing into some sort of understanding.

The Ramsay house is probably larger than Talland House, big enough for a family of ten, plus six house guests, two of whom, like Kitty Lushington and Leo Maxse, will become engaged before the visit is over. Like the Stephen children, the Ramsay offspring are accustomed to a house full of visitors: 'The eight sons and daughters of Mr and Mrs. Ramsay sought their bedrooms, their fastnesses in a house where there was no other privacy to debate anything, everything; Tansley's tie; the passing of the Reform Bill; sea-birds and butterflies; people; while the sun poured into those attics.' In the attic rooms, the slanting sun also lights up an array of children's summertime paraphernalia – 'bats, flannels, straw hats, ink-pots, paint-pots, beetles, and the skulls of small birds' – which were probably all drawn from life. There is a vivid summery air, from the 'seaweed pinned to the wall a smell of salt and weeds, which was in the towels too, gritty with sand from bathing'.[27] So the elements of an ideal childhood summer are posted round the room, as they must have been for the Stephen children. But then, as in life, a mournful interlude breaks the spell of ordinary anticipation.

Woolf described the novel's shape as an 'H'. In the middle section – the bridge of the 'H' – the family is set to return after an absence of ten years. But, as with the Stephen family, the Ramsays suffer a series of untimely deaths. Mrs Ramsay's sudden passing is relayed succinctly in brackets: '(Mr Ramsay stumbling along a passage stretched his arms out one dark morning . . .).' But as Mrs Ramsay has died suddenly the night before, his arms 'remained empty'.[28] As Stella and Thoby

The living room at Monk's House, Virginia and Leonard's summer house in East Sussex. 'That shall be our address for ever and ever.'

were now absent from Woolf's life, the Ramsay's son Andrew has been killed in the war and their daughter Prue has died in childbirth.

In these pages, as in *Jacob's Room*, Woolf wants to show the spirit of past life through the objects and atmosphere of a deserted room. She was, she explained, trying 'to give an empty house . . . the passage of time, all eyeless and featureless with nothing to cling to'.[29] All of the characters were present in the first part of the novel, and most of the visitors return for the last, but in the middle section, the house is empty, abandoned to the 'airs' that creep through, touching on a flap of wallpaper here, a stair tread there, a chest of drawers, enumerating domestic details that are so mundanely familiar, triggering feelings of both comfort and loss:

> So with the house empty and the doors locked and the mattresses rolled round, those stray airs . . . blustered in, brushed bare boards, nibbled and fanned, met . . . only hangings that flapped, wood that creaked, the bare legs of tables, saucepans and china already furred, tarnished, cracked. What people had shed and left – a pair of shoes, a shooting cap, some faded skirts and coats in the wardrobes.[30]

The Ramsay family and their guests return in the latter chapters, with Mr Ramsay determined to make the trip to the lighthouse. It was an adventure that had not been allowed years ago, owing to bad weather and Mr Ramsay's intransigence. In the boat, he and his daughter Cam look back towards land, trying to pick out their house on the shore. It is a familiar exercise, that squinting to locate a spot of familiarity in a distant landscape. 'See the little house?' Mr Ramsay asks, but Cam 'could no longer make out which was their house. All looked distant and peaceful and strange.'[31]

When Woolf was a child, it probably was possible to see Talland House from the water, sitting up on the hill above Porthminster Beach. And it is still possible to watch the boats on the water from its sloped garden, and to see in the distance the white spike of Godrevy Lighthouse, whose visitor book recorded two visits from the Stephen family and one signature from Woolf.*

In 1894 the news that a hotel was going to be built, obstructing the view of the sea, prompted Leslie Stephen to announce that it would probably be the family's last summer in St Ives. Then Julia Stephen died in 1895, and the fate of summer holidays was decided. The family never again stayed at Talland House, and following her mother's death, Woolf experienced her first mental and emotional breakdown, aged fifteen.

When the Stephen children returned to Talland House in 1905, they didn't attempt to approach the new family living there, but instead peered through the hedge for a glimpse of their own shared past. In her diary, Woolf noted the 'two lighted windows' and the stone urns, 'there on the terrace . . . against the bank of tall flowers', like the urns Mr Ramsay walks around while reciting his lines from Tennyson (and like those at Bourton where Mrs Dalloway is kissed by Sally Seton all those years ago). She describes the familiar sensation of a long-abandoned place that feels 'as though we had

---

* The lighthouse visitor book containing Virginia's name and that of her father, brother and sister was sold by Bonham's auction house, London, in 2011.

but left it in the morning'. Yet however taken the Stephens are with the sight of their much-loved former home, they understand that 'if we advanced the spell was broken. The lights were not our lights; the voices were the voices of strangers. We hung there like ghosts in the shade of the hedge, & at the sound of footsteps we turned away.'[32]

In 'A Sketch of the Past', Woolf writes of what she says is 'her most important memory':

> lying half asleep, half awake, in bed in the nursery at St Ives. It is of hearing the waves breaking, one, two, one, two, and sending a splash of water over the beach; and then breaking, one two, one, two, behind a blind. It is of hearing the blind draw its little acorn across the floor as the wind blew the blind out . . . feeling the purest ecstasy I can conceive.[33]

As an adult, Woolf could no longer enter the house in real life, but she could roam freely in its rooms and garden in her imagination. She could once again populate it with characters from her past, who could rouse its sleepy frame to life. Like the ghost couple in her short story 'The Haunted House' (1921), Woolf could revisit the place of her former happiness in her own memory and mine it for moments of startling revelation or notions of the sublime.

At Monk's House, it seems Woolf had finally found her own version of the summer retreat of her childhood. As well as spending summer there, she and Leonard went for weeks at Easter, Christmas and at odd weekends. They had guests to stay, walked the fields and worked on their respective projects.

She proudly used income from her writing to improve the somewhat ramshackle residence, where mice roamed rather too freely, windows leaked and indoor plumbing was nonexistent. 'We are having the kitchen rebuilt at a cost of £80', she recorded in her diary on 26 May 1920.[34] On 10 August, she detailed her chores: 'I have spent the whole afternoon yellow washing the earth closet. I can now reckon up my labours: dining room distempered & cleaned; bannisters painted blue; stairs white'.[35] She would add an indoor toilet with the proceeds from *Mrs Dalloway* and a new bedroom after *To the Lighthouse*. Vita-Sackville West remarked on the couple's childlike delight with their new plumbing: 'They both run upstairs every now and then and pull the plug just for the sheer fun of it, and come down and say, "It worked very well that time – did you hear?"'[36] Owing to Leornard's occasionally prickly nature, Woolf playfully named his rooms on the first floor 'Hedgehog Hall'.[37]

Monk's House was not turned into the work of art that Vanessa had created at nearby Charleston, but it is still rich with colour and an eclectic array of personal objects. Woolf favoured a minty green hue for the sitting room and 'pomegranate' for the dining room.[38] She told Vanessa, 'I must now go and paint the house bright yellow.'[39] Vanessa and other Bloomsbury artists are also present in art and design. She and Duncan Grant designed the painted table and chairs bearing Woolf's initials in the sitting room, and Vanessa designed the painted tiles used for the fireplace surround in Woolf's bedroom, which was added to the side of the house in 1929. In homage to her most recent novel at the time, the central oval over the fire depicts a sailboat on a blue sea with a lighthouse in the background. The corner tile is inscribed 'VB to VW, 1930'. There are also several of Vanessa's paintings on the walls and some by her son Quentin Bell.

Having written to her friend Ka Cox in 1919 that the house 'has its charms' but 'also has a great many drawbacks', Woolf noted there was still work to be done: 'We shall have to alter it considerably, I'm afraid. Still I find that a sunny house is incredibly cheery.'[40] She was no stranger to home improvements, as she had lived through the extensions being built at Hyde Park Gate. 'To house the lot of us, now a storey would be thrown out on top,' she later explained, 'now a dining room flung out at bottom. My mother, I believe, sketched what she wanted on a sheet of notepaper to save the architect's fees.'[41]

After the first week at Monk's House, Woolf wrote to her sister: 'We are now more or less settled . . . We spend all of our time picking apples and pears, which we sell in the

Virginia Woolf's writing 'lodge' in the garden of Monk's House. She began writing her first really experimental novel, *Jacob's Room*, after moving here.

village.'[42] Indeed, Leonard became a keen gardener, hiring a full-time caretaker to help with the orchard, flowers and vegetable patches he cultivated. Their commitment to Monk's House was solid. By 1934 they had built the garden lodge for Woolf to write in. With its double-doors and brick patio, it was also a pleasant place to sit out on warm days with family and friends. The Woolfs did make Monk's House a place for bringing people together. Photographs from the 1920s and '30s show T. S. Eliot in the sitting room or kitchen, E. M. Forster in the garden and groups including Vanessa and her children, Maynard Keynes, Clive Bell and Duncan Grant playing on the bowling green or arranged on the little deck in front of the writing lodge in the garden.

In 'The Haunted House', a couple become aware of a ghostly man and wife searching their former home for something left behind. 'Here we left it,' the ghostly woman says, and her partner adds, 'Oh but here too!' 'It's upstairs,' she murmurs. 'And in the garden,' he whispers. And then we read, 'But they had found it in the drawing-room.' They are trying to discover a 'buried treasure' somewhere in the house. Finally, as the ghosts observe the living couple asleep together, the woman wakes and realises, 'Oh, is this your buried treasure? The light in the heart.'

It is the love between the woman and her husband, the 'light in the heart', that the ghosts have returned to reclaim from the rooms of the house. There it 'hung upon the walls, pendant from the ceiling' like a decorative element. Household objects resonate with emotional memory, as they did for Woolf in the summer cottage of her childhood, but also now at the funny little place called Monk's House.

Though Woolf had many productive years as a writer, ill-ness again crept up on her. After she drowned herself in 1941, her ashes were buried in the garden at Monk's. Leonard Woolf continued to live there until his own death in 1969. The house was then in the care of his companion Trekkie Parsons, after which it was owned by the University of Sussex. The American writer Saul Bellow is said to have stayed at the house during that period, and took a rather less good-natured view than the Woolfs did of the cold and damp.

Virginia Woolf was one of the most influential modernist writers in English. She produced pages teeming with vivid impressions and spiritual revelations, and presented characters spinning in wonder at the mysterious patterns of human rela-tions, as well as those struggling in anxious isolation. In her most successful and revelatory novels, she brought those char-acters together in rooms, where there was at least the possibil-ity of making meaningful connections. Far from being a character of anxiety and isolation herself, her great gift was the ability to revel in everyday moments of exultation, in which the senses are heightened, the heart uplifted by trees waving, a blossom forming, birdsong trilling or by the bright glimmer of common understanding. Some of the most affect-ing moments of Woolf's fiction are those bursts of spirit, as when Peter Walsh says 'this is happiness', when Lily Briscoe finds that instead of a great revelation there were 'little daily miracles, illuminations, matches struck unexpectedly in the dark; here was one'.[43]

For Woolf, many of these moments were sparked by people she loved and admired. She wanted Monk's House to be alive with such people, and sent a stream of invitations to friends and colleagues to come and visit. To Violet Dickinson she wrote: 'We've gone and bought a house down here, with a garden full of cabbages and roses . . . Perhaps one of these days you might step out of your motor at our door.'[44] For in all of the houses of past and present, it was the people who brought those moments that would blur from life and memory into art.

Madresfield Court

TEN

Inheritance and Loss:
War and the Great English Estates

'The builders did not know the uses to which their work would descend; they made a new house with the stones of the old castle; year by year, generation after generation, they enriched and extended it . . . until . . . the place was desolate and the work all brought to nothing; *Quomodo sedet sola civitas*. Vanity of vanities, all is vanity.'*

Brideshead Revisited, Epilogue

The wars of the twentieth century wreaked havoc on the cities, lands and populations of Europe and brought cultural turbulence in their wake. The change to the old order became not only inevitable, but also immediate. The elation of victory at the end of the Great War was quickly tempered by the horrific fallout of modern warfare, the loss of 850,000 British troops, and by soldiers who came home physically and mentally ravaged.[1] The realisation of the evils that one army was able to visit upon another made people question the very concept of humanity. Old certainties gave way to new doubts. The grand narratives – those stories, religious, folkloric and mythical, that helped to define our culture, gave shape to Brit-

---

* From *Lamentations 1*: 'How lonely sits the city/that was full of people! /How like a widow has she become, /She who was great among the nations! /She who was a princess among the provinces / has become a slave.'

ish life and underpinned our system of beliefs and interpreta-tion of the world – were called into question. Old systems were blown apart, along with the social order they supported. Against the background of grim wartime realities and social changes, one of the most significant symbolic shifts to the social system of Britain was the decline of the great country estates.

The necessity of raising funds for the war effort meant increases in tax. Where the highest tax rate in 1914 had been 6 per cent, by 1918 the standard rate of income tax had risen to 30 per cent.[2] And not only income was hit hard. Death duties were also raised, so that, to our latter-day astonish-ment, some owners of great estates preferred to demolish them, rather than risk bankruptcy in trying to pay the duties owed on them. Such opposed forces of imminent destruction and revered tradition hover like tousling spirits around Groby Hall of *Parade's End* and Brideshead Castle of *Brideshead Revisited*. Both formerly grand estates are crumbling wit-nesses to the change wrought by war and social revolution. And yet neither Ford Madox Ford nor Evelyn Waugh seem to blame their decline on the cost of conflict or social mobility. Rather, in a theme that Jane Austen might have approved, it is the behaviour of the inheritors, a disregard for tradition and manners, that signals their doom. In the words of Ford's biog-rapher Max Saunders, *Parade's End* stood for 'the fracture in English Society which both precipitated and was revealed by the war'.[3]

Busby Hall in Yorkshire, the real-life inspiration for Groby Hall, and Madresfield Court in Worcestershire, which pro-vided the social setting for Brideshead Castle, are both still standing, and they remain in the families who have owned them for centuries. Yet both are degraded in their fictional forms by authors who offer fearful warnings of destruction elsewhere and of worse to come. By 1975, when the Victoria and Albert Museum hosted the exhibition *The Destruction of the Country House*, a thousand of England's great houses had been destroyed in the previous hundred years. While the National Trust had stepped in to save what it could, the reality was that this now-extinct way of life was in danger of losing its most important artefact. The great houses were now deemed an important part of British heritage and worth fighting to save, if only as museums for an aristocratic lifestyle that has become perhaps more valued as something from a storied noble past. In the fiction of Ford and Waugh, the houses are symbols of that past and for a whole system of beliefs and values that produced them.

Both war-weary novels carry a melancholy theme of inheritance and loss, but the authors share other similarities. Both volunteered to serve during their respective World Wars at a time in life when they had achieved some literary notoriety and were substantially older than most of the men they commanded or served with (Ford was forty-one when he joined in 1915; Waugh was thirty-six in 1939). Consequently, both writers used the perspective of an older, wiser soldier to reflect on the changes in society and the rupture with the past. Both writers also proceeded from similarly cultured and erudite families, but Waugh had the means to take him through Oxford and beyond, whereas Ford had to earn a living from his writing early on, owing to the untimely death of his father. As young men they struck different courses. Waugh became enamoured of the upper social class, using his allowance and whatever other means to run with the 'Bright Young People', while Ford immersed himself in less glamorous, literary circles; his closest friend, Joseph Conrad, was as impecunious as he was. Despite their diverging paths, Ford and Waugh are comparable in another important aspect of their lives. They both developed intense friendships with men whose families were inheritors of great English estates, and these influenced their best-known work. Ford's friendship with Arthur Marwood of Busby Hall and Waugh's relationships with Hugh Lygon of Madresfield Court and Alastair Graham of Barford House in Warwickshire left profound and lasting impressions on their creative imaginations, which were expressed in a vision of a 'lost' tradition of the great English estate.

Arthur Marwood emerged in various guises in Ford's subsequent novels, culminating in the depiction of the emotionally thwarted squire of Groby in *Parade's End*, while Sebastian Flyte is a conflation of Hugh Lygon and Alastair Graham, with Brideshead taking many of its features and quondam rituals from the life and home of the Earl of Beauchamp's seat at Madresfield. In the novels, both Groby and Brideshead fall under the guardianship of members of the Catholic faith, an event that brings consternation to some of the characters and in the case of Brideshead, prevents Charles Ryder from marrying the Earl's daughter and becoming caretaker of the house he so adores. The struggle with the characters' Catholicism is another way that the writers signal the conflict between the old and the modern world. Each work is unique, of course, and distinct from the other in innumerable ways, but together they speak as a sort of requiem in time-lapsed harmony to the doomed life of the grand English country house.

At the opening of *Some Do Not*, the first novel in Ford's tetralogy *Parade's End*, Christopher Tietjens, a brilliant mathematician in the government's Department of Statistics, is resisting bureaucratic pressure to 'fake' numbers of British casualties so that the French will be compelled to provide more troops in support of the war. He is also facing the decision of whether to take back his estranged wife. The beautiful, charming Sylvia ran off to the Continent with her foppish lover and now, with unapologetic hauteur, has announced her intention of returning to live with her husband and son. Christopher describes himself as 'eighteenth-century', that is, standing for some antiquated chivalry, and holds great store in observing an old-fashioned code of gentlemanly conduct. His wife has openly made him a cuckold, but divorce is out of the question: for Sylvia, because she is Catholic, and for Christopher, because 'a gentleman does not divorce his wife'.[4] Sylvia, who is determined to 'torture' her husband for the sin of not desiring her in spite of her own betrayals, takes up his ruin with alacrity, a ruin that will find its ultimate expression in the destruction of Christopher's ancestral home, Groby.

Like most writers, Ford created characters and situations that were an agglomeration of real-life models, twined with creations that were wholly of his imagination. Nevertheless, the germ of some characters is easy to spot. Sylvia takes much from his first wife, Elsie Martindale, a Catholic, whom Ford married at the age of twenty. She was only seventeen at the time, and refused to divorce him when he left her some fifteen years later for the author and journalist Violet Hunt. (Like Sylvia, Elsie also sold Ford's furniture while he was away.) It was Hunt who followed Ford down to Sussex when, after having served in the war, he left her and began living with the Australian painter Stella Bowen. When, in the fourth novel, Sylvia spies on the invalid Mark Tietjens as he lies in a thatched shelter in his brother's West Sussex garden, Ford was probably recalling the way Hunt came to peer at him and Bowen over their own farmyard fence.

These behaviours, somewhat understandable in the women Ford loved and left, are rendered as obsessive hatred in Sylvia. More important, however, is the influence of Arthur Marwood, who was a member of Ford's intimate circle of friends until 1908 and was heir to Busby Hall in Yorkshire. In the early years of his marriage, Ford lived in Winchelsea, near Rye, a small town on the southeast coast of England. Here, he was near to Joseph Conrad, to his friend and later enemy H. G. Wells, to his sometime supporter Henry James, to the American author Stephen Crane, and to Marwood, a Yorkshire intellectual who had moved to Winchelsea to ease the discomforts of tuberculosis. It was his illness that prevented Marwood from taking over the stewardship of Busby Hall, which then had to fall to his brother.

Marwood helped Ford set up the *The English Review* in 1907, but also caused Ford to lose the editorship when he became entangled in Ford and Elsie's ugly separation and decided to withdraw himself and his funds from the enterprise. It was Marwood's intellect and bearing that Ford recreated in Christopher, as well as the loss of his place in the line of succession of his ancestral home. Busby Hall, still owned and inhabited by the Marwoods, a family who can trace their descent from Edward III, also captured Ford's literary and historic imagination. Recalling Marwood's 'encyclopaedic' intellect, Ford reminisced that there was 'nothing under the sun that we did not discuss and no topic on which he could not . . . correct my assertions'. Like Christopher Tietjens, Marwood had an almost mystical way with mathematics and 'possessed the clear, eighteenth century English mind which has disappeared from the earth, leaving the earth very much poorer'.[5]

This 'eighteenth-century mind' refers to Marwood's ability to organise and rationalise his knowledge, as well as to his reverence for a 'feudal' Toryism, a system of government, privilege and obligation tied to the land and landowners. This is a key trait that links Marwood not only to Busby, but also to the cultural continuum of the English estate system. When Christopher's older brother, Mark, admits that he does not want the bother and responsibility of Groby, he sees that 'he had let his own people down pretty badly', meaning the family *and* their tenants.[6] And while he didn't feel like bothering with 'those confounded, hardheaded beggars', he did believe that 'one owed the blighters a duty . . . it is obvious that a landlord owes something to the estate from which he and his fathers have drawn their income for generations and generations'.[7] It is a belief that Christopher also carries, one that leads, rather perversely, to his being labelled a socialist by his wife.

Asked whether he is indeed a socialist, as Sylvia has been putting about town, Christopher replies: 'Of course . . . if it's Sylvia that called me a Socialist, it's not astonishing. I'm a Tory of such an extinct type that she might take me for anything.'[8] This comment alone delivers much of Christopher's character: he is convinced it is a wife's right to judge her husband, and he believes in an ancient (and idealised) tradition of noble, paternalistic landowners, revered by tenants whom they, in turn, support, educate and protect. The image is not so different from that cultivated a hundred years earlier by Walter Scott. Ford often referred to Marwood's commitment to such ideals: in fact, the one piece of writing that Marwood produced for *The English Review* outlined a scheme of minimum pay and insurance protections for employees. (It was the only way, he argued, to avoid the threat of communism.)[9]

Ford said that as the conflict of the First World War ended, he 'wondered what he [Marwood, who died in 1916] would have thought of the war and the way it was conducted'.[10] Having already written some moderately successful historical fiction (including *The Fifth Queen* trilogy), in *Parade's End* (1924–8), Ford was reaching back to the more recent past to help explain a new era. But the past is no idyll. To illustrate the social divide clearly, Christopher explains to his young lover, the suffragette Valentine Wannop, that Groby has an avenue made by his great-great-grandfather, who 'liked privacy and didn't want the house visible by vulgar people on the road'.[11] Shortly after this exchange, he breaks down. His loss of composure is caused partly by the tenderness of Miss Wannop, partly because he has been rattled by an accident involving a horse he had been driving, but mainly for the realisation that the inheritance of his centuries-old family estate is endangered owing to the unscrupulous behaviour of his wife.

His only son is probably not his son, and, because 'all his brothers were childless', there would be no flesh-and-blood Tietjens heir to Groby.

Interestingly, although Groby is referred to many times in the tetralogy that makes up *Parade's End*, none of the real action takes place there (even the destruction is told of second-hand) and Ford provides little description. Not put off by this, the filmmakers of the 2012 BBC television adaptation set several scenes at Duncombe Park in North Yorkshire. Groby's value in the novels is heavily symbolic and deeply cultural, as a solemn inheritance and a weighty totemic link with the past. It is only natural that audiences would want to see it (or some representation). Like Busby Hall, Duncombe Park is an eighteenth-century house in Yorkshire, although its style is more ornate than Marwood's North Riding seat.

Like many parents, Christopher wants to commune with his

Duncombe Park, Helmsley, North Yorkshire. The mostly eighteenth-century, neo-classical stately home was the film location for Groby in the 2012 BBC television adaptation of *Parade's End*.

son through sharing experiences of his childhood home: 'There was a deep well in the stable yard. He had meant to teach the child how, if you dropped a pebble in, you waited to count twenty-three. And there came up a whispering roar.'[12] Groby also unites Christopher with a young lance corporal in his regiment, who turns out to be a 'North Riding Yorkshire boy' and has his own childhood memories of Groby house and grounds. As he makes his rounds of the trenches, the young man recognises his superior as 'Mr. Tietjens, of Groby', defining him in the same way that Walter Scott relished referring to his characters as 'Edward Waverley of Waverley-Honour', or 'Baron Brawardine of Tully-Veolan'. The house is the family, is the man.

Later, Mark Tietjens muses on 'the symbol of Tietjens': the Groby Great Tree.[13] 'For thirty miles round Groby they made their marriage vows by Groby Great Tree', and, he recalls, 'when they were imaginatively drunk Cleveland villagers would declare – would knock you down if you denied – that Groby Great Tree was 365 foot high and Groby Well 365 feet deep. A foot for every day of the year.' The tree has further importance, as 'on special occasions . . . they would ask permission to hang rags and things from the boughs' as a sort of 'offerings to fairies'.

Their relationship to Groby defines both Christopher and the younger soldier, and the house represents for both men not only a vital bond in the grand scheme of English culture, but also, more mundanely, the comfort and safety of home: for the soldier it is his familiar corner of England, for Christopher it is his own past and his son's future. It is also a place where there exists a comfortable hierarchy. The lance corpo-

ral, whose mother is too poor to pay for art school, had been
to Groby 'of a Sunday afternoon', as a local visitor to the
grounds. They may be among those villagers who hang trinkets on Groby Great Tree. There, he had often seen Mr
Tietjens, the father, as well as Christopher himself, 'and Mr
Mark and Mr John and Miss Eleanor'. He tells Christopher
that he 'once handed Miss Eleanor her riding crop when
she dropped it', pleased with the small service rendered to
the ruling family.[14]

For General Campion – Christopher's superior officer,
godfather and troubled nemesis – Groby also has nostalgic
charm. While near the front in France, and trying to decide
what to 'do' with Christopher, he is caught in reverie: 'The
men's voices had reminded him of church bells on a Sunday.
And of his youth . . . He was sitting beside Mrs Tietjens'
hammock under the great cedar at the corner of the stone
house at Groby. The wind being from the east-north-east
the bells of Middlesbrough came to them faintly.'[15] Ultimately, he acknowledges that 'what indeed there had been
of the idyllic in his life had really all passed at Groby'.[16]

Later, when Christopher has a last-minute reconciliation
with his brother before going off to war, he sees the pave-
ments of London as Yorkshire and has 'a vision of Mark
standing on the lawn at Groby'.[17] In these memories the
house achieves mythic powers, so readers feel somewhat
cheated at being told that 'Tietjens was never going to live
at Groby'. Ford has introduced the ancestral prize only to
have his character refuse it. However, Christopher has only
given up on Groby for himself. In his altruism, he has
allowed Sylvia to live there with their son, who, as the

estate is entailed, will be its heir and (in name at least) will carry on the Tietjens dynasty. But by being entrusted with Groby, Sylvia is also allowed to inflict greater damage on her husband by threatening its existence.

Ford Madox Ford had no such ancestral home. His family were artistic, intellectual, but not terribly wealthy, nor were they great landowners. His mother was a painters' model and artist. He was the grandson, on his mother's side, of the Pre-Raphaelite painter Ford Madox Brown, and the son of Francis Hueffer, a German-born music critic. Born Ford Hermann Hueffer, he changed his name after serving in the Great War, both out of reverence for his maternal grandfather and to avoid anti-German sentiment. Ford's father died when he was in his teens, after which he went to work as a writer rather than attend university. Through family connections Ford certainly knew many people of the aristocratic upper classes, but none approached the influence of Arthur Marwood, who helped to create not only Christopher Tietjens, but also the fictional ideal of the great estate of Groby, with its 'fifteen thousand acres of farmland' and its connection to an older, nobler England.

The manor known as Busby Hall came into the Marwood family in 1587, so well before 'Dutch William' set foot on these shores, as Christopher says of Groby, and has remained with the family into the twenty-first century. The house was built in the eighteenth century, the century that defines Marwood for Ford and explains Christopher to his friends. Its plain Georgian exterior, built of ashlar (dressed) stone with elements set out in nice Palladian order, speaks more of elegant solidity than grandeur, a grand internal staircase and

Venetian window nothwithstanding.[18] Not many of Ford's letters survive, so it is difficult to know the real nature of his friendship with the person who left so great an impact on his imagination or why he came to have such a strong impression of his family home. It is not even clear whether Ford visited Busby during the years before his friendship with Marwood broke down, though he spent time in the region while waiting to be shipped out to France. He emerges for Ford just after the war, with his character and his ancestry given a new life.

For Christopher's wife Sylvia, Groby is something with which to torture her husband further, and beyond that, only a quantifiable object without value for its age or symbolic power:

> The immense old place was not so immense because of its room space, though, as far as she could remember, there must be anything between forty and sixty rooms, but because of the vast old grounds, the warren of stabling, wells, rose-walks, and fencing . . . A man's place really, the furniture very grim and the corridors on the ground floor all slabbed with great stones.[19]

'Christopher, of course, loved Groby,' according to his elder brother. 'He was younger and hadn't expected to own it.'[20] Ownership brings all the responsibility for others that Mark cannot take on. But Christopher also has feelings for history, which Ford contrasts with his supercilious friend Macmaster, who fancies himself a cultured antiquarian. Christopher, 'accustomed to what he called the grown oldnesses of a morose, rambling Yorkshire manor house . . . disliked being among collected and rather pitiful bits, which . . . made him feel ridiculous, as if he were trying to behave seriously at a fancy-dress ball'.[21] Here, as in *Howards End*, Ruskin rears his head. Mrs Duchemin, whose husband was a disciple of the man, warns Valentine Wannop: 'My dear! Not a word against John Ruskin in this house!'[22] So it is with some irony that Christopher must resort to his knowledge of old furniture to earn a living after the war. Even worse, he is forced to go into business with a disreputable American, who is flogging the 'disinterred relics' to his compatriots at home.

In the early pages of the novel, the demise of great houses is already in train. When Christopher decides to take Sylvia back, he stipulates that they will close up their large home in Mayfair and reside in somewhat more modest quarters in Gray's Inn. This will not arouse suspicion about their marriage, because so many were doing likewise since 'the Chancellor of the Exchequer . . . had been putting pressure on the great landlords, [and] the great landlords had been replying by cutting down their establishments and closing their town houses'.[23]

Like Christopher, Ford tried to create a more settled existence for himself and his pregnant girlfriend, Stella Bowen, in the Sussex countryside. There the two made a rather awkward attempt at self-sufficiency, while also maintaining an open-door policy for their literary friends from London. Unlike Tietjens, Ford and Bowen eventually took themselves on an extended stay in Paris, where Ford mingled with the leading lights of the 'lost generation' and helped found the *The Trans-*

atlantic Review. He then travelled to America, leaving England behind for good.

Christopher is less successful in evading his wife. Sylvia not only convinces her son to let Groby to Mrs de Bray Pape, she also convinces the 'vulgar' American of the necessity of cutting down Groby Great Tree, the symbolic heart of the house and family. Mark Tietjens immediately understands her motive, knowing that 'Christopher set great store by that tree' and that he would 'have his heart broken because the house suffered'.[24] Cutting down the tree is Sylvia's last act of vengeance, and one that brings about the destruction of the house itself. 'In hauling out the stump of Groby Great Tree', the wood-cutters had 'apparently brought down two-thirds of the ball-room exterior wall . . . along with the old school-rooms above it. . . . Christopher's boyhood's bedroom had practically disappeared.'[25]

Some critics, including Graham Greene, have dismissed this last chapter as an afterthought, which they feel was only added by Ford for quick cash. But the destruction of Groby Great Tree and the resultant mortification visited on Christopher's boyhood home mark the final blow not only to the man himself, but also to his ancestry and line of descent. This highly charged act of revenge also signals the end to a chapter of English history, which was not caused directly by the war, but by a change in taste and manners that crested on a wave of modernity ushered in by it, for good or ill. Ford, who was not wholly English, who fought in the First World War and returned, shell-shocked, after the Battle of the Somme to an uninterested and at times hostile audience, seemed to be lamenting the passing of an ideal, rather than a reality.

Like a frustrated archaeologist, Ford held up artefacts, mouldering 'oldnesses' that he felt connected England to its better traditions. These are the traditions, however antiquated or chivalric, which Christopher sees are being threatened by the vulgarisms of the modern world, the 'parade' of public dignity, respect, politeness, good manners and honesty that is being uprooted, taking the old culture with it.

For Evelyn Waugh, who was born into the upper-middle class and spent time as a family guest at several grand houses, and who never shied away from satirising those privileged enough to live in them, the decline of the great English house as an institution is inevitable. Regarded as one of the finest prose satirists of the twentieth century, Waugh is now ranked along-side Jonathan Swift in his critiques of English society. Also born an outsider to the grand country-estate tradition, he used his vantage point to mock the more dissolute behaviour of the upper classes. His father was an editor at the publishers Chapman & Hall, where his older brother, Alec, would also later work. Waugh had some ideas of pursuing a career in art and taught at boys' schools before earning a living as a writer. At Oxford he had fallen in with an aristocratic set, from whom he developed some antipathy for the 'bourgeois, literary Hampstead world to which his father and brother were proud to belong'.[26] But he came to view his aristocratic friends through a critical lens.

At Oxford and after, Waugh hung out with the 'Bright Young People', as newspapers called the group in 1924. These were mostly young women of the post-war generation who were experiencing new-found independence.[27] Although Waugh was on the fringes of this group, very much like his character 'Beaver' in the bleakly satirical *A Handful of Dust* (1934), he counted Elizabeth Ponsonby, the Jungman sisters and Diana Guinness among his early friends. His diaries teem with luncheons, teas, cocktail parties, extreme bouts of drinking and promises to give up alcohol. He had financial help from his family, but it was not enough to sustain his hedonistic lifestyle, and his diaries cite many occasions of being overdrawn, begging money from his parents and pawning jewellery to keep up with the moneyed crowd he ran with. In addition to the Lygons of Madresfield, he was friendly with Harold Acton, John Sutro, Lady Diana Cooper, Randolph Churchill, Nancy Mitford and the Asquiths, and became well acquainted with the dining-drinking-dancing set and their country-house parties.

By 1930, still in the thick of those associations, Waugh had been through a brief marriage (to Evelyn Gardner, dubbed 'she-Evelyn' to his 'he-Evelyn') and a wrenching split. He converted to Catholicism (which prompted him to seek annulment of his first marriage, rather than divorce) and began to critique the lifestyle of his chosen 'set'. In *Vile Bodies*, Adam Fenwick Symes remarks on the profusion of 'Masked parties, Savage parties, Victorian parties, Greek parties, Wild West parties, Russian parties, Circus parties, parties where one had to dress as somebody else, almost naked parties in St John's Wood . . . all that succession and repetition of massed humanity . . . Those vile bodies.'[28]

But it was in *Brideshead Revisited* that the louche behaviour of his friends and their place as guardians of the country's cultural heritage became more than a target for cynicism and laughter. Like Ford, Waugh was also writing about a house he did not possess. Like Beaver in *A Handful of Dust*, Waugh was a practised house visitor, having been invited to various stately homes in England and abroad, and a careful observer of upper-class country life. From 1923 he often spent weekends at Barford House, a twelve-bedroomed Regency home belonging to his friend (and possible lover) Alastair Graham.[29] The following year he was a guest at the house of the Ussher family in Ireland and pronounced it 'very ugly'. In 1926, touring Scotland with Graham while on a break from teaching at another boys' school, he stayed with the Fisher family at Higham Hall in the Lake District, which he found to be a satisfyingly 'Gothic house with turrets and castellations and a perfectly lovely view across the lake to a mountain called Skiddaw', and found Preston Hall, a grand eighteenth-century manor house in Midlothian, 'perfectly charming'.[30] On the same trip he stopped to look at Netherby and at another house at Tannadice.[31]

In 1927, while researching his book on the Pre-Raphaelites, Waugh visited Kelmscott in Gloucestershire, the former home of William Morris. It was occupied at the time by Morris's daughter May, whom Waugh described as 'very awkward and disagreeable dressed in a slipshod ramshackle way in hand-woven stuffs'. He had similar regard for the house: 'The rooms very low and dark and the whole effect rather cramped and constricted.'[32] Other visits included stays at Forthampton Court in Gloucestershire; Mells, a sixteenth-century manor house restored by Edwin Lutyens and owned by Waugh's friend, the Earl of Oxford and Asquith, later prime minister;

and Renishaw Hall, the Sitwell family seat in North Derbyshire.[33]

These experiences helped Waugh imbue Beaver with the charm and social skills of 'an experienced guest', who was 'well practised in the art of being shown over houses'. Hetton Abbey, the fictional home of Beaver's married lover, Brenda Last, takes its architectural cues from Madresfield Court, home of the Lygon family, being 'entirely rebuilt in 1864 in the Gothic style'. But its fate is a satirical doom. The stately-home setting and the role of the less wealthy visitor were familiar themes by the time he was writing *Brideshead Revisited*, but at this point Waugh was no longer interested in

Madresfield Court in Worcestershire, home to the Lygon family, whose story and lifestyle heavily influenced the writing of *Brideshead Revisited*.

merely lampooning the social elites in their grand houses and elaborate rituals.

Like Ford, Waugh took time out from his writing life to serve as a soldier and emerged from the war with a certain nostalgia for the great English house and its gentry. As Ford came out of the war haunted by the figure of Arthur Marwood, Waugh returned from battle to memories of his tragic friend Hugh Lygon, and of the hospitality of Hugh's family home at Madresfield. In *Brideshead*, the notes of mocking humour and high farce from Waugh's earlier novels have been replaced by something altogether more elegiac. And while Waugh may have had Alastair Graham in mind when he sketched the finer qualities of Sebastian Flyte (in the manuscript version of the novel he is 'Alastair', before being changed to 'Sebastian'), it was Madresfield and the Lygon family heritage coming up against the harsh judgements and economies of the modern world that broke over his novel like a mournful storm.[34]

Though Waugh knew Hugh Lygon and his older brother, Lord Elmley, at Oxford, it wasn't until Christmas 1931, several years after leaving university, that he was invited (by Hugh's sister Dorothy, or 'Coote', who became a lifelong friend) to the splendid family home. He spent several weeks at the house over various visits in 1932, and devoted hours each day to writing in his quarters in the old nursery, but Waugh didn't compose *Brideshead* while actually staying in the house.[35] In these early years of his career, he was writing a travelogue of his recent trip to Africa and a novel, *Black Mischief*. It wasn't until 1944, while on leave during the war, that he began to compose his story of the time when he went through a 'low door in the wall' and entered the beguiling world of the young aristocrats who inhabited or gravitated to Madresfield.

In *Brideshead Revisited*, the decline of the great English country house has begun. The Flyte family are victims of their own overspending and, some might say, carelessness. Like so many inheritors of grand estates, they find it necessary to sell off their London house. (The Lygons were compelled to sell off 8,000 acres of land between the wars.)[36] In the novel, it is Marchmain House, near Green Park in London, that is sacrificed. As the Flytes' youngest daughter, Cordelia, explains: 'Apparently papa has been terribly in debt for a long time. Selling Marchers has put him straight again and saved I don't know how much a year in rates.'[37] Cordelia will not be able to follow her sister and have her coming-out party at Marchmain House, as it will be pulled down and replaced by a block of flats. So the sale marks the end of another tradition. Yet its demise heralds the beginning of Charles Ryder's career as an architectural painter, when Lord Marchmain commissions him to paint the front and rear elevations of Marchmain House, works that will later be hung at Brideshead. Charles has been befriended at Oxford by the wayward Sebastian, younger brother of the Flyte family. His newfound vocation signals a trend of the period, in which numerous English stately homes were 'soon to be deserted or debased', because of family debts or taxes owed. With a degree of solemnity, Waugh says, Charles sometimes arrived, paintbox in hand, just 'a few paces ahead of the auctioneer'.[38] Like Christopher Tietjens, who makes a living hunting out less-than-precious antiques to sell to awestruck Americans, Charles also invents a career in preserving artefacts of disappearing ancient English houses for others to admire.

As with Groby, the decline of Brideshead has been set in train partly by a breakdown in family relations and the failure to produce a suitable heir. Having left his wife and taken up residence with his lover in Europe, Lord Marchmain is running two households in luxury (there were usually nineteen servants in attendance at Madresfield, who dressed in livery even when the parents were away). And he has failed, as Julia's commercially driven fiancé Rex Mottram points out, to use his money to make more money. Their dependence on land rents alone to support their entertaining lifestyle becomes unsustainable in the modern world of commerce and taxation. In addition, the elder son, Lord Brideshead ('Bridey'), has married an older widow, and so will not have children. Charles and Julia cannot marry because of the prohobitions of Catholicism. However, there is a cringe-worthy moment when the two consummate their affair and Charles sounds disturbingly like Soames Forsyte, remarking that it was 'as though a deed of conveyance of her narrow loins had been drawn and sealed' and 'I was making my first entry as the freeholder of a property I would enjoy and develop at leisure'.[39] Sebastian, the dissipated younger son, will die without issue, and so Brideshead will be without a male heir and the title long attached to the house and estate will end with the current generation.

When Waugh came to stay at Madresfield, William, the 7th Earl Beauchamp, was himself living in exile, after details of his homosexual affairs were revealed. As the scandal was being dredged up by his wife's brother, Lady Beauchamp was pressured to leave Madresfield. The seven Lygon children sided with their father and suffered the snubs from many in society. Like Lord Marchmain, who is 'a social leper' because he has left his wife for another woman, Lord Beauchamp was forced to stay away from England, in his case, being under threat of further exposure or possible imprisonment. The children were the only full-time residents at Madresfield, a house that had previously been known to accommodate dozens of guests and their servants at any one time, including the prime minister.

As Jane Mulvagh has recorded, Madresfield has a rich and fascinating history of its own. The earliest part of the house is the Great Hall, built in the twelfth century when the house was encircled with a moat. It was turned into a manor house in the fifteenth century and then largely rebuilt in the late sixteenth century in an Elizabethan style with a pink brick façade and crow-stepped gables added along with a Long Gallery running sixty feet in length.[40] In the 1860s, the 6th Earl of Beauchamp added neo-Gothic extensions on three sides, including a spire, a tower and a great hall.[41] The result was 'a vast house of 160 rooms covering two acres'. This is the house that captivated Waugh on that first visit in 1931.

Waugh acknowledged Brideshead's debt to Madresfield and the Lygons early on, though he tried to emphasise the fictional aspects of his novel over the factual. In a letter to Dorothy Lygon in 1944, he wrote: 'I am writing a very beautiful book, to bring tears, about the very rich, beautiful, high-born people who live in palaces and have no troubles except what they make themselves.' He also said that the main characters were

The baroque extravagance of Castle Howard, near York, informed much of the architectural detail of Waugh's Brideshead.

not really like the Lygons and that 'the house might be Mad [Madresfield], but isn't really Mad'.[42]

In the novel we first come to the house as it is being used (and mistreated) by troops in the Second World War. Charles's battalion is charged with readying a large country house that has been commandeered by the army for the new brigade headquarters. Charles is surprised to find that the house they are about to help turn over from one group of soldiers to another is in fact the place that so bewitched him twenty years ago, 'on a cloudless day in June, when the ditches were creamy with meadowsweet and the air heavy with all the scents of summer'. From here the story reels back to that time, in 1923, when Charles is first taken to Brideshead by Sebastian. His first glimpse is filmic:

In the early afternoon [we] came to our destination: wrought-iron gates and twin, classical lodges on a village green, an avenue, more gates, open park-land, a turn in the drive; and suddenly a new and secret landscape opened before us.[43]

Given the job of an architectural painter, Charles is granted the predilection of appreciating the rooms and decoration in elaborate terms. There is the Tapestry Room, the Painted Parlour, the 'Soanesque library', the 'Chinese drawing room'.[44] He takes note for us of everything from 'the stone-flagged, stone-vaulted passages of the servants' quarters' to the 'twin fireplaces of sculptured marble, the coved ceiling frescoed with classic deities . . . gilt mirrors and scagliola pilasters' of the hall. He is then shown the chapel, which, Sebastian explains, is 'a monument of art nouveau', whose 'whole interior had been gutted, elaborately refurnished and redecorated in the arts-and-crafts style of the last decade of the nineteenth century.'[45] The library at Madresfield might be described as 'Soanesque', and Lord Beauchamp had commissioned such a chapel for his Catholic wife. Beauchamp was an avid proponent of the Arts and Crafts style, which Waugh came to appreciate also, despite his early disapproval of Morris' Kelmscott. The primary supplicants in the chapel frescoes are the Earl and Lady Beauchamp, with each child added in succession as they were born. As someone who had 'nursed a love of architecture', Charles professes that though he had made the leap 'from the puritanism of Ruskin to the puritanism of Roger Fry, my sentiments at heart were insular and medieval.' But Brideshead, he says, 'was my conversion to the Baroque' and he describes the 'high and insolent dome, under those coffered ceilings', as well as the 'arches and broken pediments to the pillared shade' and finally the great fountain.

Apart from the library and chapel, the architecture at Madresfield is nothing like this. There is no great dome, no elaborate fountain, none of those Baroque elements that seduce Charles's aesthetic sensibilities. Much of the description was probably inspired by Castle Howard (where the 1981 television adaptation was filmed), a favourite building of Waugh's. Indeed the 'grey and gold', 'the dome and columns' recall Vanbrugh's vast masterwork. These are indications of the more symbolic conversion Waugh wanted to convey, possibly influenced by his visit to the Vatican, the single dome implying one source of light, with Nanny Hawkins hovering near it like a benign spirit, an angel painted up near the vanishing perspective. Dorothy Lygon agreed that 'there is no resemblance' between the landscape and architecture of Brideshead and Madresfield, 'except for one detail – the art-nouveau decoration of the chapel'. She noted further that 'Madresfield is a moated house of red brick, of mainly Victorian architecture superimposed on an earlier base, while Brideshead is an epitome in stone of the Palladian style he loved so much.'[46]

Of Brideshead's awe-inspiring decorative features, it is perhaps the destruction of the fountain (like the chopping down of Groby Great tree) that most clearly signals the coming vulgarization of culture. At first sight of the elaborate sculpture, Charles rejoices in 'all its clustered feats of daring and invention' of 'such a fountain as one might expect to find in a piazza of southern Italy', where in fact it had been found and purchased by Sebastian's ancestors:

An oval basin with an island of sculptured rocks at its centre; on the rocks grew, in stone, formal tropical vegetation and wild English fern . . . through them ran a dozen streams that counterfeited springs, and round them sported fan-tastic tropical animals, camels and camelopards and an ebullient lion, all vomiting water; on the rocks, to the height of the pediment, stood an Egyptian obelisk of red sandstone.[47]

Twenty years on, Charles finds that the house has been battered by the resident soldiers. The large fireplace has been damaged, the Chinese room, scene of Lord Marchmain's possible deathbed conversion, has been used as the mess, and outside a lorry driver 'went smack through the box-hedge and carried away all that balustrade'.[48] But the most tragic disfigurement seems to have been done to the baroque fountain. It is 'a tender spot with our landlady', Charles is told by an officer. The 'young officers used to lark about in it . . . and it was looking a bit the worse for wear'. The officer covered it in wire and turned off the water, but now 'all the drivers throw their cigarette-ends and the remains of the sandwiches there'. The British soldiers do not attack the house with the malice the English regiment directed at Tully-Veolan in *Waverley*, but the contrast between martial barbarity and high culture is similarly stark.

No such fountain exists at Madresfield, and Waugh could have been calling on any number of places he visited in England or Scotland, or indeed Italy. (The Atlas Fountain at Castle Howard is similarly spectacular, but lacks the tropical detail.) But the grandeur and the theme of beauty and enchantment are what he associated with the great home of his friends before the war. As Dorothy Lygon said, Waugh 'conceived Brideshead in a mood of violent nostalgia for what he thought was a vanished past; he put into it all the most regretted and missed in pre-war life'.[49] The house gave him a springboard, a spatial and social framework for his memories of people, moods and artistry.

When Charles Ryder receives his long-awaited (and dramatic) summons to at Brideshead, the rapture he glimpsed on his first brief visit is reborn: 'the house seemed painted in grisaille, save for the central golden square at the open doors', the golden square beckoning him to a life steeped in luxury and 'the languor of youth'.[50] Charles and Sebastian spend a dreamy August mostly alone at the house, which Charles remembers as an idyll, one that must necessarily end. Similarly, Waugh seems to be suggesting, the leisured lifestyle of the English gentry must also come to an end. We are forewarned at the start of the novel that the house will find its demise in the war, so the sense of nostalgia is pre-ordained.

At the novel's close, Waugh renders the great building in lyrical tones, speaking of the 'generation after generation' who had 'enriched and extended it'. And yet, he says 'that is not the last word.' He finds hope that 'something quite remote from anything the builders intended, has come out of their work, and out of the fierce little human tragedy in which I played'. It is symbolised in 'a small red flame – a beaten copper lamp of deplorable design relit before the beaten-copper doors of a tabernacle; the flame which the old knights saw from their tombs . . . that flame burns again for other soldiers, far from home.'[51] That soldier longing for his English home was probably Waugh, but could also be the someone like Yorkshireman who is pleased to find 'Tietjens of Groby' in a faraway battle camp.

The twenty-seven-year-old Aldous Huxley showed none of the grief at the passing of the old country estate and its manners in his first published book, *Crome Yellow* (1921). This was a lighthearted critique of the pretensions and drama of the country house party elite, written in the same gleefully mocking spirit in which Thomas Love Peacock had ribbed his romantically minded friends with books like *Crotchet Castle* in the early nineteenth century. Crome, where 'all the beds were ancient, hereditary pieces of furniture', was famously modeled on Garsington Manor, the Oxfordshire family manse of society hostess Lady Ottoline Morrell and her husband. The artists, poets and thinkers who gather at the fictional home of Priscilla and Henry Wimbush mirror the guests at Garsington, who included Virginia Woolf and other members of the Bloomsbury Group, and writers such as T. S. Eliot, D. H. Lawrence and Huxley himself. The Morrells also made their home a haven for conscientious objectors during the war. Rather than having their faith in old systems rocked by the horrors of war, the guests at Crome are living in worlds of solipsistic ennui. While some of the guests indulge in cosmological thought experiments, others, like the protagonist Denis Stone, suffer the tortures of unrequited love seemingly untouched by modern existential preoccupations.

Meanwhile, their host, Henry Wimbush, devotes himself to recording the history of his family and producing it on his own printing press, rather than dealing with the discomforting

T. S. Eliot, the painter Mark Gertler and Lady Ottoline Morrell at the Morrell's home, Garsington Manor, which became a hub for artists, intellectuals and pacifists in the First World War.

uncertainties of the present and future. The privately owned press – the plaything of the erudite country squires, like Walpole – is of course also a reference to the Bloomsbury-ites printing their own work for public consumption. Henry readily confesses: 'give me the past. It doesn't change; it's all there in black and white, and you can get to know about it comfortably and decorously and, above all, privately – by reading.'[52] Wimbush is also chronicling the changes to the house (like a good conservator of heritage) and is especially proud of its historic artifacts, the ancient oak pipes recently dug up, the musty muniment room. His solemn mistaking of his ancestor's concern for privies with rooms for a privy council is one of the more ridiculous moments. Huxley had yet to move on to his more disturbing visions of the dystopian future, though the philosophical Mr Scogan foresees in later years the growing of babies in 'gravid bottles' as will come to fruition in *Brave New World*. But it is Mr Scogan, the critic of the trend for imitation rustic, who identifies Crome as 'unmistakeably and aggressively a work of art'.[53] He also voices the inherent hypocrisy of the elite, saying that 'leisure and culture have to be paid for. Fortunately, however, it is not the leisured and cultured who have to pay'.[54]

Huxley's Ivor Lombard, the itinerant country-house cad, prefigures Waugh's John Beaver in *A Handful of Dust*. From Crome, he flits 'from hall to baronial hall, from castle to castle, from Elizabethan manor-house to Georgian mansion over the whole expanse of the kingdom.'[55] Some days after Ivor has left Crome, a love-stricken Mary Bracegirdle finds on her breakfast plate a picture postcard of Gobley Great Park addressed to her from the dashing Lombard. The souvenir is like that acquired by many a house-curious tourist, including the second Mrs de Winter, who buys herself a postcard of Manderley long before she becomes its ill-fated mistress. Gobley is 'a stately Georgian pile, with a façade sixteen windows wide; parterres in the foreground; huge smooth lawns receding out of the picture.' But these features are lost on poor Mary Bracegirdle, who knows that its primary attraction for Ivor is the young Zenobia and her 'welcoming smile'.[56]

Though it was his most successful novel, Waugh later came to feel somewhat embarrassed by the highly dramatic mood of

Brideshead Revisited. When it was reissued in 1959, he tried to explain his earlier romanticism and his feeling at the time that the English country estate, and those 'splendours of the recent past', had had their day. In a new preface, he voiced his surprise at 'the present cult of the English country house', which meant that these massive relics had not disappeared and were still being well looked after. He said this turn of events 'was impossible to foresee in the spring of 1944'. He had written with such 'passionate sincerity' of these 'ancestral seats', which were 'our chief national artistic achievement', because they had seemed 'doomed to decay and spoliation like the monasteries in the sixteenth century'. Fifteen years later, he felt that the houses had been better cared for than he had feared they would be, and that the English aristocracy had 'maintained its identity to a degree that then seemed impossible'. Consequently, much of his book turned out to be 'a panegyric preached over an empty coffin'.[57] There was no need to lament the death of the country house and its inhabitants, since they hadn't died off after all. However, the English aristocracy as an institution is not today what it was during Waugh's time among them, or even in the decline during the war and just after. That way of life *is* a relic of the past, however idealised (one wonders what Waugh would have made of the popularity of *Downton Abbey*) or lampooned. Yet Ford and Waugh in their very different imaginative recreations provide a sense of the place of these structures in a potent English story (while Huxley dares us to take them too seriously). They still carry some force of identity, symbols of a social system that has been lost. But they are also part of a continuing narrative, as the houses tell their own stories to new generations and perhaps become, as Waugh suggested, beacons of some ancient sense of belonging.

Menabilly House

ELEVEN

Gothic House Redux:
The Passion of Manderley,
Agatha Christie's Bloody House Parties

> There was Manderley, our Manderley, secretive and silent as it had
> always been, the grey stone shining in the moonlight of my dream, the
> mullioned windows reflecting the green lawns and the terrace. Time
> could not wreck the perfect symmetry of those walls, nor the site itself,
> a jewel in the hollow of a hand.
>
> *Rebecca*

There is perhaps no better known opening in English fiction:
'Last night I dreamt I went to Manderley again.' While the
narrator is speaking from a life that is modern for the time,
spent in hotels and motor cars, what follows in the story is
textbook Gothic, with Manderley at the centre of the pas-
sion-terror. As the narrator moves toward the iconic house in
her nightmarish dream, the gardens and drive have become
overgrown. Nature has overtaken, 'with long, tenacious fingers'. The woods are 'a menace', the elms 'tortured' and other
trees' roots are 'like skeleton claws', hydrangeas have grown
to 'monster height'. The path to the house feels elongated and
now leads to a 'labyrinth' of 'some choked wilderness, and not
to the house at all'.[1] No longer in the realm of castles,

Manderley is still a grand house promising to envelop us in stately rooms full of drama and romance. Rebecca is no Jane Eyre; Manderley is not Thornfield Hall, but it too holds a secret about a previous wife on the upper floor. She is not a raving monster, but her machinations have engendered monstrous consequences.

This tangled, frustrating, uneasy approach mirrors Daphne du Maurier's first contact with the house that became an obsession with her: Menabilly, in Cornwall. Du Maurier had been staying in and around the Cornish village of Fowey for many years before she wrote *Rebecca*, though she had only barely glimpsed the inside of the house. In those years she had often tramped through the surrounding woods, admiring the house from afar, aching to make it her own. So rather than communicating the ecstasy of possession, the opening passage of the novel is more redolent of the author's many thwarted attempts merely to get near the house of her dreams.

The detachment of Maxim de Winter in those early pages matches the cryptic isolation of Manderley, and of Menabilly. Forcing an introduction to de Winter in the hotel dining room in Monte Carlo, the gauche Mrs Van Hopper pronounces Manderley 'like fairyland'; 'perfectly enchanting', so she has heard. Her unwillingness to be detoured from her subject and de Winter's unwillingness to give her any details suggest there is something remote and mysterious about him and his wonderful house.[2] Immediately her paid companion, the future Mrs de Winter, surmises that Maxim de Winter looked like someone in a portrait, from 'a past where men walked cloaked at night, and stood in the shadow of old doorways, a past of narrow stairways and dim dungeons, a past of whispers in the dark, of shimmering rapier blades, of silent, exquisite courtesy'.[3]

The Gothic ingredients piled on in these pages only just avoid fantastic cliché owing to the fact that they come to us indirectly, through the dreams and impressions of the (nameless) second Mrs de Winter. It is the imagination of the narrator that provides the tension, the sense of eerie unease, before we know many real facts of the story. Readers must decide for themselves how much to trust these whispery impressions. A similar device is used to comic effect by Jane Austen in *Northanger Abbey*. It is the breathless Catherine Moreland, rather than the author, who indulges in Gothic fantasy, as inspired by her reading of *The Mysteries of Udolpho*, and leads her to both fear and hope that Northanger Abbey will be a place of thrilling secrets. The bedroom of the deceased Lady Tilney is kept as it was in her lifetime, but Mrs Danvers goes to creepy extremes in preserving Rebecca's room and furnishings as if she were still alive, carefully arranging her apricot nightdress inside its case, fondling her satin dressing gown and slippers.

Preoccupied with social status and all its manifestations, Mrs Van Hopper presses de Winter to confirm some of the more splendid details of Manderley: 'Isn't there a minstrels' gallery [...] and some very valuable portraits?' She also affirms that the house, like the best English estates, has been in the de Winter family 'since the Conquest'.[4] When de Winter later asks why a distasteful old creature such as Mrs Van Hopper should be interested in him, he is told 'because of Manderley'.[5] He seems to be the only person not in awe of his spectacular abode, and, rather than acknowledging its qualities or politely demurring, he is silenced by the mention of it.

The young companion wonders why the house, 'known to so many people by hearsay', should make 'a barrier between him and others'.[6] De Winter's puzzling reticence, coupled with the dream in the novel's opening passage and the hotel 'hearsay', sets up a wonderful anticipation for the revelation, both of the story's plot and of the house that is already, in the first few pages, an enigma.

The narrator's youth and sheltered upbringing make her the ideal Gothic heroine, offering a naïve, excitable introduction to the house whose appearance we have been expecting since the very first line. We gaze with her at 'the great stone hall, the wide doors open to the library', 'the exquisite staircase leading to the minstrels' gallery', the drawing room, which 'had all the formality of a room in a museum'.[7] The morning room, where the new wife is expected to write letters and check menus as Rebecca did, is 'graceful, fragile, the room of someone who has chosen every particle of furniture with great care'. It also overlooks the rhododendrons, which are 'blood red and luscious', perhaps a sign of something raging behind the antique formality.[8] Thereafter, references to the house are melodramatic, overindulged, so that the message is clear: Manderley is special in ways we may find troubling.

Like E. M. Forster, Daphne du Maurier fell in love with but was ultimately denied ownership of a house that she had lived in and adored. Born in 1907, the daughter of actor and manager Gerald du Maurier and granddaughter of the artist and novelist George du Maurier, she had enjoyed a privileged upbringing. Daphne first came across Menabilly during a family visit to the the Cornish village of Fowey in 1926, when her mother was in search of a summer retreat. The family bought a house at the water's edge in Boddinick – known as the 'Swiss Chalet', and renamed 'Ferryside' – at the docking point for the ferry between the tiny hamlets of Bodinnick and Fowey. It sits at the base of the hill ridged by 'Hall Walk', a favourite path of du Maurier, and now marked at the head-land by a monument to Sir Arthur Quiller-Couch, Cornish author and friend of the family.

By this point, du Maurier was already writing stories and had completed at least one play. Such was her love of boating around Fowey that for her twenty-first birthday she was given a rowboat called the *Annabel Lee*, which she used for fishing and exploring the waters around the headland on her own. Not wanting to return to London for the winter in 1929, Daphne convinced her parents to allow her to remain at Fer-ryside and write. Here, she completed her first novel, *The Loving Spirit*, published in 1931.

The area where the du Mauriers had decided to stake their claim for a holiday home was rife with stories of intrigue and legends of criminal undertakings. In previous centuries, the rocky coast caused many ships to founder, and these would be pillaged by 'wreckers', who would take whatever bounty could be salvaged. Smuggling was also part of the colourful history of Fowey and its surrounds. There are walks around the rugged coastal cliffs offering stunning views out to sea, but the many little coves, with further hidden caves so well used by smugglers and wreckers, obviously inspired du Mau-rier's penchant for a mystery tale of dangerous goings-on. She drew on this lore in her novels *Jamaica Inn* and *Frenchman's Creek*. By contrast, the hilly streets of Fowey and nearby

Ferryside in Bodinnick, across the water from Fowey, was the Du Maurier family's Cornish holiday home from 1926.

Polruan, across the estuary, make picture-postcard impressions. It is not hard to see what attracted du Maurier to the place even before she became obsessed with Menabilly.

Like Rebecca, du Maurier was a fearless, independent sailor. But she was also an intrepid explorer on foot, and it was on one of her early tramps through the woods behind Polridmouth, 'Pridmouth', Cove that she first encountered the deserted 'house of secrets' that would become her elusive prize. Menabilly has been in the Rashleigh family since 1573, and was largely transformed in the early eighteenth century.[9] A Victorian Rashleigh had contributed an addition to the north end in the late 1880s and replaced the 'small-paned windows' with plate glass. Du Maurier, like many others, considered the extension 'an ugly wing that conformed ill with the rest of her'.[10] One of her first projects, when she finally got her hands on Menabilly, was to restore the mullioned windows.

Menabilly, like its fictional counterpart, is set well back into the woods, and is still hardly visible from any point outside the grounds. In du Maurier's time the gardens here were full of those scarlet rhododendrons that tell of Manderley's secret passion and rage, 'massive and high they reared above my head'.[11] When du Maurier first came upon it, the house had been abandoned for some time: 'The windows were shuttered fast [...] Ivy covered the grey walls and threw tendrils round the windows.' Inside, 'family portraits stared into the silence and the dust' and the library 'had become a lumber place'.[12] Her first visit was an illicit ramble with her sister, Angela. Coming upon the long drive, they had been warned that it was 'nearly three miles long, and overgrown'. As in the opening of the novel, the walk up that twisting path felt endless, then 'we came to the lodge at four turnings, as we had been told, opened the creaking iron gates'.[13] They found the lodge deserted and were turned back before reaching the house by the onset of nightfall. It took another year before du Maurier made it through the woods and found the house in all of its broken glory. At this point Menabilly was in a dilapidated state similar to the Manderley of the narrator's gloomy dream, which sits 'like an empty shell amidst the tangle of the deep woods'.

Du Maurier's first look at the tired, deserted house and its grounds did nothing to deter her. 'The house possessed me from that day,' she wrote. However, though she obtained permission from the Rashleighs to walk through the woods whenever she liked, she could not obtain an agreement to live in it, and the house continued to stand in a state of uninhabited decay for a further fifteen years. In the meantime du

Maurier married, had children and followed her husband, Frederick 'Tommy' Browning, an officer in the Grenadier Guards, to Alexandria, where she first began sketching ideas and trying to write the story that would become *Rebecca*. She described being frustrated in her efforts and homesick for Cornwall, her beloved beaches and wooded walks. As she plotted the story, she decided that it would be 'about a young wife and her slightly older husband, living in a beautiful house that had been in his family for generations'. She had visited many such houses in Cornwall with her friend Foy Quiller-Couch (daughter of Sir Arthur), and was thinking of houses 'with extensive grounds, with woods, near to the sea, with family portraits on the walls, like the house Milton in Northamptonshire, where I had stayed as a child during the First World War'. However, this house would be 'empty, neglected, its owner absent, more like – yes, very like – the Menabilly near Fowey . . . where I had so often trespassed.'[14]

The Second World War continued to put paid to any plans of house-buying, and it was not until a return to Fowey in 1943 that du Maurier decided to make what she thought would be a futile attempt to live at Menabilly. She was by this time a successful author of five novels and two popular biographies, and had continued to spend as much time as possible in Fowey, both on her own and with her family. In 1943 she rented a cottage in nearby Readymoney cove.* To her great joy her offer to take up a lease on Menabilly was accepted, but the task of making the house fit to live in was truly daunting. It 'looked like a blitzed building', she later recalled, 'great

---

* Ferryside had been requisitioned during the war.

fungus growths from the ceiling. Moisture everywhere.' In 'The House of Secrets', an emotional and spiritual memoir of Menabilly, she recounted her satisfaction once work was under way:

> The creeper cut from the windows. The windows mended. The men upon the roof mortaring the slates. The carpenter in the house, setting up the doors. The plumber in the well, measuring the water. The electrician on the ladder, wiring the walls. And the doors and windows open that had not been open for so long. The sun warming the cold dusty rooms. Fires of brushwood in the grates. And then the scrubbing of the floors that had felt neither brush nor mop for many years.[15]

Du Maurier was wealthy, but the repairs were substantial (the roof alone is reported to have cost £30,000).[16] And all of this was done with the knowledge that the house could never really be hers, even if the current Rashleigh had wanted to sell. Menabilly, like the fictional Manderley, like the Baron Bradwardine's Tully-Veolan, and the grand houses belonging to the great families of Jane Austen's Regency world, was entailed. Du Maurier spent twenty-six years at Menabilly, years of repairs and restoration, during which her young family grew up, roamed the woodlands and the beaches, and where she entertained regularly and worked in a shed she had built specially for writing. By 1968 her lease still had some way to go, but the house was wanted by another Rashleigh family member, so they offered her a tenancy at Kilmarth, the dower house of Menabilly, in its place. Kilmarth, too, appeared in her fiction as *The House on the Strand*: this time the writing of it happened after she had moved in.

Manderley takes its seclusion from Menabilly isolated from public eyes, yet with sweeping views of the sea from the gardens, whose scarlet rhododendrons and subtropical verdure all made their way into the imposing ancestral home of the de Winter family. But although her love affair with Menabilly fires the overriding fervor of the novel, du Maurier was clear that the appearance and atmosphere of Manderley came from some particular houses from her childhood. In 1976, while considering a suggestion that she write about her early days and inspiration, she said that such a piece would have to be based on something, 'like houses and the influence they have on one's development'. She went on to enumerate those that had had lasting affect on her: 'Cumberland Terrace, where I was born', Cannon Hall in Hampstead, and those 'houses in the country which Daddy and Mummy used to take for us'.[17]

Of these, it was 'that great house Milton' that she had 'never forgot, and which was really the Rebecca house, more than Mena [Menabilly]'.[18] There was also Slyfield, a Jacobean manor house on the river Mole, which the family rented in summer and du Maurier remembered as a place of tremendous outdoor freedom.[19] Slyfield was also large and ominous, full of portraits of long-dead people who were unnerving to look at. She described the stair, which 'was not straight up like the stairs at Cumberland Terrace. The hall ... was larger, darker, somehow, and the staircase was wide, turning to a broad landing above.' Because her sister Angela was older and permitted to stay up later, the stairs 'must be climbed alone', she later related. 'They gave me a queer feeling.' It's a feeling she re-creates with chilling accuracy in *Rebecca*.

Cumberland Terrace is an early nineteenth-century block near Regent's Park in London, where du Maurier spent her earliest years. Cannon Hall, where the family moved when she was nine years old, is a grand Georgian house with a sweeping stair and gallery overlooking the large entrance hall.* It had a night nursery with its own en-suite bathroom, as well as a day nursery, which could be reached by three different routes via different rooms and stairs, including a back stair used by servants.[20] Of course, many large houses had a servants' stair like that described at Manderley, but it was Cannon Hall du Maurier remembered when the second Mrs de Winter went up the wrong stair so that she reached Rebecca's rooms in the west wing rather than her own bedroom on the other side of the house. Du Maurier left Cannon Hall in her early twenties, but she and her husband were given one of two cottages on the grounds when she married in 1932.[21]

In 1917 du Maurier and her sister were sent away from London because of fears of air raids. First they went to Cookham, a pretty riverside village in Berkshire, and then to Milton Hall, near Peterborough, a great manor house occupied by the Fitzwilliam family for over four hundred years. The Fitzwilliams were friends of her parents, and du Maurier spent two long visits at the house. Milton is an odd marriage of two long houses. If Manderley is defined by the east wing (tastefully refurbished for the second Mrs de Winter) and west wing (all exuberant Rebecca), Milton has its contrast in the

---

* Cannon Hall sold for a record £28 million in 2015 (*Evening Standard,* 22 June 2015).

The du Maurier children were sent to Milton Hall in Peterborough to escape air raids in London. The internal grandeur and contrasting architectural styles resurfaced in Manderley.

north and south fronts. The former was part of the original Elizabethan building, begun in 1594, with second-storey battlements and canted bays projecting from the façade. It looks somewhat squat, with the attic (added in 1773) rising above it, when compared to the south front, which was built in 1745–50 in the more uniform Palladian arrangement over two-and-a-half storeys. The du Maurier girls shared 'the big bedroom over the northern entrance', while their mother and younger sister had 'the even larger one, facing south'.[22] The contrast may not be as dramatic as that between Rebecca's room, overlooking the stormy sea, and the eastern prospect of the tranquil rose garden, but it presents a house with a divided character, if only in its architecture.

The rooms at Milton inspired the grand interiors of Manderley; even the Van Dyck portraits were first seen here.

Du Maurier wrote: 'The entrance hall at Milton is exactly as I described in Rebecca', with the only difference being the 'sweeping staircase coming down into the hall'.[23] This staircase was more Cannon Hall or Slyfield. However, there was an 'unused bachelor wing' at Milton that the children played in at one end of the house, and here, as in Rebecca's rooms, 'the beds were covered with dust-sheets'. Rather than feeling ominous, however, they 'made good cover for hide-and-seek.'[24]

Manderley's long, overly formal drawing room, the 'graceful, fragile' morning room, the musty-smelling library – all these came from Milton, as did the vast space of the great hall, which, Mrs Danvers explains, 'was the old banqueting hall, in the old days'.[25] Of course, it is Rebecca's rooms that both captivate and frighten the narrator. These, she is told by the purring Mrs Danvers, are in the west wing, where the rooms are 'very old'. The bedroom 'is nearly twice as large' as the new bride's own bedroom, and it is 'very beautiful', with its scrolled ceiling, tapestry chairs and carved mantelpiece. It is, simply, 'the most beautiful room in the house'.[26] Du Maurier spent a great deal of time and money refurbishing the interiors of Menabilly, so that the bedrooms were all charmingly decorated by the time she was able to have guests, but at the time she wrote *Rebecca*, these were still in a ruinous state. It was Milton's rooms that inspired Rebecca's shimmering boudoir.

At Milton Hall, the children were waited on by a butler at meals and the house was managed by a retinue of servants.[27] The hierarchies and systems probably informed the running of Manderley, with Mrs Danvers instructing the second Mrs de Winter as to which servant should perform which specific duties. Du Maurier recalled a servant from Milton, a Miss Parker, whom she described as 'a severe and rather frightening person', and said she got the idea for the black dress and chain worn by Mrs Danvers from 'a housekeeper in one of the houses I stayed at', though the rest was imaginary.[28] But if it was the interiors and lifestyle of Milton that sparked the details of Manderley, it was her own incurable attraction to Menabilly that provided the tension and the violent emotion.

Like Forster's 'View without a Room', du Maurier's earlier draft of the novel offers a more mundane afterlife of her house and main characters. It includes an epilogue that describes a now-familiar fate of English country houses, in which the ancestral pile is given over to commercial use. Here, the second Mrs de Winter laments the transformation of Manderlay from a grand family home to a country club with a golf course, squash courts and 'a swimming pool in the wilderness'. In place of the gun room, the flower room and 'my little morning room', there is 'what they call a "sun loggia", Italian style', where guests can 'sprawl about in negligée and acquire the fashionable tan'.[29] She addresses the reader cynically: 'If I were you I should toy with my cocktail in the new American bar' where the billiard room used to be. The narrator drones on bitterly, and perhaps du Maurier, or her editors, found this too much of a moan to include in the final draft. Was she decrying the increased tourism around Fowey? or the plight of so many great country houses that could not be managed without the low taxes and cheap servitude that existed before the wars? Some readers would no doubt find it a bit churlish. And she needn't have worried on that score: as of 2016, Cannon Hall, Milton Hall and Menabilly all remain privately owned residences. But lamenting the fate of the great house was becoming a trope by the time du Maurier was writing, one that later writers would re-work in a postmodern vein (see chapter 13). In the last trilogy of John Galsworthy's Forsyte novels, written in the 1930s, the heir to the old (but increasingly expensive to run) Condaford, which has been in the family since the thirteenth century, opines that what he 'hates' is 'the thought of Mr Tom Noddy or somebody buying Condaford and using it for week-end cocktail parties.'[30] The belief is that the houses deserve something better than becoming entertaining curiosities or public attractions; they deserve inhabitants, even families, who will care for them as they have through the centuries. In the final version of the novel du Maurier poured all of that frustration at not being able to get in and 'rescue' Menabilly into Max de Winter's raging unease over the fate of Manderley.

The Rashleighs continue to inhabit Menabilly today. Walking up the Esplanade along to Readymoney beach and then onto Polridmouth brings you to the lakeside cottage that was the model for the boathouse where Rebecca trysted with her lover. It is a pristine stone house, not at all like a ramshackle converted boathouse. It is also privately owned and still set in picturesque solitude on the ornamental lake created in the inlet around from Southground Point and nicely tucked back from the Gribben headland. Most of the land is still owned by the Rashleigh family, as it was in du Maurier's day and centuries before, and not a cocktail bar in sight.

Daphne du Maurier made no secret of her obsession with Menabilly, the house with which, 'in strange and eerie fashion', she had become one.[31] And though she hadn't yet lived in the house, or even spent more than a few fleeting moments inside, when writing *Rebecca*, in the inexplicable pull of Manderley, she describes her own ardent preoccupation with the house she could not have. In her memoir of Menabilly, du Maurier refers to the house as 'she', saying that it possessed her immediately, 'even as a mistress holds her lover'. 'Ours was a strange relationship for fifteen years,' she wrote, saying that she would 'put her from my mind for months at a time', and then, upon returning to Cornwall as she did regularly during that period, 'wait a day or two, then visit her in secret'.[32] The attraction has something to do with those other lives lived within its walls, lives of a single family, 'who had given her life'. Out of their emotions, 'she had woven a personality for herself, she had become what their thoughts and their desires had made her'.

Daphne du Maurier and her children at Menabilly House in Cornwall, 1945. 'The house possessed me' from the first day, she later wrote.

Written in the aftermath of leaving Menabilly, the sentiment is perhaps over-egged. But this idée fixe is what creates the excitement and the strange incongruity in *Rebecca*. The novel is named for a woman, but the first notes of obsession are sounded for a house, Manderley. And though Maxim de Winter's unnamed second wife feels haunted by her husband's love for Rebecca, it turns out that what he feels is not love but seething hate, though the crux of his hatred is not immediately apparent. The seed may have been sown by Rebecca's vulgar affairs, but his fatal deed is prompted by the threat to his ancestral home. Rebecca deliberately provokes de Winter by telling him she is pregnant by another man, but she knows this is not enough to make him lose control. So she deals the cruelest blow, revealing her designs to take Manderley from his family via the entailment, which would be conferred upon her unborn, illegitimate, child. It is the threat of dispossession that she knows he will not stand.

Like Christopher Tietjens in *Parade's End*, Maxim de Winter is doomed to lose his home through the reckless affairs of his wife. While Christopher takes the hit with some resignation (until the threat to Groby Great Tree), de Winter is driven to a murderous rage, as Rebecca hopes he will be. Those portents at the beginning of the novel – de Winter's silences – hid not grief for his dead wife, but the love for a house that doomed him to kill her. It is the kind of obsession du Maurier knew something about. In real life, du Maurier fought hard to keep Menabilly. She consulted lawyers and endeavoured to convince the Rashleigh family to allow her to stay on. In the end, in 1969 she took their offer of the lease at Kilmarth and lived there until her death in 1989.

Rebecca was popular at publication, but it found real fame when it was made into a film, directed by Alfred Hitchcock, in 1940. Many people will forever see the haunted de Winters as Laurence Olivier and Joan Fontaine. (Hitchcock based *The Birds* on another story by du Maurier, though he changed much of the plot.) Finding a suitable house was deemed of huge importance to the film's producer, David O. Selznick. But after searches in England and America, the team gave up and used images painted on glass for the external 'long shots' of the house.[33] All the interiors were purpose-built sets and the outdoor beach scenes were also shot in California. The unfortunate effect is that the house plays much less a part than it should, and the driving obsession is mostly transferred to the crazed expressions of Mrs Danvers.

If du Maurier re-invigorated the Gothic house with modern passion and intrigue, Agatha Christie turned it into something of a three-dimensional game-board in which to reconfigure characters and objects to act out the varied plots of her seventy-six novels, 158 short stories and fifteen plays. Not all of these took place in large old English mansions; her settings evolved over time to include modern houses and apartments, as well as trains, pleasure boats and archaeological encampments. She became the bestselling author of all time, and her characters emerged from the page onto stage, television and film. But it is for popularising the 'murder mystery' set in a specific place with an array of potential suspects that she is best known. In doing so, she also gave some of the grander houses new identities as places of intrigue but without the sense of terror of previous treatments. Her readers more like

Catherine Morland in excitable sleuthing mode than Mrs de Winter narrating her late encounters with evil.

Christie's first published novel, *The Mysterious Affair at Styles* (1921), is set in a large country house, Styles Court, in Sussex, and was written from her own large family home, Ashfield, in Torquay, Devon, as well as from her room at the Moorland Hotel on Dartmoor. Styles is revisited in *Curtain* (1975), though at this point it has suffered the ignominious fate (mourned so bitterly in du Maurier's early draft of *Rebecca*) of being turned into a guest house. Christie and her first husband, Archie, acquired their own large house in the countryside in Berkshire after the publication of her break-through novel, *The Murder of Roger Ackroyd*. They named the mock-Tudor house 'Styles', after the book that launched her career. *Crooked House* (1949), often noted by Christie as one of her personal favourites, features a large gabled, half-timbered mansion in London. *The Body in the Library* (1942) has classic Cluedo appeal, but *And Then There Were None* (1939), one of her best-loved tales, brought the murder mystery to a new level of cunning and, as the guests are stranded at an island residence, gave the house even more prominence as an accomplice.

There are many houses Christie knew that likely inspired her settings. She was born into a wealthy and well-housed family, so Styles Court, the country estate that became a reha-bilitation centre for British officers, could have taken its form from Ashfield, the house she grew up in and continued to use throughout her adult life, or from Abney Hall, which belonged to the family of her sister Madge's husband, James Watt. The eponymous 'Crooked House' probably took something from

her own Styles. Abney Hall in Cheshire, was a special favourite of young Agatha, who was a frequent visitor. It was 'a
wonderful house to have Christmas in if you were a child', she
wrote, 'an enormous Victorian Gothic, with quantities of
rooms, passages, unexpected steps, back staircases, front staircases, alcoves, niches' and 'three different pianos' to play.[34]
Christie wrote the novel *After the Funeral* and the short story
'The Adventure of the Christmas Pudding' while staying there,
and it featured as the Chimneys estate in two thrillers from
the 1920s, *The Secret of Chimneys* and *The Seven Dials Mystery*. It is easy to see how a childhood experience of living in
these great houses, especially one as happy as Christie's
appears to have been, allowed her to take what is ultimately a
more playful view of them than what we find in the Gothic
tradition. Although du Maurier related fond memories of
houses like Milton and Slyfield, the fact that these were wartime refuges may have cast a more serious spell on her
memory. Whatever the reason, Christie's view of these houses
is much less dramatic, and though she is fond of giving them
particular names – Styles Court, Ashley Grange, Swinley
Dean, Fernly Park, End House, Chimneys, Gossington Hall,
Nasse House, etc. – she doesn't usually concern herself with
lavish decorative details. Despite playing host to gruesome
crimes, the houses of her murderous imagination are not particularly memorable, or foreboding.

Agatha Christie didn't always need many rooms to stage a
good mystery. 'The Third Floor Flat' takes an interesting turn
as it moves into the realm of post-war apartment living. Characters trying to get into their locked flat by way of a coal
chute accidentally enter the wrong residence and find a dead

Agatha Christie and her second husband, Max Mallowan, at Greenway House in Devonshire.

body. Luckily, a dapper crime-fighter by the name of Hercule Poirot lives just upstairs and is on hand to bring the murderer to justice. In her later stories, Christie indulged the taste for more modern architecture. Though not often precisely articulated by Christie, the settings have given television producers license to use some of England's most iconic modern houses and apartment blocks as film locations. *Endless Night* (1967) features a glamorous newly built house that is the answer to the dream of the low-born narrator. Spying a parcel of land for sale, he says: 'My longing for a house, a fine and beautiful house, such a house as I could never hope to have, flowered into life then.'[35] Having said that, there isn't a lot of information about the design, apart from the description of it being 'plain, very modern . . . with shape and light'.[36]

Although Christie did not often name the buildings that had inspired her, she certainly would have got some of her ideas of modern architecture from her wartime residence in the Lawn Road flats in Hampstead (now known as the Isokon Building), where she and her second husband, Max Mallowan, went to live after their house at Sheffield Terrace was destroyed by bombing in 1940. The Lawn Road flats were built in 1934 by the architect Wells Coates, who was inspired by the new models for urban living, such as those espoused by Le Corbusier (see chapter 12). The Isokon (as the building was renamed for the original design collective responsible for the building) contains thirty-four flats and demonstrates the minimalist, streamlined aesthetic of 1930s modernism. Not only the style of architecture but the creative types who were also in residence probably contributed to Christie's appreciation for modernist design. Walter Gropius and Laszlo Maholy-Nagy of the influential Bauhaus school of art in Germany came to live there, as did the designer Marcel Breuer. It is now a Grade I-listed building, having been completely refurbished in 2003, and is considered one of London's modernist landmarks.

Born in Torquay, Christie often returned to Devon in her fiction and in real life. In 1938, as Ashfield was being encroached upon by public buildings, she bought a holiday home, Greenway, a house she had known from her childhood in Torquay. It became a much-loved home and she continued to use it until her death in 1976. In her stories, Greenway is most easily identifiable as Nasse House in *Dead Man's Folly* (1956), which begins with a group of people playing a murder-mystery game that turns into the genuine article. Here,

Christie has taken a postmodern approach, making a deliberately self-conscious reference to the fact that the characters and reader, too, are engaged in a kind of game. The boathouse where the body is found is very like the thatched little shelter at Greenway, further bringing the story out of its purely fictional world. Christie and Max had also purchased Winterbrook House in Wallingford as a second country retreat (she was still using her family home at Ashfield at the time) in 1934.

One of the more eccentric residences in Christie's fiction is the house on Indian Island in *And Then There Were None* (or, as it was originally titled, *Ten Little Niggers*). The 1939 novel is considered her masterpiece, and the location is thought by many to be based on Burgh Island, just off the south coast of Devon. The wind-lashed residence was probably inspired by the Burgh Island Hotel, an amusingly ornate, whitewashed Art Deco specimen that played host to a number of celebrities in the 1930s, including Winston Churchill, Noël Coward and Christie herself. The effect of war, which was impending as the book was being written, may have had some bearing on the atmosphere of desperate isolation and on her decision to turn the resort location into a darker scene of serial murder, though Christie noted that the main challenge to herself was how to get ten people to die 'without it becoming ridiculous'.[37]

Christie didn't present houses as objects of inexplicable, fatal obsession the way that du Maurier does, but she had her own domestic fixations. Early on in her career it was partly with the aim of helping her mother avoid having to sell Ashfield that Christie was prompted to continue writing detective

The Lawn Road flats, *c*. 1950 (now the Isokon Building), designed by Wells Coates in 1934. Christie and her husband went to live here in 1940, after their house was destroyed by bombing.

stories, or 'whodunits', a genre that had gained mass popularity with the tales of Arthur Conan Doyle. But the houses she set her stories in were more like pieces to a puzzle than places of supernatural or psychological horror. Christie, like others of her social set, spent a lot of time in the great houses of her family and friends, but two world wars had had an impact on what is now viewed as a period of a rather carefree and indulgent lifestyle. It is perhaps no coincidence that the board game Cluedo (Clue, in the US) appeared in 1949, in the wake of Christie's own popularity and when many such houses were under threat. Cluedo's inventor, Anthony E. Pratt, is reported to have said that Cluedo grew out of 'murder', a game played in country houses in which people snuck around the rooms enacting secret killings, and that he got the idea during the war when blackouts put an 'end to many entertainments, including house parties.[38]

Of course, Agatha Christie was well aware of the allure of the stately home, but she was happy to play with the setting in a way that approached pantomime, as well as parlour game, refusing to see it as a crucial cultural symbol or historical marker. In 'The Adventure of the Christmas Pudding', Hercule Poirot expresses 'horror' rather than delight at being invited to spend Christmas in 'an English country house', even though 'parts of it actually date from the fourteenth century', as he fears the cold and damp.[39] Yet like *Rebecca* and other haunting/mystery/detective stories, Christie's works still have tremendous voyeuristic appeal in offering readers (through unexplained happenings) the chance to spy into the rooms, rituals and private lives of other people and their houses. The stories set in their rooms give the houses a new life of sorts, with fresh possibilities for modern narratives, enriched by historical or even mythic links to the past, even if those links aren't at the forefront of the tale. In the further decades after the war, such links to the past were being thrown off as novelists embraced the life of the present, and future, however mundane or horrific that might appear.

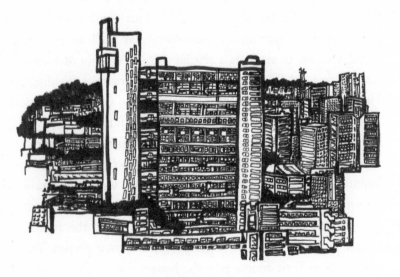

Trellick Tower

TWELVE

The Glamour, Horror and Ennui of Modern Housing: Ian Fleming, J. G. Ballard, Julian Barnes

> 'The building was a monument to good taste, to the well-designed kitchen, to sophisticated utensils and fabrics, to elegant and never ostentatious furnishings – in short to that whole aesthetic sensibility which these well-educated professional people had inherited from all the schools of industrial design, all the award-winning schemes of interior decoration institutionalized by the last quarter of the twentieth century.'
>
> J. G. Ballard, *High-Rise*

Writers like Ford Madox Ford and Evelyn Waugh may have romanticised the country manor, and even Daphne du Maurier's haunting of Manderley could be said to have played on romantic associations with the grand English pile, but housing in post-war Britain was anything but romantic. The necessity of building, and quickly, shelter to replace the 100,000 houses destroyed by the Blitz in London alone, meant there was little room for romance.[1] Coming to England as a teenager in 1946, J. G. Ballard described it as 'a terribly shabby place'. It was, he said, 'locked into the past and absolutely exhausted by the war'.[2]

In that aftermath, some architectural and planning theorists saw a clean slate on which to begin anew with modern ideas and advances in technology and ways to create new towns and solutions to urban and suburban housing. There was hope that in new buildings, dwellings could be rationalised for optimum efficiency and comfort. The architect Le Corbusier achieved fame with his radically modern designs for what he called *machines à habiter* ('machines for living'). Le Corbusier was part of a movement of 'utopian modernists' who believed that advances in technology and engineering could produce forward-looking architecture, which would promote essentially socialist ideals of offering beneficial housing to all. This attitude, combined with the need for high-density housing, resulted in the construction of what we now call tower blocks in Britain: apartment buildings of multiple storeys that might also include other amenities, such as common space at different levels, with shared walkways and stairs dubbed 'streets in the sky'. Packing many more people into a smaller footprint and offering all the modern conveniences, these models had great appeal for housing chiefs and a tremendous impact on post-war building. The first tower block was built in London in 1954, and by the end of the 1950s half a million new flats had been built, many of which were in new 'mixed' developments that included multistorey blocks.[3]

By the late 1960s, however, these same ideas were already being disparaged, as the self-contained blocks, with their isolated passageways and neglected public areas, became breeding grounds for criminal and anti-social behaviour. Into the 1970s and beyond, the housing estate and its under-maintained tower blocks provided a familiarly grim backdrop for dramas depicting crime and social desperation. Fiction in the post-war period continued to experiment with ways to express both the sense of relief and optimism of peacetime, as well as the loss of connection to the past. Some writers celebrated the new future unfettered by outmoded traditions and limitations; others saw a malaise in new consumerism and the unquestioning embrace of new technologies. The dominance of the automobile and rail led to the rise of commuter towns, while the urban centres continued to increase in population. All of this movement, development and change influenced ideas of domestic life in more ways than Thomas Hardy or E. M. Forster could have thought to imagine, or fear.

In the 1950s and '60s, Ian Fleming brought a world of glamour and intrigue to the bleak building scape of post-war Britain and to the wider reading world with his novels of megalomaniacs living in elaborate futuristic hideaways and being foiled by plucky acts of British derring-do. It was these arch-villains who provided a stage for the outlandish new architecture so eagerly, so confidently futuristic and so well exploited by the film-makers who helped to make Fleming an international household name. In the following decade, J. G. Ballard contemplated the effects of technologically driven manmade landscapes on human relationships and community. His trio of novels from the early 1970s – *Crash*, *Concrete Island* and *High-Rise* – looked at what he termed 'the communications landscape and technology'. These were brand new, modern environments created ostensibly for luxury and convenience. But, tailored to the demands of the automobile, they were designed not so much for human comfort as 'for man's absence'.[4]

Julian Barnes did not write about a specific house in the

London suburbs, but about the psychological and imaginative aura of suburban existence. (Around the same time some key American writers were looking at the social and real detachment of the suburban condition, but their adult characters expressed more hostility than Barnes's thoughtfully disenchanted protagonist.*) All pointed towards inertia in domestic life, which may not have been produced by modern housing, but was certainly at home in its thinly insulated walls.

Thanks largely to ambitious film-location managers, most of us associate Fleming's Bond characters with their ultra-luxurious lairs in exotic places. One that particularly comes to mind is *Diamonds are Forever* (1971), which includes some fantastic scenes set in a circular, boulder-inscribed desert house designed by the American avant-garde modernist John Lautner and overlooking the desert resort of Palm Springs, California.† However, that house and many other elements only exist in the film, which, like several of the cinematic versions of the novels, deviated widely from the novel. But Fleming, who wrote from his own house, Goldeneye, in Jamaica, did include some signature abodes in the written work. And he collaborated on most of the films, so the weird spaces that emerged on screen were also at least partly driven by his own fictional genius.

One of the less impressive dwellings of the novels, but no less telling of the criminal psyche, is the home of the eponymous Mr Goldfinger, 'a pretentious sort of place at Reculver, at the mouth of the Thames'.⁵ Though it has its own charm,

---

* See, for example, Richard Yates's *Revolutionary Road* or John Updike's *Rabbit* tetralogy.
† Lautner's fantastically futuristic houses appear in many Hollywood films, including *Body Double*, *A Single Man* and *The Big Lebowski*, as well as numerous music videos.

this area of the coast is not exactly glamorous, and the Grange is no futuristic wonder: it is large and expensive, and, as Bond describes it, 'a heavy, ugly, turn-of-the-century mansion with a glass-enclosed portico and sun parlour' that smelled of 'trapped sunshine, rubber plants and dead flies'.[6] The interiors are classic English heirloom reproduction, as if Goldfinger, the self-conscious émigré, is putting on the part of the English gentleman: the gloomy hall/living room is furnished with floor-to-ceiling panelling and 'Rothschildian pieces of furniture of the Second Empire'. There's not much to inspire admiration in the villain's taste, and Bond is unimpressed: 'What a dump!'[7] It is as if to say that the days of the old English country house having any appeal or authority are gone, though Goldfinger, being a foreigner, is perhaps not aware of this. Still, of course, Bond goes exploring; as he says, 'The secrets of a house are in the bedrooms and bathrooms.'[8]

Perhaps owing to the dispiriting post-war cityscape of his home country, Fleming saved the really amazing mod cons for his criminal bases abroad. Dr No's Caribbean hideout is worlds away from Goldfinger's English fustiness. Dug into an island cliff-face, it is, Bond says, a 'mink-lined prison', decorated with cool colour schemes and plush pile carpets. The pièce de résistance is the sixty-foot-long, high-ceilinged room, 'lined on three sides with books to the ceiling'. These bibliographic monoliths are only a distraction. The really noteworthy room feature is the giant glass wall onto the sea, through which Bond and the beautiful Honeychile Rider admire 'a silver swarm of anchovies', 'the twenty-foot tendrils of a Portuguese man-o'-war' and 'a long dark shadow' that can only be one thing.[9]

On Her Majesty's Secret Service (1963) and *You Only Live Twice* (1964) belong to the trilogy of novels dealing with Bond's arch-nemesis, Ernst Stavro Blofeld. The former puts the villain on top of a Swiss mountain, next to the Piz Gloria hotel and restaurant, in a discreet hideaway made of granite, with a flat concrete roof for landing helicopters. Inside is a modernist haven, with 'upholstered aluminium chaise longues' sat on a veranda offering (deadly) vertiginous vistas.[10] In *You Only Live Twice*, Bond gets to explore Blofeld's semi-ruined Japanese castle, a 'soaring black-and-gold pile' with 'winged turrets' soaring up like 'vast bat-wings against the stars.'[11] The castle is surrounded by a 'garden of death', full of poisonous vegetation and volcanic fumaroles. Blofeld, in a manner Horace Walpole would have admired, wanders around his demonic demesne dressed in the protective armour of a samurai, so as to avoid coming into contact with his fatal specimens.

Apart from Goldfinger's antiquated mansion, none of these is an English house. Fleming was looking far forward into the technological future with his ideas for underwater, sky-high and computerised pieds-a-terror, but was also using some time-honoured tropes. His scenarios play with both country-house whodunit and Gothic kitsch-horror, which he turns to futuristic fantasy. It is easy to see how readers still reeling from the after-effects of war and rationing became enticed by the offer of an insider's tour of dazzling places – the French Riviera, the Swiss Alps, the tropics – and a chance to enter a brilliant world of glamorous and exciting escapist fantasy. As he travels from ski slopes to island pleasure palaces, James Bond invites us into the pages of high-end shelter magazines, showing off the brand items – a Knole sofa, a Wilton carpet – and raising anticipation for the stylish sex and violence to follow.

Although his fictional settings are usually in far-flung locations, Fleming is often linked with one of the most famous modernist architects to work in England. Ërno Goldfinger's best-known contributions to the London cityscape are the Balfron Tower in Limehouse (1963) and Trellick Tower in Kensington, finished in 1972. Both were built in the uncompromising Brutalist style that became popular during the post-war building spree, beginning in the 1950s. The term comes from the French *béton brut*, or 'raw concrete', since the builders were exploiting the efficiency and relative cheapness of exposed concrete, rather than concrete that was covered with render or a combination of more appealing materials. The towers are monolithic in appearance, rough concrete exteriors with very little ornament, the modular forms demonstrating a

In the 1930s Goldfinger demolished three Victorian houses to built this modernist terrace on Willow Road in Hampstead. The project provoked the ire of neighbourhood conservationists.

spare functionalism. Such buildings drew harsh opposition, even before problems in the systems began to emerge.

In the 1930s, long before these more ambitious commissions, Goldfinger had built a low-lying modernist house on Willow Road, in Hampstead, north London. There is abundant lore and some fact to an argument that arose between Fleming and Goldfinger to do with this project. The house provoked the ire of the local preservation society, both because of its radically modern style and because the architect had torn down some Victorian houses in order to build it. Whether Fleming actively objected to Goldfinger's house design is not certain. However, he did have a dispute with the architect when, on hearing that his name was being used for the maniacal protagonist, the latter tried to stop publication of the novel. According to Andrew Lycett (and other Fleming biographers), the Goldfinger character was based on an American commodities magnate, Charles Engelhard. But Fleming got the villain's *name* from his friend John Blackwell, who was related by marriage to Ërno Goldfinger and was, reportedly, not a fan of the architect's oeuvre.[12] But there are some similarities between Fleming's character and the architect: Ërno Goldfinger was born in Hungary and moved with his wife to the UK in 1934; Auric Goldfinger, of the novel, is a Latvian émigré, who also came to the UK in the 1930s. The architect's reputation as an egotistical and uncompromising figure did not make the link any less plausible. (There is also a strain of thinly veiled anti-Semitism in the criticism of both.) Fleming reacted angrily to Goldfinger's attempts to halt the release of the book, and put it to his publishers that they should change the name to 'Goldprick' instead.[13]

Fleming did most of his writing from the much more sedate quarters at Goldeneye, the house he built in the late 1940s on land near the seaside village of Orcabessa, on Jamaica's northeast coast. The name 'Goldeneye' came from a wartime operation Fleming had been involved with when he worked for the Naval Intelligence Division, which he joined in 1939.[14] He had first visited the island during the war, and afterwards it became a regular retreat. Before building Goldeneye, he stayed at Bellevue, a large villa belonging to his friends Ivar and Sheila Bryce. For his own house, Fleming designed a large, open living room and comparatively modest bedrooms. It was built in traditional island style, foregoing glass in the windows and using louvered jalousies to create an open-air environment with wide verandas. The house does not appear as the base of any evil overlord in the novels, but there are glimpses of Goldeneye in the occasional places of respite the hero finds, usually with a beautiful, scantily clad woman by his side.

Fleming's grandfather was a wealthy financier who had made money investing in railroads, oil and in the financial markets. He and his wife bought an estate in Oxfordshire in 1903 and a house, which they demolished to build a many-chimneyed Jacobean-style mansion with forty-four bedrooms. It was here, at Joyce Grove, that Fleming spent his younger years, and possibly where Goldfinger's 'heavy, ugly' house with its 'Rothschildean' furnishings got its inspiration. Fleming also lived at various addresses in London, including flats on Ebury Street in Belgravia and Carlyle Mansions in Chelsea. But it was at Goldeneye in 1952 that Fleming began writing *Casino Royale*, the first novel to feature the debonair British spy, James Bond. And it was at Goldeneye and other

The sprawling Oxfordshire manor house at Joyce Grove, which Ian Fleming's grandfather began building in 1904.

sites around his regular holiday home in Jamaica that he envisioned many of the exotic settings for his heroes and villains that provided such an antidote to the grim realities of postwar Britain for his readers, and, by 1962, for cinema audiences worldwide.

A year after the cinematic release of *The Man with the Golden Gun*, J. G. Ballard published a novel that also featured malignant acts taking place in idyllic surroundings. But rather than looking beyond Britain, Ballard focused his gaze on London developments, marrying consumerist ideals of luxury housing with the social problems caused by crowded urban environments. *High-Rise* begins with two thousand hopeful residents entering a forty-storey apartment tower, feeling that they have bought into a life of domestic ease. With its smooth, modern design and high-end conveniences, it is the kind of place that

Bond might stage a tryst with a beautiful double agent. However, the novel ends not with a satisfying triumph over evil, but with the dwellings, halls, shops and corridors being devastated by a brutalism that has less to do with architectural design than with the human malevolence it has somehow inspired.

Ballard makes clear his antipathy for the development. The apartments are described as 'cells' in the cliff-face. Rather than being a beneficent machine for living, the building is 'a huge machine designed to serve, not the collective body of tenants, but the individual resident in isolation'. Its array of services – air-conditioning, garbage chutes, electrically operated features – were all things that 'a century earlier' we would have required 'an army of tireless servants' to provide.[15] It is a pointed irony, then, that the architect who dresses largely in white and lives in the penthouse at the top of the building, like some 'fallen angel', is married to a woman who grew up in a country house and is at first uncomfortable in the building's automated and cloistered lifestyle.

The flats in Ballard's dystopia are occupied not by social-housing tenants, as those in the tower blocks that were dotted around London and other UK cities by this time, but by 'professionals', who are nonetheless grouped by wealth. The lower nine floors are 'home to the "proletariat" of film technicians, air-hostesses and the like', while the middle section, up to the thirty-fifth floor, is made up of 'docile members of the professions – doctors, and lawyers, accountants and tax specialists'. The top five floors contain 'the discreet oligarchy of minor tycoons and entrepreneurs, television actresses and careerist academics'. This last group has access to the high-speed lifts, carpeted stairs and 'superior services'.[16]

It is not difficult to foretell how grievances might erupt in a building that is seen by its residents as both 'a hanging paradise' and a 'glorified tenement'.

Robert Laing, a physiology lecturer, is one of the main protagonists of the story, and has his first hostile encounter involving a dispute over the shared rubbish chute. As he negotiates the social strata of the building, he soon realises that 'people in high-rises tended not to care about tenants more than two floors below them'. Glitches in the building's electricity supply and malfunctions in some of the lifts servicing the lower floors ignite an internal class war. Unpleasant confrontations in the public spaces rapidly escalate into physical violence. Like most of the residents Laing becomes drawn in, rather than repelled, by the growing depravity as tenants raid each other's apartments and are reduced to the 'three obsessions' of 'security, food and sex'.[17] Ballard describes clashes taken to surreal extremes, arguing that the building itself demanded this behaviour, being 'an architecture designed for war, on the unconscious level if no other'.[18] The 2016 film of the novel tried to cope with this vision through heavy use of stylised montages of 1970s architecture and interiors blended with the scenes of hedonism and casual viciousness that permeate the book, to little success. This is partly due to the relentlessness of the narrative itself, which catalogues scene after scene of primal beings battling through apartments that have been torn apart and barricaded, where mounds of rubbish line every space and where domestic animals are killed for food.

Ballard, who was no admirer of England's 'green and pleasant land' and was quick to embrace the cool promise of modernity after the war, nevertheless found worrying portents in the high-rise tower blocks going up in cities in the UK and the USA. In London, the buildings that had promised so much were proving to be problematic, attracting crime and vandalism and sometimes failing to function. The idea of 'streets in the sky' with amenities at different levels, moving living space into the vertical, had demonstrated worrying cracks and earned swathes of vocal detractors. Ballard never cited these projects directly, but he claimed to have carried out his own research into criminal behaviour and concluded that a 'degree of criminality is affected by liberty of movement; it's higher in cul-de-sacs. And high-rises are cul-de-sacs: 2,000 people jammed together in the air.'[19]

Although Ballard never made direct comparisons between the novel and the Brutalist towers that were going up during the time he was writing, those buildings certainly can be seen as structures that are better off with 'man's absence'. As pristine edifices they can appear pleasingly sculptural, but are less so when their balconies are dotted with the detritus of everyday life, and further degraded by poor maintenance, graffiti and general neglect. Ballard's environments of uniform luxury become dehumanising, but rather than engendering mindless conformity, as in Aldous Huxley's *Brave New World*, they result in 'the regression of middle-class professionals into a state of barbarism'.

The novel is often associated with Goldfinger's Trellick Tower, which by the time Ballard was writing *High-Rise* had had a series of problems and a lot of bad press. Even before its opening, there were crises, both in its own construction and in other projects.* In 1968, a fire in the Ronan Point tower block in London caused most of the twenty-three floors to collapse and the deaths of three people. The disaster fuelled popular agitation against tower blocks, so that by the time Trellick Tower was completed in 1972, it seemed doomed to fail. (Goldfinger later identified the problem at Ronan Point as having been caused by the use of precast, rather than poured, concrete, but not many people by that stage were prepared to listen.)[20] The 'drying rooms' that Goldfinger had designed in the ground-floor amenities block were vandalised before they were finished. These rooms were his attempt to convince the tenants not to air their laundry on the balconies (and so ruin the appearance of the tower), but they never functioned properly.[21] Just before Christmas 1972, a fire hydrant on the twelfth floor was tampered with, causing flooding through the elevator shafts, which meant that the block had no water, heat or electricity during the holidays. The tower became so firmly linked with crime and social decay that some council-housing tenants lobbied not to be housed there.[22] (It should be noted that at least some of Goldfinger's assumptions were correct: in the twenty-first century, improvements in maintenance and security have made the Trellick Tower a desirable address.)†

Rather than making his fictional model a replication of social-housing schemes, or naming any of the council-run tower blocks as inspiration, Ballard set his story in a deliberately upscale version, citing its genesis in his experiences of

---

* To be fair to Goldfinger, and to other architects of the tower-block genre, these problems had a lot to do with poor construction, and lack of maintenance and security, which were sacrificed to benefit municipal budgets.

† At the time of writing, a one-bedroom flat in the Trellick Tower can be purchased for around a quarter of a million pounds.

luxury high-rise living in London and abroad. He described a complex of office and residential blocks in his parents' neighbourhood near Victoria, which were, he said, mostly inhabited by 'rich business people' with 'Rolls-Royces and immodestly appointed flats, huge rents'. Yet the residents, he said, 'spent all their time bickering with one another' over issues of 'the most incredible triviality', such as who needed to pay for a potted-plant display on the seventeenth-floor landing and whose curtains didn't match. He found similarly petty grievances rising among tenants in an upscale apartment block where he stayed on the Costa Brava in Spain. Again, these were mostly occupied by educated professionals, but Ballard reported 'an enormous amount of antagonism between the people in the lower floors and the people in the top'.[23] Interestingly, Ballard

Trellick Tower, designed by Ërno Goldfinger to be a 'utopian modernist' solution to the postwar housing shortage, became a symbol of design failure.

placed the shops and amenities for his high-rise on an interme-
diate floor (the tenth), as Le Corbusier had done in his ground-
breaking utopian model, the Unité d'Habitation in Marseilles,
which becomes another cause of tension between the residents
in the novel.* Goldfinger felt that locating services up inside the
building would be detrimental to residents on lower floors,
and so at Trellick Tower he chose to place these amenities –
nursery, doctor's surgery, laundry – at ground level.

Another immediate provocation for the high-rise setting of
the book probably came from the development of the London
Docklands at about the time that Ballard was writing. Developers were attempting a regeneration of land among the old
warehouses and abandoned shipping yards of a long-desolate
waterfront district by introducing a scheme of high-rise towers
for office and residential use. The first tower in this development was finished in the 1980s, but plans had already been
underway for ambitious building projects in the disused ports
since the early 1970s. Ballard specifically sites his fictional
tower in a square mile 'of abandoned dockland and ware-
housing' in London, so the Docklands development provides
some ambient background. But Ballard seems particularly
keen to demonstrate that the luxury high-rise is as prone to
criminality as its less fortunate relations in subsidised estates.
In fact, the professional classes in the world of Ballard's imagining become more deviant, relishing their descent into inhu-
manity as more buildings are finished and occupied around
them. The five towers in the fictional development overlook
an ornamental lake, which remains an empty concrete basin

---

* Unité d'Habitation in Marseilles is now mostly inhabited by the type of middle-class professionals Ballard addressed in his novel.

(a sign of promise unfulfilled), while the tenants of the first tower fall into savagery reminiscent of the adolescent boys in William Golding's *Lord of the Flies*, an equally disturbing fable of human depravity.

The failure of community was impelled by what Ballard saw as the modern sense of isolation caused by urban planning, which was not only designed for cars, but also demanded continuous movement, as on a raised motorway, where stopping even for emergencies was difficult and dangerous. It is a condition that has sped far beyond what Margaret and Helen Schlegel in *Howards End* fear in the 'craze for motion', and Ballard takes the idea to worrying extremes in *Concrete Island*. As the action in *High-Rise* goes on, it is easy to feel that Ballard goes too far, that the violence and vice continue without any seeming purpose. The decision of the residents to remain there, even to defend the building from outsiders, is just too divorced from reality to make a compelling narrative. But both the violence and the willingness to participate in its vicious circle echo other scenes from the author's own life.

In his focus on the luxury high-rise, he seems to have found a vessel in which to channel the worst tendencies of the human psyche he had witnessed as a child in 1930s Shanghai, both before and during the war. Ballard grew up in Shanghai, where his father ran a textile printing company, in the International Settlement, a collection of large, European-style houses staffed by servants and isolated from the gritty conditions of the city. The family home was expressly English, a 'three-storey, half-timbered structure in Surrey stockbroker style'.[24] Similarly, other, mostly European-born, businessmen in the neighbourhood built houses in imitation of their own national traditions. Families led lives of comparative luxury, while dismissing or ignoring the starving peasants at their gates, who were brutally treated first by the Chinese authorities, then by the occupying Japanese soldiers. At this time, Ballard says, Shanghai had been ravaged by endless civil war, famine and floods, and 'thousands of destitute Chinese roamed the streets'.[25] As a boy being driven to school, he often saw dead bodies or coffins lying by the side of the road. After the Japanese invasion of 1937 not much changed for the European families, except that the Chinese peasants, their fields and villages bombed out, became more desperate to enter the International Settlement, and were just as desperately repelled by the European inhabitants.

As the war intensified, in 1943 the Ballard family was interned in the Lunghua camp. The author describes a stimulating, if circumscribed, life there that became more dangerous as the Japanese began to lose the war. Ballard wrote explicitly of his experiences at Lunghua in his novel *Empire of the Sun* (1984), but I would argue that the knife-edge atmosphere of Shanghai and the camp permeates the earlier novels, particularly the embattled high-rise. Ballard takes care to describe how conditions started to deteriorate *after* the Japanese guards abandoned the camp and before the American troops managed to take Shanghai. No longer ruled by a menacing authority, inmates became querulous, and most chose to stay in their prison, fearful of the world beyond the barbed wire fences, and confident they would be rescued by Allied forces. Airdrops of badly needed food parcels, though fairly distributed among inmates, were greedily hoarded, and any that went astray were fiercely hunted down, even torn from the grasps of starving Chinese families, and returned to the now un-guarded camp. Ballard's story of British families who remained in the camp, 'defending their caches of Spam, Klim (powdered milk) and Lucky Strike cigarettes' six months after the war ended has the ring of wartime myth.[26] But it also helps to explain the psychology of his fictional high-rise, in which people feel secure in their prison, fighting among each other but more afraid of the world outside. This fierce desperation is disturbing enough as fact, but in the world of the novel it becomes curiously difficult to fathom, one of the problems many readers have with the book. The central paradox in the novel is that this ultimate achievement in luxury housing is inhabited by people reduced to their most savage selves.

Ballard's life when his family returned to England did not bring him a feeling of great relief or hope. It was not the won-derful return to civilization that we (or he) might have imag-ined. Instead, he found a country where 'large sections of London and the Midlands were vast bomb sites'.[27] And though they had won the war, Britain, according to Ballard, had the feeling of a country that had lost. There was 'rationed food, clothing, petrol' and a pervasive sense of diminished hope and confidence. On top of this, he found a class system that, with its codes of deference and unquestioning loyalties, 'cultivated second-rateness and low expectations'.[28]

During the war and after, Ballard spoke of his admiration for the Americans, who seemed to embrace modernity rather than shrink from it, and of new technologies, lacking any nos-talgia for a great British past. But by the 1970s, when he was writing *High-Rise*, he began to question the new technological landscape and its effect on human relationships, communities and sense of self. It might seem an unlikely comparison, but what Ballard was doing was similar in some ways to a line of authors before him, even those such as Jane Austen, in that he chronicled the encouraged by of a living space that was popular at the time. Where Austen showed us the elaborate courtesies, intrigues and injustices abetted by country-house society, Ballard revealed the menacing effects of compact vertical living on inhabitants whose places in the tower are determined by socio-economic hierarchies.

Ballard's more extreme scenarios may be in the realm of science fiction or fantasy, but his underlying assertion that the vertical container for living could have a serious social and psychological impact are not so easily dismissed.* His decision to focus on a luxury high-rise inhabited by the educated and the wealthy, rather than on the typical tower blocks built for social housing, was perhaps to make the point clearly that it was the design of the building, not the class of the residents, which brought about such a hellish downward spiral of human behaviour. It is a telling irony that in Ballard's technologically advanced high-rise, warfare is ignited largely by an everyday facilities failure: the breakdown of the lifts. As Nigel Warburton, biographer of Ernö Goldfinger, has pointed out, surveys of tower-block residents have confirmed that faulty lifts are one of the most common complaints.[29]

As an adult and father of three children, Ballard himself lived most of his life in England, in 'a little suburban house' in Shepperton, near the old film studios. He remarked that journalists who turned up to interview him were often surprised,

---

* See, for example, research for the Policy Exchange conducted by Alex Morton and Nicholas Boys Smith in 2013.

as they were 'expecting a miasma of drug addiction and per-
version of every conceivable kind', but instead found this
'easy-going man playing with his golden retriever and bringing up a family of happy young children'.[30] The madness, it
seems, was securely locked up in the past, and the high-rise.

In 1962, the year before James Bond first appeared in print,
Anthony Burgess presented a futuristic view of Britain that
was no less terrifying, perhaps more so than what Ballard
would envision, since its horrors were not confined to a single
building or group. However, in line with expectations at the
time, it is not surprising that the sociopath at the centre of *A
Clockwork Orange* lives in a battered tower block, complete
with graffiti-riven lobby, or that he is experimented on in an
institution and only finds a drop of human kindness in an out-
of-the-way 'Mansion' in 'Oldtown' (whose occupants he has
previously submitted to a vicious attack); the mansion referring to some more civilised kind of life from the past. The film
of the novel features a dark array of dystopian vignettes readily available in Brutalist London social-housing developments
of the mid-century. Thamesmead South, which along with
Trellick Tower has become synonymous with the failure of
such developments, was used as the location for the protagonist's home in the 1971 film.

As in *High-Rise*, the architecture of *A Clockwork Orange*
seems to contribute to the degradation of human behavior.
Burgess's dystopian vision is enhanced by a backdrop of bleak
public buildings (the 'beat-up biblio', the 'bolshy flatblock').
On his way into his family's apartment in Municipal Flatblock 18A, Alex coolly notes a girl lying bleeding on the

ground and evidence that another woman has been raped. Using the book's disturbing 'nadsat' slang, Alex also relates, with about the same degree of emotion, that the lift has been 'tolchocked real horror show this night, the metal doors all buckled', so he has to walk the ten flights upstairs.[31] Even here among so much casual cruelty and destruction, the failure of community is signalled by a broken elevator.

That language of his character, a fusion of English slang with elements of Russian, and the focus on state-induced institutionalised behaviour-management, invites comparison with Western fears of communism and enforced, inhuman building design. The idea of soulless (and amoral) uniformity is something many easily associated with the ominous Brutalism of tower blocks.

Decades before the residential tower seemed the answer to housing the urban millions in the post-war years, the newly formed suburbs, connected via new train lines reaching out of London to the edges of the countryside, offered the chance to swap the crowding and hazards of city living for fresh air and space, and a much more peaceful and settled existence. Perhaps too much so. In *Metroland*, Julian Barnes brings the suburban experience to the fore by scripting the thoughts of bored and wishful teens, testing a tentative swagger, loping beneath the sodium street lamps, whose orange tinge turns red to brown.* Published in 1980, the novel begins in 1963, just a year after Burgess gave us teenagers whose hunger for experience drove them to the extremes of moral behaviour. Barnes's

---

* This focus contrasts with the dissatisfied adults of suburban America that Richard Yates and John Updike were writing about around the same time.

A 1928 guide to the routes and neighbourhoods of Metro-land, areas covered by the ambitious Metropolitan Railway project, 'the child of the First World War forgotten in the Second'.

suburban young men, however, thrive on pseudo-intellectual banter and attempts to rile the older generation through clever turns at language and feigned insouciance.

The title refers to the neighbourhoods reachable by the Metropolitan railway when it was extended beyond the edges of northwest London in the 1890s and early 1900s. The line provided access to new housing outside, but within easy commuting distance of, the city centre. Developers keen to attract residents came up with the sobriquet 'Metro-land' as part of a campaign that included adorning trains and other public spaces with charmingly illustrated posters showcasing the greener, more tranquil experiences available to those who desired a life beyond the urban jungle at 'Sandy Lodge Golf Course, Pinner Hill, Moor Park, Chorleywood'.[32] The poet John Betjeman composed poems about Metroland and hosted a documentary on the developments in 1973.* As Betjeman pronounced, Metroland was 'the child of the First World War, forgotten in the second'.[33] The Metropolitan line never fulfilled its early promise of connecting the entire country, and by the Second World War, it was no longer aspiring.

By the time Barnes's novel takes place, 'Metroland' has become a byword for settled suburbia. Although *Metroland* is mostly a coming-of-age piece, and the protagonist spends some formative time in Paris, the backdrop of suburbia's unflagging evenness is key to the aura of adolescent ennui. Gone is the frisson of neighbours, of communal anxiety (or hope), the ecstasy of spiritual connection. The name Metroland, Barnes's character tells us, 'gave the string of rural suburbs a spurious integrity'.[34] Nowadays the posters advertising the various locations in easy reach from London along the new rail routes are objects of quaint nostalgia, inciting neither the fear of the urban towers, nor the lyrical charm of the country cottage.

Barnes's character describes the 'thin corridor of land' that was opened up when the Metropolitan Railway pushed west in the 1880s. To Christopher Lloyd, the area has 'no geographical or ideological unity', and it wasn't drawing people for what was there but for what was convenient to travel to: 'You lived there because it was an easy area to get out of.'[35] Accordingly, it is the daily journeys into London that provide the opportunities for Christopher to scrutinise and dismiss other passengers and the infrastructure of his every day. An experienced commuter at the age of sixteen, he has 'studied

---

* A determined advocate of architectural preservation, Betjeman campaigned against the demolition of St Pancras Rail Station when it was under threat in the 1960s.

the rolling stock' and memorised the character of train compartments: 'I knew all the advertisements by heart, and all the varieties of decoration on the barrel-vaulted ceilings.'[36] The house becomes not so much an anchor, as Forster would have it, as a station-stop, on the way somewhere else. From his comfortable but unremarkable bedroom, Chris imagines getting 'out there' to something 'vague and marvelous as the Empyrean', which is 'capital-L Life'.[37] In the end, he returns to live and bring up his own family in the very place he grew up; whatever tantalising opportunities he had heard calling from the world around him had grown quiet. And it is the return to the place, rather than the loss of it, that is the disappointment.

It is not for love of his childhood home that Christopher returns to the suburbs. 'Metroland is about defeat', the author said later. 'I wanted to write about youthful aspiration coming to a compromised end.' The suburban setting provided 'a background metaphor of disappointment' for the character, as it had for the larger aims of Metroland itself. The idea in the early years that these 'pan-European trains would run from Manchester and Birmingham, pick up passengers in London, and continue through to the great cities of the Continent', that these trains would then be linked to Paris via a Channel Tunnel, had not, by the time that Barnes was writing, fulfilled its promise: 'This London suburb where I grew up was conceived in the hope, the anticipation, of great horizons, great journeys. But in fact that never came to pass.'[38]

In the novel, Chris summarises the monotony of his surroundings in the lazy activities of a Sunday: 'Sunday was the day for which Metroland was created.' It is not an opportunity for rest or freedom, but one for lying in bed, 'wondering how to kill the day'. Along with the sounds of the church bells and the train is 'the patterned roar of motor mowers', and when these were quiet 'you might catch the quiet chomp of shears' and finally 'the gentle squeak of chamois on boot and bonnet'. Betjeman's quirky television programme makes room for just such a montage. Of the sounds of garden hoses and children playing outside, the Sundays that were 'always peaceful, and always sunny', Chris says, 'I loathed them.'[39] If Burgess's teen is horrifying in his response to ugly surroundings, Barnes's character greets his peaceful, carefree world with the willful petulance and disdain that suggests he will make good on his promise to find life outside of Metroland.

But it is not to be. In Part III of the novel we meet Chris, now with wife, young child and mortgage. Years after making his dreamt-of sojourn to Paris and having a liaison with a young French woman, he finds, 'it's certainly ironic to be back in Metroland'.[40] Though he claims satisfaction with his life, there's no pleasing nostalgia, no notable fondness for the street of 'sensible detached houses', many, as Betjeman points out in his documentary, with romantic-sounding names – 'Ravenshoe', 'Vue de Provence'. These appear in carved in Gothic letters on panels of wood screwed into the trees.[41] They are names meant to conjure older or more beautiful places, but in the new development, they have a hollow ring. Chris's return to Metroland is no happy homecoming to a place of familial roots, like Groby, to a dreamy recollection of summer at Brideshead, or an embrace of spirited connections as at Howards End. There is some comfort here, but it is a 'lazy pleasure' in the familiarly ordinary, the facts of his own kitchen, 'the smooth, clean, dry expanse of stainless steel' on the counter, 'the table laid for breakfast, the neat line of cups on their hooks, the onions giving off a crepuscular glisten from their hanging basket'. The light from the sodium street lamp outside turns the stripes on his pyjamas brown, as it had the red of his own mother's coat, quietly shading him into the dull tones of suburbia.

Although Fleming, Ballard and Barnes took diverging approaches to the living spaces of postwar Britain, they are unified by their refusal to confer any sense of inherent value, even the value of nostalgia, on the rooms, flats, and houses of their characters. Not even the architect of Ballard's high-rise is particularly fond of the building, though he refuses to leave. As tenant of the topmost flat, he considers himself 'lord of the manor' though he recognises that 'this huge building he had helped to design was moribund'. But rather than recoil at its dehumanising effects, he relishes the fact that the building has helped people to a 'new life' and 'a pattern of social organization that would become the paradigm of all future high-rise blocks'.[42] This is grim stuff, locating the high-rise more in the tradition of the crumbling Gothic manor than in a critique of urban development, although there are no secret tunnels of escape and no one looking to use them if there were. Along with Goldfinger's musty English house and the stunningly modern lairs of Bond villains, the high-rise and the anonymous suburban dwelling all signal a change in attitude toward the English house in literature. Rather than being places of narrative inspiration, invention, childhood fancy or cultural significance, these fictional homes constitute a negative presence in the lives and aspirations of their characters. For these authors the view of the current and future housing landscape is without art or promise.

Canford School

THIRTEEN

Looking Backwards: The English Country House Through a Post-Modern Lens

'The English country house is as archaic as the osprey. The few left fulfilling the purpose for which they were built are inexorably doomed.'

James Lees-Milne, *The Destruction of the Country House, 1974*

Reviewing *Metroland* in 1980, the critic John Sutherland observed a trend for authors towards 'the Victorian practise of antedating', that is, setting their stories in some definable period of the past.[1] He goes on to mention an observation by the nineteenth-century Danish philosopher Søren Kierkegaard that life is lived forward, but understood backward. Of course, authors throughout history have set their stories in the remote or recent past. Horace Walpole claimed to be relating a story set down 'between 1095, the aera of the first crusade, and 1243, the date of the last'; in *Waverley* Walter Scott said he was telling us about the events that happened 'sixty years since'; Evelyn Waugh's Charles Ryder gives us his impressions of Brideshead 'more than twenty years ago', that is, in 1923. But in the late twentieth century, what we might call 'country house fiction' was taking a new and more critical view.

Instead of presenting the country house as an enduring symbol of some enchanted epoch, writers like Kazuo Ishiguro, Ian McEwan and Alan Hollinghurst showed them to be either nondescript or disappointing relics that could not carry the weight of genuine cultural sigificance. Waugh had voiced a stirring tribute to the ability of the stately home to evoke the atmosphere of another life and time, but his successors several decades on saw the country house as a cipher for disappointment and deceit and challenged those associations with some sort of English idyll. In 2011 Blake Morrison commented that 'novels with an English country-house setting are among the most acclaimed written in recent years'.[2] It is tempting to attribute this to a postmillennial attempt by authors to locate their stories in a moment of charmed innocence, albeit one that is later defiled. But the postmodern writers examined here replaced the romantic image of the ancient noble seat with one of architectural pastiche and decay, in which the authenticity of its significance, as well as its symbolic value, is called into question.

Many people felt the world had lost its innocence in the First World War, but the second conflict in Europe proved even more revealing of human barbarity, and the scale of destruction marked a watershed in our collective history. If man hadn't deserved being kicked out of paradise before the Nazi atrocities, he certainly did now. It would be easy to find consolation in looking back to a time of cultural certainties embodied in the old traditions, manners and estates of the British upper classes as Ford and Waugh had done. Social hierarchies applied structures we may not agree with, but which provided comfort, at least, in being knowable. And yet these were failing systems. However soppy we may have been about old England in the immediate aftermath of the war, at the turn of the millennium the view was less rose-coloured.

In 1989 Kazuo Ishiguro won acclaim for his novel *The Remains of the Day*, a story told by the head butler of a large manor house, Darlington Hall. The novel's present is 1956, but the narrator, Stevens, is in thrall to events from before the Second World War. Ian McEwan's *Atonement* (2001) and Alan Hollinghurst's *The Stranger's Child* (2011) also look back to the pre-war period, presenting the consequences of earlier dramas being played out in the cold light of post-war scrutiny. Although centred on lives lived through traditional English country houses, these novels attempt not to romanticise but to reveal these 'blessed acres of English ground' as an elegant mask for hypocrisy unable to resist the telling effects of time. This isn't new, of course. *Atonement* opens with a quote from *Northanger Abbey*, which brings the English manor house full circle as a fiction writer's tool.

As Ishiguro's novel opens, Stevens, the butler of Darlington Hall, is about to set out on a journey away from the place where he has served for more than thirty years. In all that time, it seems, he has never taken such a holiday, and claims to have enjoyed doing his duty to the house and Lord Darlington. But Lord Darlington has passed away, and the Hall has been bought by Mr Farraday, a wealthy, amiable American. It is, of course, the unconventional Mr Farraday who has made the bold suggestion that Stevens should such a trip. In this small act, separating the butler from the house to which he has been attached for most of his life, the author introduces the anachronistic problem of these houses in the modern world, and he provides the tension of the novel. What will happen to Stevens when Mr Farraday and Darlington Hall no longer have a use for him or his kind? What happens to people who cannot let go of the idea of a glorious past, even once they understand it was never as glorious as they had believed?

What we know of Darlington Hall is mainly to do with its size. Asked to reduce the live-in staff of the house to no more than four, Stevens recalls a time when the house was run by a 'skeleton team of six', before that it was seventeen, and at one point as many as twenty-eight.[3] Stevens accepts the request with the same implacable manner with which he has always run things, whether he is attending to his duties while his father is upstairs on his deathbed or refusing to drop his professional mask when the housekeeper, Miss Kenton, is trying to elicit a fragment of human sympathy. Under his plan, he reveals proudly, almost all the 'attractive parts' of the house could remain in use. These are 'the extensive servants' quarters – including the back corridor, the two still rooms and the old laundry' – as well as 'all the main ground-floor rooms and a generous number of guest rooms'. However, 'the guest corridor up on the second floor would be dust-sheeted'. Stevens finds the work might be just manageable with the four full-time servants, plus a part-time gardener and two cleaners. This practical mental note-taking by Stevens tell us that this is a very large house indeed, while his pages of careful ruminations on how to achieve the perfect balance of care attests to the butler's exacting standards.

For a story so rooted in a particular house, there is little description of Darlington Hall, which tells us something of the author's attitude, that the specifics of the house do not matter here. We learn that like many a grand old English estate, Darlington Hall has been in the same family for centuries. It has a banqueting hall with a 'high and magnificent ceiling', which used to contain a great dining table and could seat thirty or more guests, fifty at a push, with extensions. Nowadays the room is used 'as a sort of gallery'.[4] Still, if Mr Farraday wishes to entertain, he can get 'up to a dozen' in the dining room. In addition to the study, there are also presumably ample public rooms. This is Stevens's 'universe'. But there are any number of English country houses with banqueting halls and high ceilings, and whether Darlington is a stone-clad Georgian pile or a red-brick Tudor, we are not told. What is important is that we see that Stevens' years of self-sacrifice and dedication to this or any house may have been wasted.

Stevens himself is not only from another era, but seems never to have left it. For his new outing he is wearing a suit that has been passed on to him by one of Lord Darlington's guests, 'in 1931 or 1932'. He relies on guidebooks written during the thirties, but is convinced that much of the information will still be up to date, since 'I do not imagine German bombs have altered our countryside so significantly'.[5] In this he may be right, but he hasn't allowed that the world beyond the gates of Darlington Hall might have changed in the normal course of time. The purpose of his journey is to visit the former housekeeper of Darlington, Miss Kenton, who left some twenty years previously when she got married and moved to Cornwall, in 1936. It is this period, when Lord Darlington was at the height of influence, rather than any

383

attachment to the house, that is Stevens's imaginative centre.

Stevens is convinced that in a recent letter from Miss Kenton he has detected 'an unmistakable nostalgia for Darlington Hall' and plans to entice her back with the offer of a job.[6] He has reread the letter a number of times and his assumption, it emerges, hinges on a single remark:

> I was so fond of that view from the second-floor bedrooms overlooking the lawn with the downs visible in the distance. Is it still like that? On summer evenings there was a sort of magical quality to that view and I will confess to you now I used to waste many precious minutes standing at one of those windows just enchanted by it.[7]

If Stevens weren't so fixated on the *idea* of Darlington, he would realise that it is the view rather than the house that Miss Kenton remembers so well. Despite his devotion, Stevens has never given himself time to be enchanted by his surroundings inside or out, or indeed wasted any 'precious minutes' in contemplation of them. It seems that rather than spurring him to any poetic feelings for the place, the letter has inspired him to recapture Miss Kenton so she can feel them for him. The idea that they might run off together and live anywhere but Darlington is not even a passing fancy: he never makes the least romantic gesture. But his recollections of Miss Kenton show him reaching for the closest thing to love that he, in his stilted professional encumbrance, can ever approach, since he is already in a platonic relationship with Darlington.

The omission of any more detail about Darlington Hall suggests that rather than being infused with symbolic or emotional meaning, it is merely a backdrop, one that has become so familiar that it requires no description. Whatever great families lived and died there, whatever historic events may have taken place, whether Elizabeth I slept in one of the bedrooms or ate wild boar in the dining room, whether Shakespeare set a sword-fighting scene in the garden is not important to Stevens or the narrative. Ishiguro isn't so interested in recalling the great houses of the past as in drawing attention to the relationship with them, and to a reverence that might be undeserved or at least unsatisfying.

Ishiguro presents Stevens as an intelligent man, who sees the folly in 'clinging as some do to tradition merely for its own sake', but cling he does, for far more desperate reasons. His father was in service before him and he measures his own strivings for butlerian perfection against a formidable paternal model. Stevens' loyalty was to Lord Darlington, and after his

Though the description of Darlington Hall is minimal, various stately homes, like Dyrham Park in Gloucestershire, were used by film-makers in 1993 to give the house prominence on screen.

employer's death, Stevens continues to live for the running of Darlington Hall. As his employer's power and influence has since fallen into disrepute, the only 'greatness' that exists is in Stevens dogged attachment to Darlington.

Rather than oozing nostalgia for a golden era, Ishiguro's story shows the dangers of being stuck in time, the way the house itself is, with its need for an army of servants. Stevens is acting on an impulse from decades earlier with an assumption, or hope, that Miss Kenton will want to step once more through the great doors of Darlington with him. Only instead of the 'low door in the wall' that Charles Ryder finds leading to 'an enclosed and enchanted garden', it is a passage leading to the past.[8] Stevens's pride in the stalwart integrity of his profession, he comes to realise, has no value in the modern world outside of Darlington and even there, his new master is only a passing visitor, hosting no grand parties, and no 'events of global significance' take place there any longer. Darlington, with many of its rooms 'under wraps', is an underused relic. As is Stevens himself, for all of his hard-won composure and unquestioning loyalty.

The grand disappointment of the novel is that Stevens's absolute obeisance to his master, so prized among the butler fraternity, is worse than valueless, tainted by Darlington's mixing with Ribbentrop and other Nazi apologists in the run-up to the war. So much so that on meeting strangers, Stevens cannot enjoy the benefit of trading on his master's great estate and name; rather he avoids even mentioning his long and devoted service to his lordship. This causes some awkwardness when Mr Farraday's American friend wants Stevens to vouch for the house's historic pedigree. Mrs Wakefield comments that a stone arch in the dining room 'looks seventeenth century', but perhaps isn't. As the butler refuses to be drawn on his previous associations with the house, and to confirm or deny the authenticity of the building, Mrs Wakefield pronounces that the arch, and many other elements of the house then are 'mock', they are 'very skilful, but mock'.[9] Stevens, the last member of its impeccable household, is also thought to be 'mock', which annoys Mr Farraday, who has told his friends that he is 'the real thing. A real old English butler'. And yet this scene, like Farraday's attempts to draw the butler into 'banter', illustrate how the house's new American owner fails to take the house or Stevens' position seriously. Both are curiosities rather than objects of reverence.

The Remains of the Day is not primarily, or even largely, about a house or its fate. The overriding theme, the author has said, is based on the metaphor of the butler, the idea that most of us are butlers, too, in that we are not powerful leaders or noblemen, but we work for those people and a lot of us, like Stevens, try to do the best job we can.[10] Rather than standing for some lost sense of tradition, Darlington Hall is more symbolic of Stevens's devotion to his work, and perhaps of Stevens himself: his punctiliousness and reserve are there in the order and polish of the rooms. He points out with some pride that Lady Astor found the silver at Darlington 'unrivalled', yet he doesn't profess any real regard for the house itself, certainly no passionate connection or sense of wonder.

Darlington Hall is a metaphor, too. What little time Ishiguro spends describing it is mainly to let us know that it is an authentic nobleman's house that is now too big and too expensive to keep fully in operation. The house is an anachronism, as is Stevens, and, by extension, our view that such houses are noble in themselves or inherently of great importance is outdated. Stevens still believes that 'debates are conducted, and crucial decisions arrived at, in the privacy and calm of the great houses of this country'.[11] We know this to be no longer true, if it ever was, as we understand the debate over which parts of the house are 'mock' and which are genuine to be a modern exercise that may have more to do with perception than reality. When Stevens recovers from his emotional awakening, he decides to return to Darlington Hall, largely because he has no other options that he can see. According to his American master, he is 'part of the package', a remark that makes it sound more like an entertainment offering than a cultural icon.

There is no actual house that is the real-life counterpart to Darlington Hall, at least not one that the author felt important enough to point out. The house and the life it represents inspire no panegyric from the author; there are no ghosts, no nostalgia. There is only the painful realisation that Darlington Hall holds no other meaning for Stevens, that his life has not been devoted to a glorious landmark in the cultural and political terrain, but to an idea that might only ever have been 'mock' instead of real.

In his 2001 novel *Atonement* Ian McEwan also questions the relevance of the English country house of old as cultural icon. *Atonement* casts a dispiriting glance backward, showing that far from being in a state of blissful naïveté, the pre-war psyche could be just as complicit in evil as anything during or after.

The manor house and the class it represents are degenerating. The members of the elite cannot be depended upon to look after their stately homes any more than they can be expected to nurture their own moral judgment.

Atonement begins and ends at the mansion belonging to the Tallis family, but the house is no dignified antique pile. Built only a generation ago by the Tallis patriarch, who made his fortune with a series of patents on 'padlocks, bolts, latches and hasps', the house, 'barely forty years old' and made of 'bright orange brick', is a tasteless extravagance constructed by a member of the nouveau riche, rather than a guardian of English history.[12]

It is the events of the 'long hot summer of 1935' that haunt the book to the end. These are narrated by the youngest member of the family, thirteen-year-old Briony, whose obsession does not centre on her ancestral home but on her love of romantic fiction, and, it must be said, on herself. A devotee of the Gothic, with its 'hidden drawers, lockable diaries and cryptographic systems', she is concerned that there is nothing 'sufficiently interesting or shameful' in her own life 'to merit hiding'.[13] However, mimicking country-house entertainments of old, Briony has written a play to celebrate her older brother, Leon, coming to stay, and is busily rehearsing her cousins for their roles. Her sister, Cecilia, is back from a half-hearted career at Cambridge, having an increasingly serious flirtation with Robbie Turner, the cleaning lady's son, who has also just emerged from Cambridge bearing a 'first' and hoping to study medicine. Briony's father, who is involved in shadowy defense department affairs, stays in the city and her mother spends most days in bed, subdued by migraines. As we will learn after the climactic events have taken place, Briony is directing more than just her adolescent staging of *The Trials of Arabella*.

The guests at Tallis house are not at an old-fashioned house party, but the house's ample rooms and grounds do the job of most such houses in fiction in providing secreted spaces for conflict, intrigue and illicit sex. Briony's cousins arrive as the result of Mrs Tallis' sister being in the midst of divorce: Lola, fifteen, overly perfumed and with vermillion-painted toenails, and her twin younger brothers. Leon brings home a brash friend, Paul Marshall, and the collisions begin. In the sultry summer atmosphere, Cecilia and Robbie have a tryst in the library, cousin Lola is raped out in the grounds and Briony, like the practised fiction writer that she will become, convinces herself and others that Robbie is the guilty man.

In the early pages of the novel, we are conscious of the inferiority of the Tallis home and of its inability to inspire. The characters are aware of this too: in a telling scene Briony literally turns her back on the house, preferring the view of a landscape of 'timeless, unchanging calm', which only adds to the certainty that she must get away. We also become aware that it is Briony who holds us in her grasp as the self-conscious narrator of the story. Her 'atonement' is in rewriting the tale with a somewhat happier ending. The Tallis house itself has had some rewrites too, and not very good ones, first by Briony's grandfather, then at the end of the book, by a hotelier. The 'squat lead-paned Baronial Gothic', which would be 'condemned one day by Pevsner, or one of his team' is the second incarnation. It had replaced 'an Adam-style house' (i.e. one that was probably more elegant) that had burned down in the 1880s. The 'artificial lake and island with its two stone bridges supporting the driveway' and a 'crumbling stuccoed temple' were all that remained of the previous house.[14] Rather than acquiring more grace and dignity with age, the house has become more artificial, a late-nineteenth-century imitation of something Gothic and baronial that fails to evoke anything like a sense of grandeur. A temple on the island in an artificial lake was 'built in the style of Nicholas Revett in the late 1780s'. The patio fountain was 'a half-scale reproduction of Bernini's Triton in the Piazza Barberini in Rome'.[15] As Briony makes postmodern intrustions on the text, the house's failed aesthetic has the ring of late-twentieth-century, albeit crumbling, postmodern pastiche.

In addition to being disappointing in style and bearing, the house and grounds have been neglected to a degree that would send a man like Stevens into paroxysms of schedule-making. The tall windows in the dining room can't be opened 'because their frames had warped long ago', and 'an aroma of warmed dust' rises from the Persian carpet to meet the diners'.[16] Like Waugh's doomed lovers, Cecilia and Robbie have a testy exchange at the fountain. But here, too, the ornate fountain statuary has been sullied and neglected. The dolphin has its mouth 'stopped with moss and algae' and the Triton himself sits in a shell grown mossy owing to the weak trickle of the water.[17]

Similarly the island temple has been allowed to decay. Its damp walls are peeling and 'clumsy repairs' in the nineteenth century had caused them to turn brown in patches, 'giving it a mottled, diseased appearance'. Anyone who may have thought this story would erupt into the mournful tones of *Howards*

End or *Brideshead* might want to look away now, as, else-where in the temple 'exposed laths, themselves rotting away, showed through like the ribs of a starving animal'. The house and outbuildings have had little care or respect even from the family who live in them:

> The double doors that opened into a circular chamber with a domed roof, had long ago been removed, and the stone floor was thickly covered in leaves and leaf mould and the drop-pings of various birds and animals that wandered in and out. All the panes were gone from the pretty, Georgian windows, smashed by Leon and his friends in the late twenties. The tall niches that had once contained statuary were empty but for the filthy ruins of spider webs.[18]

Even before the tragedy that ruins young Robbie's life, the Tallis house is a catalogue of failures, its neglected structure redolent of late-modern Gothic. It has suffered the depreda-tions of time but also abuse from its own people. As at Charles Dickens's Satis House, the dusty, mouldering surfaces signal a more serious moral torpor among the inhabitants.

Those inhabitants are representative of the English higher class, but the impovershied state of the house is warning that this is a hollow entitlement. Although Robbie has managed to rise above his station, achieving better than Cecilia, and prob-ably even Leon, we are reminded of his humble origins when he returns to his mother's bungalow on the Tallis property. As Cecilia drifts languidly in the summer heat through the many large rooms of her family home, the lawn, the patio of the fountain, Robbie squeezes into the small bedroom, bathroom and 'cubicle wedged between them he called his study', up under the eaves of his mother's roof.[19] There might be shades of the keeper's cottage at Wragby Hall here, but Robbie is no Mellors. Although he has certainly stirred the passions of Cecilia, he has availed himself of her father's offer to pay for his education, even his medical school, so there are shades of Mr Tallis behaving as Ford's Tory landlords of old. Yet the family, rallying around Briony, who until now has been a child of benign neglect, will end up destroying Robbie without much real thought.

In speaking about his inspirations for the story, Ian McEwan avoided naming any single house, but cited both *Northanger Abbey* and L. P. Hartley's novel, *The Go-Between* (1952), as influences. In *Northanger Abbey*, McEwan says, Catherine Morland is 'a young girl whose head is stuffed with Gothic novels', and it is partly a 'huge indulgence in literary models' that results in Briony's misjudgement: 'She wants things to fit with the story she has in her head.'[20] The novel's epigraph is a passage from *Northanger Abbey* in which Henry Tilney is upbraiding Catherine Morland for engaging in Gothic fantasy by inventing intrigues about his family. For Catherine Morland, being inside the Abbey stokes her imagination to bursting. For Briony, it is the *lack* of imaginative triggers at the Tallis house that drives her to invent them for herself. And yet the house and its atmosphere of moral decay make her invention more dangerous.

Hartley's novel tells the story of a thirteen-year-old boy who has befriended the son of a wealthier family and is invited to stay with them at their country house, Brandham Hall, in Norfolk. But his friend soon falls ill, leaving Leo to his own devices, trying to parse the customs and behaviours of the country-house elite. When the elder sister of the family takes him under her wing, Leo becomes entangled in her affair with a local farmer, as he is asked to run secret messages between the lovers. Events at Brandham Hall also take place during an unusually hot summer, and they too end tragically. For Leo, Brandham Hall marks a loss of innocence, and its only symbolism is to emphasise the ruthlessness with which the upper class will protect its own.

Atonement, like the classic country-house novel, plays on the proximity between staff and masters in timeless 'upstairs-downstairs' fashion. Traditionally, these novels bring people from widely different classes (though usually not the middle classes) together in the same spaces. The rules are that, despite any proximal familiarity, the twain shall not mix. But fiction thrives on rule-breakers, and country houses provide ample space and opportunity for inappropriate assignations and scandal, and the miscegenation of high- and low-born. Jane Eyre is essentially a servant who marries the lord; Fanny Price is a poor relation who is only shown kindness by servants but marries the baronet's son. Tess Durbeyfield is raped and made pregnant by her well-to-do cousin when she goes to work at his family's manor house. Lady Chatterley becomes mesmerised by her husband's gamekeeper. Sebastian Flyte periodically retreats from his family to Nanny's rooms up in the dome of Brideshead. *The Remains of the Day* is more downstairs than up, but Stevens measures his life in polished spoons, that is, by the comings and goings of the people above his class in a kind of house that could never belong to him.

However, in the past the great house held some attraction,

even if it was later found to be a mask for evil. In *Atonement* McEwan hints from the very beginning that the Tallis house is no Pemberley. Like Darlington Hall, it is not particularly loved or revered by its inhabitants; as a late-Victorian mish-mash, it has no architectural integrity even for twenty-first-century readers to admire. It doesn't even have value for the family. By the end of the novel, the Tallis home has been dealt the same fate as many other large English manors in the modern era: it has become a country-house hotel, appropriately named 'Tilney's'. On her visit at the end of the novel, Briony is not especially saddened by the changes made. She notes the portrait 'which my grandfather imported to give the family some lineage'. Here the re-writing of history is laid bare. Many an owner of a grand estate filled it with ancestral paintings that were not his own, and over time, authentic or not, these were absorbed into the fabric and appeal of the house. But the Tallis home never was appealing, so its new incarnation is less tragic than fitting. In fact rather than bemoaning the house's use by the public at large, as Mrs de Winter had of Manderlay in du Maurier's draft of *Rebecca* (see chapter 11), Briony welcomes its new role, 'the building itself surely embraced more human happiness now, as a hotel, than it did when I lived here'.[21]

Alan Hollinghurst went back to life in a grand English house at the turn of the century to address another kind of taboo, not of relationships between aristos and the help, but between people of the same sex. In doing so, he too, presented a less romantic idea of the historic country house. *The Stranger's Child* (2011) steps through and around two large family homes: Two Acres and Corley Court. The story opens at Two Acres, home to the upper-middle-class Sawle family in a suburb on what will become the northern fringes of London. It is a large house, but modest in comparison to Corley Court, home of George Sawle's Cambridge friend, the pretty, charismatic poet Cecil Valance. Of the two, it is the grander home, the birthplace of the poet who has achieved fame by dying young, that survives, though adapted and changed. The other is too large to maintain in the modern world and too middling in cultural values for historic preservation. Two Acres is first abandoned, and then torn down. But the overriding theme is to do with the unreliability of historical narrative, and of the associations it creates with artefacts like the English stately home.

It is Cecil's home, Corley Court, that will become a monument to its best-known son. But it is the Sawle home that Cecil has commemorated in a poem, in a tradition dating back centuries (and indulged by the likes of Walter Scott, so that Two Acres is immortalised as 'Two blessèd acres of English ground'). The poem is meant for his lover, George Sawle, but the lines are later thought to have been written for George's sister, Daphne. After Cecil is killed in the war, the poem is acquired for the nation, living on as an ode of misunderstanding. References to the life of the poet Rupert Brooke help to emphasise the enormity of deception and the vast ability of human beings to honour ideals over reality.

Though the poem 'Two Acres' becomes a national treasure, Cecil's home of Corley Court becomes the focus of remembrance of the young war poet. Daphne marries his brother, Dudley, who confesses, 'I can't help feeling slightly mortified that my brother Cecil, heir to a baronetcy and three thousand acres, not to mention one of the ugliest houses in the south of England, should be best remembered for his ode to a suburban garden.'[22] There is ample class snobbery in this, especially since, like the Tallis home, Corley Court is not beautiful and is not well loved by its inheritors. In all its late-Victorian Gothicism, it is no picture of ancient elegance. Only fifty years old, its 'Victorian absurdities', as Dudley calls them, are gruesome with aspiration and grief: the 'jelly-mould dome' in the dining room, its 'monstrous oak table' in the hall, the 'glaring plate glass in Gothic windows' and heraldic shields, 'the unrestful patterns of red, white and black brick', the glassed-in arcade leading to the chapel containing Cecil's tomb and effigy.[23] But it becomes, like the poem, a source of national pride. Both achieve significance well beyond what they deserve, which leads to the point that we can't always believe what we read about these houses and their link to greatness (to the profound disappointment of disciples like Stevens of Darlington Hall).

Ironically, if the house was ugly and pointless to begin with, it becomes more so when Dudley insists on hiring the leggy Eva Riley to redecorate. Although the hall with its 'gloomy panelling and Gothic windows, in which the Valance coat of arms was repeated insistently' and fireplace 'designed like a castle, with battlements instead of a mantelpiece and turrets on either side' has so far managed to escape the decorator's touch, the drawing room now had an 'off-white dazzle', like 'a room in some extremely expensive sanatorium'. The clutter of old furniture in 'cane and chintz and heavy-fringed velvet' had been replaced by 'comfortable modern chairs in grey loose covers'.[24] The 'coffered ceiling, with its twelve inset panels depicting the months, had been smoothly boxed in'. Daphne had found the old drawing room with its heavy curtains a good place to hide away, but as Henry James might appreciate, the new, lighter, brighter room offers 'no such refuge'.[25]

No one else bewails the changes to the old home. Dudley is pleased with the result and praises the change to his mother, who now shares Corley Court with her younger son and his wife and children. Remarking on a trend of the age, Dudley tells her, 'You know a lot of the best people nowadays are getting rid of these Victorian absurdities. You should run over and see what the Witherses have done at Badly-Madly, Mamma. They've pulled down the bell tower, and put an Olympic swimming-pool in its place.' To which Eva adds, 'At Madderleigh [...] they got to work long ago. They boxed in the dining-room there in the Eighties, I believe.'[26] Indeed, many such houses were 'done up' or modernised between the wars. Eva is a character in the spirit of renowned society decorators like Sybil Colefax and Syrie Maugham, who during the 1920s and 30s chased after commissions among their country house-owning friends, helping them swap dark, overly furnished rooms for lighter, more airy showpieces. As Adrian Tinniswood observes in *The Long Weekend*, interior decoration at the time was 'an intense and competitive business', whose rise was ascribed to a combination of factors, from the increasing divorce rate to a lively property market.[27]

Like Charles and Sebastian in *Brideshead Revisited*, George and Cecil share a charmed interlude at Corley Court that makes the memories most painful for George in later years (especially as everyone has agreed that Cecil was in love with his sister, rather than with him). Like Brideshead, Corley Court was requisitioned during the Second World War, giving it perhaps a bit of historic gravitas. Dudley announces that he has written his own 'satirical country-house novel', *The Long Gallery*, 'in the tradition of Peacock', a story that 'casts a merrily merciless eye over three generations of the Mersham family'.[28] This places Dudley in the literary-country-house continuum, but one of mockery; more Huxley and Peacock than Ford and Waugh (see chapter 10). He also writes a novel called *The Long Gallery*. Corley's architecture is disliked by Dudley and has inspired no aesthetic conversion in George. Cecil's most famous poem, as we know, was about a love affair that had nothing to do with country houses or their lifestyle.

Decades later, Paul Bryant, a literary biographer, has 'outed' Cecil and George, much to the family's dismay. In a scene that is doubly ironic (for both house and poet), Bryant reads Cecil's poem not as a work of lyric genius, but as a literal guide, helping him to locate the site of Two Acres. Most of the land has, at this point, been sold to a developer, who has erected an advertisement for 'Old Acres', which will encompass 'Six Executive Homes'.[29] It's a fate somewhat worse than that of being transformed into a hotel. Toward the close of the novel it is 2008, and the house, despite being the subject of a famous poem, a celebration of the English pastoral idyll, has been demolished. Meanwhile, Corley Court has become a boys' boarding school. The novel ends with another curious researcher chasing after mementoes of the young war poet, this time at Mattocks, a 'sort of Arts and Crafts' house belonging to a friend and likely lover of both Hubert Sawle

(Daphne and George's brother), and of Cecil Valance. This house, too, is about to be demolished as another Valance heir sets about burning the last of the tenant's papers, sealing off any further reaches into the family's contentious history.

Speaking of his early interest in architecture, Hollinghurst recalled being 'an architect from the age of six or so . . . I designed country houses when I went away to boarding school.'[30] It was the spaces and ornaments of his school experiences that were used as the model for Corley Court. One of these schools was Canford in Dorset, which had been a manor house before becoming a school in 1923. Like the fictional Valance home, the core buildings were constructed in the nineteenth century. Canford owes the main part of its Victorian Gothicness to designs by Edward Blore, who also had a hand in finishing Buckingham Palace and contributed to Walter Scott's Abbotsford.*[31] 'Being a beautiful and interesting old house it made a profound impression on me from an early stage,' Hollinghurst has said.[32] Far from abhorring the Victorian style that so offends Dudley Valance, Hollinghurst says that he was 'defending Victorian buildings' in the book, although 'I tried to make this Victorian house heavier' and 'fiercer than my old school'. It is another irony in the book, that as the author says, Dudley's 'hatred of the house is what preserved it', because the practice of covering over ('boxing in') all those features is what saved them.[33]

Hollinghurst also revealed an interest in architecture and old houses in *The Swimming Pool Library* (1988), in which a

---

* Later works were carried out by Sir Charles Barry.

young architectural researcher, aptly named William Beckwith (echoing the master of Fonthill, see chapter 2), is invited to help an aging lord write his life story. The process impresses on the younger man the suffocating life of homosexuality during Lord Nantwich's lifetime, inviting comparisons with the seclusion and isolation of the house itself.

For the architectural aspects of *The Line of Beauty*, Hollinghurst was inspired, he said, by observations of houses in Kensington that 'impressed me with their scale and aloofness' and the thoughts of 'what might be going on there'.[34] When Nick Guest enters the house of a Tory MP in Notting Hill, he relishes the quality and space of the rooms in a way that is easy for all of us fellow voyeurs to comprehend. He 'loved

© Canford School

In creating Corley Court, Alan Hollinghurst was partly recalling his time at Canford School in Dorset, which dates from the medieval period but is largely Victorian.

letting himself in [...] and feeling the still security of the house'.[35] Nick, the author explains, 'itemises [the house] floor by floor and takes imaginative possession of it'.[36] Nick's big project is to write a screenplay for an adaptation of Henry James's *The Spoils of Poynton*, which goes some way to explaining his own aesthetic sense of houses. Although Hollinghurst's narratives are attentive to physical detail, his aim is not to be definitive. As he says, 'a house is envisioned afresh by every person who reads a story'.[37]

Themes about the interpretations of history, guarding secrets, why we revere grand old houses and what we think they mean for us, all trail through the rooms and gardens and across the pages as the years pass in *The Stranger's Child*, a book laden with references to houses, their atmospheres and fortunes. The fate of Corley Court is foreshadowed in the early pages of the novel. During pre-dinner drinks in the drawing room at Two Acres, Hubert Sawle remarks that Queen Adelaide used to live at the nearby Priory. Another guest adds that later on in its history, 'it was a very excellent hotel':

> '"And now a school," said Hubert, with a bleak little snuffle.'
> '"A sad fate!" said Daphne.'[38]

And yet Hollinghurst, like McEwan and Ishiguro, is more concerned with the people in the houses than the houses themselves, and with the idea that certain assumptions, and a tendency toward blind nostalgia can easily veil unpleasant truths. Of course, in the twenty-first century there is still a taste for drama set in the English country house, even if it holds the lifestyle up for scrutiny. Film and television companies, spurred on by the immense popularity of *Downton Abbey* and of most any re-make of *Jane Eyre* or *Pride and Prejudice*, will continue to re-imagine scenes among the ancestral portraits and ornamental plasterwork of the stately manor. Location managers were no more put off by the hazy descriptions of Darlington Hall than they were by any of Austen's 'vague' architectural details, choosing various historic houses to stand in for the internal rooms, servants hall and exterior for a film that gave the house almost as much screen presence as the actors. Such cinematic renderings have injected new life into some houses that had faced uncertain futures due to the prohibitive costs of maintenance and repairs. Their starring roles in television and film put off for awhile at least, their 'inexorable doom'.

Fiction and film can breathe new life into old houses. Highclere Castle in Hampshire, the Jacobethan residence of Lord and Lady Carnarvon, has become familiar as Downton Abbey.

Following the success of *Downton Abbey*, an increase in paying visitors to Highclere Castle helped to make long-sought-after repairs possible, saving it from having to become a school or hotel anytime soon. And tourist numbers to English historic houses generally are up. The millennial view of the English country house in literature, as expressed by Ishiguro, McEwan and Hollinghurst, is not without feeling for such places and their history. But for these writers, there is a question about how and why we revere these buildings as cultural artefacts, and the sense of nostalgia is tempered by what we know of the biases and omissions of history that we often choose to ignore.

Epilogue

The house of fiction will continue to evolve and open its many windows on to the human drama that makes it so compelling. Though, in the digital age we might have to reimagine how these dramas will be staged. There are many arguments as to whether people are more 'connected' nowadays, or whether, communicating so often through the distorted immediacy of electronic devices, we are, in fact, becoming more isolated from one another. And yet, perhaps sending an email is no more impersonal than sending a note by way of the butler. With houses wired to provide all of those services formerly offered by human staff, there will be little scope for the brush between master and servant; our personal IT specialist may only need to make contact by phone.

As of old, some of us might employ people to manage all of our household technologies, leaving us reliant still on others, making them part of the community under our roof, though our 'friends', 'contacts' and 'links' may be many miles distant. Perhaps, ironically, the real challenges will come from attempts to humanise household techonology to create an atmosphere that is more 'homely'. One question facing fiction writers might be how to approach the scene when the power goes out, and we find ourselves fumbling through with only half memories of where we stored the torch, the candles, paper and pen.

It will be interesting to see how and whether British writers respond to these changes any differently than others, and whether there remains any 'house fiction' that could be perceived as distinctly British. As for housing types, we still profess a national ardour for the English cottage, for the country house and castle. The taste, especially in Britain and the US, for costume drama that inhabits such places does not appear to be on the wane, and may only become more fervent as those lives retreat further into the past. Will British fiction writers view those older building types with irony or longing? The urban apartment block has now been through enough iterations to supply a range of scenarios, from the poverty of those postwar estates that have yet to see the wrecking ball to the glass-walled spectacles created by millennial 'starchitects' in defiance of gravity, climate and force majeure. Will it be a completely automated luxury flat on the sixty-fifth floor of the Shard in London that the next boy Dickens aspires to? How many murder mysteries will be explained by faulty wiring or a signal glitch? Will home cyber menace be the new Gothic? In the houses of future fiction there are infinite windows and any one, as Henry James said, can be 'pierced by the individual vision and the pressure of the individual will' of human imagination.

Gazetteer

Chapter 1

Shandy Hall is operated by the Laurence Sterne Trust and is open to the public for special events and by appointment: laurencesternetrust.org.uk

Hagley Hall is open to the public: hagleyhall.com

Chapter 2

Strawberry Hill is maintained by the Strawberry Hill Trust and is open to the public: strawberryhillhouse.org.uk

Fonthill Abbey is privately owned but can sometimes be visited by appointment: fonthill.co.uk

Beckford's Tower and Museum, Bath is open to the public: beckfordstower.org.uk

Chapter 3

Jane Austen's House Museum in Hampshire is open to the public: jane-austens-house-museum.org.uk

Chawton House, now the Chawton House Library, is open to the public for tours and visiting scholars. It houses an exemplary library of women's writing from the long eighteenth century: chawtonhouse.org

Stoneleigh Abbey is privately owned and is open to the public: stoneleighabbey.org

Goodnestone has been recently restored and is available for hire as a holiday house: goodnestone.com

Godmersham Park House is now a college for the Association of British Dispensing Opticians but has a Heritage Centre in the grounds, which is open to the public: godmershamheritage.webs. com

The Vyne is owned by the National Trust and is open to the public: nationaltrust.org.uk/the-vyne

Chapter 4
Traquair House, run by Catherine Maxwell Stuart, 21st Lady of Traquair, and her husband, Mark Muller, is open to the public, the oldest continually inhabited house in Scotland: traquair.co.uk

Melville Castle is run as a country house hotel: melvillecastle.com

Dalkeith Palace is leased by the American University of Wisconsin.

Abbotsford is cared for by the Abbotsford Trust, and is open to the public: scottsabbotsford.co.uk

Craighall Castle is privately owned.

Drumlanrig Castle is still owned by the Buccleuch family and is open for tours and events: drumlanrigcastle.co.uk

Bowhill is open to the public: bowhillhouse.co.uk

Knole House in Kent is open to the public through the National Trust: nationaltrust.org.uk/knole

Chapter 5
The Brontë Parsonage Museum is open to the public (bronte.org. uk).

The Rydings is privately owned and not open to the public.

North Lees Hall is now owned by the Peak District National Park and is occasionally open to the public; the house can be viewed from the outside along a public footpath: peakdistrict.gov.uk/visiting/stanage-and-north-lees

Norton Conyers gardens are open to the public, the house by appointment: nortonconyers.org.uk

Chapter 6

Gad's Hill Place is in the grounds of Gad's Hill School and is under the care of the Dickens Fellowship. Tours are available by appointment: dickensfellowship.org

In the 1960s the Swiss Chalet was moved to the grounds of Eastgate House in Rochester, which appears as Westgate House in *The Pickwick Papers* and the Nun's House in *The Mystery of Edwin Drood*. Funding is currently being raised for restoration.

Restoration House is open to the public from May to September: restorationhouse.co.uk

The Charles Dickens Museum, Dickens House, Doughty Street is open to the public: dickensmuseum.com

Dickens House Museum in Broadstairs (former home of Mary Pearson Strong) is open to the public: thanet.gov.uk/the-thanet-magazine/campaigns/dickens-house-museum

Dickens' study is somewhat preserved and can be visited at the Bleak House Hotel, Broadstairs: bleakhousebroadstairs.co.uk

Chapter 7

Max Gate and Thomas Hardy's Cottage are both owned by the National Trust and are open to the public:

nationaltrust.org.uk/hardys-cottage

nationaltrust.org.uk/max-gate

Rooksnest and West Hackhurst are both privately owned.

The Rooksnest Mantelpiece built by Forster's father is still at Cambridge University in rooms that can be visited by appointment.

Piney Copse, the woodland Forster purchased near West Hackhurst, is owned by the National Trust and is open to the public: nationaltrust.org.uk/abinger-roughs-and-netley-park/features/piney-copse

Chapter 8

Coombe Leigh is now Holy Cross Preparatory School and may be visited by appointment.

Coombe Croft is now the Rokeby School and may be visited by appointment.

Foxwarren Park is privately owned.

Hardwick House is privately owned.

Leighton House is open to the public: rbkc.gov.uk/subsites/museums/leightonhousemuseum1.aspx

Lamb House is owned by the National Trust and is open to the public: nationaltrust.org.uk/lamb-house

Chapter 9

22 Hyde Park Gate has been divided into flats and is privately owned.

46 Gordon Square is now occupied by the University of London, as is Lytton Strachey's former house at no. 51.

The houses on Fitzroy Square and Brunswick Square are both privately owned.

The houses on Tavistock Square and Mecklenburgh Square were destroyed during the Blitz.

Hogarth House has been joined with the neighbouring property and now contains offices.

Monk's House is owned by the National Trust and is open to the public: nationaltrust.org.uk/monks-house

Talland House is privately owned and contains holiday flats. It is not open to the public.

Chapter 10

Busby Hall is privately owned.

Madresfield can be visited by appointment: elmley.org.uk/madresfield-court

Castle Howard is open to the public: castlehoward.co.uk

Garsington Manor is privately owned.

Chapter 11

Greenway is owned by the National Trust and is open to the public.

The Isokon Building (Lawn Road flats) are privately owned and let, but the gallery, which tells the story of the building, has public opening hours.

Chapter 12

Ian Fleming's villa in Jamaica is now part of the Goldeneye resort and is available for holiday lets: theianflemingvilla.com

Trellick Tower is a building of privately owned and rented flats but the entrance lobby and some flats are occasionally open to the public through Open House London: openhouselondon.org.uk

Goldfinger house, Willow Road is owned by the National Trust and open to the public: nationaltrust.org.uk/2-willow-road

Chapter 13

Dyrham Park is open to the public through the National Trust: nationaltrust.org.uk/dyrham-park

Canford is still run as a school for boarding and day pupils, but some areas can be visited by the public: canford.com/Open-to-the-Public

Notes

Unless otherwise noted, references to novels are given by chapter or volume.

Introduction

1 Andrew Motion, in conversation with Rowan Moore and Alan Hollinghurst, 'Writing Houses: Dwelling on Dwellings', Kings Place, London, 19 September 2011.

2 *Beowulf*, trans. Seamus Heaney (London: Faber and Faber, 1999), 3.

3 Ibid., 5.

4 Henry James, 'Preface' to *The Portrait of a Lady*, Everyman's Library (New York: Alfred A. Knopf), 13.

5 Ibid., 15.

6 Ibid., 18.

7 'Howards End' by Lionel Trilling, 367, in E. M. Forster, *Howards End* (London: Penguin Books, 2012) 363–381.

8 E. M. Forster, 'Three Countries', in *The Hills of Devi and Other Indian Writings* (London: Edward Arnold, 1983), 294.

9 *Howards End*, ch. 17.

Chapter 1
Shandy Hall: The Birth of the House in Fiction

1 Arthur H. Cash, *Laurence Sterne: The Later Years* (London and New York: Methuen & Co., 1986), 70.

2 *Tristram Shandy*, vol. I, ch. XX (subsequent references to the novel Tristram Shandy will be given in the form of the original volumes and chapters, published from 1760 onward, followed by the later divisions used in the Everyman edition (New York: Alfred A. Knopf, 1991), where these differ).

3 Ian Campbell Ross, *Laurence Sterne, A Life* (Oxford: Oxford University Press, 2001), 202.

4 'Horace Walpole on Tristram Shandy', 4 April 1760, in Alan B. Howes, *Laurence Sterne: The Critical Heritage* (London: Routledge & Kegan Paul, 1974), 55.

5 Mary Granville Delany to Anne Granville Dewes, Spring 1760, in Howes, *Laurence Sterne*, 61.

6 Letter from an unidentified correspondent to *The Universal Magazine of Knowledge and Pleasure* 26 (April 1760): 189–90, in Howes, *Laurence Sterne*, 63.

7 Arthur H. Cash, *Laurence Sterne: The Later Years* (London and New York: Methuen & Co., 1986), 70.

8 Ibid., 109 n4.

9 Laurence Sterne to Catherine Fourmantel, 16–22 March 1760, no. 52, in Lewis Perry Curtis, ed., *Letters of Laurence Sterne* (Oxford: Clarendon Press, 1967) (first edition 1935), 102.

10 In Ross, *Laurence Sterne*, 2; John Croft, 'Anecdotes of Sterne Vulgarly Tristram Shandy', in W. A. S. Hewins, ed., *The Whitefoord Papers* (Oxford, 1898), 227.

11 Cash, *Laurence Sterne*, 18, Sir Thomas Robinson of Newby, Yorkshire, later Baron Grantham, to his son Thomas, 27 May 1760.

12 Ross, *Laurence Sterne*, 11–12.

13 www.measuringworth.com/ukcompare (accessed on 26 February 2015).

14 Cash, *Laurence Sterne*, 29.

15 Laurence Sterne to Robert Dodsley, May 23, 1759, no. 37, in Curtis, 74.

16 Laurence Sterne to Robert Dodsley, October 1759 no. 39, in Curtis, 80.

17 Ross, *Laurence Sterne*, 48.

18 Ibid., 208.

19 Dedication from the first edition, *The Life and Opinions of Tristram Shandy, Gentleman* (London, 1760).

20 Laurence Sterne, 'Journal to Eliza', 28 May–2 June, 1767, in Curtis, 346.

21 Laurence Sterne to the Bishop of Gloucester, June 9, 1760, no. 61 in Curtis, 112.

22 Laurence Sterne to Mrs Fenton, August 3, 1760, no. 66 in Curtis, 120.

23 Laurence Sterne to Robert Foley, September 29, 1764, no.132 in Curtis, 227–8.

24 Laurence Sterne to Robert Foley, November 16, 1764, no. 136 in Curtis, 233–4.

25 *Tristram Shandy*, vol. IX, ch. I / vol. III, ch. LXXIX.

26 Max Byrd, *Tristram Shandy* (London: George Allen & Unwin, 1985), 13.

27 *Tristram Shandy*, 'Author's Preface', vol. III following ch. XX / vol. I following ch. LXIV.

28 *Tristram Shandy*, vol. III, ch. X / vol. I ch. LIV.

29 *Tristram Shandy*, vol. III, ch. XXIX / vol. I ch. LXXIII.

30 *Tristram Shandy*, vol. III, ch. XXX / vol. I ch. LXXIV.

31 *Tristram Shandy*, vol. IV, ch. X / vol. II ch. X.

32 *Tristram Shandy*, vol. IV, ch. XIII / vol. II ch. XIII.

33 Laurence Sterne to John Hall Stevenson, July 28, 1761, no. 78 in Curtis, 142.

34 Laurence Sterne to Lady ---, September 21, 1761, no. 79 in Curtis, 143.

35 Cash, *Laurence Sterne*, 58.

36 Ibid, 101, n.112.
37 Laurence Sterne to unidentified correspondent June 7, 1767, no. 200 in Curtis, 353.
38 'Journal to Eliza', June 29, 1767, in Curts 366–7.
39 Cash, *Laurence Sterne*, 293.
40 'Journal to Eliza', June 16, 1767, in Curtis, 358.
41 'Journal to Eliza', June 28, 1767, in Curtis, 367.
42 Henry Fielding, *The History of Tom Jones: A Foundling with Introduction* by Martin Battestin, Fredson Bowers ed. in two vols. (Oxford: Clarendon Press), vol. I, Bk I ch. IV, 42.
43 Tom Jones, vol. I, Bk I ch. IV, 42n. Bowers notes various connections between Paradise Hall and Sharpham Park, as well as with Hagley Hall.
44 Daniel Defoe, *Robinson Crusoe*, 'The Journal' (London: Penguin Books, 2001), 60.
45 *Tristram Shandy*, vol. IX, ch. XXXII / vol. III, ch. CX.

Chapter 2
Stawberry Hill: The Invention of the Gothic Novel

1 Timothy Mowl, *Horace Walpole, The Great Outsider* (London: John Murray, 1996), 1.
2 Dan Cruickshank, ed., *Sir Banister Fletcher's A History of Architecture* (Oxford: Architectural Press, 1996), 452.
3 Horace Walpole to Horace Mann, 4 March 1753, in John Iddon, *Strawberry Hill and Horace Walpole: Essential Guide* (London: Scala Publishers, 2011), 6.
4 Horace Walpole to Hon. H. S. Conway, 8 June 1747, in *The Correspondence of H. Walpole with G. Montagu*, vol. 1, 1735–1759 (London: Henry Colburn, 1837), 108. Although Gothic Revival houses were not yet common, there was a taste for Gothic follies such as the one at Hagley Hall and at Stainborough Castle (1752). See Kevin Rogers, 'Walpole's Gothic, Creative a Fictive History', in *Horace Walpole's Strawberry Hill*, edited by Michael Snodin with the assistance of Cynthia Roman (New Haven and London: the Lewis Walpole Library, Yale University, Yale Center for British Art, Victoria and Albert Museum, in association with Yale University Press, 2009) 59–73.
5 Ibid.
6 Kevin Rogers, 'Walpole's Gothic', 69.
7 Horace Walpole to Rev. William Cole, 9 March 1765, in W. S. Lewis, ed., *Selected Letters of Horace Walpole* (New Haven and London: Yale University Press, 1973), 122.
8 See Preface to the first edition of *The Castle of Otranto*.
9 Horace Walpole to Rev. William Cole, 9 March 1765, in Lewis, *Selected Letters of Horace Walpole*, 122.
10 Walpole, *The Castle of Otranto*, ch. I.

11 *The Monthly Review* 31 (February 1765): 97.

12 *The Monthly Review* 32 (May 1765): 394.

13 *The Castle of Otranto*, ch. I.

14 Horace Walpole to Rev. William Cole, 9 March 1765, in Lewis, 122.

15 *The General Magazine and Impartial Review* (December 1791).

16 Horace Walpole to Hon. H. S. Conway in *Correspondence*, vol. II, 5 August 1761, 94. Walpole continues, 'if they had not the substantial use of amusing me while I live, they would be worth little indeed.'

17 Horace Walpole to Richard Bentley, 3 November 1754, in Lewis, 57.

18 Ibid.

19 Horace Walpole to George Montagu, Esq., 4 July 1760, in *The Correspondence of H. Walpole with G. Montagu*, vol. 2, 1760–9 (London: Henry Coburn, 1837), 18.

20 Horace Walpole to George Montagu, Esq., 19 July 1760, in *The Correspondence of H. Walpole with G. Montagu*, vol. 2, 20.

21 Horace Walpole to George Montagu, Esq., 28 September 1749, in *The Correspondence of H. Walpole with G. Montagu*, vol. 1, 145.

22 Horace Walpole to Hon. H. S. Conway, 7 January 1772, in *Correspondence*, vol. 3, 434.

23 Mowl, *The Great Outsider*, 148.

24 Samuel Taylor Coleridge, in *The Critical Review*, February 1797.

25 Ann Radcliffe, *They Mysteries of Udolpho*, ch. XXVII.

26 *Northanger Abbey*, ch. 20.

27 Ibid.

28 Brian Fothergill, *Beckford of Fonthill* (London: Faber and Faber, 1979), 34.

29 James Lees-Milne, *William Beckford* (London: Century, 1990), 20.

30 Ibid., 4.

31 Fothergill, *Beckford*, 113.

32 William Beckford, *Vathek* (Oxford: Oxford University Press, Oxford World Classics, 1998), 1.

33 Beckford, *Vathek*, 4.

34 Lees-Milne, *William Beckford*, 59-60.

35 Ibid., 74–6.

36 Ibid., 74.

37 Beckford, *Vathek*, 4.

38 Lees-Milne, *William Beckford*, 84–5.

39 Barbara Benedict and Deirdre Le Faye, introduction to *Northanger Abbey*, The Cambridge Edition of the Works of Jane Austen (Cambridge: Cambridge University Press, 2006), xxx.

40 Thomas Love Peacock, *Nightmare Abbey*, ch. III.

Chapter 3
Pride and Property: Women and Houses in Regency England

1 For change in social protocols and architecture, see Mark Girouard, *Life in*

the English Country House (London: Yale University Press, 1978).

2 Ibid., 19.

3 Ibid., 236.

4 *Mansfield Park*, vol. II, ch. 1 / ch. 19. For Austen novels, volume and chapter of early editions are followed by those of later editions where they differ.

5 Nikolaus Pevsner, 'The Architectural Setting of Jane Austen's Novels', in *Journal of the Warburg and Courtauld Institutes* 31 (1968), 404–22.

6 See Vladimir Nabokov, 'Mansfield Park' in Fredson Bowers, ed., *Lectures on Literature* (New York: Harcourt Brace and Company, 1980), 9–62.

7 *Sense and Sensibility*, vol. I, ch. II.

8 *Pride and Prejudice*, vol. I, ch. XVII / ch. 40.

9 Ibid., ch. XVII.

10 *Mansfield Park*, vol. II, ch. II / ch. 21.

11 Ibid., ch. 5.

12 See Tony Tanner, *Jane Austen* (Basingstoke: Macmillan, 1986), 17.

13 Girouard, *Life*, 191

14 Jane Austen to Cassandra Austen, 20–21 November 1800, no. 27, in Deirdre Le Faye, ed., *Jane Austen's Letters* (Oxford: Oxford University Press, 1997), 60–1.

15 Jane Austen to Cassandra Austen, 24 December 1798, no. 15, in Ibid., 28.

16 Jane Austen to Cassandra Austen, 20 November 1800, no. 27, in Ibid., 60.

17 Girouard, *Life*, 191, 30.

18 *Sense and Sensibility*, vol. I, ch. 7

19 *Sense and Sensibility*, vol. III, ch. 6 / ch. 42.

20 *Sense and Sensibility*, vol. I, ch. III.

21 See Claire Tomalin, *Jane Austen: A Life* (London: Viking, 1997).

22 *Sense and Sensibility*, vol I, ch. V.

23 *Mansfield Park*, vol. I, ch I.

24 *Sense and Sensibility*, vol. I, ch. VI.

25 Jane Austen to Cassandra Austen, 14–15 January 1796, no. 2, in Le Faye, 4,

26 *Sense and Sensibility*, vol. III, ch. I / ch. 37.

27 See William Austen-Leigh and Richard Arthur Austen-Leigh, *Jane Austen, A Family Record*, revised and enlarged by Deirdre Le Faye (London: The British Library, 1989) 2.

28 *Northanger Abbey*, vol. I, ch. III.

29 Jane Austen to Cassandra Austen, 30 June–1 July 1808, no. 55, in Le Faye, 136–9.

30 *Pride and Prejudice*, vol. 3, ch. 1 / ch. 43.

31 *Pride and Prejudice*, vol. II, ch. VI / ch. 29; vol. I, ch. XVI.

32 Pevsner, 408.

33 Jane Austen to Cassandra Austen, 23 September 1813, no. 89, in Le Faye, 224–8

34 Jane Austen to Cassandra Austen, 25 September 1813, no. 90, in Le Faye, 229–32.

35 Jane Austen to Cassandra Austen, 18 December 1798, no. 14, in Le Faye, 25–8.

36 Jane Austen to Cassandra Austen, 3 November 1813, no. 95, in Le Faye, 247–50.

37 6 November 1813, no. 96, in Le Faye, 251–4.

38 *Sense and Sensibility*, vol. I, ch. XIII.

39 Constance Hill, *Jane Austen: Her Homes and Her Friends* (Oxford: The Bodley Head, 1923), 161–2.

40 Pevsner, xxx

41 *Mansfield Park*, ch. 6.

42 Ibid., ch. 9.

43 Ibid., ch. 6.

44 *Pride and Prejudice*, vol. III, ch. I. / ch. 43

45 *Evelina*, vol. III, ch. VI.

46 Jane Austen to Francis Austen, 26 July 1809, no. 69, in Le Faye, 177.

47 Margaret Anne Doody, *Introduction to Jane Austen, Sense and Sensibility* (Oxford: Oxford University Press, Oxford World's Classics, 1990), xii.

48 Moira Goff, John Goldfinch, Karen Limper-Herz and Helen Peden, with an Introduction by Amanda Goodrich, *Georgians Revealed, Life, Style and the Making of Modern Britain* (London: The British Library, 2013), 46.

49 Frances Burney, 1774, *Fanny Burney's Diary, A Selection from the Diary and Letters*, ed. John Wain (London: The Folio Society, 1961), 16.

50 Frances Burney, October 18th 1774 in *The Early Journals and Letters of Fanny Burney*, ed. Lars E. Troide (Oxford: Clarendon Press, 1990), vol. II, 52.

Chapter 4
Ancient and Romantic: Walter Scott's Baronial Halls

1 John Sutherland, *The Life of Walter Scott* (Oxford: Blackwell, 1995), 8.

2 Walter Scott, 'Memoirs', in David Hewitt, ed., *Scott on Himself: A Selection of the Autobiographical Writings of Sir Walter Scott* (Edinburgh: Scottish Academic Press, 1981), 13.

3 Ibid., 29.

4 Ibid., 37.

5 J. G. Lockhart, *Memoirs of the Life of Sir Walter Scott*, 5 vols, 1837–8, repr., Boston and New York, 1902, vol. I, 124, in Sutherland, 33.

6 James Reed, *Walter Scott: Landscape and Locality* (London: The Athlone Press, 1980), 51.

7 Lockhart I, 193 in Sutherland, 45.

8 Lockhart I, 419 in Sutherland, 105.

9 Sutherland, 105.

10 Walter Scott to Lady Abercorn, 30 September 1810, in H. J. C. Grierson, ed., *The Letters of Sir Walter Scott, 1808–1811* (London: Constable & Co, 1932–7), 377–8.

11 Abbotsford, *A Short Guide to the Home of Sir Walter Scott* (Melrose: The Abbotsford Trust), 54.

12 Walter Scott to Charles Carpenter 25 August 1811, in Grierson, vol. 2, 536.

13 Walter Scott to John Bacon Sawrey Morritt, 1 July 1811, in Grierson, vol. 2, 508.

14 Sutherland, 29.

15 http://www.douglashistory.co.uk/history/Places/bothwell-house.htm [accessed on 3 May 2016.]

16 Walter Scott to Charles Carpenter, 25 August 1811, in Grierson, vol. 2, 537.

17 Walter Scott to Robert Surtees, 19 December 1811, in Grierson, vol. 2, 30.

18 Walter Scott to Matthew Hartstonge, 21 August 1813, Grierson, vol. 3, 318.

19 Walter Scott to John Bacon Sawrey Morritt, 2 November 1815, Grierson, vol. 4, 112.

20 Andrew Hook, introduction, in Walter Scott, *Waverley* (London: Penguin Books Ltd, 1972), 9.

21 Walter Scott to John Bacon Sawrey Morritt, 28 July 1814, in Grierson, vol. 3, 477.

22 *Waverley*, ch. 6.

23 *The Antiquarian*, ch. 1.

24 *Waverley*, ch. 9 n1.

25 Ibid., ch. 8.

26 Ibid., ch. 9, n3.

27 Ibid., ch. 8.

28 Ibid., ch. 63.

29 Ibid., ch. 63.

30 David Daiches, 'Scott and Scotland' 38–60, in *Scott Bicentenary Essays, Selected Papers Read at the Sir Walter Scott Bicentenary Conference*, ed. Alan Bell (Edinburgh and London: Scottish Academic Press, 1973) 53.

31 Walter Scott to Joanna Baillie, 4 April 1812, in Grierson, vol. 3, 99.

32 Walter Scott to D. Terry, 28 December 1816, in Grierson, vol. 4, 335–6.

33 Ibid.

34 Walter Scott to Lady Louisa Stuart, 20 September 1812, in Grierson, vol. 3, 164.

35 Walter Scott to D. Terry, 28 December 1816, in Grierson, vol. 4, 339.

36 Walter Scott to D. Terry, March [? March] 1817, in Grierson, vol. 4, 398.

37 Walter Scott to D. Terry, 28 December 1816, in Grierson, vol. 4, 333-4.

38 Walter Scott to Joanna Baillie, 26 November 1816, in Grierson, vol. 4, 301–2.

39 Grierson, vol. 1, xxxix.

40 Amount calculated by www.measuringworth.com, aaccessed on 6 May 2016.

41 Walter Scott, Sunday 18 December 1825, in *The Journal of Walter Scott* (Oxford: Clarendon Press, 1972), 38.

42 Sutherland, 341

43 Reed, 51.
44 Walter Scott to Joanna Baillie, 4 April 1812, in Grierson, vol. 3, 100.
45 George Watson, introduction, in Maria Edgeworth, *Castle Rackrent* (London: Oxford University Press, 1964), 1.
46 Walter Scott, ch. 72, 'A Postscript which should have been a Preface', in *Waverly* (London: Penguin Books, 1985), 493.
47 Virginia Woolf, *Orlando*, ch. 6.

Chapter 5
Madwoman in the Attic, Author in the Dining Room:
The Haunts of Charlotte Brontë

1   From Anne Thackeray Ritchie's account of Charlotte Brontë's visit to her father, in James Sutherland, ed. *The Oxford Book of Literary Anecdotes* (Oxford: Oxford University Press, 1975).
2   George M. Smith, the young publisher of *Jane Eyre, recounted his time with Charlotte Brontë in* H. Orel, ed., The Brontës, p. 100, *from Cornhill Magazine, New Series, 9 (December 1900):* 778–95.
3   Elizabeth Gaskell, *The Life of Charlotte Brontë* (London: Smith, Elder & Co., 1857), 74.
4   Ellen Nussey, 'Reminiscences of Charlotte Brontë (1831–1855)', in *Scribner's Monthly* 2:1 (May 1871): 18–31, quoted in Harold Orel, ed., *The Brontës, Interviews and Recollections* (London: Macmillan Press, 1997), 26.
5   Gaskell, *The Life of Charlotte Brontë*, 81.
6   Ibid., 71.
7   Ibid., 81.
8   Ibid., 98.
9   Charlotte Brontë, 'The Search after Happiness', 17 August 1829: British Museum, in Winifred Gérin, *Charlotte Brontë: The Evolution of Genius* (Oxford: Clarendon Press, 1967), 45
10 Gaskell, *The Life of Charlotte Brontë*, 170
11 Robert Southey to Charlotte Brontë, 12 March 1837 in *The Letters of Charlotte Bronte with a Selection of Letters by Family and Friends*, 3 vols, ed. Margaret Smith (Oxford: Clarendon Press, 1995), vol I, 166–7.
12 From the *Roe Head Journal*, 11 August 1836, quoted in Gérin, 103–4.
13 CB to Ellen Nussey, 11 September 1833 in Margaret Smith, ed., *Selected Letters*, vol. I, 124.
14 Charlotte Brontë to Ellen Nussey, 9 June 1838, in Smith, ed., *Selected Letters*, vol. 2 (Oxford: Oxford University Press, 2007).
15 CB to Emily J. Brontë, 8 June 1839 in *Selected Letters*, vol. I, 190–91.
16 CB to Ellen Nussey, 30 June 1839 in *Selected Letters*, vol. I, 193.
17 CB to Ellen Nussey, 8 June 1839 in *Selected Letters*, vol. I, 191.
18 Charlotte Brontë to Ellen Nussey, 7 August 1841, in *Selected Letters*, vol. I, 32.

19 William Thackeray to W. S. Williams, 23 October 1847, in *The Brontës, The Critical Heritage*, ed. Miriam Allott (London and Boston: Routledge and Kegan Paul, 1974), No. 6, 70.
20 H. F. Charley, unsigned review, *Athenaeum*, 23 October 1847, 1100–1, in Allott, No. 7, 71.
21 Claire Harman, *Charlotte Brontë: A Life* (London: Viking, 2015), 263.
22 Elizabeth Rigby, Quarterly Review, December 1848, in Allott, 70.
23 *Jane Eyre*, ch. XI.
24 Ibid.
25 Ibid.
26 Ibid., ch. II.
27 Ibid., ch. III.
28 Ibid., ch. XI.
29 Ibid.
30 Gaskell, *The Life of Charlotte Brontë*, 362.
31 *Jane Eyre*, ch XI.
32 Ibid.
33 Ibid. ch. XII.
34 Ibid. ch. XVII.
35 Ibid.
36 Ibid.
37 Charlotte Brontë to Ellen Nussey, 4 July 1834, in Smith, 4.
38 *Jane Eyre*, ch. XII.
39 Harman, *Charlotte Brontë*, 196.
40 Ibid.
41 Herber E. Wroot, 'The Persons and Places of the Brontë Novels', in *Transactions and Other Publications of the Brontë Society* (January 1906), 1–21.
42 Conversation with Sir James Graham, 14 September 2015.
43 Wroot, *Transactions*, 15.
44 Susan E. James, 'Is Thurland Castle "Thornfield Hall"?', in Brontë Society Transactions 25:2 (October 2000): 147–53.
45 *Jane Eyre*, ch. XI.
46 Ibid.
47 Conversation with Sir James Graham.
48 *Jane Eyre*, ch. XX.
49 Ibid., 181
50 George Lewes, 'Recent Novel, French and English', Fraser's Magazine, December 1847, in Allott. 57.
51 Ellen Nussey, in Orel, 26.
52 Charlotte Brontë to Ellen Nussey, 21 May 1854, in Smith, vol. 3, 263.
53 Mary Taylor to Elizabeth Gaskell, 30 July 1857, in Orel, 114.
54 *Jane Eyre*, ch. XXXVII.

Chapter 6
Charles Dickens: A Child's View of Home

1   Charles Dickens to W. W. F. Cerjat, 19 January 1857, Graham Storey and Kathleen Tillotson, eds, *The Letters of Charles Dickens, 1856–1858*, vol. 8 (Oxford: Clarendon Press, 1995), 266.

2   Gad's Hill Place visitor information, Higham, Kent.

3   Charles Dickens to William Wills, 9 February 1855, *The Letters of Charles Dickens*, Storey and Tillotson, eds, vol. VII, 531.

4   Charles Dickens, *A Christmas Carol*, Stave Two.

5   *Old Curiosity Shop*, ch. IV.

6   *David Copperfield*, ch. III.

7   Ibid., ch. II.

8   *Old Curiosity Shop*, ch. X.

9   Ibid., ch. XXI.

10 Ibid., ch. XXII.

11 Ibid., ch. XXII.

12 *Bleak House*, ch. LXIV.

13 *David Copperfield*, ch. XIII.

14 *Old Curiosity Shop*, ch. IX.

15 John Forster, The Life of Charles Dickens, vol. 1 (London: Chapman and Hall Limited, 1911), 13.

16 *Great Expectations*, ch. VIII.

17 Ibid., ch. XX/iv, xiii

18 See Restoration House information: http://www.restorationhouse.co.uk

19 *Great Expectation*, ch. XXII.

20 Forster, vol. 2, 242.

21 *Great Expectation*, ch. VII.

22 Ibid., ch. VIII.

23 Ibid., ch. VIII.

24 Ibid., ch. VIII.

25 Ibid., ch. XI.

26 Ibid., ch. XI.

27 Ibid., ch. XXV.

28 Claire Tomalin, *Charles Dickens: A Life* (London: Penguin, 2012), 102.

29 Charles Dickens to W. W. F. De Cerjat, 7 July 1858, in Storey and Tillotson, eds, *The Letters of Charles Dickens*, vol. 8, 597.

30 Charles Dickens to Miss Burdett Coutts, 22 May 1857, in ibid., 330.

31 Charles Dickens to WFF De Cerjat, 7 July 1858, in ibid., 598.

32 Charles Dickens to Miss Burdett Coutts, 9 Feb 1856, in ibid., 51.

33 Charles Dickens to T. Fields, [summer?] 1865, in *Letters*, vol. II, 79.

34 Michael Slater, *Charles Dickens* (London: Yale University Press, 2009), 532.

35 Forster, *The Life of Charles Dickens*, vol. I, 13.

36 Ibid.

37 Ibid., 28.

38 *Oliver Twist*, bk III, ch. 13.
39 Charles Dickens to Thomas Mitton, 14 April 1845, in Storey and Tillotson, eds, *The Letters of Charles Dickens, 1844–1846*, vol. 4 (Oxford: Clarendon Press, 1995), 297–8, quoted in Frances Armstrong, *Dickens and the Concept of Home* (Ann Arbor and London: University of Michigan Press, 1990), 160, n. 2.
40 Charles Dickens, Jr., 7 March 1894 in *All the Year Round*.
41 *David Copperfield*, ch. XIII.
42 Forster, *The Life of Charles Dickens*, 235.
43 Charles Dickens to Miss Mary Dickens, 11/13 June 1859, in *Letters*, ed. Storey and Tillotson, vol. 9, 77.
44 Charles Dickens to W. C. Macready, 15 March 1857, in ibid., vol. 8, 302.
45 Tomalin, *Charles* Dickens, 358–61.
46 Charles Dickens, 'St Giles Rookery' in Sketches by Boz, 1839.
47 Ibid., 203.
48 Charles Dickens to W. F. Cerjat, 7 July 1858, in *Letters*, ed. Storey and Tillotson, vol. 8, 598.
49 *Great Expectations*, ch. XVII.
50 Forster, *The Life of Charles* Dickens, vol II, 235.
51 Ibid., vol. II, 5.
52 Tomalin, *Charles Dickens*, 402.

Chapter 7
For the Love of an English Cottage: Thomas Hardy and E. M. Forster

1 Michael Millgate, *Thomas Hardy, A Biography* (Oxford: Oxford University Press, 1982), 79.
2 As told to W. Lyon Phelps, in *The Architectural Notebook of Thomas Hardy*, 18.
3 *Jude the Obscure*, part II, ch. I.
4 Norman Page, 'Art and Aesthetics', in Dale Kramer, ed., *The Cambridge Companion to Thomas Hardy* (Cambridge: Cambridge University Press, 1999), 38–53, 45–6.
5 *The Architectural Notebook of Thomas Hardy*, 160 (Hardy's numbering).
6 Ibid., 24–5.
7 *Jude the Obscure*, part II, I.
8 Ibid.
9 Florence Emily Hardy, *The Life of Thomas Hardy 1840–1928* (London: Macmillan, 1962), 31
10 *The Laodicean*, bk I, ch. VIII
11 Ibid., bk II, ch. II.
12 *Jude the Obscure*, part II I.
13 Thomas Hardy, 'Memories of Church Restoration', in *The Society for the Protection of Ancient Buildings: the General Meeting of the Society; Twenty-Ninth Annual Report of the Committee; and Paper Read by Thomas*

Hardy, Esq., June, 1906, London, 1906, 59–80, in Harold Orel, ed., *Thomas Hardy's Personal Writings* (London Macmillan, 1967), 203–18.

14 Hardy, *The Life of Thomas Hardy*, 35.

15 Ibid., 36.

16 Ibid., 48.

17 Anonymous, 'Celebrities at Home', Mr Hardy at Max Gate, Dorchester, in *The World* (February 1886), 6–7, in James Gibson, ed., *Thomas Hardy, Interviews and Recollections* (London: Macmillan, 1999), 20. Gibson notes that the article was possibly written by Hardy himself.

18 Florence Emily Hardy, 53.

19 *Architecture Notebook*, 9, 5.

20 Hardy, *The Life of Thomas Hardy*, 87

21 Thomas Hardy, 'How I Built Myself a House', in *Chambers's Journal of Popular Literature, Science and Arts* (18 March 1865), 161–4.

22 *Under the Greenwood Tree*, part II, ch. VI.

23 Thomas Hardy, O.M., 'Note', in Journal of the Royal Society of Arts (18 March 1927): 428–9.

24 Hardy, *The Life of Thomas* Hardy, 96.

25 Ibid., 149.

26 Ibid., 173.

27 John Newman and Nikolaus Pevsner, eds, *The Buildings of England, Dorset* (London: Penguin, 1975), 186.

28 Hardy, *The Life of Thomas Hardy*, 173.

29 Anonymous, from the series 'Representative Men at Home', in *Cassell's Saturday Journal* (28 June 1892), 944–6; reprinted in James Gibson, ed., *Thomas Hardy, Interviews and Recollections* (London: Macmillan, 1999), 36.

30 *Tess of the d'Urbervilles*, part I, ch. V.

31 Ibid.

32 Ibid.

33 *The Architectural Notebook of Thomas Hardy* (Philadelphia: George S. Macmanus Company, 1966), 78 (Hardy's numbering), 8, 159.

34 Ibid.

35 Hardy, *The Life of Thomas Hardy*, 174.

36 Anonymous, 'Celebrities at Home', in *The World* (February 1886): 6–7, in Gibson, ed., *Thomas Hardy, Interviews and Recollections*, 21.

37 Hardy, *The Life of Thomas Hardy*, 176

38 Siegfried Sassoon, 21 February 1921, in Rupert Hart-Davies, ed., Siegfried Sassoon Diaries, 1920–1922 (London: Faber and Faber, 1981), 43.

39 Nicola Beaumann, *Morgan, A Biography of E. M. Forster* (London: Hodder & Stoughton, 1993), 214.

40 *Howards End*, ch. 3, ch. 44.

41 Ibid., ch. 1.

42 Ibid., ch. 13.

43 Ibid., ch. 22.

44 Ibid.

45 Ibid, ch. 6.
46 E. M. Forster, 'Three Countries', in *The Hills of Devi and Other Indian Writings* (London: Edward Arnold, 1983), 294, 295.
47 Ibid., 294.
48 *Howards End*, ch. 3.
49 Ibid., ch.11.
50 Ibid., ch. 9.
51 Lady Faith Culme-Seymour, 'Memories of E. M. Forster', in J. H. Stape, ed., *E. M. Forster, Interviews and Recollections* (London: St Martin's Press, 1993), 81.
52 *Howards End*, ch. 11.
53 Ibid., ch. 17.
54 Ibid., ch. 6.
55 Ibid., ch. 15.
56 Ibid., ch. 18.
57 Ibid., ch. 26.
58 Ibid., ch. 25.
59 Ibid., ch. 31.
60 Ibid., ch. 32.
61 Nicola Beaumann, *Morgan: A Biography of E. M. Forster* (London: Hodder & Stoughton, 1993), 21.
62 E. M. Forster, *Marianne Thornton, A Domestic Biography* (London: Edward Arnold, 1956), 16–19.
63 Ibid., 16.
64 Ibid., 17.
65 May Buckingham, 'Some Reminiscences', in Stape, 77.
66 Forster, *Marianne Thornton*, 19.
67 *Herfordshire Express*, June 17, 1882, in Margaret Ashby, *Forster Country* (Stevenage: Flaunden Press, 1991), 13.
68 Forster, *Marianne Thornton*, 269.
69 E. M. Forster, 'Rooksnest', in *Howards End*, Abinger Edition 4 (London: Edward Arnold, 1973), 350.
70 *Howards End*, ch. 1.
71 Ibid., ch. 23.
72 Forster, 'Rooksnest', 346.
73 Forster, 'Three Countries', 293.
74 Forster, *Marianne Thornton*, 269–70.
75 Forster, 'Rooksnest', 341.
76 *Howards End*, ch. 6.
77 Ibid., ch. 7.
78 E. M. Forster, *A Room with a View* (London: Penguin Classics, 2000), 129.
79 Beauman, *Morgan*, 338.
80 Wendy Moffat, *E. M. Forster: A New Life* (London: Bloomsbury, 2010), 191.
81 E. M. Forster to Florence Berger, 2 October 1924, in Mary Lago and P. N. Furnbank, eds, *Selected Letters of E. M. Forster*, vol. 2 (London: Collins,

1985), 66.

82 E. M. Forster to Robert J. Buckingham, 9 February 1953, in Lago and Furnbank, *Selected Letters*, vol. 2, 248.

83 E. M. Forster, 'My Wood', in *Abinger Harvest* (London: Edward Arnold, 1936), 23.

84 E. M. Forster to Hilton Young, 15 February 1940, in Lago and Furnbank, *Selected Letters*, vol. 2, 172.

85 *Howards End*, ch. 4.

86 Ibid., ch 13.

87 Ibid., ch. 1.

88 Ibid., ch. 24.

89 Ibid., ch. 15.

90 E. M. Forster, 'A Room without a View', in *A Room with a View* (London: Penguin Classics, 2000), 231–3.

91 *Howards End*, ch. 44.

92 Ibid., ch. 41.

93 Evelyn Waugh, preface, *Brideshead Revisited* (London: Penguin Classics, 2000), ix.

94 Lionel Trilling, 'Howards End' in *Howards End* by E. M. Forster (London: Penguin, 2012), 381.

95 Ford Madox Ford, *Some Do Not*, in *Parade's End* (London: Penguin, 2012), part I, ch. 3, 51.

96 Aldous Huxley, *Crane Yellow*, ch. XI.

97 Julian Barnes, *Metroland*, part 1, ch. 7.

Chapter 8
The House as a Work of Art: The Aesthetic Visions of
John Galsworthy and Henry James

1 *The Man of Property*, part I, ch. 1.

2 See 'Modern Novels' unsigned article by Virginia Woolf in *The Times Literary Supplement*, April 10, 1919.

3 *The Man of Property*, part I, ch. 1.

4 Ibid., part I, ch. 6.

5 *The Man of Property*, part I, ch. 3

6 http://www.ideal-homes.org.uk/case-studies/streatham/5, accessed on 21 June 2015.

7 *The Man of Property*, 'interlude'.

8 Catherine Dupré, John Galsworthy: A Biography (London: Collins, 1976), 36.

9 John Galsworthy, 'A Portrait', in A Motley (London: William Heinemann, 1927), 6.

10 *The Man of Property*, 'interlude'.

11 John Galsworthy, 'A Portrait', 30.

12 H. V. Marrot, *The Life and Letters of John Galsworthy* (London: William

Heinemann, 1935), 30.

13   *The Man of Property*, part I, ch. 8.
14   Marrot, *Life and Letters*, 402.
15   http://www.british-history.ac.uk/survey-london/vol37/pp49-57#fnnc2
16   Unpublished Diary of Lilian Sauter, 1903, 23 October, Thursday, Cadbury Research Library, Special Collections, University of Brimingham.
17   Marrot, *Life and Letters*, 108.
18   *The Man of Property*, part I, ch. 8.
19   Ibid.
20   Ibid.
21   See the history of the Hall-Héroult process, http://www.acs.org/content/acs/en/education/whatischemistry/landmarks/aluminumprocess.html accessed on 9 June 2015.
22   *The Man of Property*, part I, ch.8.
23   Ibid., part II, ch. 13.
24   Ibid., part II, ch. 7.
25   Ibid., part I, ch. 8.
26   John Galsworthy, *To Let*, part I, ch. 1.
27   http://www.british-history.ac.uk/vch/middx/vol12/pp102-106, accessed on 15 June 2015.
28   For a more fulsome account of the artistic scene in Chelsea at the time, see *The Street of Wonderful Possibilities: Whistler, Wilde & Sargent in Tite Street* (London: Frances Lincoln, 2015).
29   Susan Weber Soros, ed., E. W. Godwin Aesthetic Movement Architect and Designer (New Haven and London: Yale University Press, 1999), 197.
30   *The Man of Property*, part I, ch. 8.
31   Charlotte Gere, with Lesely Hoskins, *The House Beautiful, Oscar Wilde and the Aesthetic Interior* (London: Lund Humphries in association with The Geffrye Museum, 2000), 98.
32   Charlotte Gere, 'Leighton House, Its Rise, Fall, and Rise' in *Apollo* 171:575 (April 2010): 54–9.
33   'The Forsyte Chronicles by John Galsworthy, The Autograph Manuscript with Some Preliminary Matter', British Library, ADD41752.
34   Henry James, 'An English New Year', in Alma Louise Lowe, ed., *English Hours* (London: William Heinemann, 1960), 170.
35   Henry James, *Portrait of a Lady*, ch. I.
36   Ibid., ch. XXII.
37   Ibid., ch. XXX.
38   Ibid., ch. XLII.
39   Ibid.
40   Henry James to J. B. Pinker, 14th June 1906 in *Henry James Letters*, vol. IV, ed. by Leon Edel (Cambridge and London: The Belnap Press of Harvard University Press, 1984).
41   See Michael Gorra, *Portrait of a Novel, Henry James and the Making of an American Masterpiece* (New York: W. W. Norton & Co., 2012) p. 47.
42   Henry James to Grace Norton, 8 June 1879, in *The Letters of Henry James*,

vol. IV, 69.

43 Henry James, preface, *The Spoils of Poynton* (London: Penguin Classics, 1987), 23–5.
44 Ibid.
45 Henry James, *The Spoils of Poynton*, ch. II.
46 Ibid., ch. I.
47 Ibid.
48 For a comparison of Poynton and Wilde's description of the home of Dorian Grey see Michele Mendelssohn, Henry James, Oscar Wilde and Aesthetic Culture (Edinburgh: Edinburgh University Press, 2007) 223.
49 *The Spoils of Poynton*, ch. II.
50 Ibid., ch. IV.
51 Ibid.
52 Ibid., ch. XXII.
53 Henry James, *The Notebooks of Henry James*, ed. by F. O. Matthiesson and Kenneth B. Murdock (New York and Oxford: Oxford University Press, 1947), 137.
54 'Preface' to *The Spoils of Poynton*.
55 Henry James to Arthur Christopher Benson, 25 September 1897, in Leon Edel, ed., *The Letters of Henry James*, vol. IV, 1895–1916, 57.
56 Fred Kaplan, *Henry James: The Imagination of Genius, A Biography* (London: Hodder & Stoughton, 1992), 420.
57 The National Trust, Henry James and Lamb House, Rye (1999), 9.
58 Quoted in Kaplan, *The Imagination of* Genius, 429
59 Henry James, 'New York Revisited', in Leon Edel, ed., *The American Scene* (London: Rupert Hart-Davis, 1968), 76–7.
60 'New York, Social Notes', in Edel, ed., *The American Scene*, 167.

Chapter 9
Rooms of Her Own: Virginia Woolf's Houses of Memory

1 Lyndall Gordon, *Virginia Woolf: A Writer's Life* (Oxford: Oxford University Press, 1984), 51.
2 Quentin Bell, *Virginia Woolf, A Biography*, vol. 1: 1882–1912, 22.
3 'A Sketch of the Past' (1939–40), in *Virginia Woolf, Moments of Being* (London: Chatto & Windus, 1976), 150.
4 Ibid., 150–1
5 '22 Hyde Park Gate', in *Moments of Being*, 31–2
6 Thursday 28 June 1923, in *The Diary of Virginia Woolf*, 5 vils edited by Anne Olivier Bell, assisted by Andrew McNeillie, vol. 2: 1920–1924 (London: The Hogarth Press, 1978), 250.
7 Ibid.
8 'Old Bloomsbury' (1921–2), in *Moments of Being*, 46–7.
9 VW 23 October 1918, *The Diary of Virginia Woolf*, vol. 1: 1915–1919 (New York: Harcourt Brace, 1977), 206.
10 'Old Bloomsbury' in *Moments of Being*, 187–8.

11 Virginia Woolf to Ka Cox, 12 August 1919, in Nigel Nicolson, ed., *The Question of Things Happening: The Letters of Virginia Woolf, 1912–1922* (London: The Hogarth Press, 1976), 382.

12 VW 10 April 1920, in *The Diary of Virginia Woolf*, vol. 2: 1920–1924, 28.

13 *Jacob's Room*, ch. III.

14 Ibid., ch. XI.

15 Laurence Sterne, *The Life and Opinions of Tristram Shandy, Gentleman*, vol. III, ch. IX / I Liii

16 Virginia Woolf, *Mrs Dalloway* (London: Vintage, 2000), 1.

17 Ibid., 107.

18 A Sketch of the Past', in *Moments of Being*, 79.

19 Bell, *Virginia Woolf*, vol. 1: 1882–1912, 32.

20 Virginia Woolf, *To the Lighthouse*, part I, ch. 1.

21 VW Sunday 19 September 1920, in *The Diary of Virginia Woolf*, vol. 2, 1920–1924, 67.

22 VW 22 March 1921, in *The Diary of Virginia Woolf*, vol. 2: 1920–1924, 103.

23 'A Sketch of the Past', in *Moments of Being*, 81.

24 Ibid., 93.

25 Ibid., 159.

26 *To the Lighthouse*, part III, ch. 1.

27 Ibid., part I, ch. 1.

28 Ibid.

29 VW 18 April 1926, in *The Diary of Virginia Woolf*, vol. 2: 1920–1924, 76.

30 *To the Lighthouse*, part II, ch. 3.

31 Ibid., part I, ch. 1.

32 Virginia Woolf, 11 August 1905, in Mitchell A. Leaska, ed., *A Passionate Apprentice: The Early Journals 1897–1909* (The Hogarth Press: London, 1990), 282.

33 From 'A Sketch of the Past' in *Moments of Being*, 78.

34 VW 26 May 1920, in *The Diary of Virginia Woolf*, vol. II, 42

35 VW 10 August 1920 in ibid., 56.

36 Vita Sackville-West to Harold Nicholson, June 1926, in Hermione Lee, *Virginia Woolf* (London: Vintage, 1997), 501.

37 Lyndall Gordon, *Virginia Woolf, A Writer's Life* (Oxford: Oxford University Press, 1984), 249.

38 Virginia Woolf to Lady Robert Cecil, February 1920, in *The Question of Things Happening*, 423.

39 VW to VB, 1 May 1920, in ibid., 432.

40 Virginia Woolf to Ka Cox, 9 October 1919, in *The Question of Things Happening*, 390.

41 'Old Bloomsbury', in *Moments of Being*, 44.

42 VW to VB, 7 September 1919, in *The Question of Things Happening*, 387.

43 *To the Lighthouse*, part III, ch. 3.

44 VW to Violet Dickenson, 11 August 1919, in *The Question of Things Happening*, 381.

Chapter 10
Inheritance and Loss: War and the Great English Estates

1   Asa Briggs, *A Social History of England, From the Ice Age to the Channel Tunnel* (London: Weidenfeld & Nicolson, 1994), 279.
2   'Taxation During the First World War', http://www.parliament.uk/about/living-heritage/transformingsociety/private-lives/taxation/overview/firstworldwar. Accessed on 8 July 2015.
3   Max Saunders, *Ford Madox Ford: A Dual Life*, volume I: *The World Before the War* (Oxford: Oxford University Press, 1996), 3.
4   Ford Madox Ford, *Some Do Not*, ch. IV, in *Parade's End*.
5   Saunders, *A Dual Life*, 3.
6   Ford Madox Ford, *The Last Post*, ch. V, in *Parade's End*.
7   Ibid.
8   Ford Madox Ford, *No More Parades*, part III, ch. II, in *Parade's End*.
9   Ford Madox Ford, *Return to Yesterday*, ed. Bill Hutchings (Manchester: Carcanet, 1999), 288.
10 Ford Madox Ford, *It was the Nightingale* (London: William Heinemann, 1939), 202.
11 Ford, *Some Do Not*, part I, ch. VII.
12 Ibid.
13 Ford, *The Last Post*, part I, ch. IV.
14 Ford Madox Ford, *A Man Could Stand Up*, part II, ch. VI, in *Parade's End*.
15 Ford, *No More Parades*, part III, ch. II.
16 Ibid.
17 Ford, *Some Do Not*, part II, ch. III.
18 See Nikolaus Pevsner, *The Buildings of England BE29 Yorkshire: The North Riding* (Harmondsworth Middlesex: Penguin, 1966) 104.
19 Ford, *No More Parades*, part II, ch. II.
20 Ford, *The Last Post*, part I, ch. IV.
21 Ford, *Some Do Not*, part I, ch. III.
22 Ibid., ch. V.
23 Ibid., part II, ch. I
24 Ford, *The Last Post*, part I, ch. VI, ch. IV.
25 Ibid., part II, ch. II
26 Michael Davie, ed., *The Diaries of Evelyn Waugh* (London: Weidenfeld & Nicolson, 1976), 158.
27 Ibid., 159.
28 Evelyn Waugh, *Vile Bodies*, ch. 8.
29 http://www.barfordheritage.org/content/places/barford-house – Accessed on 31 July 2015.
30 Evelyn Waugh, 'Higham, Bassenthwaite Lake, Cockermouth, Cumberland', 4 August 1926, in Davie, *Diaries*, 257.
31 Ibid., 259.
32 6 October 1927, in Davie, *Diaires*, 291.

33 See Davie, *Diaries*, 325–7, 394.
34 Manuscript reads 'Sebastian', see Philip Eade, *Evelyn Waugh, A Life Revisited* (London: Weidenfeld, 2016).
35 See *Madresfield: The Real Brideshead* by Jane Mulvagh, a compelling story of the house, its history and the family who has inhabited it continuously since the twelfth century.
36 Jane Mulvagh, *Madresfield: The Real Brideshead* (New York: Doubleday, 2008), 32
37 Evelyn Waugh, *Brideshead Revisited, The Sacred and Profane Memories of Captain Charles Ryder*, book II, ch. 3 .
38 Ibid., book III, ch. 1.
39 Ibid.
40 Mulvagh, *Madresfield*, 64.
41 Ibid., 139
42 Evelyn Waugh to Dorothy Lygon, 23 March 1944, quoted in Mulvagh, *Madresfield*, 31.
43 Waugh, *Brideshead Revisited*, book I, ch. 1.
44 Ibid.
45 Ibid.
46 Dorothy Lygon, 'Madresfield and Brideshead', in David Pryce-Jones, ed., *Evelyn Waugh and his World* (London: Weidenfeld & Nicolson, 1973), 54.
47 Waugh, *Brideshead Revisited*, book I, ch. 3.
48 Ibid., 'Epilogue'.
49 Lygon, 'Madresfield and Brideshead' in Pryce-Jones, *Evelyn Waugh and his World*, 54.
50 Waugh, *Brideshead Revisited*, book I, ch. 3.
51 Ibid., 'Epilogue'.
52 Aldous Huxley, *Chrome Yellow*, ch. XXVIII.
53 Ibid., ch. XI.
54 Ibid., ch. XXII.
55 Ibid., ch. XX.
56 Ibid., ch. XXIV.
57 Evelyn Waugh, 'Preface' to *Brideshead Revisited*, 1959.

Chapter 11
Gothic House Redux: The Passion of Manderley, Agatha Christie's Bloody House Parties

1 Daphne du Maurier, *Rebecca*, ch. 1.
2 Ibid., ch. 3.
3 Ibid.
4 Ibid.
5 Ibid., ch. 4.
6 Ibid.
7 Ibid., chs 7 and 8.

8 Ibid., ch. 8.
9 Peter Beacham and Nikolaus Pevsner, 'Menabilly', in *The Buildings of England: Cornwall* (London: Yale University Press, 2014), 347–8.
10 Daphne du Maurier, 'The House of Secrets', in *The Rebecca Notebook: And Other Memories* (London: Virago, 2004), 138.
11 Ibid., 137.
12 Ibid., 138, 139.
13 Ibid., 134.
14 Ibid., 4.
15 Ibid., 143.
16 Margaret Forster, *Daphne du Maurier* (London: Arrow Books, 1993), 317.
17 Daphne du Maurier to Oriel Malet, 9 January 1976, in Oriel Malet, ed., *Letters from Menabilly: Portrait of a Friendship* (London: Weidenfeld & Nicolson, 1993), 277
18 Ibid.
19 Daphne du Maurier, *Growing Pains* (London: Victor Gollancz, 1977), 24–6.
20 Ibid., 36.
21 Forster, 101.
22 Du Maurier, *Growing Pains*, 43.
23 Martyn Shallcross, *The Private World of Daphne du Maurier* (London: Robson Books, 1998), 81.
24 Du Maurier, *Growing Pains*, 45.
25 Du Maurier, *Rebecca*, ch. 7.
26 Ibid.
27 Judith Cook, *Daphne: A Portrait of Daphne du Maurier* (London: Bantam Press, 1991), 43.
28 Shallcross, *Private World*, 81.
29 Daphne du Maurier, 'The Rebecca Epilogue', in *The Rebecca Notebook*, 42.
30 John Galsworthy, 'Flowering Wilderness' (Book 8 of The Forsyte Saga), ch. XXXiii
31 'The House of Secrets', 144.
32 Ibid., 139.
33 Shallcross, *Private World*, 93.
34 Agatha Christie, *An Autobiography* (London: Harper Collins, 1993), 38–9.
35 Agatha Christie, *Endless Night*, ch 1.
36 Ibid., ch. 14.
37 Christie, *An Autobiography*, 236.
38 Ann Treneman, 'Mr. Pratt in the Old People's Home, with an Empty Pocket', *Independent*, 12 November 1998.
39 Agatha Christie, *The Adventures of the Christmas Pudding*, ch. 1.

Chapter 12
The Glamour, Horror and Ennui of Modern Housing:
Ian Fleming, J. G. Ballard, Julian Barnes

1 Peter Ackroyd, *London, The Biography* (London: Vintage, 2000), 749.
2 Travis Elborough, 'An Investigative Spirit', interview with the author, in J. G. Ballard, *High-Rise* (London: Harper Perennial, 2006), 12.
3 'The History of Council Housing' (Bristol: The University of the West of England, 2008). http://fet.uwe.ac.uk/conweb/house_ages/council_housing/print.htm Accessed on 27 August 2016.
4 J. G. Ballard, *High Rise*, ch. 2.
5 Ian Fleming, *Goldfinger*, ch. 6.
6 Ibid., ch. 10.
7 Ibid.
8 Ibid.
9 Ian Fleming, *Dr. No*, ch. 14.
10 Ian Fleming, *On Her Majesty's Secret Service*, ch. 11.
11 Ian Fleming, *You Only Live Twice*, ch. 16.
12 Andrew Lycett, *Ian Fleming* (London: Phoenix, 1996), 328.
13 Ibid., 345.
14 Ibid., 99.
15 Ballard, *High Rise*, ch. 1.
16 Ibid., ch. 5.
17 Ibid., ch. 14.
18 Ibid., ch. 1.
19 J. G. Ballard interview in Philippe R. Hupp, in Simon Sellers and Dan O'Hara, eds, *Extreme Metaphors, Interviews with J. G. Ballard, 1967–2008* (London: Fourth Estate, 2012), 80.
20 Nigel Warburton, *Ernö Goldfinger, The Life of an Architect* (London: Routledge, 2004), 162.
21 Ibid., 166.
22 Ibid., 168.
23 Interview with Jon Savage, in Sellers and O'Hara, *Extreme Metaphors*, 107, 112.
24 J. G. Ballard, *Miracles of Life* (London: HarperCollins, 2008), 11.
25 Ibid.
26 Ibid., 115.
27 Ibid., 122.
28 Ibid., 125.
29 Warburton, *Goldfinger*, 160.
30 Interview by Will Self, in Sellers and O'Hara, *Extreme Metaphors*, 315.
31 Anthony Burgess, *A Clockwork Orange*, ch. 3.
32 Julian Barnes, *Metroland*, part I, ch. 5.
33 John Betjeman in *Metro-Land*, directed by Edward Mirzoeff, DD Home Entertainment for BBC Television, 1973.
34 Barnes, *Metroland*, part I, ch. 5.

35 Ibid.
36 Ibid.
37 Ibid., part I, ch. 10.
38 Julian Barnes, interview by Shusha Guppy, in 'The Art of Fiction No. 165', *The Paris Review*, issue 157, winter 2000.
39 Barnes, *Metroland*, part I, ch. 7.
40 Ibid., part III, ch. 1.
41 Ibid.
42 Ballard, *High Rise*, ch. 7

Chapter 13
Looking Backwards: The English Country House
Through a Post-Modern Lens

 1 John Sutherland, 'Looking Back', in *The London Review of Books* 2:10 (22 May 1980): 27–8.
 2 Blake Morrison, 'The Country House and the English Novel', *Guardian*, 11 June 2011.
 3 Kazuo Ishiguro, *The Remains of the Day* (New York: Alfred A. Knopf, 1990), 6–7.
 4 Ibid., 71–2.
 5 Ibid., 11.
 6 Ibid., 9.
 7 Ibid., 49.
 8 Evelyn Waugh, *Brideshead Revisited*, book I, ch. 1.
 9 Ishiguro, *Remains*, 123.
10 Susannah Hunnewell, 'Kazuo Ishiguro, The Art of Fiction No. 196', in *The Paris Review* 184 (Spring 2008).
11 Ishiguro, *Remains*, 115.
12 Ian McEwan, *Atonement* (London: Jonathan Cape, 2001), part I, ch. 2.
13 Ibid., part I, ch. 1.
14 Ibid., part I, ch. 2.
15 Ibid.
16 Ibid.
17 Ibid.
18 Ibid., part I, ch. 7.
19 Ibid., part I, ch. 8.
20 John Sutherland, 'Life was Clearly Too Interesting in the War', interview with Ian McEwan, *Guardian*, 3 January 2002.
21 McEwan, *Atonement*.
22 Alan Hollinghurst, *The Stranger's Child* (London: Picador, 2011), 124.
23 Ibid., 128, 141.
24 Ibid., 113.
25 Ibid., 114.
26 Ibid., 129.
27 Tinniswood, 155.

28 Hollingshurst, *The Stranger's Child*, 396.
29 Ibid., 437.
30 Alan Hollinghurst, in conversation with Andrew Motion and Rowan Moore, 'Writing Houses, Dwelling on Dwellings', Kings Place, London, 19 September 2011.
31 'Our History', Canford School website. http://www.canford.com/history-and-archive.aspx Accessed on 12 September 2016.
32 Stephen Moss, 'Alan Hollinghurst: Sex on the Brain', *Guardian*, 18 June 2011.
33 Hollinghurst, 'Writing Houses, Dwelling on Dwellings'.
34 Ibid.
35 Alan Hollingshurst, *The Line of Beauty* (London: Picador, 2004), 5.
36 Hollinghurst, 'Writing Houses'
37 Hollinghurst, 'Writing Houses'
38 Hollingshurst, *The Stranger's Child*, 18.

Bibliography

Chapter 1
Shandy Hall: The Birth of the House of Fiction

Main Texts:

Henry Fielding, *The History of Tom Jones, A Foundling*, 1749

Samuel Richardson, *Clarissa*, 1748

Laurence Sterne, *The Life and Opinions of Tristram Shandy, Gentleman*, 1759–1767

Resources:

Byrd, Max, *Tristram Shandy* (London: George Allen & Unwin, 1985)

Cash, Arthur, *Laurence Sterne, The Later Years* (London and New York: Methuen & Co., 1986)

Curtis, Lewis Perry, ed., *The Letters of Laurence Sterne* (Oxford: Clarendon Press, 1967 [first edition 1935])

Fielding, Henry, *The History of Tom Jones, A Foundling*, Fredson Bowers and Martin C. Battestin, eds, (Oxford: Oxford University Press and Weslyan University Press, the Weslyan Edition of the Works of Henry Fielding, 1974)

Howes, Alan B., ed., *Sterne: The Critical Heritage* (London: Routledge and Kegan Paul, 1974)

Lewis, W. S., ed., *The Yale Edition of Horace Walpole's Correspondence, Vol. XV Correspondence with Sir David Dalrymple* (New Haven: Yale University Press, 1951)

Ross, Ian Campbell, *Laurence Sterne, A Life* (Oxford: Oxford University Press, 2002)

Chapter 2
Strawberry Hill: The Invention of the Gothic Novel

Main Texts:

Jane Austen, *Northanger Abbey*, 1817

William Beckford *Vathek*, 1786

Thomas Love Peacock *Nightmare Abbey*, 1818

Bibliography

Ann Radcliffe, *The Mysteries of Udolpho*, 1794
Horace Walpole, *The Castle of Otranto*, 1764

Resources:

Benedict, Barbara and Deirdre Le Faye, eds., *Northanger Abbey*, The Cambridge Edition (Cambridge: Cambridge University Press, 2006)

Copeland, Edward, and Juliet McMaster, eds, *The Cambridge Companion to Jane Austen* (Cambridge: Cambridge University Press, 2011)

Cruickshank, Dan, ed., *Sir Banister Fletcher's A History of Architecture*, Twentieth edition (Oxford: Architectural Press, 1996)

Fothergill, Brian, Beckford of Fonthill (London: Faber and Faber, 1979)

Iddon, Johh, ed., *Strawberry Hill and Horace Walpole* (London: Scala Publishers Ltd, 2011)

Lees-Milne, James, *William Beckford* (London: Century, 1990)

Lewis, W. S., ed., *Selected Letters of Horace Walpole* (New Haven and London: Yale University Press, 1973)

Mills, Howard, *Peacock, His Circle and his Age* (Cambridge: CUP, 1969)

Mowl, Timothy, *Horace Walpole, The Great Outsider* (London: John Murray, 1996)

Snodin, Michael, ed., *Horace Walpole's Strawberry Hill* (London: Yale University Press, 2010)

Walpole, Horace, *The Correspondence of H. Walpole with G. Montagu*, 3 Vols (London: Henry Colburn, Publisher, 1837)

The Critical Review, February 1797

The General Magazine and Impartial Review, December 1791

Chapter 3
Pride and Property: Women and Houses in Regency England

Main Texts:

Jane Austen: *Sense and Sensibility*, 1811; *Pride and Prejudice*, 1813; *Mansfield Park*, 1814; *Emma*, 1815; *Persuasion*, 1818

Fanny Burney: *Evelina*, 1778; *Cecilia*, 1782

Resources:

Cecil, David, *A Portrait of Jane Austen* (London: Constable, 1978)

Harman, Claire, *Fanny Burney, A Biography* (London: Flamingo, 2001)

Hill, Constance *Jane Austen, Her Homes & Her Friends* (London: John Lane, 1902)

Girouard, Mark, *Life in the English Country House* (London: Yale University Press, 1978)

Goff, Moira, John Goldfinch, Karen Limper-Herz and Helen Peden, *Georgians Revealed, Life, Style and the Making of Modern Britain* (London: The British Library, 2013)

Grey, J. David, ed., *The Jane Austen Handbook with A Dictionary of Jane Austen's Life and Works* (London: The Athlone Press, 1986)

Le Faye, Deirdre, ed., *Jane Austen's Letters, New Edition* (Oxford: Oxford University Press, 1997)

Nabokov, Vladimir, 'Mansfield Park' in *Lectures on Literature*, ed. Fredson Bowers (New York: Harcourt Brace and Company, 1980)

Pevsner, Nikolaus, 'The Architectural Setting of Jane Austen's Novels', *Journal of the Warburg and Courtauld Institutes*, vol. 31 (1968), 404–22

Tanner, Tony, *Jane Austen* (Basingstoke: Macmillan, 1986)

Tomalin, Claire, *Jane Austen: A Life* (London: Viking, 1997)

Chapter 4
Ancient and Romantic: Walter Scott's Baronial Halls

Main texts:

Maria Edgeworth, *Castle Rackrent*

Walter Scott: *The Lay of the Last Minstrel,* 1812; *Waverley,* 1814; *Guy Mannering,* 1815; *Rob Roy,* 1817; *The Antiquary,* 1816; *The Bride of Lammermoor,* 1819

Virginia Woolf, *Orlando: A Biography,* 1928

Resources:

Bell, Alan, ed., *Scott Bicentenary Essays: Selected Papers Read at the Sir Walter Scott Bicentenary Conference* (Edinburgh: Scottish Academic Press, 1973)

Grierson, H. J. C., Davidson Cook, W. M. Parker, et al., *The Letters of Walter Scott 1787–1807*, Centenary Edition (London: Constable & Co Ltd, 1932)

Hewitt, David ed., *Scott on Himself: A Selection of the Autobiographical Writings of Sir Walter Scott* (Edinburgh: Scottish Academic Press, 1981)

Lockhart, J. G., *Memoirs of the Life of Sir Walter Scott, bart.* (Edinburgh: Robert Cadell, 1848)

Reed, James, *Walter Scott: Landscape and Locality* (London: The Athlone Press, 1980)

Scott, Walter, *The Journal of Walter Scott* (Oxford: the Clarendon Press, 1972)

Sutherland, John, *The Life of Walter Scott* (Oxford: Blackwell, 1995)

Abbotsford, A Short Guide to the Home of Sir Walter Scott

Chapter 5
Madwoman in the Attic, Author in the Dining Room: The Haunts of Charlotte Brontë

Main Texts:

Anne Brontë, *The Tenant of Wildfell Hall,* 1848

Charlotte Brontë, *Jane Eyre,* 1847

Emily Brontë, *Wuthering Heights,* 1847

Bibliography

Resources:

Allott, Miriam, ed., *Charlotte Brontë: Jane Eyre and Villette, A Casebook* London: Macmillan, 1973)

The Brontë Society, *Brontë Parsonage Museum* (London: Scala, 2013)

Gaskell, Elizabeth, *The Life of Charlotte Brontë*, ed. with introduction by Winifred Gérin (London: The Folio Society, 1971)

Gérin, Winifred, *Charlotte Brontë, The Evolution of Genius* (Oxford: Oxford University Press, 1969)

Gordon, Lyndall, *Charlotte Brontë: A Passionate Life* (London: Virago, 1994)

Harman, Claire, *Charlotte Brontë: A Life* (London: Viking, 2015)

Smith, Margaret, ed., *The Letters of Charlotte Brontë, with a selection of letters from family and friends* (Oxford: Clarendon Press, 2000).

Sutherland, James, ed., *The Oxford Book of Literary Anecdotes* (Oxford: Oxford University Press, 1975)

Wood, G. Bernard, *Historic Homes of Yorkshire* (Edinburgh: Oliver and Boyd, 1957)

Chapter 6
Charles Dickens: A Child's View of Home

Main Texts:

Charles Dickens: *The Pickwick Papers*, 1837; *The Old Curiosity Shop*, 1841; *Dombey and Son*, 1848; *David Copperfield*, 1849; *Bleak House*, 1853; *Great Expectations*,1861; *The Mystery of Edwin Drood*, 1870

Resources:

Ackroyd, Peter, *Dickens* (New York: HarperCollins, 1990)

Armstrong, Frances, *Dickens and the Concept of Home* (Ann Arbor and London: University of Michigan Press, 1990)

Forster, John, *The Life of Charles Dickens in Two Volumes* (London: Chapman and Hall Limited, 1911)

Kaplan, Fred, *Dickens, A Biography* (London: Hodder & Stoughton, 1988)

Slater, Michael, *Charles Dickens* (London: Yale University Press, 2009)

Slater, Michael, and John Drew, eds., *The Dent Uniform Edition of Dickens' Journalism, Volume 4, The Uncommercial Traveller and Other Papers, 1859–70* (London: J. M. Dent, 2000)

Storey, Graham, and Kathleen Tillotsen, eds, *The Letters of Charles Dickens* (Oxford: Clarendon Press, 1995)

Tomalin, Claire, *Charles Dickens: A Life* (London: Viking, 2011)

Chapter 7
For the Love of an English Cottage: Thomas Hardy and E. M. Forster

Main Texts:

E. M. Forster: *A Room with a View*, 1908; *Howard's End*, 1910

Thomas Hardy: *Under the Greenwood Tree*, 1872; *The Laodicean*, 1881; *Tess of the d'Urbervilles*, 1891; *Jude the Obscure*, 1895

D. H. Lawrence: *Lady Chatterley's Lover*, 1928

Resources:

Ashby, Margaret, *Forster Country* (Stevenage: Flaunden Press, 1991)

Beaumann, Nicola, *Morgan, A Biography of E. M. Forster* (London: Hodder & Stoughton, 1993)

Forster, E. M., *Abinger Harvest* (London: Edward Arnold, 1936)

Forster, E. M., *The Hills of Devi and Other Indian Writings* (London: Edward Arnold, 1983)

Forster, E. M., *Howards End, Abinger Edition 4* (London: Edward Arnold, 1973)

Forster, E. M., *Marianne Thornton, A Domestic Biography* (London: Edward Arnold, 1956)

Gibson, James, ed., *Thomas Hardy Interviews and Recollections*, (London: Macmillan, 1999)

Hardy, Florence Emily, *The Life of Thomas Hardy 1840–1928* (London: Macmillan, 1962)

Hart-Davies, Rupert, ed., *Siegfried Sassoon Diaries, 1920–1922* (London: Faber and Faber, 1981)

Kramer, Dale, ed., *The Cambridge Companion to Thomas Hardy* (Cambridge: Cambridge University Press, 1999)

Lago, Mary and P. N. Furnbank, eds, *Selected Letters of E. M. Forster* (Collins, 1985)

Millgate, Michael, *Thomas Hardy, A Biography* (Oxford: Oxford University Press, 1982)

Newman, John and Nikolaus Pevsner, eds, *The Buildings of England, Dorset* (London: Penguin, 1975)

Phelps, W. Lyon, ed., *The Architectural Notebook of Thomas Hardy* (Philadelphia: The George S Macmanus Company, 1966)

Stape, J. H., ed., *E. M. Forster, Interviews and Recollections* (London: St Martin's Press, 1973)

Chambers's Journal of Popular Science and Art, 18 March, 1865

Journal of Royal Society of Arts, 18 March, 1927

Chapter 8
The House as a Work of Art: the Aesthetic Visions of John Galsworthy and Henry James

Main texts:

John Galsworthy, *The Forsyte Saga*, nine books in three volumes, published 1906–1921

Henry James, *The Portrait of a Lady*, 1881; *The Spoils of Poynton*, 1897

Bibliography

Resources:

Cox, Devon, *The Street of Wonderful Possibilities: Whistler, Wilde & Sargent in Tite Street* (London: Frances Lincoln Limited, 2015)

Croot, Partricia E. C., ed., *A History of the County of Middlesex: Volume 12, Chelsea* (Martlesham: Boydell & Brewer, 2004)

Dupré, Catherine, *John Galsworthy, A Biography* (London: Collins, 1976)

Galsworthy, John, *A Msotley* (London: William Heinemann, 1927)

James, Henry, *The American Scene* edited by Leon Edel (London: Rupert Hart-Davis, 1968)

Edel, Leon, ed., *Henry James Letters* 4 vols (London: The Belknap Press of Harvard University Press, 1984)

Edel, Leon, *The Life of Henry James*, 5 vols (London: Collins, 1953–72)

Garnett, Oliver, *Henry James and Lamb House*, Rye (Swindon: The National Trust, 1999)

James, Henry, *English Hours*, edited with an Introduction by Alma Louise Lowe (London: Heinemann, 1960)

Kaplan, Fred, *Henry James The Imagination of Genius, A Biography* (London: Hodder and Stoughton, 1992)

Marrot, H. V., *The Life and Letters of John Galsworthy* (London: William Heinemann Ltd, 1935)

Unpublished Diary of Lilian Sauter, 1903, Cadbury Research Library, University of Birmingham

Soros, Susan Wehr, ed., *E. W. Godwin Aesthetic Movement Architect and Designer* (New Haven and London: Bard Centre for Studies in Decorative Arts and Yale University Press, 1999)

Tinniswood, Adrian, *The Long Weekend: Life in the English Country House Between the Wars* (London: Jonathan Cape, 2016)

Chapter 9
Rooms of Her Own: Virginia Woolf's Houses of Memory

Main texts:

Virginia Woolf: *Jacob's Room*, 1922; *Mrs Dalloway*, 1925; *To the Lighthouse*, 1927

Resources:

Bell, Anne Olivier, ed., assisted by Andrew McNeillie, *The Diary of Virginia Woolf*, 4 vols (London: The Hogarth Press, 1978)

Bell, Quentin, *Virginia Woolf, A Biography*, 2 vols (London: Hogarth Press, 1972)

Gordon, Lyndall, *Virginia Woolf, A Writer's Life*, (Oxford: Oxford University Press, 1984)

Harris, Alexandra, *Viriginia Woolf* (London: Thames and Hudson, 2011)

Nicolson, Nigel, ed., *The Letters of Virginia Woolf*, 6 vols (London: Hogarth Press, 1975–80)

Lee, Hermione, *Virginia Woolf* (London: Chatto & Windus, 1996)

Woolf, Virginia, *Moments of Being: Autobiographical Writings*, edited by Jeanne Schulkin, with an introduction by Hermione Lee (London: Pimlico, 2002)

Woolf, Virginia, *A Passionate Apprentice: The Early Journals of Virginia Woolf 1897–1909*, edited by Mitchell A. Leaska (London: The Hogarth Press, 1990)

Chapter 10
Inheritance and Loss: War and the Great English Estates

Main Texts:

Ford Madox Ford, *Parade's End*, 4 vols (1924–28)

Evelyn Waugh, *Vile Bodies*, 1930; *A Handful of Dust*, 1934; *Brideshead Revisited*, 1945

Resources:

Briggs, Asa, *A Social History of England, From the Ice Age to the Channel Tunnel*, (London: Weidenfeld and Nicolson, 1994)

Davie, Michael, ed., *The Diaries of Evelyn Waugh* (London: Weidenfeld and Nicolson, 1976)

Eade, Philip, *Evelyn Waugh, A Life Revisited* (London: Weidenfeld and Nicolson, 2016)

Judd, Alan, *Ford Madox Ford* (London: Collins 1990)

Madox Ford, Ford, *It was the Nightingale* (London: Heineman, 1934)

Madox Ford, Ford, *Return to Yesterday*, edited with introduction by Bill Hutchings (Manchester: Carcanet, 1999)

Pryce-Jones, David, ed., *Evelyn Waugh and His World* (London: Weidenfeld and Nicolson, 1973)

Saunders, Max, *Ford Madox Ford, A Dual Life*, 2 vols (Oxford: Oxford University Press, 1996)

Mulvagh, Jane, *Madresfield, the Real Brideshead* (London: Doubleday, 2008)

Chapter 11
Gothic House Redux: The Passion of Manderley, Agatha Christie's Bloody House Parties

Main Texts:

Daphne du Maurier, *Jamaica Inn*, 1936; *Rebecca*, 1938; *The House on the Strand*, 1969

Agatha Christie: *The Mysterious Affair at Styles*, 1921; *The Secret of Chimneys*,1925; *The Murder of Roger Ackroyd*, 1926; *the Seven Dials Mystery*,1929; *And then there Were None*,1939; *The Crooked House*, 1949; *The Adventure of the Christmas Pudding*, 1960, *Endless Night*, 1967

Bibliography

Resources:

Beacham, Peter, and Nikolaus Pevsner, *The Buildings of England, Cornwall* (London: Yale University Press, 2014)

Bunson, Matthew, *The Complete Agatha Christie, An Agatha Christie Encyclopedia* (New York: Pocket Books, 2000)

Christie, Agatha, *An Autobiography* (London: HarperCollins, 1993)

Cook, Judith, *Daphne, A Portrait of Daphne du Maurier* (London: Bantam Press, 1991)

Du Maurier, Daphne, *Growing Pains* (London: Victor Gollancz Ltd, 1977)

Du Maurier, Daphne, *The Rebecca Notebook & Other Memories* (London: Virago, 2004)

Forster, Margaret *Daphne du Maurier* (London: Arrow Books, 1993)

Malet, Oriel, ed., *Letters from Menabilly, Portrait of a Friendship* (London: Weidenfeld & Nicolson, 1993)

Newman, John, *West Kent and the Weald, The Buildings of England* edited by Nikolaus Pevsner (London: Penguin, 1976)

Shallcross, Martyn, *The Private World of Daphne du Maurier* (London: Robson Books, 1998)

Chapter 12
The Glamour, Horror and Ennui of Modern Housing:
Ian Fleming, J.G. Ballard, Julian Barnes

Main Texts:

J. G. Ballard: *Crash*, 1973; *Concrete Island*, 1974; *High-Rise*, 1975

Julian Barnes, *Metroland*, 1980

Anthony Burgess, *A Clockwork Orange*, 1962

Ian Fleming: *Goldfinger*, 1959; *Dr No*, 1957; *You Only Live Twice*, 1967

Resources:

Ballard, J. G., 'An Investigative Spirit', interview by Travis Elborough in *High-Rise* (London: Harper Perennial, 2006)

Ballard, J. G., *Miracles of Life, Shanghai to Shepperton, an Autobiography* (London: Fourth Estate, 2008)

Barnes, Julian, in 'The Art of Fiction' No. 165, *The Paris Review* issue 157, Winter 2000, interviewed by Shusha Guppy

Betjeman, John in *Metro-Land*, directed by Edward Mirzoeff, DD Home Entertainment for BBC Television, 1973

Lycett, Andrew, *Ian Fleming* (London: Phoenix, 1996)

Sellers, Simon and Dan O'Hara, eds., *Extreme Metaphors, Interviews with J. G. Ballard, 1967–2008* (London: Fourth Estate, 2012)

Warburton, Nigel, *Ernö Goldfinger, The Life of an Architect* (London: Routledge, 2004)

Chapter 13
Looking Backwards: The English Country House through a
Post-Modern Lens

Main Texts:

Alan Hollinghurst, *The Swimming Pool Library*, 1988; *The Line of Beauty*, 2004; *The Stranger's Child*, 2011

Kazuo Ishiguro, *The Remains of the Day,* 1989

Ian McEwan, *Atonement,* 2001

Resources:

Moss, Stephen, 'Alan Hollinghurst: Sex on the Brain', the *Guardian*, 18 June 2011

Ishiguro, Kazuo, in 'The Art of Fiction No. 196', *The Paris Review* issue No. 184, Spring 2008, interview by Susannah Hunnewell

McEwan, Ian, 'Life was Clearly Too Interesting in the War', interviewed by John Sutherland at the Cheltenham festival, published in the *Guardian*, 3 January 2002

Morrison, Blake, 'The Country House and the English Novel', in the *Guardian*, 11 June 2011

Strong, Roy, Marcus Binney, John Harris, eds., *The Destruction of the Country House 1875–1975* (London: Thames and Hudson, 1974)

Sutherland, John, 'Looking Back' in *The London Review of Books*, 22 May, 1980, vol. II, No. 10

Tinniswood, Adrian, *The Long Weekend, Life in the English Country House Between the Wars* (London: Jonathan Cape, 2016)

Acknowledgements

Anyone who has ever been involved in making a book understands that it is, in the end, a collaborative effort. Like most writers I was helped by the generosity, patience and advice of many. Thanks to the Arts Council for supporting the project. To Michael Alcock, who first believed in and encouraged this undertaking; Guilland Sutherland for reading, commenting, warning, being a jolly travel companion and for fearless picture research. To Jane Dietrich for reading and proofreading each chapter as I churned them out and protesting interest in every one; Robyn Read for reading early chapters and offering judicious and extremely apt comments; Harriet Winterburn for her brilliantly original illustrations and for agreeing to go on a journey which was probably a lot longer than she thought she had signed up for; Rachel Jones for luminous company (and driving) on so many actual journeys.

So many people at the houses I visited were generous with their time and information. Thanks to Patrick Wildgust at Shandy Hall, for being an early supporter of the book and so generous a host; Chris Pearson for historical information about the Hall and photos. Thanks to Strawberry Hill for letting us film the pitch video there. To Charles Jencks and the Duke of Buccleuch for a brilliant evening at Drumlanrig Castle. To Sir James Graham for showing me around his family home, Norton Conyers, and relating its fascinating history. Thanks to Stephen Martin at Gads Hill and Robert Tucker at Restoration House for sharing their knowledge and love of the houses; to Peter Hughes for a kind welcome (and volunteer chauffeuring!) at Madresfield.

Dr Tim Parnell and Dr Ben Woolley gave helpful research advice. Staff at the Cadbury Research Library, University of Birmingham helped me sift through all of the Galsworthy material (with large magnifying glass!), which led to the discovery of the unpublished drawings of Robin Hill at the British Library. Andrew Sanders generously let me raid his wonderful library.

Thanks to the team at Unbound, especially Mathew Clayton, for rescuing a project that was in great need of a boost, and Anna Simpson for her patience, good humour and enthusiasm, and to Elain McAlpine, for taking on such a mammoth editing task, and with such skill. To all of the supporters of the book, it couldn't have happened without you.

My greatest thanks to Lucas, for living with this project for such a long time, being my best editor, buoying me up and being patient all those weekends and holidays while I was lost to it, and for many things too numerous and basic to name.

Index

Index

Index

Playfair, James, 107
Poe, Edgar Allan
    The Fall of the House of Usher, 167–8
Point Hill, 256–7
Pollock, Sir Frederick, 265
Ponsonby, Elizabeth, 307
Pope, Alexander, 35
Pound, Ezra, 236
Powderham Castle, 71
Pratt, Anthony E., 348
Preston Hall, 308
Prior Park, 24
Pugin, A. W. N., 44
Punch, 181

Queen Anne revival, 198, 214, 229, 240, 246
Quiller-Couch, Sir Arthur, 329
Quiller-Couch, Foy, 332

Radcliffe, Ann
    The Mysteries of Udolpho, 47–8, 128, 327
Reed, James, 101
Renishaw Hall, 309
Repton, Humphry, 88
Restoration House, 41, 159, 165–6, 168–72
Revett, Nicholas, 391
Reynolds, Joshua, 4
Richardson, Samuel, 23–4, 58, 93
    Clarissa, 64
    Pamela, 23, 64
Rochester Cathedral, 175
Roe Head School, 134–5, 140
Rokeby Castle, 103, 105, 123
Ronan Point, 364
Rooksnest, 215–18, 220, 223
Rose, Charles, 251
Rossetti, Dante Gabriel, 241
Rothenstein, William, 243
Rouen Cathedral, 44
Roxburgh Castle, 100
Royal Society of Arts, 196
Ruskin, John, xiii, 224, 239, 243, 304, 315
Rydings, The, 136, 144–5

Sackville-West, Vita, 124, 285
St Pancras Station, 374n
Sandby, Paul, 34
Sandy Knowe, 98–9
Sandys, Lord (Lord Chamberlain), 32, 76

Sargent, John Singer, 241
Sassoon, Siegfried, 204
Saunders, Max, 292
Sauter, George, 235–6
Scott, Charlotte (née Carpenter), 102, 109, 121
Scott, Walter, xiii, xvi, xviii, 59, 97–125, 128, 179, 203, 298, 300, 396, 400
    The Bride of Lammermoor, 103
    Cadyow Castle, 103
    Castle Dangerous, 121
    Guy Mannering, 103, 116
    The Heart of Midlothian, 106, 117
    The Lady of the Lake, 102, 104
    The Lay of the Last Minstrel, 104–5
    The Lord of the Isles, 116
    Marmion, 104
    Minstrelsy of the Scottish Border, 102
    Rob Roy, 103, 114
    Rokeby, 103
    Waverley, 100, 103, 108–16, 122–3, 317, 379
    Young Lochinvar, 107
Seeley, Benton, 69n
Selznick, David O., 342
Shakespeare, William, 36, 174, 385
Shandy Hall, xvi, 1–23, 26–7, 58
Sharpham Park, 24
Shaw, Norman, 243
Shelley, Mary
    Frankenstein, 57
Shelley, Percy Bysshe, 57–8
Sidgwick, Henry, 279
Sidney, Sir Philip, 103
Single Man, A, 354n
Skene, James, 120
Skibo Castle, 122
Slape Manor, 201
Slyfield, 334, 337, 344
Smith, T. Roger, 193
Smith, William, 122
Smollett, Tobias, 93
    The Adventures of Peregrine Pickle, 173
Society for the Protection of Ancient Buildings, 190n
Southey, Robert, 134–5
Stafford House, 204
Stephen, Adrian, 261, 267n
Stephen, Julia, 277, 283
Stephen, Leslie, 261–2, 271, 277, 281, 283
Stephen, Stella, 261, 278, 281

453

Index

Unbound is the world's first crowdfunding publisher, established in 2011.

We believe that wonderful things can happen when you clear a path for people who share a passion. That's why we've built a platform that brings together readers and authors to crowdfund books they believe in – and give fresh ideas that don't fit the traditional mould the chance they deserve.

This book is in your hands because readers made it possible. Everyone who pledged their support is listed below. Join them by visiting unbound.com and supporting a book today.

Gina R. Collia
Patricia Colyer
David Cooke
Andy Cowle
Rachel Craven
Caroline Dakers
Rachel Darling
Deanna Davenport
Alison Davidson
Matt & Owen Davies
Peter Dawson
Gerald de Groot
Miranda Dickinson
Emily Dietrich
J. Kimball Dietrich
Jane Shaw Dietrich
Lucas Dietrich
Kevin Donnellon
Jenny Doughty
Vivienne Dunstan
Jennie Ensor
Barbara Fairfax
Alex Fiennes
Joseph Figueira
Paul Fischer
Christine FitzGerald
Fiona Fitzsimons
Hannah Flinders
Nick Fordy
Mark Gamble
David Gettman
Pilar Aceves Goeders
Andy Gollifer
Chris Gostick
Jack Gowrie
Laura Grace
Jane Griffiths
Peter Grundy

Camilla Guinness
Ewan Guinness
Felicity Guinness
Lorna Guinness
Rachael Hale
Dani Hall
David Smith Hall
Mariann Hardey
Wendy Harper
Jane Hayward
Jude Henderson
Andrea Henry
Linden Hibbert
E O Higgins
Catherine Hills
Lorna Hobbs
Abi Holloway
Stephen Hoppe
Antony Howard
Joy Howard
Charlie Humphries
Gil Huntley
Jennifer Hurstfield
Davina Jackson
Michelle Jervis
Alex Johnson
Meghan Jones
Philip Jones
Anita Kaushal
Hilary Kemp
Joseph Kennedy
Dan Kieran
Jill Kieran
Mags Kubicek
Margit Lammertz
Alison Lawrence
Anna Lawrence
Mark Lawson

Rupert Lewis

Tamasin Little

Una Lynch

José Machado

Seonaid Mackenzie-Murray

Gillian Mackie

Selina Macnair

Claire Madge

Catherine Makin

Philippa Manasseh

Melissa Marsh

Dave Martin

Shannon Martin

Michelle Matthews

Elain McAlpine

Martine McDonagh

Julie Schofield Mendoza

Fiona Merrikin

John Mitchinson

Keith Moss

Edith Mueller

Kabir Mulji

Rosaleen Mulji

Annie Nagem

Helen Nash

Carlo Navato

Emma Neale

David Neill

Christina Norton

Rolf Nyhus

Mary Ore

P

Neil Palfreyman

Jim Parfitt

James Parker

Julia Parker

Gill Parrott

Lesley Pearson

Penny Pepper

Debbie Phillips

Mark Robert Phillips

Jack Pinter

Irene Pizzie

Sanya Polescuk

Justin Pollard

Marguerite Ponce

John Porter

Edward Powell

Rhian Heulwen Price

Efthymia Priki

Will Pryce

Vesna Radojevic

Martin Read

Robyn Read

Deborah Rees

Margaret Reeves

Steve Reeves

Julia Reimer

Ellen Richardson

Simon Ricketts

Suzanne Robey

Roslyn Russell

Michael Rusted

Teraza Salmon

Bernie Sammon

Danny Scheinmann

Constanze Schweda

Alison Scott

Stephanie Scott

Laura Shepperson-Smith

Keith Sherratt

Linda Shoare

Tara Silva

Ollie Simpson

Ian Skewis

Paul Skinner

Megan Smedley
Nigel Smith
Richard Soundy
Martin Spencer-Whitton
Liam Spinage
Janet Sporleder
Teresa Squires
Daniel Stilwell
Guilland Sutherland
Justine Taylor
Maisie Taylor
Bill Timmerman
Harriet Walsh

Christopher Watson
Annie Weeks
Senaka Weeraman
Robert Whelan
Beth Wilburn
Patrick Wildgust
Keeley Wilson
Robyn Wessler Wisinski
Claudia Woodlingfield
Stacey Woods
Benjamin Woolley
Jack Woolley